LONGINGS OF THE HEART

LONGINGS

of the

HEART

The Story of Elsie Machle White

BY GEORGENE SEARFOSS

ISBN: 9781701090491

In memory of Thomas R. Searfoss and Connie White Frasche

Their support and guidance from the early stages of development was appreciated

Introduction

Elsie Machle White was co-author of Our Neighbors, The Chinese, published in 1945 by Rinehart & Company, Inc. The authors of this book were Josephine Budd Vaughan, and Elsie Machle White. She was not only a writer, but a "Gold Star Mother", the wife of WWI Flying Ace, Wilber White, who was killed in France in 1918. His heroism was noted in the movies "*Wings*" and "*Fly Boys*". When Elsie died in 1978 in Baltimore, Maryland, she left a house full of unpublished manuscripts, letters, photos, and documents spanning almost 70 years. Upon her death, the family directed friends and neighbors to clean out the house. Almost forty years later, this author began to type the fading letters. By contacting neighbors and members of the family, my husband and I put together a story of Elsie's life. She survived personal tragedy because of her strong will and encouragement of friends. Through it all, was her undying love for Billy White, a handsome college sweetheart, who became a WWI flying ace with the 147th Aero Squadron. The parents of two children, one deaf since birth, the burden of responsibility was shared with the White Family. Eventually, the children grew up under their care as Aunt Helen became their surrogate mother. While Elsie struggled with illness, acquiring an education, and finding a job, she was faced with the dilemma of motherhood, finding the right school for her deaf child, a career in biology, or writing. Many WWI historians have wondered about the private or personal life of Wilber. Perhaps this will answer those questions. Any errors or grammatical errors are quoted exactly as previously written and were not changed or edited including misspellings, or misspelled names.

I thank the following people for their input to our research project, sharing of information, or contribution toward our book about Elsie Machle White. There were over 1,400 letters to re-type, as well as documents, and pictures to review. Jerry and Mary Watson, Jonathan Calley, Archivist, National WWI Museum at Liberty Memorial, David Koch, Reference Archivist, Presbyterian Historical Society, Mary Margaret Brewer, Dr. Douglas Machle, Douglas Smith Archivist, Mercersburg Academy, Dale Hansen, Vol. Archivist, Fifth Avenue Presbyterian Church, Betty Bolden and Brigette C. Kamsler, Project Archivist, Burke Library, Columbia University, Constance White Frasche, Faith Nelons, Nancy McDonnell, Jennifer Wagner, Minnesota Historical Society, Rebecca Davis, Anne Green, Nancy Stover, Researcher & Genealogist, Centre County Historical Museum & Library, Denise D. Monbarren, Special Collection Librarian, The College of Wooster Libraries, Carol Seylor, Westminster Presbyterian Church, and Charlene Chesnut, M'Lissa Kesterman, Cincinnati Museum Center, Michael Szajewski, Ball State University, Ellen Manno, Penn State University, Ian Benson, Wooster University, Roger Snyder of Endeavor Presbyterian Church and Alyssa Machle John.

I'm especially grateful to Jerry and Mary Watson who read the manuscript and gave me insight. Jerry's knowledge of missionaries and YMCA work was useful.

I valued the guidance Carol Wooley and Nancy McDonnell made to the manuscript.

Many thanks to Bob Frasche and David White for their encouragement and sharing of personal family photos for this project

CHAPTER 1

China 1889-1898

It began on a tree lined street in Baltimore where York Road and Greenmount Avenue met at E. 42nd Street. That is where Elsie Machle White and Victor Machle lived. The brother and sister occupied a brown clapboard house across the street from Boundary United Methodist Church where my husband, Rev. Thomas R. Searfoss led a congregation of gasoline Christians, so named because of the exit of white families to the suburbs after the 1960 blockbusting of stable white neighborhoods in the vicinity of Memorial Stadium. The couple lived in a boarded-up house since the roving gangs of teenagers robbed and vandalized their house. Up in years, they lived in poverty and poor health, cared for by Victor's barber and his wife, their power of attorney. It wasn't until after their deaths that the story of their lives revealed their connections to events in history through a collection of 1,400 letters, documents and photographs.

Their story began when Ella May Wood and Edward Charles Machle were married in the Wharton Street Presbyterian Church in Philadelphia, Pennsylvania on July 31, 1889. This church had flourished for decades then, as often happens in cities, the demographics changed in the area and its attendance was impacted negatively. Later – in 1907 – it was re-christened as the St. John Negomucene Church, serving the many South Philadelphia

Slovakian people known as the "South Siders", and said by some of the church that it was "much nicer than any of the shitty North Philadelphia Churches of that time." Ella Wood graduated from Germantown High School.

Edward Machle attended Moore's Hill College, Wooster College, and graduated from Jefferson Medical College in Philadelphia. He also attended the Cincinnati College of Pharmacy in 1909 and the Cincinnati Dental College. At Philadelphia in 1887 after hearing Forman & Wilder of the Student Volunteer movement, an organized movement to recruit college and university students for missionary service, he volunteered as a foreign missionary. The Student Volunteer Movement for Foreign Missions began in July 1886 at a summer student conference held on the campus of the Mount Hermon School in Northfield, Massachusetts. Northfield conference was designed to provide Bible study, evangelism and promotion of YMCA work. The Northfield missionary uprising was led by four volunteers Robert Wilder, John R. Mott, William P. Taylor, and I. Riley of Princeton, Cornell, DePauw, and Yale. Robert Wilder, led the group interested in missions, and later joined with John Forman, who had not been at Northfield, but was one of the original volunteers at Princeton, New Jersey. This was a big step for Edward in many ways. He had been raised in the Roman Catholic Church by his parents, immigrants from Germany, and would soon be commissioned by the Presbyterian Foreign Board of Missions of the Presbyterian Church to be an "itinerant" medical missionary to China. It was hoped such missionaries would be married before departing for their overseas appointment and so it was that Ella and Edward found each other and, as newlyweds from the Wharton Church, they set off for China a few days later and arriving on a train that had brought them over the Rockies, after leaving Cincinnati on the third of August. learn

the language soon, retain our health and be the means of turning many to righteousness." It would not be easy!

They would soon learn that this mission work was not going
to be easy in any way. Traveling with the Machle's to the mission
field in China was Louise Johnston. When Edward was 21 years
old, he united with the Auburn Presbyterian Church in Auburn,
Ohio. Miss Johnston, was his Sunday School teacher and is credited with his early education in protestant religion. It was later,
while at Wooster University, that he became interested in missionary work in China. Louise Johnston concluded in a letter to
her cousin that they would sail on the 21ˢᵗ instead of the 19ᵗʰ and
asked that everyone would think of us, while sending her kindest
regards to the good people of the Wharton Street Church.

Ella May Wood Machle was the oldest daughter of Howard
Craven Wood and Hannah Clay Edelman Wood. She was born
on October 28, 1859 in Jenkintown, Springfield, Montgomery
County, Pennsylvania. She had two brothers Elmer J. and Walter
A. and three sisters Bertha, Alwida and Elizabeth Worthington
who was nicknamed Bessie. Howard's father Joshua was known
to sell produce off the back of his wagon while Howard farmed
for a living at the age of 18. He eventually learned the harness
making trade. After Ella graduated from Germantown High
School, she began teaching. There was interest in Northfield
but for reasons unknown, she didn't pursue it. Instead, she began teaching in South Philadelphia at the family Presbyterian
church where she met Edward.

Edward's parents, Adam George Machle and Mary were both
born in Bavaria, Germany and moved to Auburn, Ohio where
Adam worked as a night watchman at Burnt Woods Park. Adam
and Mary had six children, Edward Charles, Herman W., Anna
M., Harry J, Jeremiah B. (nicknamed Jerry) and Luella.

Ella and Edward and Louise Johnston left San Francisco on September 21 and sailed to China on the Steamship <u>Rio de Janeiro</u>. Edward recounted that they would sail directly to Shanghai but, they went first to Yokohama then to Hong Kong, finally taking another steamship to Shanghai which would deposit other missionaries at their respective destinations located along the coast. They expected it would take six days to go from Yokohama, Japan to Hong Kong,

Having arrived in Yokohama, Ella and Edward make their way to Hong Kong, then to Shanghai, eventually to Canton, where in a letter to her parents written November 3, 1889, Ella shares that "we expect to stay in Canton for a year and perhaps two as it is the best place to learn the language...We are boarding with Mr. and Mrs. Wisner (missionaries in Canton) but intend to keep house as soon as we can get the things together to do so." Ella is frustrated by the difficulty of getting this done in the time she would like it done. "You cannot make anyone hurry here so I do not know when the time will be. This is the way of doing business. You want furniture, of course. You go to the store, make a drawing of what you want stating exactly price, length, etc., and then wait till it is ready. You want a room cleaned. Two men are hired to do it and sometimes they go off at noon and that is the last you see of them. This is a nice house, large enough for two small families like ours when the extra room for the servants is finished. Our room is a large oblong room containing two large windows and three doors. One opens into the large veranda, one into a wall, one into a bathroom and one into Miss Johnston's room so you can see I was right first, there are four doors."

There is a lot of hustle and bustle all about them as they experience the energy of the Chinese villagers. Ella and Ed live next to a church which is next to a pig market. "They (Chinese villagers) carry pigs in wicker baskets as well as their chickens, ducks, and cats. Yesterday a pig got out and caused quite an excitement for a few minutes. Can you imagine never having any Sunday, but day in and day out hearing the noise and bustle attendant upon the cutting of stones carrying burdens, building houses, buying and selling…they live with the 4th of July almost every day. Sometime in the middle of the night we are awakened by a great explosion of fire crackers outside." Ed gets Ella a lamp for a present. Ella saw a "vase lamp and Ed bought her a pair…They were very pretty indeed and I am very proud of them. While we were looking at them it began to rain. The streets are very narrow and the roofs almost meet just leaving a little opening for daylight so that when it rains, it is worse than standing under a water spout to be in the street with the water pouring on you from each side and splashing up the stones so that you think it is running up and down. After waiting for it to stop, Ed sent for a chair for me as I had on a thin white dress, which is not very suitable for a promenade as you can imagine. Mr. (Oscar) Wisner gave the men instructions as to my destinations and off I was borne. Everyone gets out of the way for a chair or any heavy burden as the men who are carrying it continually give warning of their coming and on this occasion volunteered the extra information that it was a foreign devil which is their name for us the same as we at home call them John Chinaman. So every few steps they would say in Chinese, of course, 'get out of the way, here comes a foreign devil,' but one thing makes us very serene, we only understand 'F.D.' and there is no danger so they can talk all they want."

In time the washstand and two tables come. "The washstand is very pretty with a colored marble top and two large drawers, and a little sort of shelf at the back made of wood on which we can stand our tooth mugs, etc. it is large enough for two bowls making it a very nice partnership concern. The little table is on the opposite side of the room and supports a large plate glass mirror, the other table is for the dining room and is the only furniture we have for there yet." Ella adds that, "perhaps you had better not say anything about our furniture outside as some people are so silly they don't seem to think missionaries should have anything comfortable." Missionaries often filled their homes with furniture and small household items much like they had at home, which to the Chinese seemed both elegant and at the same time a rejection of their own ways of living. Ed continues to his language lessons and soon takes his first writing lesson. Ella struggles with the language at nearly every level. None of this is easy for either one of them. Yet they persist, learning the Chinese way as they make their adjustments to the new life abroad in a foreign land.

As Ella, Edward, and Miss Johnston continue their preparation to go to Lien Chow, new opportunities present themselves for insight into the Chinese culture. On the eve of going to Lien Chow for seven weeks Ella wrote a letter to her family in Philadelphia. The Sunday before they left, "we had an invitation to go in next door to a Chinese Christian wedding." They decided to go. "Miss Johnston wore her dark green sateen and I wore my black and white plaid as a light dress would be out of place and anything that attracts too much attention even from those who have some years in the school. When we entered the room which was occupied by men only, they all stood up to receive us and remained standing until we were seated. We were accorded the seat of honor, at least we suppose so, at the head of the room, next on our right was the teacher and on our left the groom who was standing about the middle of the room at first and as soon as we were seated he saluted us by shaking his own hands and bowing. Then we all stood up again and the teacher offered a prayer after which Miss Johnston was invited to play No. 7 in the green hymnbook and then they sang in Chinese and we in English. I forgot to say that before the prayer the bride was led in by the woman in waiting, for although she had large feet she must needs walk in though they were small swaying to and fro and supported by her woman. She never raised her head and often covered her face with her hands. After the hymn the teacher made a speech and then the doctor was called upon and made his 2nd speech at a wedding. I think he was more composed this time. Then the refreshments were passed around. candy of which each one took a small piece, and oranges in sections, besides very good tea in small cups. When you were served, you waited until all the other cups on the waiter were given out when you bowed to all your neighbors, their being supplied, and then drank the tea. You did the same with the candy and juice of the orange...After the tea we sang *There's a Land* and then Miss Johnston was requested to speak. She and Ed both spoke through an interpreter of course. Another man spoke after that and then there was a great time, the waiting woman talking to the bride and trying to make her take the waiter which now contained two cups of tea. She had not given her husband any and now she was to give it to him. After quite a time and in the midst of much laughing on the part of the men, she finally got to her husband with it when a few difficulty arose. He would not take it. Then he was talked to and at last he took the cup and put it on the table without drinking any of it when they all laughed again and the bride covered her face with her hands. We saw that on receiving the tea each one laid an offering on the waiter, neatly done up in red paper so we sent out for some and each of us wrapped ten cents in a paper ready to give. This did not escape their attention and for the second time we were served with tea. After singing the doxology and repeating what I suppose was the Lord's Prayer, we made our exit...Carefully instructed as to what word we should use on going and that after bowing when we got to the end of the room...

we were surprised and amused to hear almost all of them say 'Goodbye' in perfectly good English, much better I am quite sure than our Chinese."

Ella, Edward, and Miss Johnston went to Lien Chow with Dr. (B. C.) Henry. Seven weeks would be spent there, acquainting themselves with the surroundings, some of the people, and getting a sense of their future home. This took them nearly through Christmas in 1889, returning to Canton December 20. Ed and Miss Johnston gave Ella a beautiful brown lacquered set of trays decorated with different varieties of ferns, Ella shared with her sister in a December 27 letter that, "I like them very much. There are four in the set." Ella also added to Bessie, that, "Lien Chow, our expected future home is a beautiful place."

In this letter to Ella's father, Edward describes a unique procedure he experiences as he walks through a main but narrow street of Canton. Near the end of this letter he announces the birth of his and Ella's first child Elsie:

"E. C. Machle
Canton, China
May 8, 1890

"Dear Mr. Wood,

"I thought I would write a few lines to you about some of the extraordinary things that happen in China. I hardly know whether it would be best to begin with what is the most extraordinary thing with me, though very ordinary to people older, and I am sure younger than myself.

"Well to begin, a few days ago when passing through one of the main, though nevertheless narrow streets of Canton

on my way to the hospital under the management of Dr. Kerr, I heard a voice which reminded me of the even rumbling of heavy machinery at home. Wishing to satisfy myself to a certainty, entered the building from whence the sound proceeded and found the machines in use to be anything but large machines of foreign manufactures. Three men were treading on three large granite slabs shaped thus. (A picture is drawn of a disc shaped on one side with a half moon shape, the other side was flat.)

"The convex surface rested upon a wooden roller which played upon a concave surface in the floor. Between the roller and concavity was spread a yard of goods from a bolt of blue cloth. The picture which I saw was something like this, only there were three of them. (Another picture was drawn.) You see as the man presser with one foot at one end of the granite slab, the roller runs up the opposite side of the concave surface and when according to his superior judgment and years of persevering practice the roller has gone sufficiently up this side he quickly proceeds upon the other end of the slab sending the roller up the side from whence it just started. This swaying of the body and rolling of the cloth was performed after twenty times for each yard of cloth. Then the man stepped down from his pedestal pulled the yard of cloth that he had so curiously ironed until a fresh yard was properly adjusted for the roller. Thus he continued (I think for I did not wait) to the end of the bolt or both infinitive.

"Here is a puzzle. How did he get the fresh yard of blue cloth under that roller with such an enormous weight upon it?

"You know by this time the purpose of the machine. Its function is to perform the last smoothing process to cloth in a dyer's establishment

"I had gone but a short distance further when another extraordinary thing burst upon my view. It was the dried duck and goose store. Of these there are many in Canton. The sole object of the proprietors of these stores is the sale of these dainties. Imagine a store with the front of it entirely gone – no windows or doors to be seen. In this open front are long festoons of strung wishbones, goose and duck heads, gizzards and feet, thousands in number all dried with the flesh still on them, on a stand below these decorations and extending almost across the open front, were displayed things manifold. There were unstrung head, fresh gizzards, wishbones out in the midst of those, towering somewhat like the grand enduring pyramids of Egypt, were intestines. You ask are they eaten? Certainly. I have seen many a Chinaman pushing boiled ones down his throat.

"Looking within the store, I saw the three walls literally covered with dried semi-translucent ducks and geese. (Aren't you hungry and doesn't your mouth water?) I am fond of ducks and geese as prepared at home but such a sight of walls overlaid with gold like Solomon's temple, but with these ducks and geese, and the open doorway beautifully and attractively decorated with such festoons and garlands for the stomach, although remotely suggestive of Xmas decorations was not conducive to a good appetite. I have thought how nice, useful and fattening it would be if my friends at home would ornament Xmas trees with

such delicacies instead of using popcorn, cranberries and inedible rainbow-colored glass balls. Please ponder over and attempt to digest what I have given you. If either of the Wharton Street Sunday Schools, Presbyterian or Methodist, wish such decorations, I shall be willing to accommodate them.

Excuse brief description. I could give but a casual glance at my Chinese rolling mill and dried goose establishment. Shall investigate more thoroughly when more leisure.

I walked rapidly for about three squares when I was brought to a sudden standstill by some motionless objects spread upon a piece of matting in the street. A glance was sufficient to make out dead monkeys. I tried to think of the use of dead monkeys and concluded they were for medicine. I have since found out that I am right. Conversing with my almond eyes teacher afterwards on medicine, monkey stew and tiger meat tea were brought prominently into view as panaceas.

Tiger meat and bones are the great strengtheners among the Chinese and bear bile makes one courageous. I had some opposition in this line one day from a "Chinese quack". While at a small place called Kong How dispensing medicine in the Chinese vian[sic]schoolhouse, my brother in the profession was deliberately placing the dried flesh from a leg of a tiger and selling it to a small company of women. When I left he was still extoling his wares. Every disease the women could think of was curable by this medicine. I might as well confess that the opposition was too strong(?). I rejoice, though with a sad heart, that only women bought his delicious tidbits.

Now last but not least, as I think how to express myself, these words of Tennyson from "The Miller's Daughter" came to mind. "The still affection of the heart became the outward breathing type." In other words, "Unto us a child is born, unto us a daughter is given, and her name shall be called Elsie Edelman Machle. Pray for her welfare. The little stranger came on the third of May, the 31ˢᵗ anniversary of her father's birthday. Hereafter there will be the celebration of a double birthday at our home. She has an abundance of hair, weighs 7 pounds and looks like---well wait a few months and you will see her picture when you can decide for yourself.

"You have at last arrived at the responsible position of 'Grandpa'. Let your influence in that capacity be felt clear across both the continent and the great dep. I regret that you will not see her until she is 8 years old.

"Ella is getting along nicely. She had a remarkably easy time. You will find in this letter a lock of baby's hair. See how curly it is. Did you ever see longer? With best regards and kind remembrances to her grandpa, grandma, uncles, aunts etc., in your prayers. With much love to all the dear ones. She will be a week-old tonight at 1 o'clock. How you hold up your head, heart, her looks will not matter, now you all have one more to remember.

I am, Your Son,

"There is such a little room here and I would like to say so much. Aunt Bessie will like Elsie as a name I know. Just think before I get an answer to this, Elsie will be in short dresses if she lives. On Wednesday evening prayer meeting was here and Mr. Noyes made the closing prayer and then prayed so beautifully and simply for the life just come amongst us. If she only has a good" (unfinished letter......).

They called her *E So* – Little Dumpling. Within a short time, she became a chubby baby. Ella and Edward initially disagreed on her name. They eventually came down to three. Ella wrote to her mother that, "At last we had three. Ethel, Edna, and Elsie. One of Ed's nieces is named Edna so that is how Elsie got her name. I never knew of anyone of that name excepting Bessie's Elsie and I did not know it was even an abbreviation for Elizabeth until after she was named, of course. I would not change it. We will spell her middle name Edelman which is the proper way. But it was still "Little Dumpling" that captured the essence of the newborn Elsie.

When she was two weeks old Ella wrote her mother that Elsie knew her father's voice. Ella added, "the Amah (nurse) thinks she is very smart indeed." And she was, at a little over one year old Ella recounts to her sister, Alwilda that, "yesterday she (Elsie) amused us by saying, *No,ah,*" in a very emphatic manner. This is more comical to us than it may appear to you as it is an English word and a Chinese Termination. The Chinese language has many terminations such *as ah, ha, bak, ka &c.* For about a week she(Elsie) has been able to tell us when she did not wish anything, in true Chinese style with a certain shake of the hands that one born to the manor can accomplish." Before Elsie could walk she was able to speak and understand at least three different

Chinese dialects she picked up from her "nurses Miss Nyrup, *A Ho*, and *A Why*, at Macao. This was before she could communicate well and understand the English language. In a short time, Ella would find this beneficial.

CHAPTER 2

Sam Kong to Lien Chow
1898-1905

Edward was a quick learner of the Chinese language. He had great abilities and was offered a position as a court interpreter at the Peking Legation. But his heart was in his work. He believed that he could be of greater aid to the Presbyterian Mission as a doctor than to the Government as an interpreter. There were challenges, not only with the language but with the religion. The native people were suspicious of Christianity and resisted attending services on Sunday and believed in superstition. Buddhism was the early religion of the region before the folk religion of Taoism. Tao emphasized living in harmony which was more philosophical than religious. As an itinerant, Mr. Edwards, the Christian missionary, and Dr. Machle went to Hunan, Kang Hau, Tung Pi and Chung Ten Wan. He was gone for weeks at a time and Ella kept busy by writing to her family in Philadelphia. This would become the pattern of his life as an itinerant medical missionary, but a life that was more complex for Ella.

Elsie's birth kept Ella in Macao while Edward travelled. A brief letter to her mother about the event, "Well, I got back from Macao just one week before the event which came off as you know, on the 3rd of May. Miss Nyrup, the nurse, was with the French Consul's wife but left her and came to me in time and so did the doctors. Then as soon as it could be arranged we all came down to Macao. I can nurse Elsie enough to satisfy her about every other time."

Pretty soon, she became a fat three-month old on a supplemental diet, so she was nicknamed "Little Dumpling". Ella writes to her family on August 5, 1891 that, "Little Dumpling imitates the horse and dog as well as the cry of the nannie very well and is much interested in them all. She tries to say Elsie but only gets *Ah tee.* What with the hot weather, the prickly(?) heat and cutting teeth besides change of *Ahma*'s makes her quite cross, but Miss Johnston says she never saw a baby keep as well and look as well as she does under the circumstances. It is a good thing she can walk she is so fat and heavy". With Elsie's birth, Ella continued her lessons with the plan to "one day start a school". Her biggest obstacle was the Chinese language, "John Wesley said the devil invented it to keep the gospel out of China…A missionary was once visiting a family who were mourning the death of a near relative. Wishing to ask whether they had buried the corpse, he used the right word, but misplaced the aspirate, so he really asked whether they had murdered their relative."

Within four months after Elsie's birth, "Ed started for Lien Chow and took Elsie a short distance. She came back with her hand full of purple asters and white bean flowers. Yesterday she amused us by saying '*No, ah*' in a very emphatic manner. This is more comical to us than it may appear to you as it is an English word and a Ch Termination. The Ch language has many terminations such as *ah, ha, bak, ka.* For about a week she has been able to tell us when she did not wish anything, in true Chinese style with a certain shake of the hands that only one to the manor born can accomplish. The hand appears in danger of falling off at the wrist and every finger is an exclamation point or point of negation according to the occasions.

While visiting Santa Sancha, Macao in January 1891, Ella writes to her mother, "This you need not keep but I thought I would tell you that Elsie looks so cute that we cannot help kissing her. She gets very indignant if her wants are not attended to at once and cries most lustily when we are not in time to prevent her wetting herself. I am so glad she is so particular. Mr. J. C. Thomson's little son who is not ten months old has called Elsie for a long time and says a number of other words both Chinese and English."

On January 30, 1891, Ella wrote this letter to her mother, "This afternoon about 3 o'clock it was so delightfully warm and pleasant that I went down to the Point and seated myself in an easy chair with my umbrella raised to keep off the sun and a book and paper to read. I had about finished the paper when *A Ho* came with Elsie and put her in my lap while she went off to do a little ironing. Elsie was quite contented to sit in my lap and talk to me and play with the fringe of my shawl for fully an hour.

"Now, I must tell you what Elsie eats as you know I have not nursed her for a long time. At first, she had milk (condensed) but that was too rich, when she began to have boils so we changed to fresh milk which we can get here at 10 cents a pint and gave it to her without any sugar. She seemed to enjoy it but when she began to cut her teeth, we were obliged to change again and give her rice water and a little milk to which we added beef extract. At present she gets a large bottle full of rice water and beef extract to which I add from four to eight teaspoonsfuls of the so-called cream which rises to the top of the milk and on which she seems to thrive. I diminish or increase the milk according to the condition of her bowels. She is fed every four hours by the clock. The Chinese think it very strange to feed a child that way instead of just whenever they appear to be hungry. The first thing Mrs.

Thomson's woman told her was that my baby was fed and put to sleep just like her son, Herbert.

Sam Kong and Lien Chow Mission

One report from a member of the Presbyterian Board of Missions describes, "Lien Chow, 200 miles north west of Canton by water was long an outstation of Canton. Also known as the Guang-dong Province, it was an important point, lying near the province of Hanan, which was almost untouched by missionary effort and within easy reach of the Ius (an aboriginal tribe). Correspondence between Mrs. Machle and relatives indicates that also working in the field by 1891 were Rev. Henry, Miss E. M. Butler, and Miss Johnston. A chapel was leased in 1879 by Mr. B. C. Henry of the American Presbyterian Church and a church was organized in 1886 with a Chinese pastor. A chapel was built at Sam Kong. Soon, a hospital opened in 1891 and a woman's ward added in 1895. Property for a hospital was secured, but the opposition was so great that it was not occupied until 1897." Some of the opposition was the result of superstition. "A temple, belonging to the neighboring village of Hau Tsin, with its twenty-two idols was purchased by Dr. Machle. A plot of ground adjoining a temple near the Women's Hospital was also secured, and hopes were entertained that the temple itself would be sold and transformed into a temple for the worship of the true God" as well as, "the repairing and straightening of the road to Sam Kong, so that it will be suitable for jinrikshas." Also planned was a bridge across the Lien Chow River, of foreign construction. Dr. Machle was, "asked to take the lead in pushing the matter. A resident of Lien Chow offered one thousand dollars to start the fund." But not all these plans were executed until years later. Ella later mentioned that the road repair to Sam Kong was abandoned by 1896.

As Ella found herself alone while Ed travelled, often visiting the Ius, an aboriginal tribe inhabiting the hill country close to Lien Chow, doubt about her choices resurfaced and reflected in her September letter to her family when she started putting Doubting Castle as her return address, "Doubting Castle is only my own private name not to be given to the public." She reflects that, "I feel as though I could not be thankful enough to him", referring to Edward, "for all he has done for me and my loved ones and it makes me feel so ashamed of my frequent doubts and fears. I know it cannot be all sunshine with you at home and I often steam my eyes to read between the lines, but I can appreciate your kindness and love in sending me such cheerful interesting letters and I am so glad you can get along so well without me. But feel sure you will always miss me some even when I remember that often I was not as lovable as I might have been, but here again, I know you have almost forgotten how very disagreeable I was at times so think it a good thing to remind you of it fearing you will come to think I was better than I was, although I did try and I think we all did, to contribute to each other's happiness and I do not think the time will ever come when I shall look on the arrival of the mail with indifference and some have told me they do now when once they watched with the greatest anxiety. Several have told me this and if I had been younger when I married no doubt it might have been partially so in my case, but I doubt. From my observation of different families and their feelings in regard to each other, I have come to the conclusion that we are a very affectionate one, although far from an ideal one...You must pardon this letter's lack of news if it does not contain any in consequence of my moralizing, but somehow I just feel like talking to you all this way this time before doing anything else...this letter will not go until some time in September...how long the times seems when you look forward and how short when you look backward. Everything is quiet and peaceful here nor has there been the slightest of disturbance since our arrival. We are looking forward with great pleasure to Mr. and Mrs. Lingle joining us in the fall perhaps not till November. When the people up here speak their own dialect pure and simple it is almost impossible to understand a word it is so different from the Cantonese but one good thing they understand the Cantonese. I think sometimes the difference worries Elsie. First, she had *A Ho*, after she began to understand who speaks a dialect different from this. Then she had *A Mui* who speaks Cantonese, and now she has *E So* with her Sam Kong dialect with no m's at all and a different word entirely for you, but she will have to worry through like the rest of us with the advantage that she is younger."

"I do not know enough of the language to talk doctrine in one day...I sent the boy to have my shoes mended as it had a little hole on the side about at the ankle bone. When he brought it back, I could not help laughing as it had a great clumsy patch sewed on the outside...I sent it back in a hurry with instruction as to how it should be mended and it came back looking quite respectable." Misinterpretation was the norm as Ella shared another shoe story, "I have concluded to tell you about a pair I had made for Ed. His were about played out...he wrote obliging him to wear his rubbers even if the day was warm. I had no measure but the shoemaker had made him a pair of slippers with an old one for a sample and said he knew how and had the measure. On Tuesday he brought them. The soles turned up like pointed sleigh runners and they were short and narrow, no possibility of Ed ever getting them on and that after our combined directions in regard to their make. I told him they would not do, too muchee narrow, too muchee short, too muchee pointed. Must have muchee long, muchee wide. He said can do. I bring you muchee large. You take. I said yes."

The Ius, who became known as the boat people, "often come here for treatment and to hear the organ when the watchman who was with them for several years before he became converted and knows their language speaks to them. They seem more grateful for treatment than most of the Chinese and bring presents of eggs and chickens to Ed after leaving the hospital. Not long ago one of them brought a beautiful pheasant, too pretty to eat, which Ed bought for 25 or 30 cents. It was quite good. Soon after another variety was brought also very beautiful and for which they wanted over $2 saying its flesh was much better than the other." Mr. William Hill Lingle of the American Presbyterian Mission bought it for 50 cents. "I think Ed also bought one a few days after but we were disappointed as we did not like the flavor as well as of the first. I wish I could send you some of the beautiful feathers...The trees at the foot of the mountains opposite my windows are beautiful in autumn dress. Almost every night now we see the fires in the mountains where the people are burning the tall grass. Did I tell you that sometimes when the sunlight strikes one of the mountains a certain way we can see a narrow path winding along its steep sides and disappearing at last over on the other side. We have never yet been able to discover anyone on it. It leads to the Iu country." The Yangtze River flows through the valley between the Nan Mountains which rise several thousand feet.

As the oldest, and feeling responsible for them, she was rigid in her opinions about how her siblings should conduct their lives. Assuming her family knew of their plans, she writes to Bertha in April of 1890, "It rather astonished me to read that you did not clearly understand why we were going to Lien Chow. Now if you had said you did not understand why we remained so long in Canton, I would not have been surprised. My dear, Lien Chow is our appointed Station to which we are to go as soon as we know enough of the language to commence work. The Board is very anxious that we should occupy the place at the earliest possible date and we are just as anxious to do so." They were assigned to Lien Chow. She writes to her Aunt Annie, "I do not get along with the language as well as Miss Johnston and Ed and feel very much discouraged at times but do not feel at all like giving up. Rev. (Oscar) Wisner was traveling with Edward spreading the word of God for those who wanted to believe, but the Chinese people were cautious in becoming Christians. The Chinese Society was not adjusted to the observance of the Sabbath, Christianity was a foreign doctrine and presented by foreigners, superstitions, effects of the use of opium, foot binding, contempt for the education of women and lack of suitable words in the language to express religious ideas."

"Elsie has no more teeth but I think she will have two more soon. Everyone says what beautiful hair and eyes and what a pretty baby. I think her eyes will be brown though, so does mamma. She often sleeps from 6 p.m. until 6 a.m. and is very regular in her habits. For over two weeks she only required food twice during the night. The other day…having slept over her time in the morning, she was fed at 11 a.m. and 3 p.m. At six she went to sleep as she could not wait for her food. At ten minutes of six the next morning as she was still making no sound I got up and walked very softly to the crib to find her with her eyes wide open, sucking her thumb. You may be sure I hurried up and prepared her food."

Louise Johnston became known as Grandma to Elsie. Grandma Johnston "took her up and amused her as we appreciated such behavior. She used to cry all the time her food was being prepared as she could not understand but now if she can watch the operation she is perfectly contented. I know you would just hug her as we do when she looks on with her eyes full of interest in every movement. She will be seven months old December 3 and has been in short clothes since she was about 3½ months old…She wears flannel dresses now…white or rather a dirty gray after the woman washes them for with all my showing and telling she will rub them and perhaps wash them last in a little bit of dirty water…when the tailor made a new collar for an old dress she had given him as a pattern and cut a piece out of her new black dress to line it. That is one of the prices we pay and looked at in that light it is a very little matter, but sometimes we do not think of it first."

Within a few weeks, Ella and Ed took her out for a ride, "We got two Jenrickshas and took her out riding to see Macao. She seemed to enjoy it very much so today as I had to go to the shops I took her again and then along the bay and out a short distance before coming home. She was just as pleased as she was yesterday and smiled at the Portuguese woman and the Chinese who took notice of her. She is not at all afraid of the Chinese as a rule although she is a little timid when one of her own color speaks to her. Does that not seem funny…She certainly knows who she likes and who she does not."

Ella continued to play the older sister role to her younger siblings, but she had a tendency to lecture Bessie about her male friends, "And you my dear, I am sorry to hear you told Ephe you'd marry to be near your sister Ella, but you would be sure to be disappointed and it would serve you right if you married for anything but love. Remember that, my darling. And also, be sure he loves you, whoever he may be. No matter if he has been in love a dozen times before only so you are the last one and you are all right. If he cannot be positive on that point or only loves you as much as he does half dozen other girls that he knows don't you have him even if you feel sure you will never have another chance as long as you live. You are laughing at your old sister and asking what in the world she means, I know, but I tell you this is not an old maid's advice although I made such a narrow escape at last...Be sure you're right, then go ahead."

She never hesitated to advise Bessie on the subject of men, "I am glad you told me about Mr. Ware and I hope you will treat him very well. Do not give him too large doses of religion. It is better to live religion more than one talks it and I think you do my dear. Now don't show too plainly that you would say no anymore than yes for surely he has not asked yet and perhaps he never will. I do not think it ridiculous for him to think two weeks long now do you? Why two weeks is very long under some circumstances...But Bessie, if you ever do become engaged, do not consent to be married for a year at the very least. That is short enough time I am sure. 'Do not do as I do but do as I say'."

Ella had her hands full dealing with a very bright child and tells her mother in a letter home, "The teacher took Elsie downstairs to see around and she took off her ring. I had just written to Clara telling her how good she was and did not take it off and I had been praising her which I think put her in mind of it. She came upstairs saying it was very bad, and mamma would whip her hard but I took the ring away instead. She is a little busy body always getting into mischief but still she helps me in a number of ways."

Once her sister asked her to write freely about herself, but instead, she diverted her attention to her daily schedule, "Sunday, as every other morning at 6 or 6:30, the boy brings up some hot water. By the time we are dressed, the bell rings for breakfast. After breakfast prayers, not on Sunday, then the teachers arrive and the lessons begin (Chinese language) and continue with various interruptions until 12:30 o'clock, then we have dinner during which time Miss Johnston reads aloud for half an hour with the best authors...After dinner, if it is not too late, she and Ed take gymnastic exercises, but I think it does more harm than good on a full stomach and so do not indulge. By this time, the teachers have returned and the lessons begin again and last until 4 o'clock which is the time to get on your hat and go over to Shameen to walk getting home in time for supper at 5:30 or 6:00." Although, while in Macao, Ella liked to take, "a dip in the sea...Enjoyed it very much and just got back into the house."

Elsie appreciated the little surprises like the violets growing in the moss along the bank, "I was just wishing it were possible for me to be a fairy for a minute or long enough to transfer the flowers on my table to yours, but I can tell you how they look. Imagine a little nile green cup without any handles more like a little bowl about 1½ inches high and 3 inches in diameter in which on a bed of moss are placed some beautiful sweet scented violets that stand up out of the moss as though they were growing there. We gathered them yesterday while out walking and when I came home I put them in a vase while Miss Johnston put hers in a pretty little wine glass. Afterward I thought of the cup and have been admiring them ever since. At once I thought how delighted you at home would be and also how Clara would enjoy them. We could not pick all we wished as Miss Elsie would come right to the edge of the bank to me and then start to Miss Johnston who was farther on, keeping us in fear all the time that she would fall into the moat. We cannot make her afraid of falling into the water. She always says she has no fear and wishes to walk in it. On Thursday, I gave her a toothbrush, one of those that J. W. sent and showed her how to clean her teeth. We laughed so at her! She would take some water in her mouth and try to spit it out as I did but always swallowed it and spit afterward looking up in a surprised way every time. She brushes her teeth pretty well for a novice but is not particular as to where she gets the water so no doubt I will have to superintend the operation for some time yet. I have commenced in earnest to teach her English fearing she will never be able to master the L's, th's, and R's if I delay. It is so much easier to make her understand by talking in her native tongue that I forget…she likes to stand or sit on the window sill on market day which is every fifth day here and look at the people as well as chatter to them. Papa-ke's, the latter a Chinese termination to his name is very much used by her. Everything she sees she immediately asks if it is Papa-ke's or says it is Papa-ke's much to our amusement. She calls me once in a while and chatters with all the proper inflections so that anyone would think she was talking if at a distance."

The Chinese language, of which there were five, was necessary to communicate with the help. It was also necessary if Ella had hopes of teaching in the school when she wrote to Bessie, "Would you like to know how a Chinese school is conducted? This one is a day school under the charge of the Baste Mission and supported by the German Government. The teacher is an intelligent looking Chinese woman with several assistants. Some of the little things were writing, some were studying the Bible and some the three character Classic (Christian) which begins with the story of Adam and Eve. They have adopted the Romanized system which meets with much favor. You can easily imagine that the characters are not easy and sometimes one single character according to its tone marks may stand for twenty different things. Well, suppose a certain character stands for shut, which is called him with a certain tone mark with another mark it means something else. If the children study nothing but the characters to write, they must make each different character to stand for the different tones while if it is Romanized, it is only necessary to make the proper tone mark for the one work – yim, yim, yim yip, yim, yim, yim yip yip yip – the first take a higher tone than the last, the one marked thus is salt if properly said but do not venture to say any of them before a Chinaman as you might say something dreadful. I think I will look them up...You can judge by this how much easier it is to write by the Romanized methods... Some quite little tots were writing very well making the vowels and some consonants and the others were studying from the different books as I told you before."

Perhaps Ella began using Doubting Castle as a return address after reading *Pilgrims Progress,* a story written by John Bunyan in 1678. He was a Christian "realist." He wrote Doubting Castle as a message to the present day Christian. The central character was Christian; the pilgrim who leaves his home, family and city, which is threatened by destruction...the pilgrim, convicted of sin, searches for salvation and is in mortal fear of being cast out eternally from God's presence (Tangelder, 1995, p. 2). Bunyan wrote, "A castle called Doubting Castle, the owner whereof was Giant Despair...they came to the Delectable Mountains...A great horror and darkness fell upon Christians...So I awoke, and behold it was a dream...He that is down, needs fear no fall, He that is low, no pride" (Bartlett, 1891). "We are very glad to have neighbors, but we are not lonely as we are all too busy. I do not seem to accomplish anything and have about given up all hope of ever doing one-tenth, if that, of what I looked forward to doing. It is such a disappointment to me." Although she may have been disappointed in her ability to learn the language fluently and start working in the field, she was sending money to her family with instructions. Often the instructions were to send veg-etable or flower seeds, but she relied on them to shop for their clothing, shoes, eve eyeglasses, "He wants you to go to The Economy Shirt Store at 10th & South Street and buy him three pair of suspenders @ about 50 cts".

"We are in the prefecture of Lien Chow but 10 miles from the city itself. The people there are still very much opposed to foreigners but the truth is slowly spreading...it is highly prob-able that Mr. T. L. McBryde could secure a house or any place in which to live at Lien Chow as Ed's medical assistant was unable to rent a house after it was found out that he was a Christian. A poor woman had rented part of her house to him as she sorely needed money but the authorities made her tell him he could not have it although he had spent several dollars in making necessary repairs. He had not the heart to make her refund all the money he had spent. He is a Chinamen and a doctor so you can see that is not much chance for foreigners yet as Doctors always are treated well if anyone is. One day when Ed was there at Lien Chow and walking by a store some man said, 'Let's kill him'. 'No!' said the other, he buys so many things'. The amount he buys seems a great deal to them who are accustomed to buying so many cash worth at a time. In all probability the man only made the remark to see if Ed would be frightened."

Ella gave birth to a son, Victor Heuer Machle on August 23, 1892. "I have my hands full especially now that I have a little son as well as a little daughter to care for...he will be the opposite of Elsie. Slow and deliberate in all that he does. He does not eat as much as Elsie did when a week old but he wants it more frequently when awake." But as she describes when he was nearly five years old, "Victor is full of mischief...I think he has some very sweet ways. One morning he came up to me

28

and said, 'Mrs. Machle, I love you very much', at the same time taking my hand and kissing it like a knight of old or he will notice when I change my dress and tell me it is becoming." He is "always getting his toes trampled on or stubbing them or cutting them and yet in spite of it all he likes to go barefoot...he pinched his finger under a board and hurt it so that he cried a long time. But it was this mischievous side that got him into trouble as described by Harrydell Hallmark in an article in the Sunday Philadelphia Press, "Many years ago, when Dr. Machle first went to China, the family missed the oldest boy, Victor. He was a reckless youngster, owning his little Chinese 'boy', and racing the streets and learning the dialect as only a child can do. At the end of a long, hot day the Chinese boy came to the house very frightened and said that Victor was gone. The entire town was searched by the Chinese who were attached to the Machle household. For days, the hunt went on, but no child was found.

Mrs. Machle was in a state of intense anxiety, and, as the days lengthened to weeks, Victor was given up for lost. They believed that he had been drowned, or killed in some way, and nothing could be gotten from the Chinese boy.

One day, months later, a frightened-looking coolie came running into the yard with Victor clinging to his hand. The coolie was so exhausted from the long journey that he could not explain himself, and the only satisfaction the family could get was out of Victor's baby story. They believed that the coolie had stolen the boy and was bringing him back for reward.

Dr. Machle's great gift, however, is his remarkable knowledge of the Chinese dialect, and when he came home he got the full story from the man.

The coolie had been passing through a Chinese town far away, and had been attracted to the slave market where young slaves were being sold. He idly watched the proceedings without interest. In a moment, a roar went up from the crowd as a small foreign child was placed on the stand for sale. The fact of a 'foreign devil's' child being sold delighted the crowd, and every man wished he had the price in his pocket to buy the boy and make his life a living death. No name was given as the auctioneer ran over the selling qualities of the child, but suddenly the coolie pushed his way through the crowd and got close to the selling block. He had recognized the boy's face, and was sure it was the son and heir of the great American doctor who had saved his life in Sam Kong.

Pretending that he was a bidder, he asked the child his name. Victor at once told him.

"Is your father a doctor?" was the next question.

At his affirmative answer, the coolie made up his mind to his course of action. He had his fish money in his pocket, and bought the boy with it, then carried him by stealth to his father. Had he made his purchase known, hundreds would have betrayed him and detained the child. It needed all the ways that are dark and the tricks that are vain, for which the 'Heathen Chinese is peculiar' to get the boy back to his country.

One can imagine the devotion of Dr. Machle to this coolie. Victor had been stolen by a tricky coolie and carried to a slave market where the man thought he could get a good price for him. The child was playing alone, and the man led him out of sound of his voice by promises of adventure.

Victor told the story himself last winter when he was in Philadelphia with great glee and interest, but to Mrs. Machle the episode has nothing but heartache in it?"

She found that it was easier to understand the language if she applied it to everyday life, "I have the teacher write my recipes in Chinese opposite the English and then the cook copies them so in time I will have a nice cookbook...I cannot help learning a little by talking to the servants and that is a good comfort. Today, I learned the expression for cleaver. Miss Butler has used it and then having told me what it was has no doubt she noticed by blank expression. Then every night I take accounts with the cook and write down the Chinese names of the things in English. You must know and the English name by it if I never heard it before---Just stopped to take accounts and could not think of the name for carrots after I had written the Chinese name and had to ask Miss Johnston. The cook had them fixed a very fine scalloped or pointed, around the edges and with a nice dressing today... .I have commenced to study again but Elsie takes more time than I can give to my books still I learn a little every day and if I do not forget more than I remember, I will know of the language in time."

In 1894 Dr. Eleanor Chesnut arrived to take charge of the women's hospital. Work on the house and dispensary was in progress in Lien Chow but they settled in Sam Kong, where Ed was, "busy supervising the completion of our house, studying, attending Bible readings, and seeing patients. He is really obliged to send some and looking forward to the time when we can join him...our house is not on a hill but in a valley between two high mountains so that Mt. Hope would not suit would it? The valley is large enough to afford us a chance to get a sweep of wind from either side for which we are very thankful. We think that the mountains are much higher than we at first supposed as they look just as near when we are two or three miles away". At least the new house in Lien Chow would be their new home. They were living in quarters located on the second floor of the dispensary and looked forward to a house.

Elsie, "Has a large hand for her age and a very fat arm. Ed was saying yesterday that she certainly takes after him for fat. Even when he was sick with malaria, while going to college in Wooster, the class paper had this...Smith for Longitude— Machle for Latitude, and he is shorter than ever now. He said if I could only put extra flaps on his pantaloons as I did on his drawers he would be all right but as it is he cannot even sigh about it until he takes them off, while his coats and vests are giving all the time."

Then Ella became ill, "I am getting well but it is slow work on account of having lost so much blood. I have been out on the veranda once and have sat up in a chair several times. Ed said he told you all about it, but I am sure he did not tell you how carefully and tenderly he has nursed me nor of his efforts to get everything that can be got to make me comfortable and aid in my recovery." Later, she describes, "I have found grape juice to be of great benefit in sickness and weakness of any kind. It is said to be a very rapid blood maker and gave me a good start on the way back to health."

The Machle family was growing when Ella gave birth to twins; Howard Wood and Amy Worthington who were born on December 3, 1894. Ella writes on July 3, 1895 to her mother when they were seven months old, "Amy points and says, moon! Moon! And then tries to say some Chinese verses, Sz Ta tells her. The other night she saw a double reflection in a glass door reflection in a glass door folded against another one. She was much interested, found the moon and then looked in the room back of the door. I asked her what made it and she looked at one very gravely and said, 'I don't know.' She is very fond of saying it as it is the only sentence in English that she knows. Perhaps not a very good one but convenient. She cut three teeth at once a short time ago and feels better that they are through. She has lost several pounds but still weighs heavier than Howard who only weighs 20 pounds now and looks sick, but better than he did when Ed came home. He is weak and does not care to run around and play. Perhaps the change to Lien Chow will do him good. We expect to go the last of this month or the beginning of next. This morning Amy saw the donkey in the back yard and was delighted while Howard put his hand to his heart and said he was afraid".

Li Hong Zhang, the Viceroy, played a diplomatic role in negotiating a settlement in the Boxer Rebellion. It was an honor for the ladies of his family to visit. Ella was, "helping Dr. Mary Niles and Dr. E. L. Bliss to entertain a number of the ladies of the Viceroy's family. Two or three wives, two of them of equal rank with a son of each and a number of attendants. From thirty to forty small attendants, also came with them. They came in chairs and went home in a steam launch. One of the ladies could read, and as they all talked Mandarin it was very fortunate that Dr. Niles had a Mandarin New Testament which after some coaxing the one who could read, read to the others, but she did not understand the meaning. I do not know whether she took the book with her or not. They were just as anxious to see upstairs as the rest of the people, the "Tai Tai" one of the first wives or head wives got Elsie to get in the crib and then covered her over and put down the mosquito bar and patted her. She also tried Dr. Bliss's bed to see how it was and another one tried Dr. Niles bed. They seem to think the springs are very nice."

Before going they invited Dr. Bliss and Elsie and me to come with Dr. Niles and pay them a visit the next day which we did. They all made a great fuss over Elsie and the two young boys had her all over the yamen. Dr. Niles, I think was surprised that I allowed her to go but I did not know how to refuse and I did not want to make her afraid. She saw much more than we did. We had a lunch, a sort of broth with eggs in it, one of the ladies gave Elsie a bottle of cologne which she insisted on carrying about with her and just before we came away she fell down, broke the bottle, cut her hand a little and got some of the cologne in her eye but she only grieved over the loss of the cologne. The lady insisted on giving her another bottle also one large basket of bananas, one of oranges and four boxes of cakes. This morning Elsie went out to the hospital and gave each of the patients a banana. She says she intends to give the cakes to the cute girls school, I was glad to go as I wanted to see what the inside of a Viceroyal palace looked like. The ladies powder, and paint then like a very deep red. Their nails were stained a pinkish red. They wore gay silk shams and purple silk skirts. I forget the kind the one had one when she was here, the other had on purple silk spotted with gold and a light blue sham trimmed with green and black – another sham was light blue with figures in applique of a different shade, it also had a border in black and green and blue." It was felt that Li was trusted as he did not follow Empress Cixi's declaration of war against the foreigners. Empress Dowager Cixi came to power in 1861 after the death of Xianfeng Emperor and during her reign began to withdraw her once open attitude towards foreigners when Li Hongzhang's influence became overpowering.

"Canton, China
April 5, 1895

My Own Dear Mother,

You will be surprised when I tell you that I have been helping Dr. Niles and Dr. Bliss to entertain a number of the ladies of the Viceroy's family. Two or three wives, two of them of equal rank with a son of each and a number of attendants. From thirty to forty small attendants, also came with them. They came in chairs and went home in a steam launch. One of the ladies could read, and as they all talked Mandarin it was very fortunate that Dr. Niles had a Mandarin New Testament which after some coaxing the one who could read, read to the others, but she did not understand the meaning. I do not know whether she took the book with her or not. They were just as anxious to see upstairs as the rest of the people, the Tai Tai one of the first wives or head wives got Elsie to get in the crib and then covered her over and put down the mosquito bar and patted her. She also tried Dr. Bliss's bed to see how it was and another one tried Dr. Niles bed. They seem to think the springs are very nice.

Before going they invited Dr. Bliss and Elsie and me to come with Dr. Niles and pay them a visit the next day which we did. They all made a great fuss over Elsie and the two young boys had her all over the yamen. Dr. Niles, I think was surprised that I allowed her to go but I did not know how to refuse and I did not want to make her afraid. She saw much more than we did. We had a lunch, a sort of broth with eggs in it, one of the ladies gave Elsie a bottle of cologne which she insisted on carrying about with her and just before we came away she fell down, broke the bottle, cut her hand a little and got some of the cologne in her eye but she only grieved over the loss of the cologne. The lady insisted on giving her another bottle also one large basket of bananas, one of oranges and four boxes of cakes. This morning Elsie went out to the hospital and gave each of the patients a banana. She says she intends to give the cakes to the cute girls school, I was glad to go as I wanted to see what the inside of a Viceroyal palace looked like. The ladies powder, and paint then like a very deep red. Their nails were stained a pinkish red. They wore gay silk shams and purple silk skirts. I forget the kind the one had one when she was here, the other had on purple silk spotted with gold and a light blue sham trimmed with green and black – another sham was light blue with figures in appliqué of a different shade, it also had a border in black and green and blue.

I expected to go to Fa te with Ed and take the children but he found out that Mr. McCloy who is going home on a furlough intended to have a sale, therefore he went up to see if he could buy anything we wanted so now it is too late as Victor is asleep – Ed just came in he bought a few things. Said there was not much to buy.

Last night, at church, a notice was read from the United States Consul, to the effect that a Japanese torpedo boat was seen off Fumun and that hereafter until further notice the night steamers between Canton and Hong Kong will be discontinued and that all boats running will do so at their own risk which is the same as saying they cannot protect them. We were also advised to be circumspect. Action preparations are being made for the defense of the city by the Chinese who are much excited. There are

36

doubts as to whether the Japs have any intention of coming here and if they do we will know it in time to go to Macao if it is necessary. Miss Noyes decided this morning to allow all the pupils who desired to do so to go home and all those who were not afraid to remain here. It is a great responsibility for the ladies and I am glad they have decided what to do. They are not afraid of the Japs but of the Chinese thieves and rowdies if the Japs do come. I will write soon again and hope I may hear from you in the mail which is due on the 11th.

I was so sorry to hear of your all having so much sickness and hope you are all well. Give my love to Rush and Maggie, Court and Tillie and all the other aunties and uncles and cousins and friends.

With love to all the dear ones.

Your Loving Daughter,

Ella W. Machle

Elsie says peppermint makes a cold burn in her mouth.

PERSONAL

I have sent a letter to Clara which she will send to you to read and send to Della York.

I have my black dress made and this week expect to have that Alapaca[sic] one I brought from home made up. I bought some pretty India silk to go with it.

37

I wish Mrs. Campbell's dream had been true. I think I will try and write to Mrs. Homes in the next mail but do not tell her so, as I might not get time. Have you sent the box from home yet? All the rest came all right. Don't you think it pays to get soap by the box?

"Miss Johnston wrote and asked Elsie if she felt larger now. She was 5 years old. Elsie – 'feel larger! I cannot feel larger but I am larger. Of course people cannot feel larger.' Is she not a very literal young lady. Victor has just come in to sell me some 'bean curd' which is a favorite and cheap dish with the Chinese. Of course I hope to come back to China again when our furlough is up but no one can say positively only (D.V.) Another thing if we keep well and stay until our term is up we will in all probability have to wait until the following April or May as it would not do to bring the children home from this hot climate into the rigors of an American winter and for the same reason we will probably not start back the next spring that is that we will not be able to come back right into a hot summer here if we wish to gain any benefit from our stay at home but we have not made any plans at all yet. I am only telling you what we will probably do. Sometimes Ed says he does not know whether he will come back or not but that is when he is discouraged.

Indecision continued to exist, "We are still undecided as to where we will be when we get home. One thing is certain we want the children to go to school as soon as possible and I think Amy would enjoy the kindergarten"...Currently, "Victor and Elsie go and study with the Chinese teacher. Elsie in the Four Character Classic and Victor in the Three. At 10 a.m. I have prayers with the servants and on Monday and Tuesday, I got the school to hear the girls recite and ask them questions. Every day there is the rice to give out and always sewing if there is nothing else and Elsie's English lessons. You will find her away[*sic*] behind, I fear, when we get home. It is so hard to keep her regularly at her studies without any incentive. She likes to play too much." Louise Johnson later wrote to Elsie in 1908, "When you all came home to the United States, I was asked to see that all the rubbish was removed to prepare the rooms for Dr. Chesnut...those were happy days when you and your father and mother and I were the only ones from America living in the large house at Sam Kong, where you used to run from room to room after dinner and shriek with delight when your father suddenly sprang out of some retreat and caught you."

From 1895 to July 31, 1897 Ella and Edward were located in Sam Kong while the house was being built. Until the well was completed Ella and the children stayed in Sam Kong. Elsie, Victor, Amy and Howard were developing with the usual stages of childhood. There were bouts of colds, measles, and poor health. Victor and Howard were especially susceptible.

A letter to Bertha in July describes their preparation to move to Lien Chow. "Victor and two little Chinese children are playing in the hammock which I put up on the porch the next morning after we got here. We did not expect to come over until the well was done but Howard was so ill Edward thought the change might do him good. He really seems a little better but it is too soon to tell. We will not go back to Sam Kong to stay but will wait until there is a heavy rain when Miss Johnston will come over and see to the house here while I go over and finish packing, get the things on the boat ready to float down here. It would cost much more to come overland. By the looks of the clouds it bids fair to rain in a short time but we cannot tell whether it will be sufficient for the little boats to go up to Sam Kong. At this point I got up to close the door as the wind had begun to blow and then closed a window on turning around what was my surprise to see the large rug rolled up with my chair, a stool, and a large bottle of ink inside. I had a lot of work cleaning up here, had to stop again today (Sunday) and close up as we have just had another storm of wind and rain. It lasted only a little while but blew the rug that I had put on the porch railing to dry down below. You really must forgive the bad construction of my sentences as I am sitting on a spring chair and Ed is reading scraps here and there to which I pay half attention. We came over last Thursday, Amy, Howard, Victor, Sz Ta, the wash woman, cook, boy and myself. Ed came the day before and had the locks put on the outside doors. We got here the next day at candle light. The kitchen is not finished yet so the cooking is done outside in the yard quite in picnic style. We intend to go back to Sam Kong only to pack up our things and put them on the boats. Sam Kong River is very rapid and shallow so a succession of dams are made all the way from Lien Chow to Sam Kong in order to make it navigable even for small boats. The exciting part of our trip is going up or shooting down one of these dams. Sometimes one or more of those poling lose their balance and go over but they are up and at work almost before one has time to exclaim. Sometimes the pole breaks with the same result. We can get a boat for $3.80 and they will load and unload the goods.".

On August 26, 1897. Ella described Elsie's dream in a letter to her sister Alwida, "I must tell you Elsie's dream as she told me. 'Mamma, I was sorry you were asleep because God showed me his picture book and I would liked to have had you see it too, only it was a roll like the kind they used when Jesus was on earth. When He opened the roll I saw a little baby just like a real one then I saw Mary and Jesus and some men with Him. I think they must have been His disciples. He looked very beautiful and bright, as bright as silver but Mary was in the shadow. Then I saw David!" How did you know it was David? "By the sheep, of course! Then,

I saw some deer. O, it was all very beautiful and I do wish you could have seen it." "Mamma when I told the Chinese about it they said I had been dreaming but I was wide awake all the time.' I did not contradict her."

CHAPTER 3

Furlough in America

The Machle family arrived at the home of Ella's parents at Haverford Street in Philadelphia in April of 1898. For Victor, Elsie, Amy Worthington and Howard Wood Machle it was their first visit to America, but they realized it was very different from their life in China. They stayed with Ella's family that spring, escaping the heat of summer by heading to the Bell family farm in Ohio. The Bell family were relatives of Louise Johnston. Ella taught the children the three-R's but lacked the advanced textbooks, musical acumen and supplies for her "irrepressible" daughter. Victor was behind in lessons, "susceptible to colds", and perhaps the best way to describe him was "accident prone". The children were progressing and began writing letters, "Howard and Amy are writing letters one to Elsie, and you, and one to Miss Medtart."

"Dear Miss Medhtart[sic], Tomorrow is the Fourth of July and we are to have a picnic. There will not be very many people at our picnic because there are only ten of us here at lienchow. We expect to have a good time. We will fire off fire crackers and play games. Howard and I had a guinea pig which the dog Puk wa killed. Father brought it from Tungpke[sic]. Dr. Chesnut then gave us a pair of

43

rabbit both of which the dog killed. Mrs. Edwards bought Isaac a pair of brown rabbit. Ours were white. One little rabbit had its leg broken and died the other little one and the papa rabbit got out of the cage and ran away so there is only one left. We have lessons at home mamma is our tacher[sic]. In four weeks we hope to go to Macau for a month.

Your loving little friend, Amy Machle."

As you can imagine, Elsie felt the excitement in Ella as she packed trunks for the trip to America, prepared the house and wrote final letters to family directing them to write to her on the Empress of India, c/o Canadian S.S. Co. Vancouver, and "think of us on the river coming nearer to home." Needless to say, it was a bittersweet preparation knowing that Elsie had grown intellectually which prompted a decision to place Victor and Elsie before returning to China. Both Victor and Edward required medical treatment for injuries that required more than the medical facilities in China could provide. Edward's surgery was scheduled in Philadelphia when they returned home. He needed time to recuperate before engaging in public speaking events that required traveling to other cities.

During 1898, letters to her father and mother described the difficulties of building a new home and digging a well for water, "We have been up on the hill determining the depts. of the Artesian well that Mr. Alexander came up to superintend sinking. It seems almost too good to be true that we are to have well up on the hill with the prospect of having the water piped to four houses on time." By February 19, Howard sent a letter saying mamma was ill. There was a flurry of letter writing activity as Ella dealt with packing for furlough and concern about her

mother, "I received Howard's letter telling of mamma's illness."
Later that day she wrote a note to her, "I will only write a short
letter as I do not wish to tire you. I hope that you will take very
good care of yourself until I get home to help take care of you."
Hannah Clay Edelman Wood died on March 3, 1898 before Ella
got home to see her.

Ella was anxious to leave Lien Chow and recounts the experience to her sister Bertha on March 9, 1898, "Here we are on the
boat going down the Lien Chow River, having left Lien Chow at
1:45. We were ready an hour or more before the captain. A number of the native Christians came down to the boat to see us off.
The pastor Rev. Kwan Loi is with us but will leave at Lung So Tan
where we also have some Christians. It is a beautiful day. God
has been very good to us. We prayed for rain and we got it and
now when we cannot have fire, the weather has moderated and
we are very comfortable with it. Mr. Lingle came over and Miss
Johnston was here. They both stayed on the boat until we were
ready to start. We will probably reach Ham Kong on Saturday
morning and perhaps spend the Sabbath there. Our boat is a
new one and we can arrange everything very comfortably.

"Friday Morning: It took us a long time to get the beds ready
last night and I was glad to be down when at last all was done.

"Edward, Victor, Elsie and I slept in one big bed made up on
the floor of the boat. As soon as it was made the four children
were put in and then Sam So and I began the struggle with the
second one. Edward who had been helping first with one and
then with another of the children went to bed to give us a chance
to make up the other bed. First, we put a little mattress against
the side of the boat to keep out the wind then put the rest of the
boards in to cover the hold after which we had to go on all fours
or squat as we cannot stand up excepting right in the centre[*sic*]
of the boat. After putting down a number of quilts, blankets

&c. I pulled the twins out of our bed and handed them over to Sam So who put them in the bed we had just made, after which she laid down on a mattress by them and then the cook boy and another young man having put up a curtain made their bed as best they could among the baskets, boxes, and safe, next in the row. All of us slept well but were awake at the break of day when the men began to stir and the boat to go. Today it is cloudy but not cold. Howard is sleeping and now I must stop and put Amy to sleep. Victor cried for his nurse this morning and wished to know when we were going back to Sam Kong.

"Monday Afternoon: Here we are in the boat again after a very pleasant visit with the friends at Kang How. We arrived there on Saturday afternoon and have had good weather all the time. Today it is almost perfect. We have been very fortunate so far in having good weather and I hope it will last until we reach Canton. The children have kept quite well. Howard has a cold in his eye from his ride to Kang How as there was a high wind and no cover on his chair.

"They have a beautiful bed of roses red, cream, pink and almost white. Elsie brought a bunch over with her. Mrs. Reed had some bread made for us which will last us until we reach Canton. After dinner we were so sleepy that we all laid[*sic*] down and all the children went to sleep. Howard is scarcely awake yet. Victor is playing with him and Amy is calling to the boat woman's little baby. Elsie is writing a letter to her Aunt May and Edward is reading. We both forgot there was an Aunt May which made us all laugh as Elsie was so pleased to think she knew. What Aunt May, we said? 'You haven't any Aunt May'. 'Yes, I have, Uncle Walter's wife'.

"Tuesday Morning: It is now 12 noon and the boat is on the North River and we have passed all the rapids. As we entered the river the boat people spread out a tray containing a chicken and a number of cups of wine also two lighted tapers. Just as we got opposite the temple which is not far from the bank fire crackers were set off and now I think they have eaten the chicken. We are having another beautiful day. At the entrance to the North river stones are cut for the rice mills. A number were on the bank partly finished. We have passed several beautiful bamboo groves and also great stacks of grass which is piled up on a raft to float down the river. It is made hollow in one part and there the men or family sleep. Some of the hills and mountains are quite thickly wooded but...most are bare excepting for the long grass, which the people use as fuel, and a few stunted bushes. Every year the mountain sides are burned off for fear of tigers, leopards and other wild beasts. It is a grand sight to see them at night!

"Edward thinks we shall certainly reach Canton by Friday.

"Wednesday, March 16: It is almost noon of another beautiful day and we are making good progress although there is not much wind. We stopped at Tsing Yun this morning while the cook bought some fresh vegetables and a little fruit and then off we went again. I am glad we passed that city in the daylight as it is noted for its robber bands and more than one boat has been plundered that anchored there overnight. Edward fired his pistol last night for the first time, just to let anyone who might be meditating plunder that we were prepared.

"Monday Evening: I am afraid I will miss the <u>Rio</u> and I did want you to have this letter as I know you will be anxious to hear from us.

"We arrived safely on Saturday morning and have been very busy ever since. The children stood the trip quite well, only at the last Victor and the rest took cold. I hope they may soon be better. Tell mamma and papa to be of good cheer that we will soon be home."

On board the <u>Hau Nam</u> Steamer on April 14, 1898, "Here I am on the steamer on the way to Hong Kong to get my dresses from the dressmakers." Located at No. 10, Sai Hing Street in Canton, Yut Cheong was the most reliable dressmaker and manufacturer of all kinds of silk, linen, and grass cloth. It was the custom for the missionaries to use the most reliable merchants for their personal needs. "I hear that we will be detained for inspection before we are allowed to land on account of the plague. It seems rather absurd when they have the plague in Hong Kong. I hope we may not be detained long, or else I shall have to come up on the Saturday steamer instead of tomorrow. Last week I forgot my shawl and of course never got it back again. I thought I would be alone but fortunately Miss Elda Patterson was on taking a young Chinese woman to Hong Kong. They dare not trust a young Chinese woman to go about alone. It is a delightful day for travelling, almost covers the sun and there is a breeze not too strong for comfort. While we were in Hong Kong last week, Howard had a boil on his eyelid that had to be lanced. It is well now. We are very pleasantly situated at Mrs. J. J. Boggs, but we will be glad when the time comes to start. Next Monday, a week, we take the steamer for Hong Kong, the Empress of India sails on Wednesday. O, how I wish I was at home now! The time seems very long.

"Sunday Morning: Before we got to Hong Kong the ship lay while we waited for the doctor. It was not long before a little steam launch appeared in sight flying a yellow flag and soon the doctor was on board. We stayed on deck and were not inspected but all the Chinese were ordered in and had to pass before him as that is the only inspection possible with one doctor and so many people. While we were waiting I planned how to go to save time as I wished to come back in the morning. I got through by ten o'clock and was too tired to sleep for about an hour. At five I was up and dressed. When I got downstairs and found it was so early I went back and tried to sleep but kept listening for the clock and could not do it. Before I started the landlady became much excited as a number of Chinese had commenced to pile their goods against the side of her house and she feared they were from a house where they had plague. She was pouring buckets of water down on them when I left.

"There were three cases of plague on board coming up, one in a dying condition. We stayed on deck in the air. They do not inspect at this end of the line.

"This will be the last letter from China. It will come by the <u>Doric</u> which sails on Tuesday. Mrs. B. C. Henry and her two daughters go on the <u>Doric</u> to Japan for Mrs. Henry's health. I did hope to get another letter before I started. Last mail brought no letter, the mail before said mamma was worse and the doctor gave little hope. I hope I may hear better news in this mail.

"We are all well and impatient to be off. With much love to all the dear ones. Any letter addressed to me, passenger on <u>Empress of India</u>, will be delivered on board."

They arrived in Trumansburg, New York after Ella and Edward placed the children in the care of her sister, Bertha in Philadelphia, "I hope you are all well and that the children have not given you too much trouble. I have been thinking of you... and pray that no harm may come to any of you while I am away. Do not let the children forget their prayers. Amy and Howard can repeat 'Now I lay Me' after you."

After leaving the children with Bertha, Ella and Dr. Mary Niles arrived at Clifton Springs, New York on June 7, "I had a very pleasant journey, met a number of nice people on the train who were on their way to Clifton Springs, Dr. & Mrs. Hepburn, Mr. Henry Grant, Miss Correll and Miss Vail of the Methodist Church."

"Clifton Springs was originally known as Sulphur Springs because of the mineral springs that run through the town." There were different types of healing springs offered along with well-planned exercise. It was, "Integrated healthcare that nurtured the mind, body and spirit with the goal of promoting wellness and individual health." The grounds, "had lovely pathways through the trees and gardens for patients to spend quiet peaceful walks." It was a peaceful setting yet offered, "The Baths" which, "put people up against a wall and sprayed them with 98 to 105 degree water and then with cold water down to 70 degrees or less." It was followed by rub downs with wet salt until the skin showed a good glow. This was all part of the medical treatments at Clifton Springs Sanitarium.

Arthur Judson Brown, Secretary of the Missions Board, emphasized in his work how noble it was 'to grasp the great thought that the Chinese is not only a man, but our brother man, made like ourselves in the image of God.' "The Missionary Mind" or "contact between missionaries in the field and their domestic constituents" (Reed, 1983) not only solicited support for foreign mission but served as a tool to implement policy change which could only be generated by public opinion. Dr. Machle was contacted by Presbyterian Missionary Societies and churches for speaking engagements in Philadelphia, New Jersey and Ohio. He was also interviewed by the Philadelphia Press for an article by Harrydell Hallmark which detailed their life in China.

After arriving in America Dr. Machle's first priority was having the skin graft on his leg. He was 14 years old when his tibia was crushed in an accident while working in a furniture store in Cincinnati, Ohio. The first part of their furlough was spent in Philadelphia where Edward had his surgery, allowing Ella an opportunity to visit all her friends, family and favorite places with her children. For many relatives, it was the first opportunity to get acquainted with Edward since they left for China shortly after they were married. Edward's surgery went well and during his recuperation arrangements were made with Presbyterian churches in the Frankford area for speaking engagements before going to Columbus, Ohio in August 1899 to spend time with his family. Ella writes from Columbus to her father, "Friday at 4:20 p.m. we left Cincinnati for Colorado. Edward's mother, Sister Annie, Brother Harry, and his wife Ida, and Anne's husband Frank Lamping saw us off. Ida and I took the children and went to the hospital to say goodbye to Edward while Annie and mother went on with the telescope. Where we change cars, we were fortunate enough to meet Frank on his way to the station and he helped us on and off of the car with the children. We had sent a telegram on to Jerry so thought, of course, he and Ellie would be there to meet us at Colorado, but the operator made a mistake in the date and no one came. I telephoned out to the barracks but could get no reply so about 8:15 p.m. checked my parcels and started with the four children to find the place."

Jerry, the Post Commissary Sergeant at Fort Snelling planned to meet them at the Post, when Ella, "Asked a policeman who directed me to a certain car which took me to the barracks but away on the opposite side from where Jerry lives. Fortunately, a little boy at my request went along to show us the way and took us to a house where a family having a similar name lived. The woman knew about where Jerry lived and went with us to the gate. Jerry was just saying that we would be there before that the next day when we walked in. They were all so sorry we had had such a time. The children soon had something to eat and were put to bed and we followed as we were quite tired.

"I expected to start for Wooster today but Jerry decided that I must wait until tomorrow. It looks like rain but then it is so hard to tell here with so much smoke. They all seemed to think that I did remarkably well to find the place as soon as I did and laughed at me for coming in the recruit's gate. I told them I was a 'raw recruit'...Yesterday 350 recruits started from here which kept Jerry busy until almost 2 p.m. He says there are very few soldiers left in the country. They have a very pretty place with a large yard – a grape arbor and some fruit and shade trees. There are a great many beautiful shade trees in the parade grounds. I had a peep at the mess room where over six hundred men can be seated at once and at their sleeping quarters. The grounds are certainly beautiful and of course, well kept. Jerry would rather not go to Cuba or Manila again but he may be ordered to do so. He says he has had all he wants of Cuba but if sent to Manila he will certainly come and see us at Lien Chow.

A month later they stopped in Millersburg, Ohio, to visit with Mary Bell, a relative of Hannah Louise Johnston. Mary's husband, Frank was a farmer who died years earlier, leaving her with ten children to raise. While visiting the farm, Elsie wrote a note to her Aunt Anna, "The kitty could not get in any other way because it was not wanted in the house. It would climb up the screen door till it got to the hole in the screen and then would climb down on the other side safe and sound on the floor. Write to me soon, I am always your loving, Elsie E. Machle...P.S. Please give my love to little William...good afternoon...address till September 7, West View Farm, Wooster Wayne Co. Ohio" with a picture drawn of Victor feeding the chickens in the farmyard; Victor wrote his cousin William, "I have been riding on a nice black horse...Elsie found some tiny little mice while she was help-ing pitch the sheaves of wheat...The other night just before dark while I was coming home with Mr. Frank Bell from driving the cows' home, I heard something say, Bah! Bah! Bah! and I was frightened as I feared it might eat men, and asked Mrs. Bell what it was and she said a sheep so I am not afraid."

The Presbyterian Homes for Children of Foreign Missionaries
In June 1897 the bitter part of the furlough was placing Elsie and
Victor in the missionary home, whose object was to strengthen
the work in the field for their parents. Ella had been working
on the application for admission for more than a year. Elsie was
located on the second floor of Westminster, an elegant Victorian
home that once belonged to the college president. Her roommate was Edith Fulton. It was a sparsely furnished room. Victor,
the youngest of the "mishkids" was placed in Livingstone, a
larger, more austere looking home. Each of the children had
housemothers. Elsie's housemother was Mrs. Mary Trenholm
and Victor's was Miss Cornelia Sherman. They assumed guard-
ianship over the children. Both women as Ella described them,
"Had difficult positions and a great family of girls and boys with
different dispositions requiring different treatment besides the
oversight of their clothing, accounts." Instruction were given by
Ella to the housemothers to write once a week about the children's progress. Since Mrs. Trenholm had control over the accounts, Elsie did not have access to her allowance. At Westminster
Home she was under the watchful eye of the matron. Matron
and 'inmate was a term commonly used on census records before 1920. Though the role of housemother was referred to as
matron, while residents in her care were known as inmates, or as
Merriam-Webster's Dictionary of the English Language defines
as, "A person who lodges or dwells in the same apartment or
house with another; a fellow lodger." Ella once warned her sister, "She is the matron, but I rather think she does not like to be
called that, so be careful when you write, not to offend in that
way. I think that is the way I found out she did not like it."

The school environment and rules governing visits with Victor
on Friday's was complicated by Ella's expectation that Elsie would
look out for her brother. Rule number five was, "Brothers may

call on their sisters at Westminster between four and five o'clock on Sunday afternoons. Aside from this there must be no Sunday visiting." From the moment he was able to walk, Victor was incorrigible. Ella now urged Elsie to help him 'do good,' 'be kind,' 'be honest.' Elsie, too, was faced with cultural adjustments. She left behind several young Chinese friends vowing that someday she would return and now she was in the position of parenting her brother. The differences between China and America became more obvious to the children who were referred to as "mishkids." A term similar to PK, or preacher's kid, that created labeling or ostracism outside of the Wooster campus.

After returning to Lien Chow on December 5, 1899, Ella soon learned her expectations regarding contact with the children by mail was only as good as the mail delivery. Mail delivery between America and China depended on the weather, steamer's arrival and departure, Chinese holidays or lost mail. It took nearly three weeks regardless of the delivery system. Ella's letters were pointed, "Where is that nice long letter we had hoped to get in the last mail? Do not neglect to write my dear one or there may come a time when you will bitterly regret it." Then, she frets, "The Russians have been molesting vessels just carrying passengers and cargo, so mail has come irregularly." She never hesitated to share her disappointment when her sister didn't share enough information. The separation created anxiety. The children were growing up and she wanted to know what they looked like, requesting current photos to see how they were developing.

Amy or "*Ah Ming* is what the Chinese called Amy, meaning bright, clear, beautiful. Her name translated has almost the same sound as in English and the same sound as in English and the same meaning." After having malaria, she wrote this note to Elsie, "I am sick now and I want to go back home and see you. But mother will not let me. So, I must stay here." This letter had stick figures at the top in colored pencil, "I do not think that I could bear to leave Mamma. I send hugs and kisses. I am your sister, Amy." There are letters that indicate Ella coached Amy as she writes to Victor, "I hope that you have a good time with the boys. I hope that Elsie will soon send those books. Mamma has two pigeons. They are still young...I have finished the Sum sz King and the Se sz King. I am commencing in the second reader. Your loving little sister."

By July 17, 1900, there was growing concern when Ella wrote to her father: "How your hearts must have been filled with anxiety and terror when the news reached you of the state of affairs in Pekin[*sic*] and Tiensin and vicinity. We cannot believe that it is true that so many of our friends and countrymen have been murdered. Yesterday we received the China Mail in which the rumor that all the foreigners in Pekin had undoubtedly been murdered was said to be only too true, but yet we cannot believe it and will wait and hope until we cannot do so any longer. Li Heung Chung is holding the reins with a firm hand in Canton and is anxious that the "powers" confine their operations to the north. We also hope and pray that each may be the case. It would not be right and God would surely punish the Christian powers if they allow such butchery to go on and do not try to stop it. They have waited too long already thus sacrificing valuable lives. After the first excitement had subsided in Canton everyone settled down to his usual occupation big and little. We have been sent for by special messenger twice – our seven dollar letters we call them but there is really no reason as to why we should go. The people have never seemed more friendly. If it were necessary for us to leave here for a time we would probably go to the Iu country, but we do not anticipate any danger and thank God every day for this undeserved mercy, that while so many have been called upon to suffer we have been kept in peace. I would be terribly afraid of a mob and would want to go away in a hurry if there were any indications of an uprising."

By the end of the month, her letters shared even more concern when, "we received a letter from the American Consul telling us to come to Macao or Hong Kong...we are far from the seat of war. The official has put out a very good proclamation sent from Canton by Li Heung Chung. The disturbance caused by the advent of three Italian priests who attempted to escape from Hang Chow, Hunan...disguised as Chinese...were discovered after they were on a boat to go to Canton...Cries of 'Kill! Kill the foreign devils' was heard on all sides...the official pretended to arrest them but really gave them an escort...we hope...that they were not dragged back to be killed."

By August 13, Ella again writes to her father about the situation, "there has been no change...one of the 'dragon heads' ... of the Triad Society who was trying to inaugurate a rising was captured at Sing Tsz...went to a rich man of the place and tried to induce him to put out the necessary money, but the man being peacefully inclined...refused to help...we still do not know who is to succeed *Li Heung Chung* if he is not allowed to return to Canton. He has refused to take the field against the foreigners as he has been ordered. He himself cannot say positively that the 'edict' he received is genuine. His mission as mediator and 'stave-er-off'...I feel sorry for him. So old...not in love with foreigners yet through policy inclined to treat them well...now having his hands tied by this mysterious edict from no one knows whom...we feel we are about as safe here as anywhere."

By the end of August, they left Lien Chow by boat, keeping in the background away from open doors, and went to Hong Kong to find a safe place to live. By the time they arrived, news reached them that Pekin had been taken.

Yet there was also tension between Ella and Louise. It seems that Miss Johnston was in America and word came back to Ella that she took a Chinese man home with her. He was studying at Wooster University. Ella wrote to her saying, "I did not care to have Elsie or Victor go anywhere in his company...if she did not leave the Chinese man with her I would be glad to have her near the children as she is very fond of them and they of her."

It was Wooster's summer break and on July 20, 1902 Elsie was visiting Mary Bell at Westview Farm and writes to her Aunt Bert in Philadelphia describing her ventures, "I hope you are well. I know I have not written to you very often. I am out in the country now, and I and Victor are having lots of fun.

"I got a letter from mother the other day and so did Victor. They keep lots of chickens here and have an incubator and hatch little chicks which are very cute. It is a very pretty place. They have had ripe apples for over a week.

"It has been raining for too[*sic*] days write[*sic*] along. They have four little kittens here. There is one pure white," but a letter from Ella on October 14 established her control over the situation. "I did not give Elsie permission to manage her own correspondence. Mrs. Trenholm made a mistake. I said Elsie's letters to me I would like to have her send just as she wrote them without inspection as I could then see what progress she was making and she would feel free to write as her heart dictated. Do you think that strange? That I should wish her to feel free to write to me without inspection?"

On the other hand, when Elsie finished her lessons in arithmetic she was expected to send them to her mother for Mrs. Edwards, wife of Rev. Rees Edwards. Mrs. Edwards taught arithmetic to Amy and Howard and needed the advanced textbook, "If you have finished with yours, please send it by mail." Ella then proposed that she, "ask Mrs. Trenholm to let you buy the first practical arithmetic used in Wooster at present, and also the first mental arithmetic...and send in the next mail."

"Elsie and Victor are in the country about forty miles from Wooster", writes Ella to her father, "I heard that Victor had had the measles and that Elsie has had an operation on her throat. I have not heard the particulars. They have a very nice home in Wooster. Perhaps some time you can go see them. Haven't you a friend who would give you a pass? Wooster is a nice country town. The rents and living are cheap. Ten dollars a month secures a very nice house of seven rooms and summer kitchen with wood house and garden. Elsie and Victor are in the country about forty miles from Wooster." Late November, word came to Ella and Edward of Elsie's illness with scarlet fever. Then, Victor underwent surgery for an undisclosed injury by Dr. Joseph Stoll, the Wooster University physician. Ella's cousin, Clara Cloud, wrote to Ella on January 1904 that Elsie had diphtheria. A letter arrives from Papa to Elsie showing his concern, "You have had scarlet fever and now diphtheria. These two diseases are unknown at Lien Chow. If you had been with us you would not have suffered from either one of them. As far as your physical being is concerned, you have not been benefitted by a residence in America." Later her mother wrote, "How grateful you must feel to Mrs. Trenholm for all her love and care while you were shut upstairs. How hard it was for her to have to go up and down with your food and take care of all the others besides...she never... said a word to us about it when she wrote, but we knew through Grandma Johnston." Again, the emphasis was on their behavior, "Do not worry if your averages are lower, if your conduct marks are higher. I want you to have fun, but let it be the kind that leaves no sting behind." The message is repeated to Victor, "Do you try to keep your teacher by being kind and gentle and loving and honest. Never cheat, Victor. It will only harm you and cause you to be disliked."

Ella never hesitated to have a teaching moment in her correspondence whether it was to Elsie or Victor about the reports of bad behavior, "It is know, to know anything, not no and meant, not ment. You generally spell very well, but I thought you would like to know that you made these two mistakes. Sometimes you write to, for too. No doubt if you looked over your letter before sending, you would notice such a mistake" and to Victor, "Ask me some questions if you want to know." They were also interested in their lessons and would ask if they took drawing, music, instrumental or vocal lessons. It seemed important to be able to entertain others with their voice or music. There was the suggestion that she may, "Learn to like to sew. It is very important to know how...because a dress does not fit, without knowing how to remedy it is very foolish." Then, the emphasis on reading! "In one of your letters, you said you had begun to read the Bible through—now I think you would get more profit from it if you left that until later and read it by topics or by books. For instance, begin with the word faith or light, or peace, and read what the Bible says or walk. It is surprising how many there are, telling us how to walk...when you read a book for pleasure, get all the enjoyment out of it you can, but I am not at all pleased to have you read so many novels. It is not good for you...I like to have you enjoy yourself, but do not be silly about the boys...another thing dear, never tell, or listen to an unclean or wrong story. You need not be ashamed to speak out, and say you will not listen, and if you lose a friend by it, be sure she was not worth keeping."

As she became more active in school she developed an interest in joining clubs and was particularly interested in sports. She wanted to join the tennis club and Ella suggested only, "If it is not too expensive. You could have a simple white flannel waist and a dark blue skirt and you would have to take great care of your racquet as racquets are expensive…if Mrs. Trenholm thinks the members are all right, I think it would be very nice, but I do not want you to neglect your music or your studies."

By March 19, 1903, Papa writes to his dear boy, Victor, and shares with him that, "The highest military official leaves tomorrow for Canton and another man takes his place. I sent him some potted jam, honey and canned fruits because we were friends. He gave me a monkey that was very kind to everybody and did not bite, although it was tantalized. I put it in some medicine (chloroform) until it was dead and put it in some medicine (pickle) so as to preserve for the medical students who will soon study anatomy."

Rumors of more trouble was spreading. An article in The Washington Times writes of Chinese mobs menacing American engineers. Within the month, Ella writes to her daughter on April 30, and says, "The time will surely come if you live long enough, when you will understand our anxiety for your welfare and you will regret with bitter tears, if you wait until it is too late to write to us. Suppose one sad day, you should receive a letter from father saying I had gone home to Heaven, and that you would never see me again on earth, would you not feel sad to think how often the weeks slipped by and you neglected to send the letter you knew would gladden my heart and quiet my fears, and would it not be the same, if it were from me you received the same sad words about your father. Again, Ella writes to her sister, "Do you know I have longed more to be at home this last year than ever since I came to China…I do want to learn as Paul did…to be content."

On the other hand Elsie's letters were descriptive, full of activities, as well as reports on her studies with no indication that she was aware of the troubles in China. One letter upset Ella which generated this response, "I am glad you had a good time on Halloween, but I do not admire the method of the boys in celebrating it. My dear girl, do not nag at Victor, but try to persuade him by other methods. Do try to help him. We feel so sad to think he is disgracing us by his conduct...and a letter to Victor, "do be a good, dear boy. Ask God to help you. Cut your bad companions. Be ashamed to use bad language." Later, Papa writes to Elsie that, "Victor has already disgraced his parents and I do not want you to. Try to get him to be obedient and honest. I want you to write all you hear and see about him. Do not think you a tale-bearing because we wish to know. When one asks to know about another, it is not tale-bearing if a person's tells that one most interested in the culprit." At the same time, Elsie kept up her correspondence to her Chinese friends, Naamwo and Seung Wu, the youngest daughter of Rev. Kwaan Loi. In late July, Harriet Noyes sends Seung Wu's letter sharing her concern for Elsie and hoping to hear from her soon. Some of her letters to her mother share her homesickness for the family and as her mother writes, "My dear girlie, I often feel as you do that I would give anything to see you and Victor, but I know it is best for you to be in the homeland and I feel sure you will make good use of your time. Do help Victor all you can my dear. Be a good kind sister to him. Do not scold him but love him into being good. My heart is very sad when I think of him, but I know the Lord is as near him in America, as he would be in China."

Ella received word in June that Grandpa Wood was dying and she hoped Elsie would go to see him before he passed away.

Papa, on the other hand, directs his daughter to be more frugal, [Elsie] "you are fourteen years old...we decided to give you a larger allowance and permit you to purchase your own things... render an account to both Mrs. Trenholm and us occasionally. Get an account book and write everything you buy, even to the stick of candy…we have allowed you $80." Other decisions developed when Ella writes to sister Bessie that she expects to start a new plan…to keep a correspondence book and write down when she receives a letter and when she sends one out. This is instilled in Elsie as well.

In August, of 1903, the correspondence focuses on textbooks when Ella writes to Elsie, "Amy and Howard have commenced to study again. I want you to send me by return mail <u>two new</u> 2nd Readers. You sent an old third Reader but they are not ready for that yet." A year later, she sent money for "new ones…and send them at once…Amy says she wants to write for this mail, but she has not done it." Just as Amy's letters share her insecurities about being separated from Victor and Elsie, there was a tone of insecurity about being away from her parents, especially her mother. I imagine it was hard to be separated for seven years at a time. The children wrote these notes,

> *"Dear Elsie, I wold[sic] like to see you but I cannot see you. Because you are far away from me, but I love you.*
>
> *Howard."*
>
> *"I want to see you very much, but I cannot see you for a long long time yet for I am far away from you. I am, learning now to knit and sew and I finished a quilt the other day."* Ella writes a note at this point, *"for her doll's bed…I have a little yellow dog. Its name is yellow just like his hair.*
>
> *Your Loving Little Sister, Amy W. Machle"*

It was mid-October when Ella described the arrival of Dr. Chesnut and Miss Patterson to her father in a letter, "Dr. Chesnut arrived here on Saturday afternoon with our new missionary Miss Patterson who is to have charge of the Girls' School...we had been inquiring all week of the boats arriving whether their boat had been seen and where as we did not wish them to come in on us unawares. On Saturday morning the hospital preacher started on foot down the bank of the river and not long after he had gone the elder who had been to Canton to Presbytery and came up in Mr. Scheirer's boat and Tung Seen Shang our helper at Tung Pae, greeted me with peace in our yard and at the same time handed me a letter which proved to be from Dr. Chesnut saying they could hardly wait to see us. That they hoped we could come meet them. They were at the Dragon's Beard Falls so we knew they would be near the pagoda below the city early in the afternoon. I had planned to let everyone go and stay and watch the house but Mrs. Edwards was not willing to go without me so we had two boats and away we went. Mr. Scheirer's boat with Dr. Chesnut and Miss Patterson came along side and the journey was over. Fire crakers[*sic*] were set off, the gong was beaten, Edward blew his horn and both American and Chinese flags and people waved a greeting. We did not mind the rain as the boats did not leak and it stopped while we were outside on the front of the boat waiting for them. We all took supper together and enjoyed ourselves very much. We think we shall like the new missionary." Elda G. Patterson was born in Washington, Pennsylvania on March 30, 1868 and was a teacher at West Middletown, Pennsylvania before leaving for China in 1903. By November 1, "Last night we reached Sam Kong just a short time after the sun set. The men wished to anchor at four o'clock but father told them that they must go to Sam Kong. Mr. Edwards and father and Mok Sin Shang and Howard helped row.

Howard enjoys rowing very much and I have to make him rest every once in a while, or when the sun is too hot…we have a new missionary who came with Dr. Chesnut, Miss Elda Patterson, so there are two now at the station you have not seen, Mr. Edwards, Scheirer and Miss Patterson."

A letter from Papa to Elsie in mid-November, "He[Howard] and Amy will be 8 years old in December. When we return to America in four years more they will be 12 years old. You and Victor will never see them again as a little boy and girl. They have started a letter apiece for Ella's sister, Aunt Bert. They write very little each day."

Victor rarely wrote a letter unless he had an ulterior motive to gain information. Imagine Amy's surprise when he sent this letter in July of 1904, "I suppose that you thought that I would never write to you, but you can see that I have not yet forgotten your letter that you wrote to me. There has been pretty fine weather for three days but all the rest of the time it would rain, rain, rain nothing but rain all the day. As you said in your letter, you are having a nice time and I am glad to hear so how much money have you got to spend on fun. I wish you would tell me for I would like to know and if you do not tell me I will not write you any more letters. I cannot write straight[sic] because I have not got any lines. I hope you may be able to see that. I have not much to say but all I have to say I will of course. I want to ask you if you are going to the Western College with the other girls or the Northfield. This week I am going to send you a box of faug[sic]…I will be at the home all summer and you may send your letter at 52 College Wooster, Ohio, Wayne County. I was up to the Medina Bee Hives largest bee farm in the world and I brought home a pocket full of bee's wax. The man that owns the bee farm, Mr. Root, he took a picture of the hold bunch of us and he is going to send each one of us a picture…he is going to send each of us a picture so you not think he is kind. Good bye from Victor."

Life seemed simple for Elsie. It was either her need for $30 to attend the St. Louis Exposition or making plans to go to Chautauqua. If she goes to the Exposition, Victor could not go with her because he was too small, but they allowed him to go to Chautauqua. In the midst of deciding, Papa writes about a disturbance in Lien Chow in early May. "The people did not want lottery gambling in their town so when the place opened, they tore down the house, burnt all the things in it, then went to the houses of two of the gentry and took out all the furniture from their houses and burnt them on the parade grounds. These two gentry helped the gamblers to open up the lottery shop. When they got through with the three houses, they went towards the city. The city gates were closed, so they broke through one of the closed gateways and went to the great yamen. It was closed. They broke it open and rescued two men whom the official had unjustly seized and who were good gentry...nothing happened to us for the people numbering 4000 were good people and not rowdies and gamblers." Within the month, Ella's letters shared the death of Rev. Richard Noyes, who died of the plague, and Rev. Edward Scheirer who died of a liver abscess.

At the end of the 1904 school year, Elsie had to make a decision about enrolling in Prep School. Ella, Edward and Elsie focused on Western, Northfield or Wooster and since Ella recommended Northfield and believed the contact with earnest Christian workers was very inspiring, the school would be good for Elsie, "I and mamma have talked about your entering the prep department of the University of Wooster. I wrote in my last of the conditions. I hope you will comply with them." Ella urged her daughter to consider going away from Wooster because there were advantages in leaving Wooster. But she had friends at

Wooster, as well as concerns about Victor's welfare, so Elsie chose Wooster to start Prep School in the fall.

By November, the Machle's were vacationing in Macao while Edward attended the annual meeting, "Returning up the river after the annual meeting in Canton, Howard developed diphtheria halfway to Lien Chou. They had to decide whether to run back to Canton for antitoxin or continue up river. They decided to continue on home but to send a runner to Canton to get the medicine. That runner hadn't returned after several days so they sent out a second runner who made it to Canton and back in record time with the antitoxin…but with only enough for Howard. Howard didn't survive and Amy lost her twin brother who was also buried in the Lien Chou cemetery." On November 29, Ella's father, Howard Wood died and was buried in Hillside, Pennsylvania just below Willow Grove although word would not reach Ella until weeks later. "Howard you know has gone to a better land." Edward writes to Ella's family in Philadelphia. He "loved to sing." Edward wrote to Elsie shortly after his death, "Yesterday was the twins' birthday and Howard was missed by us very much. Amy enjoyed herself after being cooped up for two weeks. She had diphtheria also but the lord graciously restored her. The antitoxin came too late for Howard but was the means with God's blessing of saving dear Amy. You have now a little brother hardly nine years old…in heaven awaiting your coming…dear Howard had many admirable traits. Kind, sunshiny, and musical and energetic. I had built many hopes on him in his natural life. My sadness is brightened by thinking of him with the King of Kings and Lord of Lords singing the sweet songs of heaven where there is no sorrow, no crying, no night. Make your life useful and beautiful with kind acts, with furvent[*sic*] faith in Christ."

Bert received a letter in December, "Amy had an attack of diphtheria, beginning just two weeks after Howard passed away, but she made a rapid recovery. Edward only using the anti-toxin twice giving her in all three thousand units. We are so thankful she has been spared to us...I think all of us have had sore throats...and Sunday before last November 30, Edward's throat was so inflamed that I was much alarmed but it yielded to ordinary treatment and that night (no the night before) the special messenger came with the extra anti-toxin which we will have on hand...we are all disinfected again...if you fear, burn this letter." Even though there was concern about the trouble in Kwangtung Province, they never believed it would affect them. Elsie had no way of knowing what lie ahead for her family, even though Ella's letters and the trouble in China seemed to have dampened the spirits of everyone. To Elsie, a fourteen-year old, it was important to concentrate on school.

CHAPTER 4
Lien Chow 1905

Rumors of trouble in North China circulated since The Boxer Uprising began. Ella mentioned Kwang How in a letter home and the trepidation she felt about visiting the city. That was normal when reports of attacks on the missionaries and destruction of property by robbers and mobs prevailed. They had become familiar with the Chinese term "foreign devil," or the American label of "John Chinaman." Dr. Eleanor Chesnut, remained in Lien Chow when the Machle's left Lien Chow on August 11 to vacation at the Peak in Hong Kong before going on to Macao for the Annual Meeting. It was a trip they looked forward to. They would meet with other missionaries in a social setting and relax. The year before while at the Macao Hotel, they were entertained by the Commander of Police when the String Band played many enjoyable tunes. The new missionaries, Rev. and Mrs. John Rogers Peale met Dr. Machle and took a boat down river to Lien Chow, a trip of two to three weeks. Mr. and Mrs. Edwards, another family assigned to the Lien Chow Mission sailed April 25, 1905, for America for their first furlough so the Mission needed the new arrivals to carry the work load.

The previous year was difficult for the Machle's with the death of Reverends' Noyes and Scheirer. Then, Dr. Machle's father died in Cincinnati, Ohio, and Ella was struggling with exhaustion and despair from the loss of Howard. Ella put a lot of herself in raising the children, even from afar, and wrote to Elsie and Victor daily with suggestions and guidance in their daily life. In January 1905, Ella wrote to Elsie, "Mrs. Burgoyne told me about your Grandfather Machle's death. She went to see your Grandma Machle the other day. This is what she wrote me about him, "So suddenly he was taken, no sickness nor warning whatever. He was night watchman at Burnet Woods Park and left home at nine o'clock in his usual cheerful way, stopping at the drug store for the evening papers and then going directly to the park, not a long walk arriving there, he went into the house, greeted his comrades within, sat down and was gone. They talked of Edward and family and showed me a picture of Howard. It seems to me that Howard is not gone. I cannot make it seem real to myself."

Ella put equally as much work into the school she started for the local children which was growing in attendance. They had worked hard to build the Mission house, men's and women's hospital, and care for the residents of this city of 12,000, situated in the western portion of the Province of Kwangtung, at the head of the Gulf of Tong King, not far from the treaty port of Pakhoi. Dr. Machle's associate, Dr. Eleanor Chesnut, had the same compassion for the people as both traveled on horseback and jinricksha across the area to treat the people. Dr. Chesnut started a class for nurses at the women's hospital. In recent months, she started training Mrs. Goo Kim, from Honolulu as a medical student. It wasn't unusual for Dr. Machle and Dr. Chesnut to be involved in the lives of the Chinese people. Each of them had hostlers to help them with their horses, chores, housework, and children, and it became part of their way of life to deal with the Chinese anger which had been mounting in the North China region but had not affected them in the Kwangtung Province.

Lien Chow was the most successful Mission and one area where there was little trouble.

Rev. John Rogers Peale and Rebecca Gillespie Peale, left New Bloomfield, Pennsylvania in June, arriving in Canton in early October to fill the post of Rev. Edward Scheirer. After arriving by boat on the evening of October 27th, Dr. Edward Machle walked up to the men's hospital to see how things were going, only to find the village involved in a festival held to celebrate Ta Tsin, or Ta Tsiu. The spelling in the Cantonese pronunciation, is a festival according to the lunar calendar. October 28, 1905 was the first day of the tenth lunar month that year or the new moon. It wasn't celebrated every year, although there is a Taoist renewal ceremony which had been going on for three days.

This is a summary of the newspaper articles that began appearing in Honolulu and Oregon on November 10, 1905. The Oregonion reported that, "As he approached the hospital, he saw a child with a cannon and picked up the cannon which a boy was preparing to fire. At the same time, Dr. Machle told the boy to tell three old men to come out and speak to him. He thought it would be better than going in the temple and disturbing their worship. Three old men came to Dr. Machle at the entrance to the hospital. They agreed with the doctor that it was not right to build on the mission ground but asked that as it was the last day of the feast that the mat shed be allowed to remain." They promised not to build in the same place next year. Therefore, the cannon was handed back to the elders and the matter was settled.

In a letter from Dr. Machle, he describes the mat shed as a gambling place. Another newspaper account from the Oregonion adds this account, "Dr. Eleanor Chesnut arrived at the women's hospital and saw the commotion generated by the discussion with the elders. Several of the young ruffians, objected to Dr. Machle's interference and struck him on the arm with a bamboo stick and threw a brick at him, causing a gash on his forehead. At this point, Dr. Machle didn't think the event was that serious and went up to his house to get a card to send in to let the officials know what had happened." Then the mob set fire to the hospitals and started toward the missionary compound. The group headed to a small temple, behind which there was a cave. Dr. Chesnut left and went down to the river to the yamen but could not get through on account of the crowd and was taken on board a guard boat. She tried to leave to go back to the other missionaries and was escorted by a guard back to the house. At the house, all of them gathered in an upper room while Dr. Machle sent a man to the officials. They came with attendants, but the soldiers were unarmed. With the exception of Dr. Machle and Elda Patterson, a nurse missionary at the hospital, Ella, Amy, Dr. Chesnut, Rebecca and Rev. John Rogers Peale were all murdered. The tragedy was complicated by the Boxer Uprising in the north and the anger generated by the disrespect of the Chinese culture, superstitions, and society. The missionary movement often forced upon them by outsiders known as the Foreign Devils and the wealthy investors in the railroad as well as development of sacred land contributed to this tragedy.

Edward wrote a note to the other survivor, Elda Patterson on November 20, "We all reached here on Sunday, yesterday, at 11 a.m. A large body of soldiers with officials received us at the lower end of the city below the Yuk Ying Tung, saluted us and then received us at Lien Chow by Nam Yun Tou, official landing. All the officials made their calls upon us and we informed them as the day is Sunday we would return the call the next day.

"On Sunday afternoon, we went to the burned buildings and gave the Consul-general the whole story of the burning in order. He said we had a beautiful place. He did not realize we had such a large plant. The buildings he said were certainly fired separately, one could not catch from the other. The grave-yard with its broken tombstones, five new graves and razed walls were a sad sight. There is nothing wicked the mob did not do. On the walls of the church many vile epithets and phrases were written with the charred wood. Both cemetery and church they desecrated. The church tower with its golden cross is still un-touched by fire. Thus far, we have found four reasons, the boy-cott, the hatred of foreigners in general, the greed for loot, and the spoiling of their fung-shui." Another reason was the ill feel-ing about the building of the Hankow Railroad. "This morning about 9:30 we went to the yamen all the officials received us at the head official's yamen, where in a room newly papered on the walls and ceiling, we had Tim-sam (luncheon) from a long table covered with a clean piece of muslin. After a few bites and a long talk from the *to-toi*, Mr. Beattie waited to take the officials' pictures. So, we all went to a small open space just outside the reception hall where three different groups were taken by Dr. Beattie, Fulton and the Consul-general. The Consul-general's camera was worked by his stenographer.

"We then returned to our houseboats as we prefer sleeping on them. At about 3 p.m. we went to Lung Tau Sz (the cave). Here I pointed out your hiding place and mine. Mr. [Joseph] Goo Kim came over from Sam Kong with Li Yong Shang just before we started for the cave so they went along. Mr. Goo Kim showed where Mrs. Machle lay and one of his children were hid-ing and Dr. Chesnut's hiding place. Mrs. Machle hid alone just off from the steps leading down into the depths of the cave. Amy and Fanny Goo hid further back on a high place. Dr. Chesnut hid just inside the opening of that section of the cave that I had entered very deeply. Mr. and Mrs. Peale went clear to the bottom of the main corridor of the cave and quite far among the clefts and hollows.

The Consul General Captain Evans and Lieutenant Captain Dismukes took great interest in it all and went into all the places except jumping into the pit where you were. They were satisfied with just looking down into the abyss."

In a letter to friends, he wrote, "I attended the meeting out of justice to the Chinamen who committed the atrocity, being with the Joint Committee, composed of three Americans, the Consul General Lieutenant Evans, of the USS Oregon, and Lieutenant Dismukes of the USS Monadnock." Three Chinese officials took part, *Taotai Wen*, the Civil Authority, General *Chui* of the Provincial Troops, and Commodore *Kew* of the Imperial Navy.

"About thirty of the 200 scoundrels who participated in the massacre were given a hearing. Many of them were sentenced to one, three and five years' imprisonment. Three were beheaded in a public place on a sand bar just by the main bridge of Lien Chow. Thousands of persons attended the beheading. All the officials, great and small, were there.

"Many of the culprits have escaped and are in the fastnesses of the mountains. Rewards have been offered for them and they will no doubt be caught in the near future." There was punishment for the fourteen captured; three were decapitated, four were imprisoned for five years, two were disgraced by wearing the canque or yoke which was labeled with the person's name, address, and nature of the crime, and five were bambooed.[1]

Wharton Street Presbyterian Church held a service in memory of the Lien-Chou Martyrs on December 10th, 1905 at 8 p.m. The address was given by Rev. Arthur J. Brown, D.D. and the choir sang, *The Christians Good Night*. Scripture teachings were read responsively and Ella's sister, Bessie, underlined on the bulletin, "But this cometh to pass that the word may be fulfilled that is written in their law, 'They hated me without a cause.'" Mrs. Machle had been a member of the church for seven years and the bulletin quoted her favorite lines, "Build a little wall of trust around to-day: Fill it in with loving deeds and therein stay; Look not through the sheltering bars upon tomorrow; God will help you bear what comes of joy or sorrow."

DR. MACHLE IN RICKSHAW IN FRONT OF MENS HOSPITAL

ROW 1: DR. EDWARD MACHLE, ELLA, REV. REES EDWARDS
ROW 2: AMY MACHLE, DR. ELEANOR CHESNUT, HOWARD
MACHLE, MRS. REES EDWARDS HOLDING MARGARET

LIEN CHOW HOSPITAL AND RESIDENCE

ELSIE AND VICTOR MACHLE, 1904

THE NIGHT OF OCTOBER 28 SHOWING THE FIRES BURNING
AT LIEN CHOW DURING FULL MOON

CHAPTER 5

Papa Comes Home in 1906-1910

A rthur Brown sent a message to Victor and Elsie Machle on November 8, 1905 but addressed it to Elizabeth Bechtel at Wooster. He sent his condolences at the death of their mother and father. It was a simple yet unfeeling message to two very young people who despite the confusion that must have been going on, probably remembered very little of its content.

The times were uncertain in January 1906 when Elsie returned from Christmas vacation with Ella's family in Philadelphia. It had only been a few months after the massacre when she wrote the following essay for a prep school class, "The times are uncertain, that is, the time of certain trains, so it was with little surprise that we learned that No. 8 was about two hours late. We were submissive to our fate but all the romance was gone from the hour (which was one o'clock p.m.) after we had waited in the draughty Wooster station until the clock said it was three. When at last the train did pull out it was with a feeling of joy that I saw the dim lights of Wooster disappear in the distance, and I thought with no little pleasure of the time which would elapse before I would see the charming place again. The train slipped along with very little jarring (which is strange on the Pennsylvania lines) and as magazines were plentiful we were soon enjoying ourselves. After passing Pittsburg the scenery was very beautiful. The wooded slopes of the Allegheny Mountains were often colored with yellow, red and blue, while the large quarries shaded into the various colors of the rainbow. One large rock I remember distinctly. It was of the deepest red and looked as if an autumn sunset, unwilling to leave its beautiful surroundings, had chosen this place for its rest. Deep violet shades and dimmer purple were fringing the distant horizons but as the sun set they were changed first to rosy pink and golden, then fainter yellow, and finally the lightest tint of lemon faded away in the west.

"At last, just as I had almost abandoned hope of ever seeing Philadelphia, we pulled into the Broad Street Station. At first I was at a loss, for I could see no one whom I knew and being a stranger I must admit I felt a little 'weird' as I walked up toward the gate; but though trembling in my boots I put on a brave face and walking as though I owned half of Wanamakers and knew everything about the city I pushed my way past the hurrying people. I came to the gate and then I had no more time to fear, for my aunts and cousins and even one of the members of the Travelers Aid Society embraced me in rapturous embrace so glad were they all to see me.

"Then followed the usual thing. After having seen about the trunk we went to Wanamaker's tea room for dinner and all I can say is, that I am glad I did not have to pay the bill.

"Now began a season of living which, should I explain to you, would immediately cause me to be 'fired'. But I am naturally courageous, being born that way or at least attaining it at an early age, so I will risk my life, yes even the reputation of the 'uncriticizable' class of 1912, by relating to you in short some of my adventures.

"It was not long before I discovered that I had an aunt or uncle in every corner of the city and was quite delighted because I knew

I would leave just that many more places to visit. Wanamaker's (though only related by Adam) claimed my attention on the next morning even before some of my nearer relations. I went really to see his store but I am quite fond of the gentleman also. He is adding to his store and when it is finished it will be one of the most beautiful stores in the world. The ceilings are all molded beautifully and studded with many colored lights. There, may be seen anything from the finest Paris gowns to tin tops. Beautiful furs and laces, rugs from the Orient, lamps from Venice, lovely jewelry from all parts of the world. Everything that's one's heart could desire and one's purse could not buy. You open the doors of Wanamaker's and you are in fairyland.

"Street cars are used by everyone and many amusing incidents happen on them. I will only mention the time we rode on our looks. We changed cars three times yet did not have to pay a cent. It would never do to go into detail for it might shock you. I must say my conscience hurts me when I think of how we robbed the Traction Co. of three fares.

"The State House where the original of the Declaration of Independence is and many famous relics is one of the most visited buildings in Philadelphia. There may be seen the Liberty Bell and many fine portraits of Washington, and if you should enter the museum you would see an old lady who would tell you that she was the great granddaughter of Betsy Ross. Many old flags and swords were hung about the walls while in glass cases were letters written by many famous men.

"The zoo also is a great place of enjoyment and I liked the reptiles and birds best to say nothing of elephants and lions etc. Outside the zoo is the house of William Penn. It is of pretty red brick and covered with ivy. The hospital, penitentiary, and insane asylum are visited by many but I satisfied myself by viewing them from the outside for my stay was short and then I thought my time was yet to come.

"I cannot write much on the New Year's celebration but it certainly was a beautiful sight. The parade of all the clubs in costumes was down Broad Street. Dressed in fantastic garbs and dancing and singing they made a continual moving picture. There was one robe that cost over a thousand dollars and had taken months to make. It was covered with beautiful embroidery and the train took forty pages to carry it." Elsie may not have named it, but it was one of the early Mummer's Parade.

"Everything was fine I had a better time than I have ever had in my life. If anyone of you should also wish the time of your lives you should follow my receipt---four uncles (mixed with fun); six aunts (of the best quality); four cousins (they should be young); and a Xmas vacation.

Then add a good heart full of good will and mix thoroughly in Philadelphia."

Elsie's frivolous essay was a typical 12-year old version of events. But it does reveal her talent for writing. In many ways, Elsie was removed from the tragedy and probably couldn't understand the reality of the situation. Was she in shock or was she denying that it happened? The short note from Dr. Brown doesn't describe the massacre but the Ohio newspapers put it on the front page with both cartoon drawings and pictures.

In 1907 the newspaper headlines announced Dr. Edward Machles' arrival back to the U.S.A. Describing the conditions in China to an eager reporter about the latest political upheaval, he was succinct. He was home and wanted to leave the stress behind. He planned a trip to Cuba with his brother Jerry, taking courses in pharmacy and dentistry, an attempt made on his earlier furlough, meeting with the Board of Foreign Missions of the Presbyterian Church in the U.S.A. and voting for William

Howard Taft for President. Unable to return to Lien Chow, once a consideration, he started to focus on a hospital in Canton, but he needed to expand his medical knowledge. Somehow, he would arrange a visit with Elsie and Victor. But, the Board of Foreign Missions developed a new policy governing field work and the changes would have a far-reaching impact on those in foreign service abroad.

A newspaper article in the Little Falls Herald on 1907 announced, "Dr. E. C. Machle, a Presbyterian missionary, has arrived here on the steamer Doric enroute to his former home in Cincinnati...He says he believes there will be another rising of the natives before many months in consequence of the efforts of the triad to overthrow the present Manchu dynasty and place a Chinese on the throne...natives are uneasy and dare not express opinions."

Having grown up in Auburn on the outskirts of Cincinnati, Edward Machle and William Howard Taft were childhood friends. The two had occasionally seen each other since meeting over dinner at the Government House in Hong Kong in September of 1905. Taft was running for President and stumping in his hometown of Cincinnati after the Chicago Convention. Edward refers to the décor around town for the event as he writes a letter to Elsie and mentions "Billy" the nickname Edward gave Taft.

"3151 Vine Street
Cinti, Ohio
July 28, 1908

Miss Elsie Machle
c/o Charles Haupert, Superintendent
Public Schools
Wapahoneta, Ohio

"Dear Elsie,

"So you are having a fine time are you! I am glad of it.
I wouldn't mind an auto run myself this hot weather. I
hope they will not trust you with the steering gear, if they
do, goodbye to you, the machine and the telegraph pole.

"The killed chicken certainly has an aroma so look out for
the S.P.C. next time. Autoists are not supposed to hunt
game with their huge blunderbusses.

"Well! I suppose you have made many new acquain-
tances and 'Wappa' will be a place of interest to you still
more in the future.

"Today 'Billy' will spout in his brother's front yard.

"The town is adorned as a bride in American regatta to
receive his benediction.

"The newspapers of course will tell you all. I will take in
all I can of the proceedings. Everything moves here in the
usual brisk businesslike way. Even Jeretta is mopping up

the kitchen floor. Work is the order of this household and this city. All you have to do in Wappa, I suppose, is to "wallow in the lap of luxury." I want no broken heads, arms or legs to come to me, so do be careful.

With love,

Your Papa"

The letter was addressed to Elsie at the public schools in Wapahoneta, Ohio, but Elsie was still a resident of the mission school in Wooster. Is it possible that she took a summer class in 'Wappa' which was closer to Cincinnati than Wooster?

While he was at 3151 Vine Street on furlough he completed the courses in pharmacy and dentistry at the Cincinnati College of Pharmacy, and the Cincinnati Dental College before travelling to Mantanzas, Cuba with his brother Jerry. A short note to Elsie gives little clue about the trip, "You certainly have been very kind to write to your 'dad' without receiving a reply to the first one. You may just keep on doing so. So, you are at Wooster and in the freshman class. I am so glad that you made it. I was a little afraid that you would be conditioned so much that you would feel it best to take the senior class. I know you can do anything in the study line if you are determined to do so. Well after you had a good time in 'Cinti', you will have to go to the necessary but pursue work of hard study." Cinti was short for Cincinnati, where Edward's relatives lived.

Mantanzas, Cuba

Jerry was the Post Commissary Sergeant at Fort Snelling, Ohio. He once claimed he preferred staying in the United States, but since he was in the U. S. Military he never knew where he would be sent. While in Cuba, his wife Ida, and their daughters worked at the Congregationalist Church. Dr. Machle sent his agenda to Elsie, "In two days", it was October 10, "I sail from Cuba. I wish to go from New York where the boat will touch to Philadelphia and from there to Wooster where I will stop about two days at most, then to "Cinti" and by a circuitous route through Chattanooga to China.

"I have tried to get the two dress patterns for you but have not yet succeeded. It seems that the goods you want are made in the Canary Islands brought over here by venders[*sic*] and sold. The venders[sic] come to Mantanzas about three or four times a year. They were here just before I arrived. Jerry is making every effort to find a vender and may succeed yet but the time is very short indeed. If you have time, it would please your "dad" if you would work in silk worsted a cushion cover to take to China. There are printed ones which need very little work on them. As you have but little time to work an elaborate one, just get one that need a few stitches to complete it.

"It is delightfully cool here now for summer is over. Electric shows galore here. I can go every night.

"Violet is a great help here in the Congregationalist Church. She plays the organ; teaches in the Sunday school and attends the different services. At home, she helps her mother much and takes three lessons a week in Spanish, teaches Pauline music and entertains many with her music. Nothing pleases her better than to get sheet music from her friends.

"Music for the piano and rag time songs are desired. Supposing you send her some music from Wooster and tickle her a little. Of course, you must send her the very latest for she has quite a number of songs. Jerretta isn't in it when it comes to quantity of music. Violet plays very well indeed ordinary music and gives all callers much pleasure. It would please me if you could find time for music, both vocal and instrumental. Read fewer novels and acquire a fairly good knowledge of this fascinating science.

"I hope at Wooster you will not keep up the awful sinful practice of looking for diversions on Sunday. I know you have been much better in regard to keeping the Sabbath than Jerretta, who has decidedly a non-Christian idea of Sunday pleasure. I find that those who do the least in the Sunday, go seldom to services are the ones that look upon Sunday pleasure going as right, a walk, a rest in the woods, a good book, or a good jolly walk are all right...I do not wish to preach a sermon to you for I do not think you need it.

"I received a letter from Victor the other day. He says he is having lots of fun at college and is taking French, Latin, arithmetic, physical geography, and spelling. I hope he will do good work there, for he is sadly deficient in learning for a boy of his age. He was coddled too much at Wooster. For him to remain there for his entire education would ruin him. His expenses at the Tennessee Military Institute is much greater, but if he gets what I think he needs, the money will be well spent. You may be looking for me the latter part of October. I will let you know when I will be in Wooster after I get into the States.

"I am enjoying myself here immensely. Jerry wishes me to remain quite a while longer. I think of returning to the states by way of New York. I can then see the members of the Board, the Philadelphia friends and you and afterwards run down to see Vic. Do not worry about Vic not being able to carry on the studies assigned him for the first year. They are few. He chooses one of the three language studies; German, French or Spanish. As to Latin, beginning Latin is easy and in England is taken up at nine years of age. He's a boy, that has to be made to study and I hope they in authority only will make him tow[*sic*] the line."

While Jerry stayed in Cuba, Edward arrived on the 8:07 train that rolled into Wooster on October 28. Elsie and a classmate, Bernie, met him at the station for a short visit. He would be going up to Cleveland where she met him the following Saturday for the weekend with the Machle family. Papa had a talk with her. Since she asked for twenty dollars and didn't get a response, she assumed he wouldn't give it to her. That night she wrote in her diary, "Oh! What's the use of anything anyway."

Before leaving, Edward drops a note to Elsie, "I leave here tomorrow for Wooster on the Penn line. Will have a short stop at Pittsburg…need not meet me at the station. I will come to the home if I cannot be accommodated. There will find a place for a day or two. I must be in Cinti by the 3rd, Election Day, to vote for Taft. Do not know yet whether I will go out under the Board or independent and signed Papa." It seems he had received some information from the Board and would be teaching at a non-denominational school in Canton.

It was the Week of Prayer, November 1, and the two of them went to the German Church where Elsie had been attending and spent the afternoon walking around campus and talking.   On November 2 Elsie cut her classes to see him off on the 11:05 train on his way back to Cinti. He arrived in time to vote for Taft on November 3. Before leaving on November 30 he sent her the 20 dollars she asked for and apologized for forgetting it earlier.

He was on board the S.S. <u>Tenyo Maru</u> when he wrote on the 11th of December 1908, "I have but a little while before I leave America for four years. I have thought much of you lately, wondering what will be your condition when I return. I do wish so much to get back in time for your graduation. I know you will have honor to me and so rejoice that you can go to college and prepare thoroughly for the future. You will see Victor in Cincinnati, Xmas time. Give him sisterly advice kindly…see whether you can't persuade the boy to knuckle down in his studies. Don't say anything to him in regard to my writing you."

He arrived in Canton in the middle of December and on March 4, 1909 writes, "I am teaching Chemistry and Light in the Fati School and Materia Medica, Therapeutics and Pharmacy at the Women's Medical College...being busy makes one contented...The Chinese are taking to Western Medicine. Five Medical Colleges have already been opened this year...Miss Mawson is in the country at present and will be for a month." He begins to mention Jean Mawson more often in his letters as Elsie suspects they are dating.

Prior to 1909, the organized body of missionaries in the field made decisions; but policy changes were made by Secretary Brown who influenced missionary policy, "If we are going to work for the Native Church, we must work with the Native Church" and the changing numbers and power of the Natives. Brown believed because of the growth, "In number and power, it is equally natural that this state of things should be disturbed...manifestly the Mission and the Board can no longer do as they please without reference to the judgment of such a church.

Our responsibility for a people continues after the Church is in the field, but it continues through and in cooperation with the Church and not independently of it...the recognition of its rights and privileges. We have built up Missions emphasizing their authority and dignity, and kept them separate from the Native Church, until, in some regions at least, the Mission has become such an independent centralized body, so entrenched in its station compounds and with all powers so absolutely in its hands, that the Native Church feels helpless and irritated in its presence."

"I have not heard from Victor yet. Tell him to address me at Canton and I will get it as I left my address at the post offices.

This must be a short letter tonight only to let you know that I think often of you, pray for you. When something thrilling happens, I will let you know."

Elsie received a letter from him on September 17, 1909, "I was glad to get a letter from you and Victor. Especially Victor's was exceedingly precious, for he has written me but two letters since I have been in China. School has begun and with it much hard work for me. Everything you know that I teach is through the Chinese language and so I have to prepare each lesson which takes so little time."

Whether it was because Edward was frugal or worried that the money wouldn't last, Edward scolds his daughter for mishandling money, "You know I gave you and Victor a book each to keep your accounts in and told you both how necessary it was to do so. You hooted at the idea and told your father that the money was yours and so you did not have to render accounts. I suppose you followed your own sweet will and have not rendered an account to Harry for once even. Had you followed my advice you would have known that you were running short and would not have to hustle during your vacation to make up the balance. Victor has more in bank than you have, which is very little; about $155.55. He will need this for clothing before he gets a salary sufficient to feed and clothe him. Now please Elsie, as soon as you get this, tell me what you are going to do. I haven't time to write anymore. Harry says Frank Lamping failed in business and as he had all my money except the little in bank which I ought to keep for old age, where am I to get enough to supply your needs?" Edward was parenting...wanting to have control, and not having control over his children, regarding money, their behavior and education. "In business it takes many years to get experience...Ask your Uncle Frank Lamping. I have not any complaints to make to you in regard to your studies but someone writes me from Philadelphia, saying that you used profane language when there and did not mind what people thought of you just so you could have your own way. I am sorry you left that impression on anyone…as to the profane language, it was evidently Wooster trash, slang which is utterly useless stuff. I would advise you when you go outside of Wooster that you leave Wooster slang behind, 'You if you were to be considered civilized.'"

"I see from it that you received from the Board about $150 and that you also unwisely took all that your Uncle Harry sent and no doubt spent it without giving a single thought to how much you may have in the bank at the end of the year. If you have deposited some of the money you got from either party in a bank in Wooster, well and good, if not, I fear you will not have enough to take you through college. According to Uncle Harry who has sent me your bank account, you have only $99.94 in bank." Although Edward's brother, Harry, was responsible for the financial accounts of his daughter, Elsie had the discretion to use it as she saw fit which didn't always please her father. "You should keep an account of the money you get from Uncle Harry and others and spend a few moments once in a while to see how you stand financially then you would not get into such a 'hole' as you are now."

"There is so much to sadden one here, in a great city when the gospel has only been preached about ten years. Of course, doctor from his position is compelled to associate with the educated men of the province, the leading men. They are so anxious for our education, but have been so wronged by foreigners, that they want to get rid of foreign instructor's."

Edward juggles classes, meetings, and a blossoming romantic relationship with Jean Mawson. No matter how hard he tries to keep in touch with his children, there is a void in their relationship. When he writes, it is about his work, or events around him, giving the illusion that he is out of touch with his daughter's life, "This I suppose will have to chase you up to find you somewhere out of Wooster if you are not at summer school as you contemplated doing some time ago. I am in the classroom watching my class on Light taking their written examination. One eye on this sheet and another on them is my policy. It seems to work well since I have one boy on a bench. I shall be glad when school closes. I heard from Vic the other day. Glad he stuck out his year at Park and hope he will continue to do so for that is the college for him."

The beginning of 1910 brought news of his work at the University Medical School in Canton, now under President Josiah McCracken, a University of Pennsylvania School of Medicine graduate. As a teacher of chemistry, Edward reacted to Elsie's account of a mishap with dismay, "You ought to be very careful in making experiments in chemistry. You'll blow yourself to pieces if you don't follow closely your textbook. The pieces may be so widely scattered that it would be impossible to find them all and glue you together again like a wooden dollie. You are the only daughter I have and I am very proud of you but for goodness sake don't get to look like a fellow that gone through a half dozen duals at a German University.

"I am teacher or professor of Chemistry here and I am very careful to know what I am doing. In spite of all my care I had an explosion from hydrogen gas. The transmitting tube was too large so the H (hydrogen) combined with O (oxygen). The apparatus went to pieces. I was cut on my finger (index). I took the precaution to wrap a cloth around the apparatus for fear it would explode. The glass particles could not carry very far from the apparatus. I have since made H without any explosion on burning it. All that is needed is an air tight receptacle and a fine piece of tubing...I have not yet heard from Park in regard to

Victor's illness. Your letter was the first and only information I have received. Ida sent a letter recently which she received from President of Park College saying Vic smokes and makes remarks in regard to obtaining money some way to go away from Park. He is not much in favor at Park because he violates the rules by smoking. It is too bad that he cannot obey the rules and regulations of the college in every particular. They are always for the best to the general body of students."

After returning to Canton, Edward began mentioning Jean Mawson more often in his letters, "Miss Mawson is in the country at present and will be for a month." Jean Mawson[2], a Deaconness with the Presbyterian Women's Training Institute assigned to service in South China. While at Canton Villages Mission, she met Edward Machle and soon began courting, "I had a good time down in Hong Kong for twenty days. I was entitled to 2½ months vacation but I only took 20 days. I helped other people to have a vacation who could not otherwise go. Miss Mawson was at a place called Fois Lea, a missionary residence in Hong Kong. I was at the Rhennish Mission House about two blocks away, so you see we need not walk far to see each other."

Miss Mawson has left for New Zealand and will be gone for eight or nine months. She will return from furlough with her brother," Rev. William Mawson, "Who has been home on furlough since last spring." Jean Mawson Machle was born on November 21, 1876 in Purahanui, Otago. She was a graduate of Presbyterian Women's Training Institute and one of two Deaconness accepted for service to South China in 1905.

In a letter sent from Hong Kong in March 1910, Edward was staying at Dr. Hager's house, "I should have said I have been here and shall leave tonight. I took dear Mrs. Kerr to the Hong Kong Ltr. She goes to America on furlough. As she lives in Seville you will probably see her sometime and she will tell you all about me and my girl.

"I am engaged to Miss Mawson. Her brother and family leave from Hong Kong today for New Zealand. Jean is down here to see them off. We two will return tonight to Canton. She returns to the country and I plan on teaching chemistry – light and materia medica, therapeutic and pharmacy. When we will get married is a question of long time. It is to be three years hence, unless other missionaries come out to take up the work that she is doing. When you receive this, write Miss Jean Mawson a nice letter. Yesterday, we took in the botanical gardens, parade grounds etc. of Hong Kong. As Miss Mawson works in the country, I do not see her very frequently. I want you to rejoice with me. Miss Mawson is a superbly fine, well brought up woman. I am sometimes astonished that she took me at all.

"I am glad you are having a nice time. Students generally do have. I presume you did not get the goose egg you wished (?) in mathematics. I haven't received a word from Victor yet and do not know when I will.

"This has been lying around forgotten. Must have thought I finished it. Well, you should have received it sooner you will now. You will see from this letter what I am doing; how I stand with Miss Mawson; and some other items of interest. I received a letter yesterday from Wm. H. Smith, Phila. Telling me he is ready to pay me in installments what he owes. How good of him. I have waited ten years for him to pay 300 dollars.

"I wish I could write you a long letter but time will not permit. My studies take much time. I must prepare them that is, fix the Chinese terms in my mind so as to speak intelligently to the students. I received a letter from Victor at last. He wishes to go to Wooster, next year. He can't bear being away from you, he says. I have not yet decided where to send him. It will be either Park or

Wooster. Mrs. Henry McCandless certainly had a hard time of it for awhile. Victor is just as much interested in athletics. Thinks he must write me the year's score. Wooster did shine a little this year, in outdoor sports. Did you do your share of yelling? Miss Johnston is now in Chang Sha, Hunan. Write her a letter. She says she has not heard from either of you. She has a twelve-room house, well furnished, servants etc. I sent to her twelve large boxes of things recently so she will be in full swing housekeeping very soon. Nothing interesting happening in China just now. The new government, Prince Regent, is making some changes in the higher officials. He seems to wish to get rid of the Chinese and place only Manchu's near the throne. We fear it will eventually result in a rebellion. Time, of course, will tell. I am writing this while waiting for the chapel bell to ring at 7:30. I got up earlier than usual this morning. Who is your roommate now? Where are you going to spend your summer? What about earning some money during the summer months!"

"This I suppose will have to chase you up to find you somewhere out of Wooster if you are not at summer school as you contemplated doing some time ago. I am in the classroom watching my class on Light taking their written examination. One eye on this sheet and another on them is my policy. It seems to work well since I have one boy on a bench. I shall be glad when school closes. Miss Johnston has sent me three letters requesting me to come to Cheung Sha for the summer. I am contemplating doing so. I shall go by train about 60 miles, then by steam launch to head waters of the North River; then into Hunan floating by the Siantau River northward to Cheung Sha. It will take me I calculate at least ten days. Returning to Canton, I'll go to Hankow, then down the Yangtse to Shanghai, to Hong Kong to Canton. School and college close on July 1st and reopen September 1st. Only two months of vacation and hundreds of miles to travel.

"I presume you saw in the papers the trouble there has been through mob violence at Cheung Sha. All is quiet again but rice being dear and many people poor, hunger will drive them to desperation, so the Viceroy in Canton has had a great lot of rice brought in from Chochin China, Annam etc. This will give the rice at a little cheaper rate and we hope prevent trouble in South China. Where I am on Fati across the river from the Foreign Concession all is quiet. The rains have certainly been scarce this year and Hong Kong itself has been fearing a water famine. Fields in the hill country away from streams are dried up and the young rice plants dead. This certainly is intensely hot here at present. The thermometer in my room on the third floor of the Theology Seminary registers in the evening 92 degrees F. How hot is it in the sun? I don't care to know just now. I'd feel better than I do if I did. I took dinner yesterday with Dr. & Mrs. Todd after church services. They are kind pleasant people; former missionaries but now working independently. I heard from Vic the other day. Glad he stuck out his year at Park and hope he will continue to do so for that is the college for him.

"Miss Mawson is still in New Zealand but is expected back in the fall. She sends her love and thanks for your kind gift for her. Tell Victor that she has sent her kind regards to him. I wish you would write her a letter to the following address: Miss Jean Mawson, Burns Street, Port Chalmers, New Zealand.

"She would appreciate it very much I am sure. Her folks have written to me and it is now more than right that you and Vic should send a few words.

Mrs. Machle has a share in it. I am in Hong Kong just now on our honeymoon. We were married December 27th. It was a quiet wedding because of my lame leg. We sent out no printed announcements."

CHAPTER 6

Endeavor and the Summer of 1911

Elsie went to freshman football practice in the fall of 1908 at the University of Wooster and watched a player by the name of Wilbur White. This young man who everyone called "Wilbur" was soon known by about all the students at the college as "Billy." But Elsie named him "Billy" first. When asked why, she replied because 'he looked like a Billy.' Little did anyone know, least of all "Billy" himself, that when Elsie was a small child growing up in Lien Chow, China, there was a pet donkey named "Billy" that she rode around the missionary compound where she lived. As the daughter of Presbyterian medical missionaries, her playmates were children of the cooks and missionaries, so Elsie's young world revolved around pets and playmates. The donkey had been special to her.

When Elsie graduated from the Presbyterian Homes for Children of Foreign Missionaries, she could have gone to just about any college of her choice. Instead, she elected to stay at Wooster. It was a familiar and stable environment for her, close to friends, many of whom had backgrounds similar to her own. She became close to her classmates whose families were missionaries just like her own family. Elsie was intellectually gifted in so many ways. Her Chapter interests in literature were influenced by her mother. She joined the Quadrangle Club, a group of students like herself interested in studying works of leading English philosophers and novelist of the 18th and 19th centuries. She took an active interest in drama which described her acting in the college yearbook, 'Elsie gets a good chance in Willard play to get off a big swear word and doesn't lose the opportunity.' What is more, she had a beautiful voice and sang in the college chorus. Like her, "Billy" was also a member of Quadrangle. As a Classical major with advanced composition, he sang tenor in the choral group. They had a lot in common.

Wilbur began his studies at Mercersburg Academy in Mercersburg, Pennsylvania and graduated in 1907. The Mercersburg yearbook Karux lists Wilbur on the scrub baseball team. He was also a member of the Marshall Literary Society. Wilbur was six feet tall, weighed 160 pounds and was described as 'all muscle'. Enrolling at the University of Wooster, he played tackle and halfback positions in football earning him three letters. He also played tennis, basketball, baseball, and track. After earning 10 letters, he was a member of the 'W' lettermen. Billy was a leader in every way. He was president of the Y.M.C.A. at Wooster. Whether it was the Minstrel Show, Glee Club, or Beta Theta Pi, his time was full of activities where his leadership qualities continued to add to his popularity. Elsie became interested in sports and would drop by football practice to watch the team and attend the games.

Wilbert Wallace White (Wilbur) was born on May 1, 1889 in New Haven, Connecticut to Wilbert Webster and Ella Jane Henderson White. Wilbert and Ella had four children: Helen Henderson, Wilbert Wallace, Robert Campbell and Donald Murray. Wilbur's father graduated from Wooster College in 1883. In 1885 after graduating from Xenia Theological Seminary, he married Ella Jane Henderson, a student at Wooster.

In 1896, Dr. White went to Calcutta, India on behalf of the Y.M.C.A. to work with college students and missionaries. While there, Wilbur's younger brother, Robert Campbell, died of malaria. He was named Robert Campbell after Dr. White's mother, Martha Campbell White. Martha's family were from Nankin, Ohio. Two years later they left India for America, stopping first in Great Britain where Wilbert Webster White conducted Bible studies. He did graduate work at Yale where he was awarded a Ph.D. in 1891 and returned to Xenia Theological Seminary as a professor, before becoming the Associate Director of the Moody Bible Institute. He was awarded honorary degrees from Muskegum and New York University. In 1900 he founded Bible Teachers Training College which became Winona Bible School, then The Biblical Seminary in New York. The family located in Montclair, New Jersey before moving to 541 Lexington Avenue.

Their first date was in February, 1910. By April, Billy sent her roses and she returned a note of appreciation, "Thank you so much for the lovely roses. You know better than I can express it how much I appreciated them."

When classes were over in the spring of 1911, a member of Elsie's fraternity(this was also the name for a sororiety), Kappa Kappa Gamma, Mary McKean, invited her to spend several weeks with her family in Endeavor, Pennsylvania. Mary's parents, Harper and Edna Hazel McKean had five children, Laura, Mary Grace, Hazel, Harper Khlare, and Margaret. The McKean's were an established family in Forest County where Harper was the blacksmith for the Wheeler & Dusenberry Railroad.

Because Billy received a deficiency in chemistry, he was required to enroll in summer school in order to graduate in May of 1912. However, because he was President of the Y.M.C.A. he was expected to attend the Lake Erie Student Conference at Linwood Park, Vermillion, on the outskirts of Cleveland, Ohio the week of June 16. Elsie left Wooster to spend the summer with Mary. Endeavor, located about 30 miles northeast of Oil City in Forest County, along the Allegheny National Forest, is a lumber and mill town whose early beginnings were named after the Christian Endeavor Society, the original inhabitants of the town when it was called Stowtown. East Hickory begins as a row of houses and quickly becomes Endeavor with no other identification other than sign in front of a house. From there it is a short distance to the massive saw mill now a lumber yard.

It seems that their relationship was growing into something more than a casual date when Wilbert writes to Elsie on June 17, "After I left the station, I went to Shorty Irvin's place and we went to lunch together. After that I bummed around Cleveland for a couple of hours waiting for train time. When I got to the station the first people I saw were June (McSweeney) and Ken (Johnson). They had been to the 10:25 train in the morning, but had left, thinking that you were going some other way. They were both awfully sorry to have missed you. I left about four minutes before they did, so I wasn't compelled to see anyone else pull out of that station and leave me behind. By the way, that is a feeling which I want to have very, very seldom in my life in that or any other station. I mean the feeling which I got when that 11:30 train pulled out this morning with you on it and me on the platform. When you and I are married we are going to stay together. I hope the prospect pleases. In the meantime, I suppose I'll have to be satisfied with things as they have to be." The next day Billy discovers his letter had not gone in the mail and Elsie would not receive it in time for her arrival at Endeavor. He laments that he got a poor grade in chemistry and "that chemistry has got to be on my list of credits at the end of the summer at all odds and…what the dickens am I going to do with myself after I finish college? That question has been bothering me for several years now. And

I don't know any more about it now than when I used to say I wanted to be an ask man. Help me decide will you Elsie? I'd like to know what you want me to do, or rather make of myself, when I finish college. You certainly have some opinion about it, and I don't see why you shouldn't have just as much more to say about it than anyone else. Almost everywhere I go someone tries to tell me what to do with myself, so why shouldn't you?"

Billy's annoyance with people advising him on his future when he was unsure bubbles over to Elsie, yet she is sensitive when she responds to Billy on June 19 from Endeavor by addressing him as Sir Galahad, "I am a little doubtful as to the propriety of poisoning your pure mind with an account of Mary's and my adventure after we were left to shift for ourselves in the world. We certainly did shift, though when we reached Erie even our sunny natures despaired of finding anything in that wicked town which could amuse us for three hours. We spent two hours and a half searching for picture shows only to be doomed to disappointment in the end—then we thought that the 'Empire Theatre' looked unusually attractive and decided to go there and see some high-class vaudeville but when we reached the ticket office we discovered the place had been closed for the summer. How we could have endured the monotony of the journey had we never changed cars more than three times we alone can tell. When we finally arrived at West Hickory, we were pleasantly surprised to see that some of Mary's friends had come up for us in their machine. At least the last eight miles were covered comfortably and we came into Endeavor with a grand flourish.

"I must say Endeavor is even more beautiful than I imagined it would be. Such pine and oak covered hills—such fields of daisies and buttercups. No indeed—I am certainly not going to forget my training and foist upon you a description of Endeavor scenery. Don't you know Mr. White that I am quite aware of the large portions of this country you have been fortunate enough to have seen at those seasons when the dean's displeasure was stronger than the bonds which bound you to your Alma Mater? I would not presume therefore, to tell you anything—when I really must—which you know already."

The bantering between them seems to edge them closer to a romantic pitch as he delightfully writes in his June 19 letter to Elsie, "Dearest--When that form of salutation gets tiresome to you say so and I'll change it. I don't say it as a matter of form or anything like that. I mean it, every letter and a whole lot more, and the longer I say it the more it speaks the truth."

"I walked over to Vermillion last night with your second letter and as I was going out of the gate, I ran into Roy Kennedy, he had come over from Lorain to see me. Had quite a nice time with him for an hour or so, until he had to leave, then I sneaked in the back way and went to bed about midnight. This is as bad a place for getting in late as Holden Hall. Two other Betas have arrived upon the scene of action, so the place is getting to seem a little more like home."

"I told Lichty, the man at the head, when he asked me to take the athletics, that he'd probably have to get someone else after Tuesday, but he said that he thought that probably I'd stay; so I'm expecting a little trouble when I tell him I'm leaving tomorrow. He wants me to stay and decide to go into Y.M. work permanently. But I have tomorrow if my money covers. Here's hoping.

"This certainly has been a beautiful day. The sun is just beginning to set now, and I have seldom seen a prettier one. The lake is like glass except in one or two places where the wind strikes it, and it gets a darker blue. You see that I am beginning to see things a little more in their right perspective. Never-the-less there is a big ache down deep inside of me all the time. Honestly Elsie, I thought we were fools when they spoke of love the way some of them do, but now—well they haven't said one-half of the things. They couldn't, it would be impossible."

If Billy was frustrated by the mail system, Elsie was equally as frustrated with it when she didn't receive letters from him. She began to look forward to hearing from him. On June 20, she writes, "You have no idea how disappointed I was when I went to the post office yesterday and found no letter from you there. The worst of it was Mary had a nice long one from Lakewood to read on our weary way back to the house. How I called down and muttered 'curses not loud but deep' upon the United States mail system! Good things I guess can be had only by a deal of waiting and as soon as I realized that, I decided to cease railing against fortune and wait in something like a reasonable frame of mind until it smiled again. This morning your letters came and I spent a sweet half hour listening to you ramble on in your usual nice way—I have been having pleasant experiences here which have helped me forget and remember—forget how long the time really has been and remember how much more I would rather have spent that time with Sir Galahad and listen to the sweet lies which he can tell.

"Sunday evening Mr. (Nelson Platt) Wheeler Jr., a Princeton man who is handsome—a perfect dear and who is to be married next week—came over in his big Packard and took us for a seventy-mile spin through the country. I used to think the Cedar Valley road was the loveliest road in existence. It may be the dearest, but these roads here are certainly more beautiful. We drove thro' woodland nearly all the way, following the windings of the Allegheny River for miles and miles until our road turned again toward the hills. I am sure that you would have been quite pleased to have been with us.

"This morning I got up at six (unholy hour for one so broken down in health, don't you think?) and went with Mary's little brother to take the cows to pasture. It was lots of fun to tramp behind four ugly harmless creatures, armed as we were with brown sticks four feet long, and beat them gently when they reverted to their primitive habits. I think I shall go again if Khlare will let me. After we went for the mail Mary's sister, and myself, stopped to visit the kindergarten. There were about twenty youngsters being kept out of mischief by all sorts of childish amusements. (You would be quite happy no doubt in such a place with sand and blocks and pretty colored balls to play with). The teacher naturally, wished to show off her little school to us so she bade the boys choose their partners which they did by presenting themselves with a Chesterfieldian[*sic*] bow before the girl of their choice. Little, chubby Isabel, however, aged three had no knight present himself to claim her hand and so she set up a most pathetic howl and began rubbing the tears as fast as they fell, all over her dirty face. It took teacher and a dear, little boy in blue to comfort Isabel. Another youngster while refreshments were being served, upset his cup of water on the floor. He was so ashamed that in order not to let us see what he had done, he carefully sat down in it and calmly set his empty cup before him without for a moment losing his dignity. I must admit that I almost lost mine. Such a spectacle could not fail to move even you in your most indifferent and blasé' mood…you know that little boy I told you about who sat down in the water he spilled—well he seems to be quite a prodigy. Some of the youngsters around here can't swear very well so he said to them, 'Come over, I'll teach you how to swear, it'll only take me a minute.' You see you can even get a course in artistic cursing in this place.

"Last night several of the promising young men of the village called to pay their devoirs. We had a grand time sitting in the porch swings, singing and joking. Just because I felt more like weeping than laughing, I laughed and tried to be amusing.

Some people doubtless were shocked. If it was a new sensation, they will probably come again.

"I am writing this sitting in one of the nice porch swings. There would be plenty of room for one or two more in it too. I hadn't realized that I had rambled past the four-page limit. Won't you be in a towering rage though. Well, it's your own fault. You shouldn't be so nice to talk to and then you wouldn't have all this thrust upon you." Tease him, she did, especially by mentioning other handsome men who might be suitors, however, he follows suit by challenging her.

Billy returns to Wooster for summer school and on Tuesday evening June 20 addresses her as 'Lady Fair' which was in response to the letter which addressed him as 'Sir Galahad', a poem by Alfred Lord Tennyson and Elsie's favorite poet. Tennyson, "is my favorite author, but because he has created for me a world filled with living beings who have lived in his pages. By merely closing my eyes I can see fair ladies and brave knights passing in a glittering pageant; white haired Merlin working some magic spell of 'woven paces and of waving wims'; beautiful Guinevere riding in some primeval forest beside the noble being Arthur; the poor deluded Lady of Shalott and a host of others besides."

Beta Theta Pi's had a reputation for being pranksters. They also used nicknames for the fraternity brothers' but fellow students still called him "Wilber". "How is that I don't think for a moment that the other one isn't just as true as it ever was. Nay my friend, it is times truer than ever, but your example must be followed, and if you call me Sir Galahad, I must forsooth fall into line and do all I can to keep up that delusion in your mind. No, I don't really think that it is really a delusion, for I think you know enough of me, and also of that other (you see I scratched out the other) illustrious gentleman to know that you place him in a position where I am very likely to get a severe case of the swollen cranium. I didn't say that last in exactly the right way, but perhaps you can get a little meaning out of it.

They are a competitive pair of writers, always trying to outdo the other. "Good Heavens Elsie, if your letter was dull as you tried as hard to make me believe, what in the name of goodness did you think of mine. If there was some way of getting those back and eradicating the effect they had upon you, I certainly would like to do it. However, I suppose that the evil work has been done, and that there is no way of effacing it, so I'll have to let it go. There is one thing that I would like to contradict, that is that I ever said that I couldn't wade through more than four sheets of any letter. I never said that; what you remember is that I couldn't write more than four pages, and now when I come to look back over the last few letters, that's a lie too. The first one I wrote was longer than that, wasn't it? No, I'll never admit that I said anything like that…I left Linwood Park this afternoon at 4:30 and came to Lorain where Roy Kennedy lives. We are going out in the machine in a little while, then sleep the sleep of the just. I leave here at 8 o'clock in the morning and get to Wooster at 11:15. Summer school forever! After the first plunge, I don't suppose that it will be so bad, but oh that first plunge. Mr. Lichty had quite a long argument with me today about my leaving so soon. I finally convinced him, however, that my duty lay in the clinical laboratory of the summer school of the University of Wooster and we parted friends. He is a peach of a scout, the only thing I have against him is that he always gets back to that old subject of going into Y.M.C.A. work. But I've said enough along that line already."

Always consistent, yet not sure of her feelings, Elsie never failed to write Billy every day from Endeavor. Their friendship was unusually challenging, but developing into something more serious when on June 21, after midnight, she begins her letter with "Dearest Slave of Minerva, boy this time I suppose you are up to your ears in HgSO4 or something quite as stimulating. You have a nice clean notebook with scores of pure, white empty pages in it waiting for you to put down on them all the fascinating experiments which you are going to do. Of course, I'm perfectly heartless to 'rub it in' this way, but it's perfectly safe at this distance I guess so perhaps I won't stop until I get quite ready.

"The very first things I saw this morning were two letters one from Cara (Lehman) and one from a rather nice grouch who writes to me occasionally. I hate to be wakened suddenly unless there is something very nice as an excuse for such a barbarous action. I was certainly glad someone had the nerve and the infinite kindness to disturb me.

"Yesterday evening our trunks came so we had wash to do today. Am I tired? O, dear no—a little too tired to sleep I guess at least until I finish this little talk with you. I made the craziest mistake in washing. I like the combination I suppose, so put my pink dress in the bluing water. Mrs. McKean had quite a little fit over it but rescued my poor dress from ultimate ruination. Yesterday afternoon, we took our supper up to a place called the Log Cabin. It is away up between two big hills and we had to climb up a beautiful rocky road to get to it. Billy, I would have given so many things if you could have been with us. Down in a ravine not far from the road you could have seen Bloody Run, a picturesque little creek which ran red with blood one time when some Indians did some butchering up on the hill. Along the path there were bunches of mountain laurel, ferns and flowers which I had never seen before. The cabin is built upon a huge rock. There was a big rattler killed on the very doorstep of this cabin last year but though we looked with eager eyes for a friendly welcome from one of these graceful serpents not one made an appearance.

"Tonight, we have been having some very good music. Mr. Thrum, who is quite a violinist, has been abroad, and is very nice besides, entertained us with some of the familiar selections we like best." He was known to be accompanied by Mary Alice Warden, the sister of George H., at various social events around Endeavor. Mr. Urban Thrum was one of the young foresters who eventually headed to the School of Forestry at Biltmore, Ashville, North Carolina. "There were other young men who came to be entertained and entertain. One of them, Mr. George Warden is certainly worth knowing. I think perhaps we shall be good friends for he seems to have a most delightful sense of humor and an adorable way of accepting 'knocks'. Imagine—after Mr. Thrum's playing to be asked to sing! Of course, I simply had to do it. The lucky thing is I felt like singing too. I felt rather ashamed though, to accept their thanks and compliments when I wasn't singing for them at all. *The Rosary* came last. I'm afraid I spoiled it, although Mr. Thrum was sweet enough not to say so. I wish I could hear you sing tonight—no use wishing it. Mr. White's voice can only be heard when admission is paid at the door—thank goodness not always then! I have absolutely no respect for the man that made you manager of athletics at the conference. How perfectly stupid of him to make such a blunder. Dear heart, it must be one o'clock. I must be off to dreamland and there." Elsie continues her four-page letter on June 22, "Do you suppose for a minute that four half-pages with a letter heading a quarter of a page deep on each one of them, to say nothing of sprawl writing with two inches between each word will ever be passed off on an intelligent person for four healthy full-sized pages? Never, if I'm that person. You know as well as I do that I pack a great deal more material on a sheet than you do—me thinks I hear the cry of "give us quality not quantity"— but I'm sure that remark came from the gallery—not from the nice portion of my audience. So, don't you ever stop just simply because I am humane enough to do so! Herein endeth the first lesson-selah!"

She must have been thinking about the June 17th letter when she writes: "You asked me in one of your letters to suggest something for your life work. Why, dear, you know better than I could possibly know what you want to do. Of course, it must be something in which you can put your whole heart or I'm afraid it wouldn't be worth much. Your father, I should think, would be better able to advise you than anyone else. He realized if nobody else of all those kind friends who are eternally telling you what you should be when they haven't got wits enough to appreciate what you are (oh! yes, I did it myself once didn't I)—your father realizes that there are a few things that a Christian gentleman might do besides being a Y.M.C.A. worker and not be eternally damned. Of course, you've talked it over with him before I suppose, and are still at a loss. Surely, though, you know what you would like to do—remember then that you can do absolutely anything which you really want to do. You know it—then do it and believe me that my thoughts and prayers shall be always for you."

The response comes on June 23 from Billy, "What wouldn't I have given to have been with you on that trip to the Log Cabin and then in the evening when you sang...to sit in one of those swings you talk about, or to stroll along one of those roads with you for a few fleeting hours would certainly fill my cup of joy to overflowing."

There was sunshine in Elsie's letters on June 24, "I was looking at the sunlight on the maple trees today and it made me think of smiles—your smile, perhaps, who knows as well as myself what they are really like? I suppose you are smiling right this minute—that is what I wanted you to do—it is vastly becoming.

I have thought of learning how to do it myself—but it would be humiliating wouldn't it only to be a poor second-rate manufacturer of sunbeams.

Would you really think it worthwhile to come to Endeavor over the Fourth? Mary seems to think that I am a permanent fixture in the McKean family and won't listen to my leaving before that date. Now if you are really coming I shall stay without a doubt—why I'd let a little thing like your possible advent in Endeavor make the slightest difference to me is more than I can say—but probably it will make a very slight difference. There is a boarding house or something of the sort here but whether it has all the modern conveniences such as springs and individual butter-dishes I am not well enough informed to tell you. Anyway, I would hate to raise your hopes and then have them dashed to the ground by your discovering that the sole luxury of the place consisted in a popular tiny wash basin. If you leave Wooster on the 4728 you will arrive in Endeavor at 8 or 9 the next morning without having to change cars any place except Pittsburg. Doesn't that bit of information sound good to the ears of such as you have loves ease? You will tell me, of course, just what you think is best for you to do.

"Tomorrow we are going up on what is called here the 'grub-train' to Camp No. Seven, where the big timber is. We shall be gone all day. I have never been to a big lumber camp and therefore I am quite curious to see one. Smile for me just once now, before I say goodnight and sweet dreams." What Elsie called a 'grub-train' was the W&D or Wheeler and Dusenberry private logging railroad that used rod locomotives, log rollways and loading crews in their daily operation.

Elsie stayed up until 1 a.m. when she wrote to Billy, "I don't want to write to you at all this early Monday morning but I've written to several of my other friends' so I suppose it is only just that

I should keep on scrawling measly chicken-tracks until breakfast time! Am I grouchy? Oh, dear no. Such a little sunbeam you never saw—nor would you want to see me either. This has been the worst day—rain, rain all day long, and not enough energy left in Mary and myself to make it worthwhile moving at all.

"Yesterday we took the trip we had intended to take up to Camp No. Seven. We went up on the 'grub-trains' as I thought we should. The palace car we were in was a respectable enough looking box-car with a plank in the middle-propped up on two soap boxes, for a seat. We draped ourselves over this plank and admired the scenery as we bumped serenely up the track. The beauty of the woods did a great deal to make us forget that our travelling conveniences were pretty nearly nil and none of us even thought of wanting upholstering and springs. Camp No. Seven is a good deal cleaner than the other camps we passed along the way. Such squalid looking hovels and such dirty children I never want to see again! Yet the children seemed happy and Mr. Wheeler, the man who owns everything here, said that the people who lived in these camps in the woods wouldn't leave for anything because they loved their work so. The ride back might have been nicer if it hadn't made me sick. Oh, dear, I felt like such a baby, but I wanted to die and go to Heaven quick! No chance—I lived on, of course—actually got home and to bed where I stayed and calmly let the whole McKean family wait on me. Every minute for a while, I thought perhaps the angels would sing and then you would send pretty flowers to the funeral and sing some appropriate little dirge yourself.

"You poor Sir Galahad! Of course, you couldn't find Endeavor in the guide book because it isn't there. West Hickory, however, isn't very far from here and a nice rickety stage meets all trains at West Hickory and delivers parcels, mail, and those individuals who harvest the hardwood or are simply perfectly nice enough to venture out into these wilds. Saturday or Sunday, whichever you say, we shall meet you with the band and greet you with all due respect at West Hickory. Do come, I refuse to coax. If you come, I shall have freckles all over my heart." The Hickory Valley Railroad was run by General Superintendent, George W. Warden. It ran from Hickory to Ross Run Junction; and Endeavor, to Browns with freight and lumber. The only connection with the Pennsylvania Railroad was at Hickory.

The letter telling about Mr. Wheeler was effective, "When you said that he was a Princeton man it started. When you said, 'he was handsome', it got to my throat, when he was 'a perfect dear', it came on up a little way almost into my mouth, but when you ended it up with, 'who is to be married next week,' I almost fainted as my heart settled back to its regular work.' The dialogue continues between Elsie and Billy on Sunday, June 25 when Billy writes after returning from Endeavor and giving her his fraternity pin...I know that over there among the pines of Pennsylvania somewhere 'she wears my Beta pin.'" Billy and Elsie were engaged and the fellows at the fraternity heard about it before leaving campus, "got three letters from different fellows who didn't see me before they left, and who didn't have a chance to congratulate me, and I can tell you that if you saw those letters, you would have to buy a larger hat to wear away from Endeavor."

"Last night Dous (Douglas Newton Forman) and I went down and mailed some letters, went to a moving picture show, got a malted milk at Wally's and wandered up the hill about 11 o'clock. Scotty and some of the other fellows were just starting out after some chickens. But Dous and I were too tired so went to bed. The chicken thieves came back about twelve thirty with seven chickens, think of it, seven. Such wholesale butchery I have never heard of before. Three of the seven were still alive, so they put them out in the barn and ate the other four. This morning there was a great cackling issuing from the region of the shack, and when we went out we found two nice fresh eggs. You see I may realize my dream of a chicken yard yet. But alas, Dous ate one of the eggs raw, and Walter Snyder got the other one. No setting for me out of that bunch. Tonight, the fellows are out at Dr. Stoll's cabin eating the remainder of the seven.

"One of the things which developed last night on the way up from Wally's was a Summer School Minstrel Show." Wilber was first tenor in the Glee Club and End Man in the Fifth Biennial College Minstrel at the Opera House in Wooster on March 17, 1910, in which he sang *Oh, What a Lovely Dream.* "Dous and I are both sadly in need of some very healthy financial assistance, so we are going to get up a show and give it about the last of July. There are about twelve of the glee club in town, and so we can work up a pretty good circle with the help of some of the other fellows in school. If you have any bright ideas for a farce or in the joke lines, don't let them waste away, for we need everything we can get. Will Cameron is here and so we have three of the old end men back. Kizzy will work in pretty well and if necessary we can get two more easily enough, but we can get along on four if we can't find anyone else.

"There is a little black oval framed picture hanging just above my desk here in the den. Every time I look up, you look almost right straight into my eyes. Not quite though. You are looking just over my head, but your eyes are focused on something and when I look hard enough I can make them, in my mind, focus on me."

July 4th weekend became an indelible memory for Elsie when Scotty drove Billy to Endeavor. Wooster, Ohio is approximately 175 miles from Endeavor so it wasn't an quick trip in 1911. A few days later, "Dearest—And I am glad that I have them to count over and remember—you knew you would surprise me by writing two letters on the same day. I am so glad you did for they were nice letters too and made me feel that I was being missed a little—a good deal.

"Endeavor has just been hot—that all-boiling—broiling baking hot since you left, so you haven't missed much. You found out before you asked what we drew on Wednesday night. Last night it was Lib and George again. Rex Wheeler and Roy felt like being sociable so they came up and were introduced—you want to know and you don't seem to want to know so I'm rather in a quandary sometimes just what to do…well, Rex Wheeler is quite a little bit like you. He is 'terribly' good looking—has deep blue eyes and a smile which is almost an even match for yours. He is like you in another way too—he is decently religious and if there is any one thing which I must have in a man before I can truly admire him, it is a respect for religion. Then Rex Wheeler has a chin—such a chin—with it I'm sure he'll chisel a glorious career for himself. I know you don't like my eulogies to other inhabitants of this globe but seeing that all my attempts at praising or rather giving onto Caesar only what is his due have been worked at and even been designated by that vile appellation 'flattery'. I am forced to lay my tribute at feet which do not kick!"

Later, she thoughtfully continued writing this letter, "Saturday afternoon (hotter than ever)—Dearest Sir Galahad—Who ever would have dreamed that you could just bubble over with wit and humor like you did in Mary's letter. Dear jester mine, why not pass some of that excellent wit along the line. You don't seem to think that I would appreciate it---why I can see the point to things almost as quickly as John Hattery and then to be treated as if I couldn't understand your sallies is enough to break my heart. If it wasn't so terrifically *transin equificant* dram damn all hot, I should be tempted to weep on somebody's shoulder but as it is I'm trying to keep cool. Really, I believe I like you rather well today or I wouldn't broil here by the half hour just so you'll get a letter on Monday. I thought perhaps after your two efforts in Oil City and Pittsburg there would be a dead dull calm of some kind and consequently an empty pigeonhole in the Endeavor post office, so I was only disappointed, not surprised, not to receive your letter yesterday. This morning, however, I went for the mail myself to see what was the matter. Gee, how you have spoiled me-don't you dare to stop—at least not without a week's notice. I suppose I could get used to only receiving two letters a week if I had to and such a state of things would keep you in your Career.

"Of course, you must know that ever since you told me about what Dr. (Charles) Compton said, I've thought and thought of very little else. I do so want you to show everybody next year that you "are the heir of all the ages in the foremost files of time"— and have the toughest, stiffest backbone in Christendom! If those men don't give you a chance Wilbert (I wrote that because it seems to have more dignity than Billy and I'm trying to be serious for once in my life) if they don't give you a chance God pity somebody. I'm not just sure yet whether it will be they or you or I—but somebody will need all the pity that can be spared from above.

"Please tear up all these ridiculous letters I've written, am writing and shall write to you. Do you think I want my literary reputation to say nothing of any other reputations ruined by having such things floating around with a simpleton. Answer me.

"Dear—I think as long as I have such a large bill to pay to his satanic majesty for the rest of my brimstone pit in purgatory, I wouldn't mind adding another thousand years or two to my indebtedness. You are making me be very honest and economical, however, and refuse to let me run bills at the hot gate of eternity. The question is will I ever owe the days I contracted such a debt? 'I will not'—you read me like an open book, don't you? Nothing subtle about those last words. I know it and should be ashamed. I suppose to let you know, that I know, you know—yet I'm not. Maybe you are praying for me this time so as to keep me cool and undisturbed. Will nothing stop me this afternoon! One thing would but I can't get it to do it. Shame on you Elsie—never mind Billy doesn't know what you are talking about anyway and if he did he would smile a kind, pitying smile and murmur 'poor idiot.'"

Elsie had received a long letter from Billy about a week later and she responded with, "Then you had to go and heap coals of fire on my head by sending three perfectly grand letters in this morning's mail. Twelve pages in one. Billy dear, you are a wonder. I'm in a good humor now—I got over whatever was the matter with me—forgive anything in it that is nasty and mean and cattish—I suppose it is just full of such things—all thorns and no roses at all."

A humorous reflection occurred on July 11 after Mary and Elsie spent the afternoon reading their old diaries, "Yesterday 'we' amused ourselves by reading our old 'date-books'. We discovered several interesting things which had increased in value because of their age. One thing I thought you might be interested in (you see I have to write about something—nothing really truly happens in this place you know—not since the glorious fourth—so I simply grub around until I find any little thing that I think you might condescend to let your nice eye rest upon and write it down). This is the remarkably trifling thing. After the first date I ever had with you—oh, last year some time you remember you asked me, when somebody else probably couldn't go! I had written in my date book, 'Had a much better time than I expected'. How much is that worth—nothing I suppose—yet by speaking of it, I have been able to cover almost a page. Lucky, I thought of it.

"Dear—did you see that moon last night. I stared it out of countenance—the beautiful, imprudent thing. Finally, it went behind a cloud and peeped out sheepishly at me from one black corner. Then it grew bolder and came clear out again—then I went in. I thought perhaps you might be up at Chippewa having a grand time—how unreasonable—there is no dancing there on Monday night, is there—you certainly have me wild to go to Lake George. Of course, I don't really expect to get there—but it is sweet to dream about.

"Most Gallant and Gentle Sir Galahad—Lady is at present no sight for eyes which delight in spotless beauty—for woe is me—she upset the contents of a phial of ink upon her robe and is now set down to mourn amid its trickling rivulets of Stygian blackness" writes Elsie on July 13. "The God's have favored you, however, Sir Knight for almost a thimble full of the precious writing fluid was saved for your service. Me thinks your pen has grown as mighty as your sword dear Galahad, for sweet have been the messages which have come to me bearing your sign and seal. Did you fancy that you but dreamed a dream the other night—nay 'twas no dream for I myself was there and did behold that you were the most gallant and splendid of all the knights assembled. I marveled too, that you smiled upon me when there were many fairer brighter ladies sparkling near thee. But since it is as it is, may it ever be so. You know my maiden knight, that e'er you win a crest upon your shield—three deeds must be accomplished—three foes be conquered. Even now you are upon the battlefield—to win or die—and I doubt not that the foe you fight is even now growing faint hearted before the fury of your onslaught. Yield no quarter for the day that be yours. I presume I could keep this up indefinitely, but you must have some limit of endurance though never yet have I been able to discover it. You are having a hard time though, aren't you. If you were a baby, I would send you a nice stick of peppermint candy with red stripes running around it to comfort you. As you aren't, I can't do a thing but wish that I could do something. If there had been any person in it at all, I should have arisen in the silence of Tuesday night and written you a masterpiece. I was in one of those unexplainable hilarious moods of mine—when I'm not afraid of man nor devil—so if I had written anything startling would be bound to have resulted. The next time such a mood strikes me, there shall be something doing. Yesterday, I came down from my hill-top with an awful crash. Such a reaction—it was expected though so I wasn't surprised Tuesday night the whole McKean family was kept awake by my craziness and Wednesday if anyone had stuck a pin into me, I doubt whether I should have deigned to notice it even. Mary is going to have a dinner this evening—so yesterday, we decided on the place cards and that I should make them. Did you dream I was artistic? Hardly so artistic, I wager. Yesterday, on account of my burst of artistic enthusiasm, I began mutilating dainty, oblong pieces of cardboard into place cards. Horrors, but the result of my efforts is a sickly-looking mess. Thank goodness 'colors seen by candlelight are not the same by day'—you understand—thank goodness for the candlelight. I must go and excavate the germs from the parlor now—when Elsie comes the dust must fly—not always of course—just when it's dusty. Adieu, my friend.

"You have such pretty dreams. I can't dream about you anymore. I suppose because I think about you too much, there have been dreams though. Years ago was it...in which you were a prince indeed and there were roses and music and moonlight. And all these beautiful things were placed together on 'a heaven kissing hill' away up near the stars. Why should my night angel bar you from the golden gate of my dream world now...when once she let you wonder wherever you seemed to choose? It is rather disappointing not to be able to command you to enter... or at least to give you the open sesame to my dreamland, but I'm afraid I shall have to go there alone, for all dreams to come.

"Last week, there were three rattlers killed between here and the Eddy. Yesterday evening, somebody had a brilliant idea, 'Let's go to the creek for supper.' No objections." East Hickory Creek flows past Endeavor to the Allegheny River. "We all went...who wanted to go and who didn't, was just the same. It is beautiful at the creek. I do wish I had known of the place when you were here. I certainly should have taken you down there on Tuesday afternoon in spite of my sleepiness and your desire to smoke. The memory of that afternoon is rather too vivid yet, perhaps though if it had been less bitter to me, what followed might not have been so sweet. It was different for you because you're nothing but a man anyway and coldly reasonable. Enough! Let it pass." There were rough moments in their relationship even at the beginning without explanation or reason why. Were her expectations too high, or was he insensitive to her feelings?

"No, it isn't Saturday either, it is 1:15 Sunday morning." It is July 15, "The dance is over, praise the Lord. I most sincerely hope that they don't give any more—Scotty, Burnie, Dous and myself were all hilariously out of tune—it was because each one of us was thinking of the one we would rather have there than anyone else in the world, at least I know it was so in my case and suppose at least that it was the same with the rest of them. There were a whole lot of summer school girls there and I absolutely refused to trade dances with any of the fellows who had them, consequently I made a bunch sore at me, but what care I. I'd a whole lot rather be a wallflower and sit out the whole darned program than to have to dance with some of those people."

"I told you about the fellows throwing one of the inmates of this house into Reddick's Dam didn't I"? One of the places of interest around Wooster was Reddick's Reservoir, a city water-works and picnic grove half a mile from Old Stone Quarry, a little north of corporation line. "Well, the poor kid took it so to heart and was so mopey that I finally took pity on him and asked him to help me do a stunt on the fellows here. I told him about it last Sunday morning, and he has been after me every night since then to pull it off, so tomorrow night we are going to do it. Get a bunch of old bags and put them into a tin can or coal bucket, light them, then put them out and…when they get to going good, hide them in the house somewhere and let the house fill up with smoke. Someone will wake up, and yell "fire" then we will all…I can see Satan running around like a headless chicken now. It really ought to be quite a little diversion if we can only get away with it without being caught. But if they find out who did it, there will probably be a whole lot more division, for Koshbaugh and myself at least.

"This is a beautiful night. I knew that that word is hackneyed and time worn, but it expresses just the truth. It certainly would be a night for a long drive. But, of course, there is no sense wishing for impossible things, so I'll have to be content for the time being with thoughts of you. The thoughts are with me all of the time, and I tell the charm on my rosary with a greater and stronger love every moment. Oh, Elsie darling, when you talk about the possibility of someone wanting to forget all that has passed between us, you don't know how it hurts, for I know more certainly with every beat of my heart, the heart that thinks it's every beat for you, that if that time does ever come, it will be you who will want to forget, while I, well I will have my Rosary, and no one can take that from me. I love you dearest, more than I can tell, love you more every day. You know I do dear heart, tell me that you do for I am forever yours."

Billy was in a blue mood when he wrote to Elsie from Beta Theta Pi House on Sunday, July 16, "It's been raining all afternoon, has let up a little now, and it looks like it might clear up before night. I wish it wouldn't. Days like this are great sometimes. Scotty and I left our names at the post office yesterday for mail today. The postman didn't deliver any yesterday afternoon. We started down right after dinner, ran all the way down to beat the rain...we got there all right, but the regular man wasn't at the window and he said we couldn't get our mail on Sundays...we walked back up through the rain, stopped at Boyce's for a soda after we were soaking wet and have been up here cussing that postmaster ever since.

"This house had been a veritable pandemonium all afternoon. There are five fellows who play, as rather play...here in the house, consequently in our room, they are having a band practice. Walter Snyder and his cohorts are having what he calls a "Turkish festival" in his room...it consists mostly of Japanese lanterns hung around, with the aforementioned cohorts strung around the room shouting at the top of their lungs and beating upon old pans and a couple of my tamboreens while Walter directs the music from the top of Jumbo's (Edward Chalfant) strongbox. Satan (M. A. Gregg) is trying to help me write this letter by singing *He's a College Boy*, and with each successive note, he changes the pitch. So, if this letter should by any chance contain one or two light incongruities, don't blame me.

"I just discovered this letter that I wrote to you last night in my pocket. I took it downtown to mail so that it would go out in the 4:28 and was so upset with the man in the P.O. that I forgot to mail it...two letters in one mail again.

"Say, Elsie, do I repeat a whole lot of stuff in my letters? I've often wondered if I did and have often wished that I had kept a copy of some of the ones I have written where I was either blue, tired, or in some other way entirely unfit to write to such a person as you, just to read them over when I get a little more straightened up. It is probably a mighty good thing for me that I haven't done it. Now, take that letter I wrote last night for instance. I don't remember a thing I wrote in it except the last paragraph. That is, something I couldn't forget...One thing I know, I couldn't have said and that is that I had a 'perfectly wonderful time.'

"I have just come up from a little talk with Mrs. Reynolds. She called me down to the lab to talk, said that she was tired of seeing 'pesky summer schoolers' all the time, and wanted to talk to a friend for a little while. She is a peach, and she is so good to us fellows who were here during the winter. It's a wonder that some of the other roomers don't get sore at the partiality, for she certainly shows it. Well, I went down, and we talked about a whole lot of stuff, then finally, she wanted to know what I was going to do when I finished college. Ye Gods and little Julius, will it never cease? I don't suppose so, until I decide. Of course, I told her I didn't know, and she thinks that it would be fine for me to go into the ministry. I told her to please not place her hopes too high along that line, for great as I think that line of work to be, yet, I'm afraid that I'd make a grand fizzle of that. Well, I got out of there pretty soon after that.

"Darn Adam Koshbaugh's hide, he has been in here for the last hour, trying to make some plans for the big fire scare tonight. I hinted broadly to him two or three times that I wanted him to stop. I guess that either he is too thick-headed...hint or else I'm too clumsy to make things happen. I finally had to tell him that if he didn't let me alone, I wouldn't bother with his old fire, so he got out. Poor kid, how he does want to get something on the fellows here."

Elsie has surprising news. Mary McKean's younger sister, Hazel, eloped. She writes to Billy on July 16 with the news,

"Such excitement as we've had here! Hazel, the young and beautiful, the beloved, has eloped with her devoted Paul…and has returned a happy bride." A newspaper article in the Forest Republican announces that Hazel McKean and Paul Sieger were married in Jamestown by Rev. C. T. Shaw." Imagine what suppressed emotions there were among all of us this morning when we discovered she had disappeared. Her mother and father are taking it very sensibly—they are disappointed of course, in a way because they didn't tell them about it—but her mother at least was expecting something sort—her intuition, I suppose told her something was brewing.

"Do you know that night we were up at Chippewa, Mary and Cara (Lehman) thought some rather foolish things. Of course, I've never defended you, so it was natural they would expect something foolish from me—but it made me rather furious to hear you being calmly thought of as having no sense. Listen, they didn't say you were really neglected by providence understand, but of course, anybody that would let a little moonlight and a girl persuade them into buying a plain gold band on very, very short notice hasn't really got good sense. I soon set them straight. It was all, all my fault. How I regret that night, simply because it reflected on you so that isn't the only time either that the wild strain in my nature has made you do things or not do things which you of your own sweet will would never have done or left undone. Don't misunderstand me dearest, you know what I mean. I have often realized that I'm not all that I might be—I wish I could be all you will ever need me to be instead of being what I'm afraid I shall be—a bitter disappointment. Every night, I pray to be made more worthy to be loved by you. You said once you did not know me and you said truly, you do not. But dear, I don't want you to know me too late—when nothing can be undone. Sometimes, I have thought that it is because I really do not love you that I think these things—that I doubt your constancy for a moment. But, it can't be that—for my heart tells me in every beat that I do, I do, so it must be because I care so much that I want you to have what will make you most happy. Don't think that I really ever think you don't love me. You know if I ever thought that, for a moment, I wouldn't give you more than one chance to let me know you didn't but would just slip away nicely and obligingly and let you hear me singing all the way! Such a letter—how ashamed I am of myself. You never say such things—perhaps you never think them. Oh, I'd like to talk to you for an hour or so—it would be nice wouldn't it? Do you think it would be interesting to have a catalogued list of all the emotions I range through while I'm writing one letter to you. Yes, interesting, but scarcely practical…there would be almost a great variety as those I've had when walking around the quadrangle. Is this letter about myself? Dear me, no…there is nothing self-centered about it at all…every word is about somebody else. We shall now change our mood to order…can it be done… surely…and you must listen to some dusty description of a Free Methodist prayer meeting." A short distance down the road from McKean's is a small white clapboard church not far from the East Hickory line.

"Last night, Mary and I walked with our faces toward Jesus, enjoying the beautiful night and talking earnestly all the time we walked. Suddenly, we heard something that sounded like a poor, half consumptive phonograph rasping and gasping away at a great rate. We stopped and listened…not because our musical souls were stirred by the sympathetic sounds which oozed from a house before us, but simply because we were rooted to the spot by amazement, and vulgar curiosity. It was no phonograph that was making the night hideous, but one of God's poor deluded creatures made in his image, too move's the pity shouting to almighty heaven for mercy, strength, peace and all the other fifty-seven varieties of heavenly canned goods. Shocked...I never was so shocked in my life. Others were screaming away...others were moaning piteously...still others were shouting 'Praise the Lord', 'Hallelujah-Amen' in a wild medley. Some less intelligent mortal from their number was even as we passed being converted. I thought I heard the water in the baptismal fount heave a wave or two during the ceremony, but perhaps it was only some sauer[*sic*] individual bent on attoning[*sic*] physical cleanliness since spiritual purity demanded such strenuous exertions... perhaps it was only a normal person trying out the new bath-tub. It is needless to say that in order not to shock these fellow-beings of mine while they were calling on higher heaven, Mary and I raced down the road and smothered our unwomanly laughter in our handkerchiefs—and we continued to move away from the house of prayer suppressing our laughter as best we could until the ugly helps, groans, cries, howls, prayers and amen's were mellowed and toned down into a suggestive moaning. Don't get the idea of what it was that waylaid us on our pleasant walk last night?

"Tra la. Hazel is getting all that is coming to her...she just said now that she wished somebody would hang crepe on the door so that people wouldn't grin so idiotically when they passed the house. Mary hadn't quite gotten over the shock yet...neither have I. It is rather provoking to have our plans all upset...you see Mary and I had picked out Hazel for Jim and now 'she's gone and done it.'

"I received word from my uncle that I'm going to visit someday in the near future, that he has been expecting me for the last two weeks and wonders where I am. He seems interested...very... in my future movements. Poor man, I've had him hanging in the air for a month or so already, and I haven't decided yet when I'm going to leave this place. Mary is so good...she simply won't let me go…she says not until the 1st of August, but that's too much… even if I offend her, I've got to pull out of here before then.

Billy begins to realize that Elsie truly cares for him. It's not just a budding romance, it has become deeper, so on July 17 he tells her how he feels, "The one I got today was, oh Elsie, it was a wonder. I never imagined that I could ever be made quite as happy by a letter as that one made me. You know to which part I refer, the part referring to the Rousseau's definition—you know that I have often said that the only time I feel absolutely certain that you aren't going to fly away from me sometime is when I am holding you in my arms…it isn't that I feel that you don't love me, it isn't that. It is just because I love you so absolutely that I think of you all the time. Then I get to thinking why in thunder you should ever; how you could ever, have fallen in love with me, and then I suppose that it is only natural this form thinking. Sometimes, I get frightened about whether I'm going to lose you or not. God, but it is hard to stand sometimes, I've been trying to control my thoughts a little lately and trying to make myself believe that there is no chance of your ever loving anyone else the way you do me, and well a letter like that one certainly helps a whole lot…Two weeks ago now, I was just about saying goodnight to you, after our little trip to the city. I thought at that time that I knew what love was in its fullest meaning, but now that love has grown. I loved you then, loved you more than any other being, but now, well it is too deep a thing for me to try to describe. And, thank God that I love to love you. Oh dearest, sometimes it seems as if ages had gone by since last I saw you, and heard you tell me that you love me; yet it has only been since the last week, my heart, that you told me that.

I don't suppose that you and I will ever agree about that night at Chippewa." Less than 20 miles north of Wooster via trolley, Chippewa Lake was a place for swimming, boating, and fishing.

It was a favorite spot. The night in question is a mystery. One thing for sure, Cara Lehman was with them and Billy ended up with black teeth. "Of course, it was my fault, and if I want to take the blame, please don't stop me, for there are enough things blamed upon me so that that will make very little difference anyway…please don't regret it, I don't any more at all, now that everything came out all right."

"I almost fell over when I read the news about Hazel. My, but I'm sorry about this. I don't suppose I should be if they are happy, but she was such a peach. My, what a shock it must have been for Mary and the rest of you people. It was an awful shock to me, who only knew them for a short few days, what's more, it must have been for their family and you who know her so well. I certainly hope and pray that everything is for the best."

Mary and Elsie spend the following Sunday afternoon hiking in the hills above Endeavor. She ponders the beauty of the scenery while she writes to Billy, "You should have been here today for you would have enjoyed the tramp Mary and I took up to the big rocks. The climb was steeper than I had imagined it would be, but the view from the top of the rocks and the rocks themselves are well worth the trouble it takes to see them. Daddy McKean went with us to keep the rattlers away. It really is dangerous to go up the narrow trail flanked on either side by low shrubbery and pick your way among stones and brush without being able to see more than two clear feet before you. If it hadn't rained while we were toiling up the hillside, we should undoubtedly have met a half dozen or more snakes but the rain makes them get under shelter so their rattlers won't get dampened. Mr. McKean told us about how he killed the biggest rattler known to have been killed in this state. Imagine, the creature was seven feet two in length, measured nineteen inches around and had rattlers over an inch across. Naturally, after a wild story like his was, Mary and I didn't trip along quite as gaily as we had been doing.

"The rocks are perfectly huge…some of them must be sixty feet high at least." Minister Rocks, "is one place where they are arranged so as to form a small amphitheatre[*sic*]. This little amphitheatre is a beautiful spot…romantic enough to please even you in one of your abominable indifferent moods. The rocks which form its walls are all fern covered…and there is pretty thick moss on its floor. Three or four trees like rustic pillars grow through the center and make it shady even at noon. Oh, dear, I have no idea what I'm writing…somebody is playing familiar hymns and my mind is following them. Khlare and Margaret are scrapping[*sic*] and the bride and groom are trying to bring down the only safe porch swing. How can I write when all these things are going on? Here's where I concentrate my mind on Mr. Wilbert White just to see if I can when bedlam is loose around me.

"We climbed to the top of one of the biggest of the rocks. From there we could look away down the river past West Hickory to the blue most-girdled hills beyond. Do you like huckleberries? There were just quarts of them up on top of those rocks. We ate until common sense dictated to us to leave a few for the birds…a big thunder shower caught us on our way down…just as we were when we strolled into Endeavor. I tore my dress in six shreds…you never saw such tatters…one tear was a yard long and Mr. McKean when he saw that, suggested that we hurry for fear I should leave all of it behind me. It was fun though, great fun.

"I tried to smoke a cigar today…tra-la, you can imagine how far I got." Elsie was very adventurous in every way. "I only choked about six times…and then I gave up! Mary said John Mateer wasn't in it compared to me. Nobody was shocked…they laughed

too much so all my efforts were in vain. I wanted to startle someone into a fit, but nobody tumbled into one.

"I wonder if I ever will get to Lake George...dream on if you
like...I'm crazy to go of course, but I couldn't if I would be the
least bit of trouble to your mother...you know that. You may say
that she has had you to contend with all these years and so would
be equal to almost anything...Mary and I have just returned
from a party up at Wheeler's," and on July 18. "We certainly did
have a grand good time. George, Wil(Gus) Warden, Rex and Roy
Wheeler and a cousin of theirs from Yale were the young men
present...Carolyn, the girl who thinks you are 'cute', and two
others beside Mary and myself, represented the youthful part of
the eternal feminine. I have laughed until my sides ache. Mr.
Karl Smith, Mrs. Wheeler's brother-in-law, is a perfect circus all
in himself. He gave us some high-class vaudeville...Salome[*sic*]
dancing...impersonations, and best of all, a prize-fight where he
managed to knock himself down two or three times with very
scientific blows. Mr. Roy Wheeler, who by the way is even more
sarcastic than you can be, seemed to enjoy the wrestling match
to the fullest extent. During the evening, we all sang and listened to some excellent selections on a phonograph. I'm sure
this affair has been noted as a brilliant success by all the lucky
ones' present.

"Wil(Gus) and George (Warden) left a few minutes ago.
George and I had a great 'rough-house' tonight. Mary says she
thinks we were pretty evenly matched. At any rate, he'll remember me for the awful twist I gave his hand and I'll remember him
because of a nice achy arm I have. It was great fun, but it made
me horribly tired after all the other things I've done today. Mary
and I walked to the Eddy this afternoon...dear old Eddy! When
we got there, we just stretched ourselves out on the grass and

looked up at the blue sky and the white clouds. I showed Mary, on our way home, the exact spot where we had met our rattler.

"Never mind what you wrote about the dance. You were dead tired and didn't mean at all I'm sure, that you didn't have a bit of a good time. Don't be afraid that I might not like to hear you say that you had 'a perfectly wonderful time' someplace…if you really did. You deserve to have them and I want you to get what you deserve. When you are tired, you don't care what you say…or don't you know what you say…that you write such sweet things to me. I do not get tired hearing you say some things…we never do. You don't repeat yourself in other things though…you seemed to be a little worried for fear you did.

"We were given roses tonight…a bunch of them. Roses from the wrong person have such big thorns, haven't they, yet, these of ours are very sweet. I know I shouldn't write letters to you so late at night when I am so tired…not my spirit dear…it isn't weary a bit, or I shouldn't be talking to you now…but I'm afraid I say things I should never say…When your arms are around me you know, I could tell you anything, but this way it is too much…I just had a fright…downstairs all alone again, I heard somebody or something knock a crock and plate over down in the cellar. You may be sure I'm upstairs now. This thing of having nerves is simply disgusting…I never used to have them. It's probably because I'm so tired, I scarcely know what I'm writing, but this I do know, and I shall write it even if I knew I'd go to Hell for it the next minute…I love you dearest, with 'the breath, smiles, tears of all my life' and I shall love you as long as God chooses."

"Nothing has happened today except the arrival for the day of a Mr. Marshall Merrick, who was one of Hazel's ardent admirers. He just blew in and then found out the glad news about Hazel and Paul. He's a perfect circus…a traveling man…you can imagine the line of talk he can get off. You just have to start him going and he does the rest as long as you will listen. I'm tired of being entertained, so I excused myself to come and talk with you." It's the middle of July, yet she seems to be feeling devilish after reading one of his recent letters, perhaps even peeved, "Aren't you flattered? No, of course not...you're so very used to it by this time, that you just take it for granted. 'Don't take anything for granted'...for sometimes things don't always 'pan out' that way. (Nasty, nasty, Elsie). Wil practically told me last night that he was engaged...did I tell you that before. He fancies he has in me, someone to sympathize with him...and he has, if he wants sympathy. He's as young as you are, although, he's roughed it a good deal so he's worn off a little of the tender bloom of youth...but he needs bringing up too, and if he wants it, he shall have the very best. Oh, what's the use of talking to you this way anyway? If there was anything else to talk about, I certainly wouldn't talk about all the infants in this burg. I'm going to read your morning's letter over again and see if you've asked any questions that I might answer. Here we are...speaking of things being blamed on you...you say one thing more or less wouldn't make any difference. What sort of a mood prompted you to say a thing like that! You know you care...if you don't, I've made some mistake somewhere. I just seem to pick everything you say when you're tired to pieces, don't I? Well, at least I appear interested...I am far from being indifferent anyway. I must think of something unusually startling to raise a ripple of interest or the calm sea of your indifference. Perhaps I meant that last sentence, but just as likely as not, I didn't. You see, I admit that. I have tried sometimes to amuse you...so of course, I'm glad when you are entertained. Glory Hallelujah, it's going to rain." No matter how you look at it, Elsie is incorrigible, but she gets her point across.

131

The letter of July 20 (and ½ as she noted) reflected her bad habits and wry humor, "When are you going to step down off that wonderful beautiful gold-lined cloud, lay aside your rose-colored glasses and breathe again the common air of less favored, else contented, earth-born creatures? I'll wager not until you get good and ready. The God's themselves sir, are at your service. Dame Fortune smiles and prosperity has sworn to be thy page. The world makes you feel as comfortable as a well upholstered Morris chair looks and comfy as footing the bill for the drinks and cigars (figuratively speaking). 'Every prospect pleases' and man ever taken in a cold lump isn't vile. If your highness were walking down the street and passed a darling little girl with golden curls, your highness would feel like pulling one gently that would show the tenderness in your mood. And, if you were summoned before High Heaven or the Devil to answer for yourself, you would approach either tribunal with a springy step, a half defiant, half indifferent smile, and a sublime composure… that is, if you had been summoned Wednesday afternoon. The almighty ego is triumphant, so let the rest of humanity crawl and babble on to the fulfillment of their own inevitable destinies. The puny, disfurging[*sic*] blots which fell from the careless brand of the great writer who wrote our name so perfectly! Do we (editorial) not feel all this, and more, much more, which some feeble intelligence cannot convey to our reader? How senseless of me to try to guess what sort of a complicated mood you were in. Let me say though, I know this much about your mood…I love you when you're in it…I love the freckles on your heart and the Devil-may-care and the Sir Galahad gentleness all mixed up together in this all's-right-with-the-world-and-what-isn't-doesn't-affect-me mood of yours. Am I altogether wrong in my guess, Darling of the Gods?

"Such a day as we've had of it. Most of the morning was spent getting dinner and all the afternoon was whiled away at a missionary meeting." Endeavor Presbyterian Church was formed by Mrs. Wheeler as a bible study. Most of the families associated with the mill; namely the Wheelers, Wardens, Scherer's and McKean's were active in the church which was built by N. P. Wheeler. Hence, Elsie begins to refer to those leaders of the Missionary Society as twigs and their daughters as twiglets. Its presence at the end of the street, across from the mill office seemed appropriate given the influence of the Wheelers' in its founding. "I had to go, or I certainly should have taken a long walk through the woods instead. Dear, have you ever been at a twig meeting of the mighty branch of the almighty tree of the Pennsylvania Missionary Society. Of course, you haven't. That question was purely rhetorical. You see how I am getting around to my subject...the fire and spirit with which I pursue my lectures to innocent young men is simply confounding isn't it? Well, this twig must need blossom like Aaron's rod...or rather is sprouted... there is no other explanation for the twelve varieties of grasses and ferns delicately sprinkled with mayonnaise that were thrust upon me by the sub-twiglets. I have never even in my protagonist existence when I was a little wooly, wooly lamb wondering over miles of pastureland...I have never seen so many varieties of the gem grass complacently, mutilated for human satisfaction. Fortunately, with these salads, sandwiches of unknown origin, and shrouded pedigree were coyly offered. When the refreshments were all over...the room...everyone sang plaintively, but with secret rebellion in their hearts...Praise God from whom all blessings flow'. Tonight, Rex Wheeler condescended to take Mary and me to the tennis game, but he didn't think a session on our porch would do him any good spiritually or morally, so he went about his business.

"You would have laughed had you strolled in upon us an hour ago that lunatics were at work wasting a perfectly good paper or else, that we were running a poultry farm. For would you believe it, three of the night owls of this ranch have been making ciphers, rows of them, hundreds of them, just as fast as fingers can fly and they have been engaged in this seemingly profitless occupation for two hours or more. You could never guess what it was for. We were divining by occult science, the meaning of the visions of the night, the phantoms of slumber. There is a crazy book here. Maybe you've seen it. If you have, you're a fraud for not having yelled sooner and headed me off from all that I am about to divulge. Here's where I make a plunge and slip to you the secrets learned by man's arduous cipher...making from The Ancient Oracle of the Priests of India. I performed the necessary mystic ceremony in order to discover the meaning of my awful 'dinner dream'. This is what that book said. Tra da, I haven't stopped laughing yet, 'A sign of prosperity to a man and of marriage within a year to a woman'. The foolish part about the whole process of dream interpretation is that there exists no real connection between the ciphers and your dream unless as the book tries to insist (you knew I believed in all these things didn't you? No?) insists there is a psychological connection. Well, my egg dream 'what do I care about all this? Not Elsie?' Yes, dear, but you must put up with it like a gentleman. Don't sulk, but suffer my egg dream, was not interpreted quite so satisfactorily. 'On a Tuesday, this shows an evening' boo! Billy, I'm not afraid of you. 'On a Monday, a friend, but deceitful.' You hateful deceiver. 'On all other days...rain!' Did it rain in January dear, do you remember! Of course, it simply poured. Now turn around and listen to me. In your next letter, you will please enclose a slip of paper on which you have enscribed[*sic*] ciphers? Ciphers, ciphers... think of any dream you like (this is very, very serious Billy, so you must pay attention and stop yawning...it's horribly rude to yawn anyway.) Then write ten rows of ciphers as I've indicated... just as many in each row as the spirit dictates and I shall inform you by return mail (perhaps) just which road is safest for you to travel on in the future. It's almost time for the chickens to start crowing and there I sit talking drivel to one who has, but lately conversed with the Gods.

"We'll probably not go to Chautauqua after all and I think about Wednesday of next week, I'll fly to my uncle's waiting arms and hang around until he kills the fatted calf. Yes, just drop in and see me anytime...the latch string is always out for tramps or Salvation Army rogues or just plain well-meaning gentlemen. You'd never guess what sort of a mood I'm into tonight. It is just as well sir that you are not around for I'm afraid you might not appreciate every way in which I would be bound to express my burning enthusiasm. Billy, it's great to be alive. Let's hang around this terrestrial ball as long as the music's good...will you? I'm quite satisfied with the way things have been dished out to-night, my share of the goods seems so satisfactory. I am thankful for it all...you understand...help me always to be...you can you know by always loving one who loves you."

Was she feeling as though she was taken advantage of by Billy? If so, she let him know it, "You just love to give out nice bits of startling news, don't you? Oh! I'm so glad-glad-glad. If you dare not to come now, I'll never in the world forgive you. Don't you know my heart can't be jarred and jostled about just anyway... it has work to do and must keep it up regularly until I have sus-picions that I need false teeth...then it can go to rest forever. I met George this morning quite as usual...just after I'd finished reading your letter. He looked at me as if he thought I must have seen a 'great light' and said, 'my, but your face looks bright this morning'. How could it help but be shining when the flame before the inner shrine had leaped up to make the room of my heart, warmer, brighter, purer for your coming…you know you must use your persuasive powers to persuade Jim to come with you…anybody ought to be crazy to come and see Mary if they got half a chance…of course Jim is used to being petted and babied by us…so are you, aren't you Baby Stare?"

She is unsure about when she will be leaving for Cincinnati and thinks she will be in Endeavor until August 25, arriving in time for the upcoming wedding of her cousin Eloise. Her late arrival causes a lot of family stress since she is one of the bridesmaids. But Elsie's love for Billy and need to be close to him, even though she is feeling insecure about their relationship, far outweighs her obligation to family. Later, she will understand why there is stress in the family.

Billy is in New York and receives a letter from Elsie on December 31, 1911 from Springdale, Ohio, where she is visiting Cara Lehman before going to Cincinnati to spend time with relatives. It is New Year's Eve. She begins her letter with, "This looks as if I were going to compose a theme or something equally formidable – it really means, however, that I'm going to talk to you a little while in spite of the lack of note paper on this ranch. Yesterday was mighty dreary, rain, rain, rain and no letter from you to brighten things a bit. If I hadn't been on the go every minute I should have shed tears of disappointment and rage I'm sure at the conditions of affairs and cursed softly at the gods and you. As it was, the play was absorbing, my car for Springdale late so there were other things besides you and your precious letter to entertain me! Scott has been turning the kitchen into a laundry. He's been pressing and no doubt will reappear in a short time clad fairer than the lilies. This house hasn't so very many modern conveniences – it's one of those all fashioned country houses – but it has one redeeming feature – open fire places. Right now,

I'm ensconced in a big rocking chair in front of a perfectly beautiful fire. No wonder I want to talk to you, to feel you near me. If I could only have now some of the things I've made myself miss – what wouldn't I give. You are quite right though, it is good for us to be away from each other, but dear, just as soon as I begin to resign myself to the inevitable, to tell myself there is no earthly use in longing for it cannot be then all my equanimity is destroyed by seeing you again. And then when my happiness is almost complete comes the thought that in a little while we must be parted again. If I only didn't love you so, Billy things wouldn't hurt at all. When I think to myself how sometimes I doubted if I really did love you I can't understand myself, yet I do have those doubts even yet. Until you hurt me or make me desperately happy and then I know that if I weren't quite sure that my love for you would remain unshaken through everything, I would be afraid to risk having those doubts come at all for fear my happiness would be destroyed in the process.

"We just got home from church and Cara is putting finishing touches to the dinner and refuses to be bothered by such a tyro in the culinary art as I am so I'm back again for a brief stay in Arcady. I'll have to go back to Cincy this afternoon and that will mean no more open fireplaces to sit in front of for the rest of my stay. I'd like to know when you expect to get to Bob's. Of course, it's too late for me to find out now, but if I knew I could be counting the hours, but that I suppose would make the days seem longer than ever. I just thought of something, New York, I believe, is the one spot on earth where anything can be obtained. Well I wish you'd do something for me if it won't take up too much of your time. Get me two good looking red candles with gold dragons twisted around them. You've seen that kind, haven't you? I haven't the remotest idea what the price will be but if you think it will break me please don't get them. I've scoured this town and so has my cousin, for these candles and it's all been in vain. She wants them. I don't, but I just got a hunch that I'd get them and give them to her. So please do your very, very best and as you shall prove faithful over a little thing doubtless, I mean perhaps, you shall eventually be made ruler over – whatever you like, of course...the savor of the kitchen is becoming more alluring – in a minute more Carissina will call us to begin our work of devastation. How I wish I might see you, but I shall spend my time making good resolves until I do and breaking them as soon as I see you."

She signs it, "Yours of the longing heart, Elsie."

CHAPTER 7

Cincinnati Here I Come

The Lamping's expected their niece to arrive in Cincinnati and when she didn't arrive until August 2, "These poor people were rather frightened because I didn't show up Saturday or any of the subsequent days," because Elsie did what she wanted and bemoaned, "Why is it that I never do anything smoothly". Frank and Anna Machle Lamping lived at 3145 Vine Street with their children, Eloise, Gertrude and Edward. Mary Machle, Edward's elderly mother also lived in the household. They were in the midst of planning a wedding for their daughter. Elsie was to be one of the bridesmaids, so one can imagine how stressed the family was about her late arrival.

Elsie stopped in Wooster to see Billy, delaying her arrival at her uncle's home in Cinti, "Yesterday was such a long, long day. I thought I should never arrive in Cinti", her nickname for Cincinnati, a city on the north shore of the Ohio River, and home of Proctor and Gamble and Moerleins' Beer. "However, when the pure odor of Proctor and Gamble's famous dirt chaser floated in upon me I realized that I was nearing my destination and when the delicate aroma of malt greeted me I became drunk with the joy of really being in the vicinity of Moerleins' and arose with Sadie and Sally to call myself blessed! Dear I have never been tired in my life before. It was all imagination. Eloise and

I talked until the 'wee early hours' – we had so much to say to each other."

"Eloise wrote to Mary and my uncle asking them to telegraph as to my whereabouts…every time I move about the country it causes a commotion of some sort! Vic brought your letters down to the station…He didn't know that it was just yesterday morning that I was with you."

Billy left Wooster in August and met his family in Lake George, New York. The White family owned a cottage on Lake George where families associated with the Y.M.C.A. developed a conference center for training the youth. Dr. White and his brother, J. Campbell White, worked for the Y.M.C.A. in Calcutta before J. Campbell became General Secretary of the Laymen's Missionary Movement in New York. Their sister, Leila was married to John R. Mott, whose college and international work in Y.M.C.A. later earned him a Nobel Peace Prize. The program nurtured the individual's spirit, mind and body which led to the Young People's Missionary Movement and training young people for foreign and home missions. "The more I think about it the more I want to go. I can't help feeling with my usual unreasonable pessimist that I'll never see the place or that something will happen to you. Yes, I know I've always said there was no sense in looking for things in the future. There isn't for nice things, but for catastrophes. I shall always be expecting them." There was trepidation in her writing, perhaps she was still dealing with the untimely death of her mother and sister, but little did Elsie know how this premonition would come true.

While Elsie was in Cincinnati, she corresponds with Billy at Lake George with an invitation to visit them, "No, I never received a letter from your mother – I wish I had. Perhaps it is still at Holden Hall. Billy, I wish I'd never left Wooster and you…I'm so selfish I want some of the happiness that seems to be floating around here for myself and you. Of course, I am going to smother all these thoughts of mine. I am not going to tell you anything more. I've said too much already, like I always do. Thank you dear for being so good to me while I was in Wooster...you have no idea how I felt when the 10:53 stopped at Wooster. I could never explain just what it was like, but my mental attitude was like that of a person with one hand outstretched, pleading for something and the other places to ward off an expected blow. I thought things over calmly; you might despise me just when I wanted to be loved. You understand a little don't you and know how glad I was when I saw you and knew. Dearest, the Great Light has really come, it had been shining all the time but the Door to my Inner Shrine was shut and I was looking at some other light and thought it was love. Now the Door is open and the Light has so filled the Room that there is not a dark corner for Suspicion or Doubt to lurk in. Dearest Gift of God indeed 'God's gifts put man's best dreams to shame'. I love you, love you. What I gave you before was in comparison to what I offer now as a puny tight green bud to a half-blown rose and this rose if you but breath or it shall grow to perfection, but never grow to wither forever and ever yours.

"My grandma just said, "What! Writing to him again when you haven't heard from him since you came! Something must ail you!" A letter on August 4 adds to her dilemma. "She is quite right, something does. I must write to you now if I want you to have a canned conversation for this day of the year of grace 1911, for tonight somebody has had the bad taste to request our presence at a little affair of some sort. I don't know the people, they don't know me; I don't want to know the people and as soon as they know me they won't want to prolong the acquaintance; and I haven't anything to wear anyway! Nevertheless, I expect in spite of all these draw backs to have the time of my life.

"When my aunt saw your picture she said, 'He looks like a student; as if he could concentrate his mind on one thing easily!' My respect for my aunt as a reader of character has dropped down to nil now...The concentration part wasn't a bad guess. I am referring to your ability to keep your mind pinned down to a Minstrel Show when I wanted to make you forget it. I wrote to father yesterday and told him a little news. He will be surprised, no doubt to think that anyone would really think even that they thought they might or did want his erratic daughter. I almost told him the weather had affected your mind on several occasions and that you really were not to be held responsible. Uncle told me that father expected to come home next June. I hadn't heard about it. If he does get here, then of course China for two years won't be my battle-cry any longer. I am not raising my hopes though. I refuse to give the gods a chance to laugh in their sleeves! Do you think I enjoy this persecution Lord High Inquisitor! I am expecting my Lord to prolong the torture when your prisoner has confessed the Faith – confessed and suffered for her belief and her rank heresy. Will not my Lord open his eyes and look upon his handmaiden; will he not behold her distress and have mercy upon her soul? I beseech thee, my Lord, hear me."

Frustrated with his inconsistent letter writing, Elsie complains, "Sir, if I do not receive a letter tomorrow, your name won't be on my nice-list any longer. Aren't you alarmed about your standing? Of course, you aren't. Imagine you have the same confident look now as you have when you light your pipe, on a windy night, with a guarded match. Someday I am going to make you look a little less conceited when you accomplish that little feat of yours. Beware! Lest you be undone by your 'bitter-sweet' enemy."

Billy wisely keeps in touch with Elsie and shares that he is seriously thinking of their future but frustrated as well by her misinterpretation of his words, "I am trying pretty hard to make my writing legible, so that you won't get my meaning mixed up any more than you have to. There isn't much in the letters that is capable of being mixed very much, it is all so very simple, but when you can't make out the sense, or rather make any sense out of a certain sentence, just let it go for what it is meant the whole letter means nothing more or less than that I love you....it is the most sensible thing that ever came to me. I've had more real ambition to make something of myself, more really sensible thoughts, and really sensible better times since I began to go with you, than I ever had in my whole life before. Don't think that I am saying this just to hear myself talk, or to fill up space on this piece of paper, for that is the farthest thing from my thoughts. It is the truth Elsie dear heart, and I want you to know it for the truth, I love you, and you only, and this love which has come to me is the best thing that ever happened for me at least, and I can only hope that you will never regret anything that has ever happened between us. This is a love letter. I know, for I had no more idea of saying what I have said than a rabbit has of flying in a 1915 model aeroplane.

"Say Elsie, the only decent thing for me to do, is to write to your father and ask him if he is willing to trust his daughter to a poor fool who has absolutely no prospects in this life and eternal fire in the next. Of course, I've thought of it before and meant to ask you what his address was when you were here but didn't do it. My, but I wish that he was here so that I could talk to him, but if he were, I suppose that I would be wishing that I could write it to him... I'm up in the air...should I write, or rather go and see your uncle before saying anything to your father, or what?"

Billy's youthful exuberance was displayed in a romantic letter to Elsie, when he realizes that she reciprocates his feelings for her, "I got your letter this afternoon, and oh dearest—it is as useless for me to try to describe my feelings as it is for me to think of flying to Cincinnati tonight and holding you in my arms. If a letter ever transported a person into an absolutely joyous realm, where nothing at all could disturb him, that letter of yours did it to me. I don't know just why, I knew before that you loved me, I knew it in my heart; but when that letter came, and you said it again, and said it is just the way you did…I was so absolutely happy that I cried…it is from the depths of my heart, and the most sensible one I ever wrote. Did I love you before? Yes, yes, a thousand times yes. Do I love you now? A thousand, thousand, times more than I imagined was possible. There is a verse somewhere in Revelations which says something about having to pass through great tribulation before being able to enter into the Kingdom of Heaven. I don't know what made me think of it, but if "tribulation" means triple-plated hell, Oh, well I know that I'm in Heaven now and always will be and can only thank God for the hell which gave me such a Heaven.

Elsie's desire to return to China was always with her, perhaps it was because that was home to her or perhaps it was to put closure on the grief in her heart, "Don't go to China next year Elsie, stay at home and, I'm going to say it, get married. 'Oh, what' you ask, 'love'? I shrug my shoulders and say that is all I have to offer, but what an immense amount of that there is." Was this a quandary for Elsie who has dreamed of returning to China since she left years earlier and as a "mishkid" felt the obligation to return as part of her grooming at Wooster. At this point, she followed her heart.

Billy begins to commit himself to her amidst his growing sense of misdirection about his future, "It is just half-past eight, and I wondered if I might have a little date with you. I know how you hate to be asked at the last minute, but this is such a beautiful evening that I'm sure you won't refuse just this one little appeal. It comes so directly from the heart too that if you did say that you had to study at work or some other such flimsy excuse, you would hurt the poor beggar who awaits your decision with such loudly beating heart throbs. Thank you so much dear, you don't know how happy you have made me.

This certainly is a wonderful night, and when I think of you away down there in Cincinnati, so very far away, it makes me feel like going outside and calling forth the anger of the Gods upon the moon for sending forth her brilliancy, the stars for shining so brightly, and everything in general for being so peacefully charming. Why couldn't you have stayed here in Wooster for a few days longer anyway? Why do we ever have to be away from each other? What a day it will be when we don't have to have these separations anymore. To even think of that time makes me drunk with the prospect. But, why oh, why, am I going on at this rate when you are down there in the malty city, and I am up here in this hell...I'm just writing what I think, and my thoughts can't seem to keep away from you for very long at a time. I'm glad they can't, for what I'd do if they did is more than I know.

Dave Radrick is out in the other room reading. He came over after supper, and we lay on the bed by the window watching the moon for about two hours and a half. He is going to go up to Lake George to get a little training for his work next year down at Mercersburg, or rather he will go if he gets the job down there. Did you know that he may go down there as the secretary of the Y.M.C.A. in the Academy? I'm not sure whether I told you or not. He doesn't know for sure yet, but will hear in a day or so, and in all probability will go to Silver Bay at the same time I do. We lay there talking about almost everything and everybody under the sun. Did your ears burn?

"I'm going to leave here Thursday afternoon at 4:28…will have to do some things in New York on Friday and then go up to the lake Friday night. That trip up the Hudson is a wonderful one, especially when the moon is shining and it will be on Friday night. Don't you think that there is the slightest possibility that you will be taking that same trip in about three weeks? Please come dearest. I'm not going to give up hope you see until the very last. I think I'll give you my address up at the lake so that you will be sure to have it, it will be after Thursday, Silver Bay, Lake George, N.Y."

Billy seems surprised that she hadn't received any of his letters, "I got your letter this morning, the one you wrote Saturday, and you said that you had not heard from me up till that time. My, but I'm sorry that I didn't write sooner…you really didn't think that I had stopped writing altogether did you?

"Just three more nights in this town and then I make a start anyway for New York. It is good that Dave is going with me for I am afraid if I went alone I'd never reach the gay White Way in a very sober state of mind. I never fully appreciated just why fellows went on a good big drawl: after a hard piece of work until lately. I could go get dead drunk with an absolutely clear conscience. I could be glad to do it, glory in it, and then probably cuss myself out for the rest of my living days. That is exactly the way I feel. I have no more life than a 'quart of junk', but I will have in September, don't you worry. My drooping head will be held buoyantly erect, my bloodshot eyes will be cleared by the expansive view of Lake George and will sparkle, with unexpected brilliancy, my impossible lassitude will be dropped in the deep blue water and I will come springing forward to meet you, when I see you next, with a new elasticity to my step. No, Elsie dearest, don't think I'm tired, for I'm not, don't think I'm crazy, for I'm not, I'm just in love, and I want to see you, to feel your arms around my neck, to kiss, kiss, kiss you, and to hear you say, that you love me. God, but I'd give anything I possess to see you for a little while tonight. I've told you that I love you so much that it hurts, and it is true, and I'm glad it's true, if it wasn't true, I don't know what would happen. You are my every life, my all, and if anything would happen that you should stop loving me—well I won't think of it darling, for it can't, it won't be. You are mine, God made us for each other and when that day comes when I can truly call you mine by all the laws of men as well as those of God, he only knows how great my happiness will be. Oh, how long away that day seems, how long it seems until I will see you again."

Again, Billy's rhetoric describes his trip on a New York Central Lines train, "This ride is perfectly beautiful. I've been sitting for the last two hours on the platform of the observation car which we were going thru miles and miles of Beta sky. You are probably wondering how it is that I am up here in northern Ohio where I should be...Well, yesterday my chemistry exam took so long that I couldn't make the 4:28, so decided to come to Cleveland and take the New York Central to Albany. Mother is expecting me tomorrow noon and if I waited until today to start from Wooster, then went to New York, I wouldn't get home until Sunday. So, Hug Torneau and I came to Cleveland yesterday morning, and I am now on my way to Albany. Yesterday was about the most jam full day I've had this summer. We had to go to recitation in the morning, then take exams in the afternoon. I hadn't done a bit of packing and so the time between the exam and the five-fifty car was spent in slamming things into my trunk. How mother will faint when she sees it. But I will tell you that I tossed the things in, in just about as jubulent[*sic*] a frame of mind as I have been in all summer with the exception of one or two instances, for I was getting my things together to leave Wooster summer school. My but I'm glad that is over. Never again for me.

"If you were only here too, my cup of happiness would be filled to overflowing. There I go again, cursing out the fates, when it is only a little over four weeks now until I see you again…I may have written it that way, but my how different it was inside. A little over a decade ago it was five weeks, now it is four weeks. That's why I said it the way I did.

"I'm glad that you can't see me for a few days at least," Billy writes on August 13, "for I'm afraid that if you did you would have to ask yourself the same question that Della Brown asked the night of the now-to-be forgotten Minstrel Show, 'can you love that?' No, nobody has given me a black eye, or broken my face, nobody has pulled my hair out, or any other slight inconvenience like that, I am simply sunburned. Gad what a redress there is attached to my facial epithelium. When I left Wooster on Thursday afternoon, I couldn't find my hat anywhere, at the last moment I remembered that I had left it down at Allis's so went tearing down there after it, only to find that they had all left the house and it was locked up on the inside. There was only one thing to do and so I came off without any cranial protection. In Cleveland, all of the stores were closed except the haberdashery in the Hollenden Hotel and they only carried a small line of caps. Well, I picked out one of those and made the best of it, but it wasn't much protection against the wind and sun when I got on the lake, so I awoke this morning with a most glorious red face. Whew but I am a sight. Here's hoping that it turns just a couple of shades darker before many days pass by, if it doesn't, I will almost be ashamed to go back to Wooster.

"You would have laughed if you had seen me after church this morning. Everybody in the vicinity came around and said 'hello' and then proceeded to congratulate me in most effusive terms.

It got to be funny after a while. I couldn't help thinking that they would all have to come around and do it again and with a whole lot more sincerely after they had seen the girl I have gotten. Or are they doing it because they are surprised that I could get anyone to promise to share my future with me. Probably that is what they think. Some of the questions I'm asked about you are funny too. There is a girl here from New York, with whom I ran around some last summer, who said the deuce of a funny thing this morning, she came up after church was over, and after she had said the usual 'how well you are looking' etc. she said, 'Well I suppose that I can ask you to come up and see us, even if I do have to congratulate you in the same breath'. What the dickens did she mean by that? Of course, I asked when I could come, so I'm hooked for a date with Irene Mason tomorrow night.

"I just saw something out of the corner of my eye which drove everything out of my head but thoughts of you, I turned to look out of the window and saw the moon just coming up over the tops of the mountains across the lake. My, what a night it would be for a little paddle out in the lake with you. There is just enough breeze to make it nice and rippley[*sic*], and we could float straight down the silver path the moon makes on the water, until the moon was on the other side of us then we could drift slowly back still in that path. Oh Elsie, dearest, come on up here please. Jim Sanders, a fellow from Montclair, paddled down to Uncas with me this afternoon while I mailed your letter. It got splashed a little bit enroute, but I don't think that it was blotted enough to keep it from reaching you. The reason we took it to Uncas was because no mail goes out from here on Sunday." But, the mail would be picked up on Sunday since it is a popular camping and picnic island during the summer months. "Jim graduated from Yale this year. He is a peach of a scout, the only trouble is that he impresses people who don't know him very well as being

149

just a little bit swell-headed. He, and Hal Johnson (Ken's older brother) and myself had kind of a triumvirate before we went to college. We used to run around together all of the time. Hal was married last February, and Jim has been engaged for over a year, so of course, he is quite crazy to see you. He and Hal had it all planned out that all six of us, I mean you, Jim's fiancée (Louise), Hal's wife (who by the way is Jim's sister) and us three fellows, would have a little dinner party in New York this fall before you and I went back to Wooster. There would be some class to such a party believe me, and I only hope that we can have it, or rather that you will make it possible for us to have it. Of course, if you don't come now, it will merely be postponed until some future date, so that we'll have it someday anyhow.

"Say Elsie I don't know your father's initials. Will you tell me, so that I can get my letter off to him right away?

"Next time you write, please tell me that you can come up for a few days. We are going down to the city on about the sixth of September so if you come up, say on the 24th of August. You could have just about ten days up here. Then you could get on the train there at Cincinnati and I'll meet you in Albany. I'll look up all the trains and everything if you but say the word."

By Wednesday, August 16 Billy tartly writes, "Of all the letters I ever got in my whole life from you, the one that I got today, the one you wrote Sunday, takes the prize absolutely...Sophie Johnson (Hal's wife) was the only one who got a single inkling of it. Hal finished his vacation a couple of weeks ago, and she has been staying up here with her mother for a little while. I was over at Sanders for supper last night. Well just after we had finished eating, it started raining. Sophie and I were the only ones who wanted to brave the rain, or cared enough to go for the mail, so we put on slickers and went along. She hadn't heard from Hal for two days either, so we were both kind of anxious to get there...I never wore a lighter smile, nor carried a heavier heart. We both, in fact, put up a beautiful front until the darkness of the road home hid us from each other then we subsided, it seemed by mutual consent. The next thing I knew, Sophie was pulling on my arm and saying, 'Billy White', I've asked you three times if you are going to the regatta with us on Thursday. 'I said that I didn't know', then she said, 'Oh never mind Baby Blue she'll write you a letter tomorrow'. Well I almost fell over when she said that. I wonder if I do impress everybody as being something which reminds them right away of the afore-mentioned infant of rather indigo shade, if I do I think that another straight dive into very shallow water would be just the right kind of a dose of medicine for the poor kid. Well we got back to the house and found a bunch of the young people of the place had congregated in the Sanders boat house, for a nice social evening. Three cheers for the nice social part of it. I tried to dig, but Jim cornered me and I had to stick it out...I decided to stay in the boat house all night with Jim. The upstairs of the place is fixed up into a kind of a half-open-air living room with swings etc. strung around, and as we had no one to take home, we stayed in out of the wet. I was lying out on the porch part of it, practically in the open, and just after we got to bed, the moon came out beautifully and shone right in my face. I got to sleep after a while, then the next thing I knew the sun was streaming in on my already sun burned face. It was pretty early, but I stayed there in that sunshine for two hours more trying to get up enough ambition to get up and pull my head back into the shade...I lay there until we were called for breakfast. We went down the lake in the motor-boat after breakfast and got back just in time for the noon mail...but you could have run the freckles on my heart shining in my face when I read that 'Dearest of all', but why on earth did you end it with 'not quite as ever – yet yours.'"

This is a side of Billy that gives pause to his intentions. Irene was a heartthrob from last summer; yet he had no hesitation in offering her companionship during his vacation. All their friends knew he had proposed to Elsie, so going solo didn't seem to be an option for Billy in the Lake George society. Perhaps it didn't occur to him that it may upset Elsie, "I haven't told you about my date Monday night with Irene Mason...It was a peach of a night. We went down to an old stone tower on one of the points around here and had quite a friendly little chat...Of course she wanted to know all about you, and of course, I was absolutely unable to describe you adequately. She got, I am afraid, a rather faulty idea as to how really wonderful you really are." It sounds like a fabricated tale. "However, she has some imagination and so may have been able to put my description and her imagination picture together and so came a little bit nearer hitting the right thing." Billy assumed Irene understood he was engaged to Elsie, but it didn't prevent her from asking when she could see him again?

"When I left, she wanted to know when I could come up again, but the simple life for me while at this joint, was I simply said, 'sometime soon'. Then, nothing very definite or binding about that is there?" It was hard for Billy to say no to such a request, especially since they had a history together and the lake could be a lonely place without a companion.

"I've been on an awful grouch all day, tried like the very dickens to get over it, but no good." Although not stated, Billy seems to be experiencing some regret, perhaps it was regret that he dated Irene, or guilt that he enjoyed her company when he was committed to Elsie, "It is simply a case of not being able to have what I want. Ye gads how I wish that Cincinnati was just a few hundred miles closer than it is."

There is concern that Elsie is doing too much, but Billy doesn't seem to understand what is involved in planning a wedding when he gives her advice that is purely selfish, "Listen, Elsie dearest, you are going to be dead by the time for you to get back to Wooster if you don't let up just a little. I know that things are piling up to beat the band this last week before the wedding, but please for my sake if for nothing else, take one night off and get a rest...dear heart I'm lonesome, gawd but I'm lonesome for you. Darling, you know it, and I know it more and more as the day's pass. Now and forever I love you dearest. It seems to me that no man has ever known the true meaning of that word as I know it.

"Fooled, weren't you? You thought that you wouldn't get a letter from me today, because of the canoe trip, but here it is and we went on the trip too" he writes on August 17 that, "Bolton Landing is eighteen miles on a direct line up the lake, but we followed the shore a good bit in order to keep out of the heavy south wind that was blowing right against us, we stopped at two or three places to see some people too, so we covered about twenty-five miles this morning. When we started talking of making the trip, we intended paddling back in the afternoon, but there were a number of people down there Jim wanted to see, they lived there last summer...forgot Jim completely, and finally found him down by the hotel talking to some girl he knew. Did I tell you that Jim has been engaged for about two years to a girl in Wellesley...we just barely made the boat. If we had missed that boat and had had to paddle back here tonight I would have croaked. We had to get back too for Jim leaves in the morning for Long Island where he is going to spend a couple of weeks at his fiancee's home...I mean to be able to be with his fiancée that way...I'd give anything to be with mine just at present."

Sagamore Hotel was the premier gathering spot for the wealthy families of New York and New Jersey, yet it was also part of the social fiber for the lake. A place where the elite gathered for fun and relaxation during the summer months. Billy describes one event at the Hotel, "There was a field meet for the negroe[*sic*] help…it certainly was one of the funniest things I have ever seen, worth the paddle up there if we saw nothing else. It was gotten up principally for the amusement of the guests at the hotel, and not because they thought that the darkies needed some exercise, consequently it was more or less of a farce all the way through. Some of the track suits worn by those negroes', I know would have startled even your hardened aesthetic sense. The crazy coon about six feet and a half tall wore a light blue bathing suit over his under clothing, he was one of the funniest sights I've ever seen. They had regular races, then egg races, shoe races, potatoe[*sic*] races, fat men's obstacle, and every other kind you could think of, and to cap the climax of the whole performance, they had $18 stuck up on the top of a greased pole. I've never seen anything like that greased pole exhibition, it was really a circus. They worked half an hour before they decided that they would have to split the money up between them if they wanted it, so they made a kind of a pyramid and finally housted[*sic*] one of the men high enough to get it. Almost as funny as watching the colored contingent fighting for the filthy here, was to watch the more dignified whites lose their dignity and roll around on the ground laughing at them. The people who stay down there at the Sagamore, are a pretty sporty class of people as a whole and try to let people know that they are rolling in wealth, when in all probability they are simply putting up a big bluff, a pretty poor one at that. They put on a lot of false manners and carry an overload of dignity which sits upon their shoulders just about as gracefully as the daubs of paint on their faces. Well for once they lost their dignity and really laughed, and it was mighty funny to see them suddenly remember that they were doing something

improper, then they would look sheepishly around and straight-
en up."

Billy is ecstatic about life when he writes on August 20 telling Elsie, "This has been a glorious day. Just enough clouds in
the sky to make the mountains and lake more beautiful, great
big fleecy clouds that remind you of the lather of some shaving
soaps."

As customary in the absence of Dr. White who was in China,
Billy stood at the head of the table to begin, "Carving the chick-
en…the knife was like a hoe, and they had forgotten to bring a
steel one along. I thought some of going down and putting it
on the grindstone, but the hen was sitting there in front of me
waiting to be hacked to pieces, the Wilbur's, who were out for
dinner, were sitting around with expected looks on their faces,
mother was at the other end of the table smiling sweetly at me,
and Donald was sitting at my left chuckling in glee and entering
such encouraging remarks as 'you're cleared to start', 'let me do
it', and 'give Mr. Wilbur the neck'. What could I do? Gad, how
I did whale that kid after dinner. The only thing that saved me
was that the bird was done to a turn, and I could almost pull it
to pieces…Mr. Wilbur told me that it was a very good piece of
work."

For Billy, the social calendar was full, and many of his letters
shared tales about Irene and their day trips around Silver Bay,
"Last night I went down to Uncas with Irene Mason. They hold
dances down there twice a week, so we walked down, although
I told her before we went that I didn't want to dance. When we
got down we found that the regular piano player had been called
home on account of the death of her grandmother, and that the
substitute could play dance music just about as well as Prexy can
deliver nice quiet little talks in chapel. We tried to dance one
waltz, and after I had succeeded in treading all over her feet two

or three times in my frantic effort to keep in time with the music, which besides being poor time was played entirely too fast, she decided that she didn't want to dance either, so we made tracks for the porch.

I got a letter from my favorite aunt (Kate Pollock White) the other day, it was one of congratulations and good wishes. She is the wife of J. Campbell White, perhaps you have heard of him. He's in China now with father and they are I believe the most ideally happy pair I have ever seen. They graduated from Wooster in '92.

When are you going to get back to Wooster? I'm going to leave New York on the 6th, that is the Wednesday before college opens, and will get to Wooster on Thursday morning…this is the week of the wedding isn't it? Therefore, everybody in the house down there will be so awfully busy that they won't have time for a solitary thing in the line of giving a little drop of happiness to some of the distant people who are interested…and say, don't the bridal party always indulge in a whole lot of kissing and such things. Darn weddings anyways, I wish mine was going to be this week."

Elsie's last letter was sarcastic, so Billy writes to her on August 21 defending his actions and scolding her for being so forthright, "I just got back to the cottage from the morning boat with that letter of yours which you wrote Friday night. When you were in one of those absolutely original moods of yours in which you would dare to do anything. How I wish that I could have been there. On last Friday night, I was so tired physically that I could hardly move, but if some magic rug had transported me to 3145 Vine Street and you had still been in that mood after you saw me, the tonic would have so revived me that were you going at your fastest clip would have had a hard time keeping pace.

"So, you have gotten the idea that I have been trying, in a very subtle way, to flatter you by saying that I am not having a most delightful time. It certainly has been a woefully bungled job if I have had that little piece of subtlety in mind, hasn't it? Well I suppose that I was several kinds of a fool for ever telling you that... By all the laws of good times, I should be having a dandy time up here, there are nice people, there that's the trouble, there are 'nice' people. Do you know why the Thetas aren't as good now as they used to be. They got to taking in 'nice' girls. I know that you are what I mean. I'd like to get away some place where nobody knows me and nobody cares a darn what I do. The people in Wooster know me, and most of the people up here have known me ever since I was knee high-to-a-duck. It is kind of a Y.M.C.A. and ministerial settlement right around in this vicinity, consequently I can't stroll down the road with any pipe in my mouth without feeling like an absolutely lost soul. Don't you see how it is, and why I said what I did. I'm tired of being decent, I'd like to go off on a nice great big bet just to see how it feels. I'm tired of all the things that are done so regularly around here, tired of asking the blessing, tired of hearing prayers, tired of singing hymns and going to church. That sounds awfully sacreligious[*sic*], but it is the truth. Gad, wouldn't some of my 'good friends' around Wooster like to get hold of that sentence with my name signed to it. That's what makes me so darn sick of it all, I'm such a rotten hypocrite. But why am I burdening you with all this?

"Cold, cold, cold! Ye Gods, how I did shiver, it wasn't the water as much as the air...It really is getting cold up here, we have had a fire in the fire place for the last four nights now, sleeping under double blankets, then baking in the middle of the day. It is simply great to sit around that big fire place.

"The Mason sisters, Inez and Irene, with a fellow by the name of Walter Brown and myself, are going up to Fort Ticonderoga tomorrow. We will start about eight o'clock in the morning and take a picnic lunch along, then get back home about 3 o'clock in the afternoon. We are going in a motor boat so that there won't be very much work connected with the affair." Billy's choice of words reveal his feelings underlying his actions.

"This will get to Cincinnati on the day of the wedding, give my heartiest best wishes to the bride, if you think she would care a rap for them.

"How I wish that you were here." It's 11 p.m. on Saturday night at the lake and Billy begins to show his frustration about being away from Elsie, "To compare tonight with my feelings at that time would be foolishness in its worst form, but believe me, I don't wish anything worse right now. And what is the worst part about it, is that tomorrow is Sunday, and no mail will come. Four whole days without any word from you at all. Darn weddings anyway, think what a lot this one has taken from me. 'Selfish', I heard you say; I know it, and I'm ashamed of myself for having written what I did. Weddings are the finest thing on earth, almost, and I only hope and pray that there will be another in the mighty near future, which I will be a great deal more really interested in than this one.

"Today was circus day at Silver Bay. No, not a real circus with all of its attractions but a house made circus. The men over at the Bay have a circus each year, and it is a mighty good street. They are all in training for Y.M. work, and so some are right good acrobats, so it isn't all a farce by any means. But it would take a Barnum and Bailey genius to think up more crazy sideshows and ways to extract money, than they had over there today. Wild men, snake-eaters, and all of the rest of them. Peanuts, popcorn, pink-lemonade and ice cream cones. People came from all over the Lake to see the thing, so Silver Bay was certainly a gay place this afternoon. I didn't stay very long at the show but went down to see the finals in a tennis tournament that is being played over there.

"I was up at the Mason's cottage tonight. They leave on Monday. They are mighty nice girls, but typical New Yorkers, how I hope that I am not one of those. I guess I can't be though for I'm never crazy to get back to 'the gay white way' the way they are. They want to go back and never leave it again, while I am only too glad to leave after about twenty-four hours stay.

"It is not quite 7:30 p.m. yet, and I am beginning another one of my wails to you, what is going to happen anyway." It is Sunday, August 27 and, "this time of the evening doesn't seem at all natural in the house, but mother didn't want to go over to church tonight, useless to say that I didn't, so we are staying at home.

"Our family drunk came home last night, pennyless, and still about three sheets under the wind, and asked for money to pay the liveryman who brought him from Ticonderoga. The family drunk is an old French Canadian. David Schillaire, who we have had working for us for the last three years…he takes about two weeks to get well stocked with booze. Then as a rule he is perfectly all right for about six months. He had been down on the farm until about the fourth of July, when my uncle in Canada borrowed him for a month or so to do some work for him. Dave left the Mott's place, two weeks ago yesterday, with almost two hundred dollars in his pocket, and a firm resolve in his mind to come directly home. No luck. He doesn't remember very much from the time he got to Montreal, except that he bought a dog, which according to his description is fully as big as an ordinary cow, he said that it was too big to bring along so he left it with a friend who is to send it to him. Poor Dave, sixty-two years old, strong as a bull, but he can't read or write. Mother is reading to him now in the other room. I took care of him this afternoon, he is all right now, but we always make it a point for one of us to be with him most of the time just after one of his sprees, especially on Sunday when he can't work. If we leave him alone for very long he gets to thinking about what he has done, and gets sore at himself, then goes and gets drunk again. He certainly is a character, he has been all over the United States and Canada, has made two or three fortunes, and has been swindled out of them, and the tales he can tell. He used to come in last summer when I was in bed and talk to me by the hour, at night. My how I wish that I could write him up or rather that Henry Van Dyke would get acquainted with him. Van Dyke could make a wonderful story out of Dave's life.

"Four weeks ago tonight, you were in Wooster. The kindest act of your life was committed when you boarded the train there in Pittsburg for Wooster. I don't believe you can ever realize what a reprieve that was for me. How about two weeks from tonight, do you think that you can be there or not? I won't try to tell you just how much I am hoping that you can, for it would be useless. It is just fifteen weeks ago tonight, that I first told you that I loved you, and you said it was the night. Then, later on you gave me a week to get over it, then six, and now—well now you must know dear heart that time has nothing at all to do with this except to make it stronger.

"Donald just came in to say goodnight and stood here a minute looking at your picture. Then he said, 'Gee Billy, I'm sorry Elsie couldn't come up this summer'… If that kid was to be with me all of the time, I believe that I would be a perfect model. He tries to do absolutely everything I do, and he can do most of them. How is Vic coming on the cigarette proposition. I don't quite see how he could withstand your persuasive power, but they certainly do get a hold on a person when they once get a chance. Nothing else beats a good pipe though along that line. I know that that is all that has kept me from breaking one a hundred times, that and one other thing.

"I suppose that these last few days have been our long recuperation after the strenuous days of the wedding. Or have the festivities kept right on? You had some pictures taken in your bridesmaid's dress didn't you.

"This is just a note." He writes on August 30, "I want to let you know that your letter was read and duly appreciated by mother. She said before she opened it that she knew that it must have been awfully hard for you to write us. This has been an unusually busy day around the White cottage, packing, moving, crating, and about everything else you could think of, and of course, all of the neighbors had to come in to say farewell, so between interruptions we have had a mighty full day of it...my, but I am glad to get started back to Wooster."

Once again on the Hudson River Night Lines on August 31 Billy is reviewing his day during his trip back to New York, "At last we are on our way back to the city. What a day we have put in. I was going to get up really early this morning and get started on the stuff that had to be done, but when I awoke at 6 o'clock there was hustle and pounding going on all over the place. Mother, the maid, and Dave, had been at work since 5 o'clock, so you can imagine how I felt when Dave asked me if I was really up yet. We sent him (Dave) off on the early morning boat to the farm, so I had to shut off all of the water and loosen up the pipes to keep them from freezing this winter...the boat left at 2 o'clock, and at 1:30, the men hadn't come for our trunks...the phone refused to work, so there was nothing to do but hoof it. I finally got them but if the boat hadn't been late, we would have had to have them there for a couple of days.

"There is a fellow out here from Ohio Wesleyan and he had a peach of a guitar which I had borrowed on a couple of occasions.

Mother liked the machine...the tone of it...that she wanted me to get it, so I asked him just for fun if he would sell it. He said, sure, and mother bought it right away. I fell in love with the thing the first time I played it, and it certainly was a nice surprise when I found myself carrying it off. People will get the idea that I am a regular walking orchestra, with my banjo and guitar trailing along.

Tensions in the Relationship

"I've been kind of blue for some reason or other, so far on the trip, I've been wanting something I can't have, longing for someone else who isn't here. I can now tell you how I want you tonight Elsie, it is far beyond my expressive ability, you seem so very, very far away, and the time seems to grow longer and longer until I will see you. Tell me when you are expecting to get to Wooster, I certainly hope that it will be next week."

Was it intuition that made her write these words, "I can't write a letter to you tonight that could be sent. I wrote one with my whole heart in it—but dear, it was too bitter to offer to you. It isn't fair anyway to drag you down to the depths with me every time I go. I'm such a coward though you despise cowards don't you? There is no early reason why I should tell you in detail about my every heart ache. It is good to have them isn't it—develops character...at night we were escorted to the Mechlinberg. Cincinnati's famous German Garden." Elsie's grandfather traditionally liked German cooking. Ella once wrote to her sister telling her about the German dishes he liked to eat, that she didn't, "It was quite a treat—everything very pretty and all that—everything utterly empty, empty. We got home a little after 'bedtime' you would say.

"I haven't been very nice to you very recently, have I?" It's early in the morning on September 5, when she continues, "Well,

162

it's not because I haven't wanted to be—it's simply because—well I've been on the wrong side of the cloud to see the silver lining, for days and days—perhaps I was born on that side of the cloud. Don't blame me too much—you'll do that later any way—not too much I didn't mean just enough of course—so be perfectly dear to me now and tell me you think it quite natural that a person deprived of your presence long should have *ein weren Herz!*"

When Elsie read Billy's letters about his dates with Irene Mason, tension developed between them. His letters were full of activity, day and evening, leaving her with questions about his loyalty to her. In response, she writes, "Two letters came today—the last one you wrote from blessed Lake George and the one on the steamer. You did not want me any more than I wanted to be with you. Dear heart, if I only didn't love you so much. Someday, my heart will break—you of course, can't understand why I know it will—I don't want you to either." It seems as though Elsie understands Billy's carefree attitude about socializing with other women is part of his character and she is concerned enough to put it into words, "Can't you learn to love me less Billy? Couldn't you if you tried very hard? You know that you really didn't want to love me anyway in the beginning—but no, I know, it's long past the beginning now—nothing but absolute monotony would make you really want to leave me, would it? I've thought a great deal in the last three days—too much for my peace of soul—and now I see dark spectres—waiting, watching and dearest, I'm afraid—afraid to love you anymore, but God help me I can't help it. I'm yours forever and ever—my heart is yours to keep as you will and to throw aside. You filled my life with love as a royal prince would fill an empty goblet with purple wine—and my life as the goblet was made valuable because of the priceless thing it contained. You have done so much and I so little! Try to love me less—try and I will help you." Elsie bares her soul when she pens these words to Billy, sharing her innermost thoughts about their relationship yet reflecting on his summer activities with Irene Mason, "Yes dearest, I mean it truly—do your best and Heaven help you if you don't succeed. If you do, we shall laugh together Billy, and shake hands—perhaps, you will kiss me just once more if I asked you and you know how much it would mean to me—perhaps you would just turn away and leave me, without a word. I can't bear to think of that—better to curse me than to leave me like that. Dear, I must be tired or I wouldn't write like this. I am tired of everything—tired of the endless aching in my heart—tired of trying to give the world an excuse for being here—weary of loving hopelessly, of longing and waiting—heart sick because I am what I am. I could take a drug tonight and smile myself cheerfully into Hell—only of course I won't do anything more violent than play cards and kiss my dear friend's goodnight. You understand partly don't you dear—that is enough—and if you were here, you would take me in your arms wouldn't you and tell me how beautiful everything is going to be—and I would be happy even though I would know that it couldn't be ever as you said." There is doubt in her tone, and a little fear in her inner voice, "There is still a great deal of happiness for us though—and I at least am going to drink the cup of Joy to the very dregs before it's snatched from my lips—then what will it matter, I shall have tasted and known—the sweet memories I shall keep locked deep within my heart—with them kept where they shall be inviolate, there will be molting bitter able to enter to destroy their sweetness. Dearest of all—I meant to write so differently—tomorrow you shall see."

By 10 o'clock, on September 5, she sits down and writes another letter about her feelings that their relationship had tension, "How can I write, what can I write to make you understand that even to try not to love you would be an utter impossibility with me? Not even if I tried with all my might, not even if you tried to make me stop loving you, yet I would go on loving and that love would keep on growing. So, you see it's useless to try to make me stop. You don't really want me to try do you—oh well what if you do, that is one thing that it would be absolutely impossible for me to try to do for you. Ask me anything else, and I'll make a try anyway. Dearest, I'm glad you wrote me that letter—the one you wrote Saturday. It only makes me love you all the more. Did I say once that way back there some time I didn't want to love you? It's a lie. I never meant it, I couldn't have meant it, for what would my life be now without you and without the love I have for you, absolutely empty. That's all. And the knowledge that you are mine, and you love me, makes me feel as though I had "the strength of tens", and could do anything, accomplish new thoughts of things for you. Yes, that is it "for you". You above have made me everything I am right now. Foolish? No, never that when I am talking the way I am. How, about you. Do you think that I am selfish and mean when I say that I am glad for your heartaches? I can't help it, I am. I'm sorry of course that you have to have them, because of the circumstances of them, but it makes me glad to think that they are because I am not there. That sounds awfully egotistical, but well, I can't help it. If I could only get you to look on the other side, Oh, I know you do, of course, you do, or you never would have consented to marry me, but wait dear heart, wait until the time comes when we won't have to be away from each other anymore, then they won't come I know. I had a dream the other night. I can't tell you about it now, and the heartaches were there. Oh, so many, but dear, they were all on my side, and you know that I would do anything, absolutely anything to ease those of yours, if I only could. The dream? I'll tell you about it when you are in Wooster."

Billy returned to the Beta Theta Pi House and wrote this letter on Thursday afternoon, September 7, "I'm simply writing to you to make myself feel deserving of a medal—for no letter came from you this morning and that is a thing which cannot be triflingly[*sic*] overlooked."

Elsie received Billy's reply and responded with confirmation of her love, "Dear heart, the mail man just came and luckily for him he brought me a letter—the one you wrote from Johnsons'. So—if you can't stop loving me, I want you to love me so much that your love will be able to believe and to endure and to forgive all things. I am staking my all on the belief that it is or shall be so. It has only been in these last two weeks that I have realized fully what you really mean to me—my awakening dear, has somehow been slower than yours. I thought that love was—something that my will could govern—that I might love or not love—take or discard. I thought it was all sweetness except the "sweet sorrow" of parting—I have learned. It is pleasant, indeed, to dwell among the clouds but Billy I have at last touched the earth again and found it indeed earthy. You know dear heart that not for the salvation of my soul even—yes for that, perhaps, but that only would I hurt you. Above all things, I mustn't rob you of your ideals—the material things don't matter so much—it wouldn't hurt you half so much to lose me as your ideal for which perhaps I stand as a poor inadequate representative. Believe me, I shall not go if you truly love me as you think you do—dearest this does not mean that I doubt you—if I did do you think I could write to you this way. Isn't it strange how one simply has to cross bridges before one comes to them. Even you do—but your bridges are usually made of rainbows—mine of tears." As much as Elsie tried to be honest with Billy, she seemed to know that she would commit herself to him even though she had doubts.

And his response was, "Oh, Elsie, can't you try to be a little more cheerful—constant dripping you know, they say, will wear away the hardest stone—what if my love is like a rock—the rain falls and the floods descend so often from your tearful letters that—well stop being hysterical...my, that was rough handling thems harsh words George. I shall certainly change my style of writing to something more like coca cola—it relieves fatigue." Does he seem insensitive. Perhaps.

"I got back home to Wooster on the 3:05 this afternoon... and maybe I wasn't glad to get back. But the very first thing I read when I came into the house was your letter saying that you wouldn't be here until Monday. Words fail me when I try to express my disappointment. But what in the world was the use of telling you that, you knew it already. Well, if it has to be, it has to be. I suppose, and I know that you would come earlier if you could. Someday, I may learn to take your advice and stop making beautiful air-castles about the future. They aren't all gone yet, however, no, not by a very great deal, and they aren't all going to end the way my Sunday the 10th of September one did, so I guess I'll keep on making them.

"Gee, but this is a lovely place. I am the only person in the house except Harlan, and Mrs. Reynolds. The fellows don't start to come back until tomorrow, so you can imagine how still and quiet this house feels. It makes me think of my midnight writing in summer school, only I miss Jay's anxious tours in the next room. It is raining, started about an hour ago. At first I thought that it was going to be a good heavy thunderstorm, but it has degenerated into one of those persistent downpours.

"Dave landed his job at Mercersburg. He is very enthusiastic about the possibilities down there, and I think that he will enjoy it immensely. He fired questions at me for about two hours last night in an attempt to find out something about what kind of a joint it was. I hope that he has a little idea by this time.

"Well, I suppose that I've got to get busy now and go up and fix the room so that they will look a little bit better than they do. Monday at 4:28 is the cry. I'm getting happier every minute. I love you, dearest."

It's 9:30 a.m., September 8. Billy is in a hurry, "But I want to get this off this morning so that you will get it before you leave for Wooster. I'm mighty sorry that I didn't make it plain about when I was to get back...yesterday morning I decided to keep clear out of any possible temptation to stop off so stayed in bed and intended to stay there until I got clear of this town. No chance Jim and Grange got on the train at East Liberty, rode in to the city and on the way pulled me out of bed and so all of my good intentions went to the bad, and I'm here yet...think of it, only two more days and you will be there."

CHAPTER 8

The Proposal

The fall of 1911 held a lot of promise for Elsie and Billy who were looking forward to graduation and wedding plans. Billy realized he needed Dr. Edward Machle's permission, made all the more difficult because he was located in China. But that wasn't the only item on Elsie's agenda. There was one thing more, she needed money. Elsie's letter arrived ahead of Billy's. While Edward was in Canton on September 10 he answered with, "Your last letter dated August 3rd came to hand two or three days ago when we were all in the midst of our annual meetings which took from Tuesday morning until Saturday noon. We had a session only in the morning but the committees met in the afternoons to report next day as that there was so much to attend to relative to the year's work and the preparations for the following years work that I sought my bed at about 9 p.m. not only much tired of but very weary throughout.

"My 'game leg' is not yet healed but it will in time. It is quite strong now for I walk easily with a cane. My name was mentioned at the annual meeting for Lien Chow as temporary physician until Dr. Ross, who goes with his wife and two children on furlough next spring. I could not see my way to go to Lien Chow because of the work I am doing at Canton in the Fati School. Mr.

Marshall and family will go to Lien Chow to assist Mr. Kunkle in the work.

"I'm glad to read you had a nice five weeks vacation with your school friend at Endeavor. So, Eloise has precipitated herself into the gulf of matrimony. I had heard through Aunt Anne that she was to do so in August. Well how do you like being bridesmaid? I presume you would rather be a bride any day to the fellow you love. You give me a few hints that a young man named "Billy" (W. Wallace White) thinks he can tolerate you by his side for life. I have not yet heard from your Billy that he cares a straw for you. When I do receive such an epistle, I can then say what I think. Did you refer him to your 'dad'?

"Poor girl, out of money, played the spend-thrift last year and now comes to poor, lame, old papa for help. Well! I don't mind investing a few hundred more in you seeing that it will give you a sheepskin and fully prepare you to take care of yourself. Of course, you always are welcome to live with me as a single daughter and I hope that Wilbert will come out here as a Y.M.C.A. man under the auspices of the Presbyterian Board of Foreign Missions.

"I shall write Harry to give you in installments the sum of $200 U.S.G. I wish you to tell your Billy that you are the poorest accountant I ever came across in a life-time. That's the $1666.66 U.S.G. has been spent and you have not a line of an account to show how or where it went. Tell him you are very near relative to the married woman who received $20 from her husband with the request that she write down each item with cost or price and when the $20 were used up to come to him, her husband, with the book for more. Then appeared one day with the book which had these entries; received $20, spent $20. Tell him you can do that with $1666.66 and see what he will say.

"As to coming out to me. I'd be very glad to have you but do not know where to stow you. We will have a nice new house in six or seven months...at present Jean and I are living in one room in Mr. Bogg's house now occupied by Mr. Henry. He kindly let us a room so I could be near to the school work. I have a study in the theological building about 100 feet away from the house. In a month, I expect to move into the theological seminary. Mr. Boggs, you see, is expected here in October and may wish the whole house. If so, we shall live entirely in two rooms in the theological seminary. I don't doubt that young Mr. White will be needed by his illustrious father in New York. W. W. White has been out here the last two summers giving addresses at the summer resorts in China and Japan. If you knew just what 'your Billy' is preparing for, you might do some more studying to prepare yourself more fully to help him in every time of need." It seems that Dr. Machle was referring to the article on *Progress in China* in the Washington Herald on November 19, 1911 about J. Campbell and Wilbert W. White completing a tour of the mission fields. They came in contact with 1,200 missionaries assembled at three summer conferences to study the mission situation in China and make evangelistic recommendations.

He quickly describes Jean as, "a splendid woman. I know you would love her if you knew her. Everybody likes her for her gentle, kind, unsophisticated manner and her willingness to help in every time of need. She has black crinkly hair, blue eyes, rosy cheeks, slender form, graceful ways, and sings and plays well (ahem). Don't you believe it Elsie! I'm hard as nails, only she won't believe it...Did you get the photos I sent you of your mother, myself and the wedding guests?"

Jean writes a note, "Your father has very generously given me leave to write on the back of his letter...we were so glad to hear from you again, and very happy to hear all your news. Thank you for your note to me. I appreciated that, for I know it was a rather hard thing for you to write it, and I could not blame you for putting off the task. But I want to get to your great piece of news and send you my very best wishes. Dear Elsie, I do wish for you all fullest joy and happiness both now, and in the years to come, a glad, full life of love in your home, and in work for others. Your father was so happy and 'set-up' over the news that it took some days of hazing to get him back to his normal again! He is very fond and proud of you, Elsie. I think Mr. White is very much to be congratulated. I suppose a letter will be coming from him soon…Do you know that you didn't tell us a thing about him except that he is 'glorious!' And poor 'we', all curious to know what he is like, and what he is doing. We think there must have been lots of news lost in those burnt letters!

"We have been talking a good deal over your proposal to come out here for a while. You know your welcome would be a warm one. I know how your father would love to have you with him, and how happy you would be together. But we are troubled to know whether it would be profitable for you or not. The foreigners here want someone to teach their children (I am speaking of your inquiry as to openings for teaching in English) but they can only afford a very small remuneration, not enough to tempt one lady who is here already looking for the same kind of work. At one time it might have been possible to get work as a teacher of English to wealthy families in Canton, but affairs are so disturbed here this year, another revolutionary outburst may come any day, and most of the wealthy folk have left the city and gone to Hong Kong or Macao. All these things combined make it very hard for your father to know just what to do, to indulge his inclinations and have you come, or to consider you and what will benefit you most.

"I can imagine the excitement you were all in over your cousin's wedding. We are hoping someone will tell us about it. I have heard so much about them all in Cincinnati that I feel as if I know them quite well. We have that fine photo of you with Eloise and Jeretta, hanging on the wall" and then Jean Machle followed with this short note, "You would be delighted to see how well your father is looking now, and how well he walks. The weak limp he had is hardly perceptible now. The Lien Chow people and missionaries are unfortunate in begging him to return there, but he can't be spared from Canton now. The Union Medical College have the same longings, but they can't have him yet, either. He is a very much sought-after man, and it is very hard to say just where he is most needed. At present, his duty seems plainly here. He is a dear man and it is delightful to see him rewarded and appreciated. Now I must close. It is impardonable[*sic*] to disfigure the paper in this way, but my Scotch soul won't let me waste so much edging!"

The dialogue continues between Elsie and her father over her upcoming marriage. Distance, work schedules and confusion about Billy's future vocation culminates in questions from E. C. Machle about their plans, "I received a letter from W.W.W. and shall answer him soon. He seems from his letter that he cannot get along in life without you. Well! That is the way you ought to feel also. I'm not going into a long discussion pro and con marriage; neither do I intend to tell you that to precipitate yourself into the golf of matrimony you need each other's help to keep afloat for there are no life preservers for each individual but where two have been made one a special preserver is used. I'm glad you found the man that fits exactly into your nature and is the complement of you.".

"You no doubt now experience a change in your views and can say from the bottom of your heart that love is the greatest thing in the world. It's a great transformer, renewer, elevator and makes one feel that all is not lost on this mundane sphere. Victor has written me of the good things he stored away in his bread basket at the wedding festivities. He seems to show some promise of being a man someday. He writes pleasingly of his work and wishes to join the Y.M.C.A. I soul out rejoice that his desires are tending that way. I hope you will encourage him as much as possible to take up such studies as will help him in his mental development and also his line of business.

"Eloise's wedding was certainly a swell affair and it was certainly fine that you could be there in the capacity of bridesmaid. I have a letter from Violet. She says she will write me her father's address and then does not do so. All I got out of the letter in the way of an address is that she came from Old Point Comfort to attend Eloise's wedding.

"I presume you don't know any more of the address. I think O.P.C. is in New York but I cannot be sure. My life in the east does not give me an opportunity to read the daily American newspapers and so one soon gets rusty on out of the way places. I hope Violet found time to go with you to Wooster. She would do her and you good and her mother and father will appreciate the kindness shown her very much. When I look at the photo of the trio, you, Eloise and Jerretta, I always regret that Violet was not there also. I had intended to have the four, but you naughty, procrastinating girls, put it off until just before I sailed for China and then Violet had left for about two weeks or more. I have the picture framed in gold hanging near my writing desk. Two of those...have already taken to themselves husbands and the other (you) will soon change name and affections and establish a household. The thought of my daughter marrying makes me feel like the 'Old Man' that is usually used to express the papa at the betrothal stage. Fortunately, the term is stuck on to the husband soon after the wedding and the papa has the epithet of 'Old Dad'. Such expressions and such doings is a sure sign that the world is growing as old as the 'Old Dad' and that power is being vested in the rising generation...I had better close as time is short and I have much to do today."

Up until this time, Elsie and Jean had not met except through correspondence, yet this brief note from Jean was included in his letter, "Dear Elsie, I meant to write a sheet for you, but have been so busy. Up at 6 a.m., the time for posting, so please excuse me this time. Your deluge of letters has been a most welcome one, and your affectionate messages have warmed our hearts immensely. I shall write a decently long letter just as soon as I can do it."

Billy kept letters marked SACRED, which implied that they were meant for his eyes only. He writes to E. C. Machle asking to marry Elsie.

"I am certainly very sorry that circumstances prevent the possibility of our meeting very soon, for I should much prefer making this a personal interview instead of a long-distance affair, and I imagine that you would like to look at me also. However, as it is impossible for me to speak to you personally, this letter will of necessity have to speak for me.

"To come to the point directly, I love your daughter. I love her as a man loves only one woman. Elsie has done me the honor of saying that she returns my love, and now I am writing to you to ask that you will give your consent to our marriage."

"Of course, I realize that you know absolutely nothing about me and that you will want to know something about me before you entrust Elsie to my keeping. I don't know just how to go about it, but I suppose that the best thing I can do is to give you some facts about myself. I was born May 1, 1889 and will graduate from Wooster next June. My father is Dr. Wilbert W. White of the Bible Teachers Training School in N.Y.C. I have not fully decided yet as to what my life work will be. I have been thinking of going into Y.M. work, and also some of working in with father in his school in N.Y. but the possibilities are just about as strong that I will do neither. I do not know how soon I will be in a position to support a wife. I will have nothing when I graduate from college except my diploma, but if faith, hope, and love, have anything to do with this life here on earth, it will certainly not take me long to get enough to support her."

"You may criticize me for saying anything to Elsie about my love for her, and for asking her to marry me, but Dr. Machle, it seemed impossible for me to keep it to myself, so I told her when I had nothing at all to offer her but my love. You have loved yourself, was I wrong?"

"You realize I am sure, that there are some almost insurmountable difficulties in a letter of this kind, and I have in all probability bumped against all of them; but believe me, I am sincere in my great request of you, and if it is granted will endeavor with all my power to keep Elsie as a sacred trust until God chooses to part us by death."

Dr. and Mrs. Machle respond to Billy's letter with advice and reassurance that they are looking forward to meeting him, if possible, in China. Jean Machle was gracious in her response but reassured Billy that although she had not met Elsie, she heard a lot about her and approved of their upcoming union.

"October 27, 1911

"Dear Mr. White,

"Your letter has been before me for some days. I wish we could have a plain talk together over such an important affair which either makes or mars a man. Elsie's letter giving the news, preceded yours, so I was prepared for the reception of your letter. From what you write you intend to engage in some line of work that will help on the coming of the Kingdom of our Lord and Savior. It has been the prayer of my life that my children should serve the Lord in direct Christian work; so it seems that the Lord is answering my prayer for Elsie through you.

"I am glad you love Elsie as a man only loves one woman and rejoice that the love is mutual. A diploma, fully realizing what it stands for, is a large asset in life and I have no fear but that you will provide Elsie not only with the needful things that money can buy but the true, tender and close companionship that brightens the life and home.

"I know your father, although he has long ago forgotten me. I was in his class when he was a tutor at the U. W. I

had hoped meeting him last September in Hong Kong but a change in his programme prevented.

"Mrs. A. A. Fulton gave such a glowing description of your height, curly locks, manly bearing, jolly ways and many good qualities that I have about decided Elsie has taken the pick of the lot of your men at Wooster. Of course, there is no need of a father telling you his daughter is just about perfect.

"You have my consent to marry her when in a position to support her.

"May God's richest blessing go with you and her, Wilbert!

Yours Sincerely

E. C. Machle"

"October 31, 1911

"Dear Mr. White,

"My husband has kept his letter open that I might have the pleasure of enclosing a note to you also, and of adding my good wishes to his. I have not yet met Elsie, but in her photos she looks very sweet and loveable, and always reminds me of the old-time English phrase, "of a sweet dignity'. Those who know her say she resembles her father very much, and if so, she will be a very good wife, and

you will have good reason to consider yourself fortunate. (Being only a stepmother, and 'miles removed' at that, of course I am free to say what I think!) I do trust that God will give you a long, useful, and happy life together in a life that will grow more sweet and beautiful as the years go by, full with an ever deepening love and honor for each other, and full of help and blessing for others."

By December the White family included Elsie in their Christmas plans. She received a letter from Billy's mother, Ella Henderson White on December 3 inviting her to come to New York during Christmas vacation. Elsie made other plans for Christmas, "Dear, I sent your little present off in such a rush I forgot to put the card in with it but of course you know better than I could ever express it in words just what kind of a Christmas I was wishing you, and all the other days of your life. I wished they'd keep getting happier and sweeter until you might just step from the last mortal day into the eternal one without having to acclimate yourself to the change in the weather at all ('Dear, don't write such silly things; don't you know that with you by my side I am doomed inevitably to a sour old age without a redeeming bit of sweetness in it' 'why Billy, how rude to express yourself so candidly.')"

"The Wooster crowd had a jolly time going from Wooster to Crestline." Crestline was a railroad town known for its social gatherings and decorations at Christmas time. The lovely town center attracted the college students at Christmas time and Elsie and several of her friends took the train to the seasonal dinner held in Crestline, "By the way Lenore (Hattery) and I sat in exactly the same places in which you and I had sat a few weeks ago. I was as excited by the discovery, the same train and all, that I told Lenore in order to get some sympathy."

Billy returned to 541 Lexington Avenue on Christmas Eve and wrote a heartfelt letter to Elsie sharing his disappointment at her absence, "Please, please, don't ever make me spend another Christmas Eve away from you. I've been on a grouch for the last twenty-four hours, consequently the family is sore at me. I'm sorry for them, very sorry in fact, I've tried not to let them know that I wasn't in the best of humors, but it could not be. They have kind of sensed it in the air, and so when father and I had a scrap tonight, oh just about fifteen minutes ago, it seemed almost the natural sequence of things. Father and I get along beautifully as long as we keep off certain subjects, but as soon as we get on those subjects, he loses his temper, and says a lot of stuff about things as he sees them and, of course, I see them a little differently and I get sore. The special things tonight was this Christmas basketball trip, he can't see it for dust, and for that matter I can't either. Coach wants me to come out again next Monday and join them in Ashtabula. Well, I didn't think that I would do it, but I thought that it would be fairly decent to talk it over with dad, and if he wanted me to get away from here as soon as possible, why I'd go back (to Wooster). Well, dad flew off the handle because I even thought of it, I hadn't wanted to go before, but that kind of riled me all up and so we went to it, or rather he did, and I said just enough to keep him going. Throw in a chunk of wood for fuel now and then, as it were. It's peculiar how dad and I disagree on so many things when we could have such a darn good time together. It makes me sick sometimes, and I know that most of it is my fault. All of it isn't I know that. But I have felt ever since I was old enough to disobey that I have always been under suspicion and I am a great deal of the time I know. I'm not sure what kind of crimes I'm suspected of doing, but it's there. For Heavens' sake choke the squeal[*sic*], gee whiz, I didn't know what I was writing there for a while. I didn't mean to let out such a mournful bleat. See what kind of a person this one is.

"Dear heart I love you tonight as I have never loved you before. I know it as I live. You said in the note you write me a week ago tonight that I could not understand what I was to you. Darling, I know that that comparison in such a case would be impossible, but it is impossible for me to see how you can ever understand what you are to me. I love you absolutely, utterly, earnestly, and I love you forever. God knows that you are everything to me, oh Elsie, dearest love, I want you now. And when I think of the time that must elapse before I can call you mine before the law, I, oh, dearest, I love you, love you. I've got to stop this. Goodnight darling. I am forever and ever altogether yours."

It is unclear why Elsie didn't accept the invitation from Billy to go to New York for Christmas with his family. But family matters and tension existed in both households. Elsie had pressure from her relatives in Philadelphia and New Jersey and Billy had pressure from his parents in New York. There was time to plan, or so they thought. Billy had to finish college while Elsie planned to teach at Paulding High School. Ever present was the issue of traveling to China to meet Dr. and Mrs. Machle so he could request Elsie's hand in marriage. Elsie took her father's advice not to go with Billy since his parents were once again planning to attend summer meetings in Japan. As plans began to form, it became clearer to Elsie that she would again spend the summer in Endeavor and formulate wedding plans after his return. Now, she would head to Philadelphia and New Jersey to spend time with her mother's relatives, but as time drew closer, she realized how much she wanted her father to come back for the wedding.

CHAPTER 9

Sunshine and Breezes
Dear Simpleton

The beginning of any letter should be an introduction to what lies ahead. As time went on, Elsie, more than Billy, became creative in her introduction, whatever the body of the letter held in its mysterious clutches. One of her letters in mid-1911 started with, "You really must stop writing such clever letters unless you want me to strain my funny-bone trying to keep up with your witticisms. Improving in your letter writing—dear boy—you are master of the art now in every way except one—you end too abruptly. You should lead your victim down a gentle slope and then tenderly push her off, not take her up to a mountain peak and then suddenly scream; 'jump idiot, jump' and thrust her violently over into the abyss beneath...What am I talking about? Nothing that little boy blue shouldn't hear...and nothing that he has time enough to be bothered with either." Her clever writing skills were just the beginning of an avalanche of letters between them while he was traveling to Japan and China with his parents during the summer of 1912. Many of her letters were a mere 45 pages long and implied a competitive side of Elsie, always challenging Billy with her ability to persevere even if her handwriting became larger and larger with each page.

Their letters reflect sexual tension, forgiveness, stubbornness, anger, loneliness, and deep emotional connections through words. Words that imply 'wished for actions', "There are plenty who might say that they would go with me, but there is only one for me, and she (Elsie) is not to be had. She is probably right now, let me on—sitting in one of the McKean's porch swings with some young gentleman with blue eyes. Shut up you damn fool, Billy, don't you know that you are making yourself absolutely miserable? All right, I want…but I certainly wish that I could blot out some 'images in my mind' before me. They make me unquestionably jealous…I'm going to move my bed over right next to the window as I can hear the splash of the drops on the tin roof. Then lie there and dream for a while, finally go to sleep and dream some more. I have an idea that I'm going to dream about you tonight. I'm afraid that it isn't going to be a 'music and roses' one though."

Elsie spent New Year's Eve with her friend, Clara Louise Barrett in Springfield, Ohio and Billy's letter begins with a dialogue about his writing pen. His father advises him to get another pen, and asks Elsie if she likes his writing, "I know that you love to have people change their writing all of the time, but you know that I have no definite writing of my own yet, so I'm simply hunting for the best I can find." He begins to share his dream of what he wants in their house someday, "There is going to be at least one big fireplace with some nice large easy seats around to sit in and watch the flames…if you choose first and take a fireplace, I'll take a porch…and if you take the porch first, I'll take the fireplace…I am not crazy, nor am I a simpleton, but a perfectly sane person, crazy perhaps in one or two particulars, but in all other points absolutely normal.

It wasn't unusual for him to write explanations about why he didn't write, or didn't receive her letters, or why he was too busy to write more than a few lines, then begin a dissertation on his family, "Did I ever tell you that I had three cousins, the Motts, whose hair is red? John who is a sophomore at Princeton, has brown hair, but the three younger children's is red. Not a flaming, brilliant red, the way you like it, but a yellowish, blond red. These cousins range from seven to twelve years of age, and they broke in upon John and myself this morning at 7 o'clock while we were in the midst of beautiful dreams. I was dreaming that I was lifting you across a muddy gutter into an automobile, when I awake to find Eleanor (age seven, blue eyes, pug nose, red hair) leaning over me, asking if I was asleep. She certainly is a cute kid to say the very least. Of course, we got up and had a pillow fight with them."

In late January, Elsie arrives in Paulding, Ohio, where she will be teaching for the next five months. Billy says, "I am a mutt. I've decided that absolutely, so there isn't much use in arguing the question even if you wanted to. Here I write you a measely[*sic*] scrall, telling of some of my little troubles when I know all of the time that you are having one every minute that would put all of mine combined so much in the shade that it would take a spot-light to find them. Yes, I am a mutt. No, I am a mutt, with the 'M' capitalized." Their separation was a strain on both of them and generates some guilt on Billy's part, "Here I've been thinking I was working, while you have been slaving away there over those exams. Whew! What did you ever have to say that would take you four hours on questions like those you sent me? I would have passed in my checks at about 8:10 and started to pack my trunk and order the drayman immediately. If you get through those things you deserve a gold medal and a whole lot more. But does it matter so much about those things, aren't they more a matter of form than anything else? Not that I mean to belittle your work in any way at all, but it seems to me that if you can 'produce the goods' so to speak with the kids, that that is about all that is necessary. Darn that school board anyway, why in thunderation don't they have a little vacation now and then anyway…But listen here, if you run off to Cincy and Springfield and a whole lot of other places about the last of May, don't blame me for anything that may happen to a certain young male here in Wooster. Please put a big underline right under the date when your incarceration ends.

He remembers their first date, "This is the 9th of February. Two years ago tonight, I had my first date with you. I've been thinking about that all day. How honestly glad I was when Hal couldn't come and I hadn't made my date yet…How the Thetas[3] looked cross eyed at me when we came in the door. How you accidentally called me Billy, on the way home just below the Alpha Tau house, and how scared I was all evening. It seems funny now that I was scared, and yet once in a while yet, it is the same way. I just get scared, I don't know why, but I do."

College boy's pranks seem to be common and one is described in a letter, "Ralph and George have dates with Mary (McKean) and Blix (Krichbaum) downstairs. Jumbo (Chalfant) came in a little while ago and offered Satan (Gregg) and myself $.50 if we would go down just as we were and say 'hello'. Satan was dressed for studying, he had on his class sweater and looked somewhat like a tough. I had on a pair of old grey flannel trousers, blue socks, pumps, one of the new basketball sweaters, no collar and a white skating cap. We certainly were a fine-looking pair of bums. We won the 50 cents.

"Hazel Drummond told me this morning in chapel that she had gotten a letter from you and she said that I had better go over and see if I couldn't cheer you up some."

Hazel shared what Elsie wrote earlier on February 6, "If it were not for you on earth…I'm afraid I should never win out against my lesser self…but just drift down the great stream heedlessly and lose myself." I should, "trust in your love for me, makes me strive to be something…a little worthy perhaps of what you have given to me. There are some things though that I wish to God I could tell you. If I only didn't love you so---if I could put you out of my thoughts and out of my life---yes, I know I should fail in making anything out of it—but you—perhaps you might live a fuller, richer life…I have tried my best and I still know that you do not understand…there were no nights but only eternal sunshiny days---then you never should hear these things from me. Think anything you like—but don't laugh for if you do, I shall hear it and shall never forget. Is this incoherent? 'Oh, yes, one of her moods again—how they do vary, don't they?' Perhaps you are saying it—and if you are, I know some things which I would rather be dead than know." Hazel "didn't know how near she came to speaking (Billy's) very wish at that moment…For Billy had come in the chapel early and Professor (John) Erb was standing up by the organ looking down when he saw me and smiled…I was just in the middle of some reflections about organ playing up there in the chapel with you, and thinking what it would be like if I could only send a note back and see if you wouldn't wait and hear him play for an hour, when she told me that…It seems like about the limit of time since you left not quite two weeks ago…But, oh Darling, my heart has ached for a sight of you, and to be able to hold you close again—Dearest, it hurts to think that I can't right now. Do you get tired of hearing me say it? I love you, my own love, Elsie, dearest. I love you with my whole being, and it can never be stopped, no nothing can ever turn my love from you, absolutely nothing. I couldn't stop it if I wanted to. So, I am yours forever and ever as long as you will, and then you can't make me stop loving you.

"Prepare yourself for a microscopic dissertation upon the wits of staying up late, or the evils of going to bed early, whichever you may wish to call it...for try as I would I couldn't keep my eyes shut. As soon as they were shut, a veritable panorama of all our little jaunts together came flitting along right underneath the lids...then my eyes would come open, I suppose they opened, for I would find myself staring off into space with what Mary would call my 'baby-stare'. I wanted to talk to you, I wanted to go up and scratch on your screen until you came and opened the window just so I could see you. I wanted to take you out to that sacred old chariot, where so many different emotions have gone through my being, and take you in my arms, and kiss you, kiss you brutally, until you should cry for mercy. I wanted to—oh, there are a thousand and one things I wanted to do with you, but the thing I wanted most was to feel that you were somewhere near, that you were in this vicinity, and that I could reach you somehow if I wanted to. After a while it got too awfully hard for me to stand, so I got up and lit all of the lights in the room and got one of Stewart Edward White's novels to read...past midnight before...I went to sleep."

Elsie finished up her coursework at the end of 1911 and left Wooster to teach at Paulding High School where many of the graduates went for their first teaching position. Billy, finishing up his coursework remained at Wooster. He still had a carefree attitude about life, "That would be fun sometime, take a day off and go to visit the Paulding High School and not let you know that I was coming. What would you do if I strolled in unannounced... have you heard yet whether you get the Friday after Washington's birthday or not?" A few days later he shows his disinterest for a schedule like hers, "You certainly are leading the strenuous life now, teaching five, and six classes a day...whew, why I don't attend that many two days out of the week in succession. But when you have to leave out a lesson in botany, besides teaching those other subjects with which you are more familiar, why it is a pretty heavy schedule. You tell any of those rough-necks who try to get funny that if they don't behave themselves, one of these days they will get the worst whaling they ever had in their lives. Then, when I come over, as I was sorely tempted to do...all you need to do is to point your finger, and I'll do it clear from the head guy down...from the different remarks of innumerable friends here in Wooster, there must be about two hundred graduates and ex's over there...you ought to start up an alumni association.

I guess that I'm going to go to New York with father next year. I haven't written him positively yet but intend to...tell me just what you think of it." He is displaying the characteristics of an underachiever. He has the potential but doesn't apply himself.

Again, Elsie is in rare form when she addresses him as, "Curly-head, Behold—the evening and the morning was the second day! Today was worse than yesterday, but tomorrow I feel sure is going to be a wonderfully nice day...tomorrow, perhaps, I shall get a letter from you...the hope that springs eternal...my hopes of receiving your letters are thrown in to brighten up existence, why I'm naturally altogether enchanted with it.

"You should just get a peep into some of the school-rooms in this place—you would think you had strolled into a green-house of some kind. Every window ledge—every nook and corner— even floor space is occupied by plants. Geraniums, predominate. In my room the pots are stacked three tiers high—shelves were tacked on to the window frames in order to accommodate the tender, green things. The explanation of this phenomenon is that an ancient veteran of the Civil War who seems to have a license to loaf on the high school premises and who has a terrible weakness for flowers devotes his feeble energy in raising them. My six classes today went along without very much trouble. The fault which I find with four of my classes is their unwillingness to work. They've simply been allowed to slip so long that now they won't do anything. One class was told to write a letter to President Taft—this letter to be handed in. Eight out of twenty-five came empty handed—simply saying that they didn't have time to do it. They were mightily surprised when I told them that those letters were to be handed in tomorrow—and that a percent would be subtracted from their grade for the tardiness... no doubt I shall drive you frantic telling you about the things that happen here." It wasn't long before Elsie was sharing the fun she had with one of her classes, "My but I did have fun with my freshmen class. We have been studying about the value of imagination in narration and read today as an illustration of imaginative writing a selection from *Water Babies*. Well, I didn't have a thing prepared to keep those children busy so I just sent the boys to the board trusting to luck that by the time they got there something would pop into my mind. And, my dear, the subjects did come, ridiculous ones to be sure, but, good material for the imagination to work on. The prize composition was written on this subject, 'conversation between a fish worm and a fish.' Another clever one was written on, 'an angry caterpillar'. I was simply convulsed myself at the possibilities in some of the grotesque titles my fevered brain dished out to them and had to pretend to be examining my plants in order to hide my smile."

Soon she was back in the chivalry mode and stirs his imagination with, "Such an avalanche of mail from you today—three beautifully addressed envelopes just sauntered in at noon and fairly took my breath away. I didn't deserve to be so nicely surprised after all the peevish, feverish altogether nasty things I've screamed at you in the last week...Today, I feel more like Elsie Machle than I've felt for over a month...Elsie, is tired of being tired, tired of staring at the ridiculous bunches of violets on the wall paper, tired of thinking of what may happen to, spoil the lovely dream she's been having about Sir Galahad, and roses and moonlight and an eternity in Arcady, and being absolutely tired of all that silly; foolish things she is simply going to send them scuttling back to their old dark haunts again and take out an option on all the sunlight, the restfulness and peace of soul and love, that happens to come anywhere near her. Instead of gazing at everything through a wet, dark blue glass, she vows that now she isn't going to look through a glass at all—either cuts the rest or the future – for indeed, 'unborn tomorrow, and dead yesterday why fret about them if today be sweet!' and all the todays are going to be sweet aren't they? She signs the letter, Lady Bitter-Sweet."

Billy received Elsie's Valentine, "And is now hanging here in the den where I can look at it all of the time...it certainly is a dandy, dearest you have no idea how my heart thumped when I saw the package down in the hall...I knew it was from you, and yet I was hoping in a way that it wasn't. Was that wrong to feel that way? I'll tell you why. I don't know why I am telling you but I guess it is just to let you know that I tried and failed. I wasn't going to send you anything as substantial and lasting in a material sense, but I did want you to have some roses...I saw Mr. Dewitt about them and he tried several places in Cleveland and...he couldn't get them anywhere. Did I tell you that, that was why you never got those others...you know better than I can tell you how much I appreciate it." Several days later, he announces, "The roses are going out sometime this afternoon. I hope that you will get them all right before Sunday. We had a fifty-minute student meeting this morning after chapel and decided upon the honor system in the future for Wooster. It certainly is a good thing and is a mighty big step in advance...there were some great speeches pro and con. Bess Agarten made the best one of the day. I almost fell off my chair when you mentioned Mr. Briesat as the principal over there. Peter and I used to do chemistry together when we were freshmen. He certainly is peculiar looking to say the least, but I always liked him pretty well. Jumbo and I used to have a lot of fun with him.

"This evening Bob Staley asked Miss Corey, Mr. Briesat and myself to take an auto ride. We accepted with fervor and he took us for a gay little spin. After I got home I picked up the paper and of course, was attracted by the headlines telling about the awful fate of the 'Titanic.' It's certainly horrible to think of all those people going down into the deep unknelled, uncoffined and unknown." On April 15, 1912, the ship was on a maiden voyage to New York when it struck an iceberg in the North Atlantic Sea. Almost 1,500 lives were lost and has become the most intriguing mystery to historians of sea tragedies.

Billy goes to Paulding to visit Elsie one weekend and comes back invigorated, but the sinking of the Titanic goes unnoticed in his letters, "I can hardly realize that I have really been to Paulding to see you. But I know that it is a fact, and oh my darling I am so glad that I did go, so glad that I saw you and felt you and heard you tell me that you did love me, for to tell the truth I was afraid that maybe you were beginning to feel like you did last summer. But now well, I know that everything is all right again, and although it may seem like a long time before we can begin life together, yet it isn't going to be so long in reality. I know though that I really did impose upon you while I was there. When I think of how I let you do things for me simply because I was a little tired I get so darn sore at myself, that I feel like getting someone to administer a good thrashing to me. The only thing I can do though I guess is to plead forgiveness and say that I'll try to make up for it someday. I got over to Latty about twenty minutes before train time and then the train was about half an hour late. How I cussed that driver out for coming so early, think of that time that I could have been with you when I was sitting over there in that station. Well, the train finally came and I went on board only to find every seat in the car taken. I went back to the next one and discovered that it was a Pullman. One birth was made up in the car and it was empty, so without waiting to see a porter or conductor, I rolled in. The next thing I knew, the porter was sticking his head in at the curtains with a surprised look on his face. It was daylight and I wondered if we had gone very far past Cleveland. The porter almost yelled, 'where in Hell did you come from?' I gave him my ticket and he told me I'd better get up for we were just outside Cleveland then. Well, I got down to Wooster and we played Delaware and were beaten 30-25. I wasn't any worse than some of the others on the team, and not so bad as a few of them so I can't see where my trip did very much harm to Wooster U. I know darn well that if I hadn't taken the trip, I couldn't have played so well."

Elsie isn't shy about her negative feelings about the upcoming minstrel show, "You had a dress rehearsal tonight I suppose of the Minstrel Show and are pretty weary yourself—wherefore doubtless, I shall receive a snippy little scrawl from you Friday telling me how much you would like to write to me if you could only keep your eyes open. 'Same here' – as the funny man in the *Toledo Blade* always says whenever he asks a question."

Minstrel Shows were fund raisers but also a form of entertainment. Each show consisted of comic skits, variety acts, dancing, and music, performed by white people in make-up or blackface for the purpose of playing the role of black people often portrayed as dim-witted, lazy, buffoonish, superstitious, happy-go-lucky, and musical. Elsie shares her distain for the whole idea, "You ole black niggah you – go'way I'll have nothing whatever to do with no specimen of humanity. It's just about 10 o'clock so I presume the flow of wit has commenced in the Wooster Opera House by this time—you see I've given you at least two hours to work up to something 'really fine.' How I hate to be missing the show—it pleases me to be flattering anyway doesn't it, for I might have said what I am really thinking, but what through mere courtesy I have postponed with the second page—that I don't care a rag about the old thing—so there! My sense of humor is not sufficiently developed to enjoy old jokes no matter what their pedigree may be."

Billy performed in the Minstrel Show, but wanted her to know the rehearsals didn't go well before the performance, "I know your aversion to the things, but you can stand one little wail can't you? The thing has been getting under way and the practices have been getting a little better each time, but the trouble is with the stuff we are practicing." Billy was the tenor in the group called The End Men and they, "don't seem to have any originality at all. Everything has to be written out for them and explained in detail before they can understand it at all. The jokes are even worse than the ones in the show last summer. Help! The only good thing about it seems to be the songs, and you know how very fine they are. We practiced yesterday from 1:00 till 5:00, then some more after the senior party last night. The dress rehearsal comes tonight and will take about five hours I imagine. I will never be mixed up in another one of the things. Control your laughter...then the senior party! Yes, a big exclamation point. Hazel Drummond took me. They should have for well I couldn't help thinking about you (I never can) and I guess that Hazel sensed that I didn't want to think about anything else." The day after the Minstrel Show, Billy tells Elsie that it didn't go well. "Dress rehearsal on Wednesday evening went just about as poorly as anyone of us could hope. No one laughed at the intended jokes, no one knew the words to their songs, and worst of all, no one seemed to care a bit about the thing...the tickets were gone, so the financial success of the thing was sure anyway. The curtain rang up ten minutes late, pretty good for a Wooster audience wasn't it, and we were started. The jokes went off in fine style. They were so stale to us that we didn't see how on earth anyone could possibly see any point to them...George Hackett got pretty sore at "June"(John) McSweeney and me for one of them and won't speak to us yet...the songs went mighty well and took much better than we thought."

The fraternities of Wooster had a tradition of initiating new brothers when Billy writes, "We have had to change the date of our initiation, making it one week earlier." Some of the festivities began regardless of the very cold weather and the innocence of freshmen who didn't know better than to go out in subzero weather to serenade under the dormitory windows in the middle of the night.

"I flunked history. I told you I would. That darn little mutt gave me 56 as a final. I'm going to take another exam on Friday and I guess that if I study a little before-hand, I can pass all right, but gee it makes me sore...I know that it was my own fault, and I ought to have...studied a little before the exam. The basketball team is kind of shot to pieces. Hap (John Hattery) flunked, Worth flunked, and now as a final...I have to flunk. Worth is out of it for good, I'll be all right by Saturday when we play Reserve, and Hap says that he will, so things may come out better than we think. Ralph Fulton is just about as good, if not better than Worth anyway...that young cousin, Bill, of yours, is sure some artist, but where in time did he get the idea of a Roman nose. I may have smoked a few cigarettes in my time, and may have worn a straw hat, but a Roman nose is impossible...My, won't there be an awful crash when he sees me come meandering in with my poor little insignificant Irish beak...I was interrupted and in the interim have been practicing for our initiation and studying history.

"Well, my required history is a thing of the past. I don't say that I got through, for if I was to make a candid statement…I'm afraid that I would have to say that Professor A. Gould kindly put me through…I waited while he corrected my paper with fear and trembling in my heart. Finally, he looked up and said, 'well, I guess that I can remove that flunk for you now'…You who went through your college course without failing once must know the joys to be derived from a second exam. When I handed that paper in, I had no idea that it could possibly get a passing grade.

"Some of the fellows around this house are low down mutts. Oh, I suppose that it was funny to them, but if I ever catch the fellow who has been hiding your letters after they come, I'll whale him most certainly…The mail comes generally when I am out, and so if I get a letter from Paulding, it is hid until after dinner or supper then put in a very conspicuous place. I'm going to meet the postman at the door hereafter, for your letters are too sacred to be monkeyed with by anyone, and a thousand times over by some of the people in this house…I wished that I had flunked that history so that I could have cut that game last night and gone over to Paulding. We played Reserve last night (he was the center on the basketball team) and beat them 24-23. It was an awful game, they were ahead 17-10 at the end of the first half, and consequently the second half was rough. It wasn't much better than a mad scramble after the ball all over that floor. Worth was out on account of flunking, but Hap made his stuff up and Ralph Fulton took Worth's place…I was rotten, I frankly had no qualms of any kind admitting it. My man did most of the scoring for their team. I think that I am keeping my place on that team simply because I'm captain, and I'll be darned if I'm going to let it be that way anymore…The fraternities and sororities are going to have so very many to initiate. When the people went up yesterday to get the permits, I guess that they must have almost had a riot. Prexy, "the nickname students used when referring to Rev. Louis Edward Holden, President of Wooster, "had gotten pretty sore in the morning when a whole bunch came in late to the matriculation exercises and wouldn't let them sign up. There is a rumor out that the whole bunch that were late are going to be suspended for a week. We got five permits, the Alpha Taus' didn't get any, the Phi Gams' two, the Kappas' two, and I don't know about the rest, but there weren't very many. We will get a couple more before the week is over, so you see what students the Betas are. The whole college is crazy about Prexy going up in the air.

"I saw to it that I was at home when the mailman came, and I didn't let anyone else see that mail. We have basketball games every Saturday for the next four weeks. I might perhaps persuade the coach to let me go up to Paulding from Delaware after our game down there on the 22nd, but we play them here on the 24th and I'm afraid he would say 'No!' Can't you possibly get away to come here for the Kappa initiation?

"Prexy gave a bombastic talk this morning on the code of honor seemingly very prevalent among the students here in Wooster…it was a corker…poor old Prexy, he has an awfully hard row to hoe here. Did you know that he was in a sanitarium for two months last fall for his health? He was practically a nervous wreck, and if he gives many more talks like he did this morning, he won't be loose very much longer I am sure. One kid, a Delta Tau prep, has been fired already for cribbery and there are some others on the waiting list. I certainly hope they don't rake up any former actions about chemistry notebooks, for if they do I won't last very long."

Elsie was looking forward to finishing up the last four weeks of school, "In truth I can say—only four more weeks of school—and then what? Who knows? I rather think it will be Endeavor and then summer school in spite of the fact that I received another letter from my dear Uncle Howard today asking if I wouldn't really come in June! I know better than to be very definite about my time of coming, though—for just as likely as not, I shall go in the opposite direction...You don't deserve a single line from me today...I believe it is two days since I received a letter from you...no doubt with malice aforethought, deserted me! If you weren't such an adorable boy I should use 'harsh words,' but as it is, I find myself unable to say anything except that I miss you and want you, and want you to miss, and want your loving."

His social activities superceded his studies. There was the Glee Club concert, "The best I think, that a club ever gave here in Wooster...the quartette" of which he was the tenor, "was not up to par because Bill Orbison could scarcely talk above a whisper, but everybody knew what was the matter...the Grand Opera selection written by Jack Loy was a wonder. It was a direct take off on the real thing and was awfully funny." Then the Quadrangle Club went to Candor's and Billy took Hazel Drummond, "While we were eating, Grace Knoche threw about half a glass of water on me, it started something. She got a full glass, and after that there was some time in there, believe me. Neil Kilgore helped Grace and so I came away with myself quite a little disheveled and with slightly damp hair and clothing, but they got all they wanted." In the midst of his stories about daily life during his senior year, he pours out his heart to Elsie, "I got your letter last night with the rose petals in it, you don't know how happy that letter made me dear. I'm going to be worthy of your love someday dearest, if it is in mortal man to be. I know I've been woefully indefinite about some things, but dear heart it hasn't been because I've wanted to be...one thing I know and that is that you and I can be infinitely more happy together anywhere than apart...there will be sacrifices dearest, and you know that I must feel that I don't like you to make any severe sacrifices...don't go back to Paulding next year Elsie. You can't very well I think, for you are going to be my wife before the year is out. I love you dearest with all my heart and I am forever if you will have me.

"You become more of a wonder to me every day...everything which has any connection with you, becomes more wonderful. Yesterday afternoon there was a baseball game, I was sliding in to second base with my usual grace and dexterity when my heel spike caught on the bag and I tore the ligaments in my ankle...I am in bed today...but I think I'll be able to get around tomorrow...I thought I could stand pain, but this ankle hurts like the very devil...there is one more day gone until you come again. Do you know dear that everything I think or do, all seems to be thought or done in terms of either the last time you were here, or the next time you will be here...I want you tonight. I want you to tell me of your love and let me tell you of mine. I want you to lie in my arms and tell me that you love me, and let me kiss those loving lips—God, Elsie, I'm mad for you. My head aches with the awful heartache that I have. It is just aching for a sight of you, for a touch of you, for anything my darling that means you are near. You are the sum of all things in my life, and sometimes I feel like a crook or lowdown sneak to take your love, for God knows I'm not worthy of it dearest. But I want to be someday. What is it that makes this life as much more worth living when you are near me, and I can feel that I can see you once in a while. I have gotten to almost hate this town since you have gone dear. And, as for the college part of it, it is almost unbearable. Oh, I want you dearest, sweetheart. If I could take you in my arms just once and hold you, it would help so much."

By late April, he is looking forward to Elsie's arrival in Wooster, "I feel like a criminal. That wail of mine about having such a headache, and a little bit of something else in it, must have been the only snatch you got from me for three or four days, and here I have been getting letters from you...I just couldn't write, that is all...The dramatic club is going to stage Mr. Bob, a three-act comedy, in which Jay (Kilpatrick) is the leading man, on Thursday night. Bess Agarten lost a bet to me about getting caught at the time of the University Club dance and is taking me to the show. Just ten more days and if the 10:53 is on time, I will meet you in Mansfield." Later he was glad he went to the play on April 25 and Billy is still limping from his ankle injury, "If I walk real slow, I can walk almost naturally." Billy attends the play, "It was really mighty good and the people were all fine...Jay had a part which suited him exactly, allowed him to bluster and blow as much as he wanted without bothering to touch any details. There were a couple of very tense places when Jay was making love to Irene Morley, and you could almost see the audience sitting up on their toes until the tension was loosened. Elisa Candor was fine. She was a maid, and certainly carried off her part to perfection. Bess Livingspire wasn't so good as I had thought she would be, but not one of them was close to being poor. The commencement speakers were announced this morning. Frances Scott – valedictorian, Behot (Willis Chichester Behoteguy) – salutatory, and the rest were those whom everybody thought would get them."

Each letter revealed Elsie's sharp satirical side when she wrote what was on her mind, "Good morning dearest" – what a charming way it is to start out a perfectly new day by saying 'good morning' to you. I've just finished writing to your mother—a hopeless Chop-suey of a letter and now it's your turn curley head, to receive the last withering, emaciated thoughts as they drop dully out of my brain...A spicy missive from Hazel Drummond also came today which told me practically everything which you didn't, I guess. Now my dear boy—do not become peeved at what I've just said—it may sound badly, but it doesn't mean much...Tonight as I had a special invitation to attend a Methodist missionary social meeting I couldn't decline and therefore went...The Methodist's do not seem to be as inquisitive as the Presbyterians—I think I shall try to become a Methodist! She ends the letter with a sarcastic treatise, "Be good to Marge and Hazel; call on Miriam occasionally; and whenever your mind is not occupied with Minstrel Show, Basketball; Y.M.C.A., Studies!?!; Dates; Social Functions, Fraternity Affairs; Glee Club; Forensic Pursuits; Special Dinners; Sleep; The Beauties of Lake George; Your Self and your Worthlessness; Your Accomplishments and Your Lovableness—then, squeeze in a thought for your loving, inconsistent, Elsie."

Billy's announces that his Uncle John Mott, would be in Wooster for a few days, "You've heard me speak of him before...I am glad that you didn't see him, for I assuredly would have been a very light eye-filling green with jealousy if you had, for I'm sure you would have liked him too well for my comfort. He is getting better as he gets older, has all the good qualities that I possess (see how egotistical I am becoming) with all of his own added to them, and to crown the whole things has curly hair and blue eyes...but John is a peach and I know that you two will like each other immensely. He is crazy to meet you."

The news of a cheating scandal peppered Billy's letters and by the beginning of spring he shares the latest events, "In chapel, Compy (Elias Compton) announced that definite information had been handed to him about some people who had cheated. If they would confess, he said that they could take another exam on the subject and that would end the matter. If they did not confess, severe punishment would be meted[*sic*] out to them. He repeated his little monologue this morning in chapel and added that he would give the people until the end of this week. If they did not come to him by that time, their future was in the hands of the faculty…every place you go, people ask if you are going up to confess. Punk May was caught and was expelled last Friday. No one knew about it, however, until yesterday. The case of those other three Thetas hasn't been settled yet I guess, but I kind of have a hunch that they will travel along, too. It certainly is having a mighty bad effect on the reputation of the college around the country. It is a wonder to me that nothing has gotten into the Cleveland papers about it yet. When it does, it is bound to create some commotion." Then in April, "Some news was published in the Wooster paper Friday night which made everybody up here on the hill sit up and take notice. The Executive Committee of the Board of Trustees[4] have suspended the Phi Gams' for two years from next June on account of some rough work they did in initiation. Wallace Ryall was the freshman. He is said to have been in bed for a week after the initiation on account of some internal injuries he got. It certainly is too bad. It will handicap them like everything. They have to give up their house in June and cannot exist as a Chapter until September 1914. Cannot initiate or anything else. It is all true. I was talking to Hurd Miller yesterday and he says the fellows are almost crazy down there about it. There is a little hope for them when the whole Board meets in June, but not very much." The cheating scandal coupled with the fraternity hazing had repercussions when "Lewis Severance, a wealthy donor to The College, issued an ultimatum threating to withdraw his support from the school if national Greek life persisted, stating in a letter, 'what I do on this million-dollar effort, with the General Education Board, will pledge only on condition that the fraternities surrender their charter at Wooster.' Severance's opinion and ultimatum regarding Greek life was foreshadowed in a 1910 letter to President Holden, saying that he was 'decidedly opposed to them,' and suggested that they disband their efforts and energies should be used towards the creation of two new dorms on campus. Due to Severance's threat, the Board of Trustees voted in February of 1913 on the matter, resulting in a 13-10 vote, with four members absent, to abolish the current Greek system. Angered by the results of the vote, three of the dissenting trustees resigned following the meeting. Within a year, Greek life returned to the campus in the form of 'sections.'"

Elsie writes to Billy from the high school Assembly Room on April 18, "Dear Irishman...Yesterday was a blue day...all weepy and rainy so when night came I simply couldn't write a very sunshiny letter to you...I wrote to Uncle Howard and Helen...My botany class has just weathered one of my choicest 'written lessons' but doesn't seem at all peeved at me for having handed it to them. There is one boy trying to stare me out of countenance now because I gave him a sulphuric look a few minutes ago... Calmness and sublime complacency are my long suit at present... that is outward calmness, but within, my heart is doing a number of unprescribed things. Two weeks from tomorrow! Can you realize that it is only a few days, dear, before we shall be in Arcady together. I swear I could write a canticle at the mere thought of what those golden days with you are going to give me. Tell me...may I go on dreaming and hoping without the thought of ever having a bitter awakening? Or, must I awake sometime to find that you did in truth love me but do not still? No, what may happen though...we have lived a little you and I, haven't we and nothing can ever change that."

The various accounts of Wooster social activities dominated Billy's letters. Toward the end of the school year, Billy attended social engagements; while Elsie, on the other hand, was busy completing her year at Paulding. She was anxious to join him as soon as school ended. "This is to be your birthday letter so you mustn't think of anything except red roses and moonlight and windy blue-arched days; you must think of all the sweet times we have had together—the walks, the drives and all the other Arcadian joys which the Gods have granted us; above all though, dearest,--that is, I trust it will be above all, you must think of how much I love you…I wish that I had been created as beautiful as the roses which you have so often sent to me…and never grow weary of loving…tonight I must go over to one of the teacher's houses and make place-cards for my spread Wednesday night. This week is going to go fast…there is going to be a heap of things…I just discovered that I must write a class plulrophery[*sic*] for the banquet and sing also…the last I have already refused to do---I wonder what they think I am anyway…a grouchy, old sleepy head…tomorrow though I shall write you my usual twenty volume letter." By May 9 the banquet and party is past, with a comment that she felt it was a 'fizzle' and is looking forward to joining him at Wooster: "These last days have seemed so long… not while I've been living them…tomorrow marks the commence-ment of the week which the God's grant, may not end until you hold me again close to your heart and say the sweetest words in all the world, 'I love you, Elsie.'"

He is impatiently waiting for Elsie to return. While looking forward to the end of the school year he takes time to reflect on his five years at Wooster, "Sometimes I wonder if it all has paid. Perhaps not all has, but part of it has, and the five years would have been more than useless if I hadn't met you here… The last week of your stay in Paulding. Praise the Lord. I can scarcely wait until Thursday to come…there is going to be a kind of reception, and dance and lawn fete combined for Dorothy Mullinus at McSweeney's, and June has asked me to come down, and to bring whoever I please. You know that you are the only girl I really want to take. Is there any possible chance of your getting here in time for it...then there is another party coming off on the 23rd of May at Annats. Can you stay over for that date and will you? I feel so utterly inadequate...I am so very unworthy of your love. You have seen just the best side of me, for that is the part of me that always comes to the front when you are near, and I am afraid that you have exaggerated those few good qualities that I do have, and when I do appear in my true life, it will be an awful comedown for you...but darling I don't want you to think me something that I am not. I don't know just what it is, but I feel somehow that there is so much about me that you could not love if you knew it all. I don't know why I am writing all this. I know that I love you and am going to make you happy and that is the main things...if someone would suggest or hint that I couldn't... make you happy, I'd be up in arms in a minute...you are the only person in this world I love, and you have every bit of my love for yourself alone through all eternity."

Over the next few weeks there were off again, on again, plans to attend a dance in early May, only to find that Elsie was involved in end of school banquets and activities at Paulding with an exclamation, "My little party is now a thing of the past for which, O Heavenly powers, accept my peevish thanks and grant me no more such pleasures in the near future. It's true, my training in K.K.[*sic*] stood me in good part tonight but even with such backing, I should have undoubtedly failed had not someone come to my assistance...Yesterday I received a letter from Helen (White)—it was such a nice one wishing me every happiness on earth." Then Elsie reminisces about, "A year ago tonight," May 15, "you told me something for the first time and I didn't believe you at all---and now dearest, you have gone and loved me for 'a year and a day' just to prove how mistaken I was! How things have changed since then—how differently we feel—or at least I have changed into quite a different person than I was then—and it has just been your love that has done it—or my desire to keep your love ever burning for me. Dear, you must never say again that you are not worthy of me—I can't bear to have you do it. Perhaps you don't understand that although I love you, yet it is hard to give myself to you—for better, for worse—entirely and forever, not that I do not want to be forever yours, but that I would, that I might have the strength never to be anyone's wife—much less the wife of the one whom I must needs, love more than the sun of all things. So, I have often thought and this thought was torture, but tonight I must only think of the sweetness and happiness which are waiting for us somewhere in the golden years to come and ever trusting in you, wait for you to make my sweetest dream come true."

Billy received a letter from his father saying, "That he is sailing on the 28th of June and so I suppose I'll go there too. One month from today is the last time you will appear in Paulding, Ohio, as a teacher in the high school…By the 17th of May…one more month nearer to that day and you and I will be starting our life together…I'm crazy to have this business of being away from you ended forever…the sooner we are married, the happier and better it will be for both of us…It makes it just right for commencement week. I was afraid at first that I'd have to go before the week was over, but of course won't have to now. He was in Indianapolis last Saturday and almost stopped off here in Wooster. I may go to New York sometime soon to see him about some of the final arrangements. I told him in my last letter that if he could use me there, I'd do whatever I could." Billy made a commitment to his father, but what other commitments he made or what role he would assume was still a mystery to both he and Elsie.

By June 2, they are discussing graduation gifts to each other, "Dearest Spendthrift, I feel like 'talking' at least twelve pages to you but must needs be reasonable and humane and write only four. It seems to me that in the last two or three letters you have made some suggestions and asked some questions which up to this present moment have been most persistently ignored. Really, I never remembered any of them until just now. It always takes a day or two for things to soak into my brain and today as I was sitting here writing some letters which must be written I decided to be decent and answer all I could think of...You have given me so many things already that I really wish you wouldn't give me a commencement present. Do be sensible instead of generous for once, dear, and just let me have a whiter, shinier porcelain sink when I want it! The 'luxuries' which you suggested—or rather... those that are dear to the feminine heart I admit, and must always be appreciated. There is one thing, however, which I would rather have (four silk stockings although really 'luxuries' as you say have often been enjoyed by your fellow spendthrift) but this other thing I must look into before I ask you for it—but if I can, I certainly shall let you know...After scouring this city for a pig-skin bill book I discovered the existence of the above-mentioned articles. The clerk informed me that they were too stiff to be much in demand and offered me the lone sample for fifty cents. Thinking perhaps you would like to change your order I made arrangements to have a quarter one made...Have I told you anything you wanted to know? I hope not. The best thing for me to do since you refuse to listen to me any longer is to take a nap. I intended to go to the Art Exhibit this afternoon out at Eden Park, Fine Arts Building, but my white gloves are too saturated with Cincinnati soot to make an appearance in, so I shall do the worst thing, possibly sleep when I want to do something else. 'Excuse me please.' The other spendthrift, Elsie."

She finally makes a decision which creates a line in the sand. She wrote to her father suggesting that if he couldn't possibly come in the fall, would he promise to come next spring and she would wait until he came to be married. She writes to Paulding to see if they decided on an English teacher for next year and if they haven't, offered them her services for the coming school term. She's making decisions, "In regard to you my heart has run through the whole gament[*sic*] of emotions, only I do not think I have ever really hated you, and I know that I could never despise, for you are too noble, too good to ever call forth an emotion that can only be called forth by what is low and ignoble, but you have made me feel that I myself deserved such from you some times and for that very feeling within myself, because you aroused it, I have almost hated you at times. Why should I write my miserable thoughts out for you to read, you who keep your own sealed tightly in your heart, sealed and hidden even from the eyes of her whom you swear you love as your own soul. I cannot understand—but dearest I do not want to lose your love, I must keep it, all of it, every ounce of it, I love your love and I love you; not as much as you should be loved, not as much as when my soul grows you shall be loved, but yet dearest of men, I swear that I could say unflinchingly before the soul-reading eyes of God that as much as my cramped suspicious heart is capable of loving, I love you.

You will try to be patient, long suffering and kind, will you not? You will give me time to catch up to you, to gather up what I can of the sacred wine that I have spilled along my way, to extinquish every flickering candle that burns before any shrine but your own, you will help me with your love and strengthen me with your faith in me, you will do all this, I know, and you will make me more worthy of your love, more worthy to have you and to be your wife." Later, "Our conversation over the telephone was rather unsatisfactory wasn't it? I am going up to Endeavor just as soon as ever I can, and I am going to stay until Mary feels like throwing me out. There is no use, I suppose, at this stage in the game of quarreling with my future maid-of-honor. Besides its mighty lovely of anybody to ask me to come and visit them 'indefinitely', you know. I'm going to write to Helen tonight if my temper stays sweet and tell her how much I would like to go to Lake George this summer and how very unlikely it is that I shall ever get there...you mustn't stop writing to me now because you will have a long, long vacation very soon...Do you know how many days you will be sailing over the deep, blue sea? Please tell me, I want to think of you always with the correct setting and background. 'Ultramarine' blue, 'river-of-Paradise' blue, both are infinitely becoming to your peculiar type...So you are doing 'nothing as usual'. If I had only known that sooner, I would have been glad to come over and fill up a few hundred of your empty moments. It must be very refreshing to take a rest though undisturbed save by the intelligent footsteps of a myriad tramping past your door. *Pax Dobiscum*, and a cool Fourth of July." And Elsie heads to Endeavor.

CHAPTER 10

Endeavor Forever

Elsie left Canton for Endeavor in late June after visiting her friend Blix, cherishing the quiet train ride as she contemplated what lie ahead. She knew Billy would soon leave for China, and she would again return to the McKean home for the summer. She had several choices. She could go to Cincinnati, or Philadelphia, but Mary's invitation sealed it; she chose Endeavor. She was eight years old when she left Lien Chow. An age when childhood memories of people and places seem to stick. The early years in China never left her psychic or the longing to return. If comparisons were made between Lien Chow and Endeavor, they were similar. They were situated in the midst of mountainous areas overlooking rivers with beautiful vistas and impressive rock formations. Elsie seemed fearless. She wasn't afraid of snakes and seemed to thrive on the folklore about them. The forestry culture fascinated her as much as the locals. With Billy gone, she had time to think, and plan for the possible Thanksgiving Day wedding, although she didn't know where it would take place.

Blix, as Elizabeth Gans Krichbaum was called was another college friend who left Wooster and went home to Canton, "Tomorrow Blix and I are going somewhere, we've never been there before and would dislike very much ever to be forced to go there again, nevertheless, tomorrow we're going and tomorrow

I shall tell you all about it...it would be making a great many of my sweetest dreams come true if you would come over Sunday evening and say goodbye to me again...if you possibly can...to see you again, to feel your strong arms around me, to be kissed by the sweetest lips in all the world, to be told that I am really the one you love...it is for these things...and others even sweeter... that I am living...for you, dearest; do not let me live in vain", Within a week, she heads to Endeavor for the summer, "Can I write a letter in fifteen minutes? Of course, I can, if I must. Don't you get tired of being called Sir Galahad? You know I can vary your titles infinitely...I have given you one or two other nice ones if you remember rightly, but none of them please me as well as does Sir Galahad...I dote on contrasts, but I adore things which are perfectly adapted to each other...I fancy I see a shadow of a halo descending like a ring of cigarette smoke upon your sunny head. Oh! Galahad agonists...what a strong man like you must suffer! And like a lamb before your shearers you open not your mouth. You endure all in silence and becoming humility... Just like Old Faithful, I pour out a stream, it may be muddy too, but nevertheless, it is a stream into your patient ears, every few hours. Train...I must run to the post office or you won't have a letter Wednesday and Baby-Blue will have several minutes on his hands."

There was a delay of travel plans to Japan which gave Billy an opportunity to see Elsie in Endeavor before leaving, "I'm glad you're coming...on Saturday." With plans to leave once again delayed; this time, in Vancouver, a few brief letters, telegram and a telephone call between Elsie and Billy ensued. Finally, he was on his way and would be gone for several months.

Elsie thrives on the social scene in Endeavor with the students of the Department of Forestry at the Pennsylvania State College, "Our little house party broke up Wednesday afternoon and Mary and I were both ready to turn in and get a good rest. Last night we had callers again and entertained them so well that they stayed until midnight. A dozen of the Penn State forestry boys I told you about have come down to Endeavor to camp for two weeks. It sounds interesting, and maybe, as long as there is plenty of competition we are invited to a big honor party which will begin in about ten days. Mary and I are planning perfectly stunning bathing suits for the occasion. The house party is going to be up near Tionesta some place, on the picturesque Allegheney[*sic*]. We are anticipating the time of our sweet young lives but of course shall not forget our friends of long ago no matter how exciting things may prove.

"Billy, I just invited Mary to come and have Thanksgiving dinner with us in 1913. I invited Blix some time ago. I thought I'd better tell you, so you wouldn't appear too surprised when they made their advent. My dear, I am absolutely head over heels in love with you today. What am I going to do about it? Really, it's serious this time, and I'm just afraid I shall not get over it for several hours. Did you ever feel that way yourself, Sir Galahad, I wonder?

"When you get this letter, I want you to sit down and write one to my father and tell him anything you like just so it has a good affect; this to be done of course if you haven't done so long before and if you still intend to have me at your wedding in November. Twenty weeks! Is that all? It isn't giving you much time to change your mind, is it?

"I am going to write to Satan today and Dous too, if I get around to it. Poor Satan, I'm sorry he's so unhappy, but of course it's all in the game. He isn't doing what he ought to do in regard to Hazel, but how can a girl tell him that! It will just have to work itself out, I guess, for its dangerous to meddle with other people's love affairs when, well when the course of true love isn't supposed to run smooth anyway.

"Dear heart I'm blue myself today and I should be happy knowing that you love me as you do, but I'm not and you will just have to forgive me for telling you about it. I would give anything but my immortal soul, which is not mine to give, to have you here beside me. The more I see of other men, the more those qualities which I admire in you shine out and put theirs to shame. I am not speaking disparagingly of them; it is only in the comparison with you that they suffer. I'm not saying that you are perfect, what on earth (heaven is the place for perfection), what on earth then, would I do with a perfect man on my hands? No, I want none such for my life companion because it will be hard enough as it is for me to keep the scales balanced. This is not intended to be humorous, it is a classical reference, sir. Therefore, thank heaven for your faults, one of which I believe I have discovered only to find that it is merely an overgrown virtue which doubtless will reach a normal size in a very few years. Not that I want it to, but twill be better for my character if it does. I always was self-sacrificing.

"When I wrote to Helen about going to the lake, I wasn't at all certain about going. I told her that I disliked being too 'definite' because I might have to change my plans, therefore, I never made any plans but just went ahead, and did things when I felt like it. It will be a great disappointment to me if I don't get up there and see that summer paradise and learn to know Helen and Donald. Do you know, I was going to write you the most beautiful set of steamer letters, one to be opened every day, but my brain gave out and somehow or other no brilliant ideas offered themselves, so the whole thing just fizzled out and died a natural death. It's just as well anyway. I guess for you not to see any of my delightful brilliantdom[*sic*] for two or three weeks, you'll appreciate them when they do come trailing in, written in such a small hand that you'll have to put on your professional spectacles to decipher them.

"You seemed to have had a funny streak as you were clunking along through Utah, for your letters did credit to your Irish ancestry. Mary and I received your letters about 10:30 a.m. one bright morning when we were trying to sleep off the effects of the house party. We had really slept too long and were consequently not in a very angelic mood, when like oil upon the turbulent waters; or a glass of Cincinnati's famous brew in a hot and heavy land; or the sound of the nine o'clock bell to the bored Thursday night caller; like all these things, and many, many, more, dear boy which time the weather and my disposition prevent me from belting down herein, came your sky blue missiles to refresh and comfort us.

"Cara wrote me the most absurd letter the other day, in her happiest style and consequently the Endeavor hills reechoed with our appreciative laughter. You have no idea Billy, what you miss by not having her in your list of correspondents, but I'm glad you haven't included her in your list because you'd never read my letters at all, I'm afraid, if you had.

"It will seem strange just to write to you once a week instead of seven times. I think I shall number my letters so you won't read the last over first. Be good to yourself and leave the most glorious of times but don't forget to come back to one who loves you more dearly every day."

She addresses Billy at the Sontag Hotel in Seoul, Korea on a Monday afternoon, "I've decided that to write just one letter a week and have it contain all the news in chronological order is an impossibility for me to accomplish. Therefore, you'll get a huge manuscript containing seven letters more or less every week instead of one like my last.

"Last night is a night to be remembered for Mary and I met the Betas when we've been yearning to meet for a week. Billy, they are perfect stars. I'm quite crazy about both of them. Another rather nice man came along with them but as Cara would say we were tempted by the baubles which sparkled on the manly breasts of the other men and consequently overlooked a great many of this poor fellow's virtues. We had the time of our young lives exchanging our choicest lines of talk for other choice lines of a distinctly Eastern flavor. Now let me introduce you to your brothers Mr. Kuscke (don't pronounce it) tall, light haired, blue-eyes and delightfully handsome. (Shake) And this is Mr. Bowman, medium sized, well built, with wavey[*sic*] black hair and a face which is a fitting index to the humorous character of its owner. Mr. Bowman is one of those rare young men who can act the fool eternally and still retain your respect and be asked to call again. He kept us amused until our jaws fairly ached laughing at his absurdities.

"Allow me to congratulate the Beta fraternity on having secured two such prizes. (Now, Elsie, what would you say if these two boys weren't really all you so firmly believe them to be? 'It would break my heart.)

"Tonight, we are going down to their camp and back in the light of their camp fire. It sounds nice. I only hope it will be. I shall think of you, dear as I sit gazing into the flames and shall wish as I have wished so often before that you were beside me.

"George Warden hasn't been over since Wednesday. I can't imagine what's the matter with him. He knows both of us like him awfully well so why can't he be more sociable? I'll ask him for an explanation of his conduct tomorrow. I talk as if I had a right to, don't I? Perhaps I won't find anything out for all my pas either but there's nothing like trying. We're having quite a long 'date' this afternoon aren't we? I'm up in the 'pink room' lying on the bed writing because it happens to be the only cool place in the house. Mary is downstairs overhauling her memory book. Every once in a while, she slips up here to read me some juicy morsel which she knows I will appreciate. For the most part, however, she's more 'reserved' than you are. (I might have omitted that last but it just trickled off my pen before I thought). I wrote to Satan today just to let him know that I was 'very sincerely yours, Elsie' to him. I hope he appreciates my effort. As soon as I get enough energy up I'm going to write to Dous, I've deserted most of my friends insofar as to write a lot of things which couldn't possibly interest you, and for fear I trespass again I'm going to stop talking and get busy so I'll make a suitable appearance at supper.

"Another day has scuttled into eternity and lost itself in the infinite mazes of the past, and I'm glad it's gone for it means that you are just one day nearer your coming back to me. Mary and I were lazy again today so the morning's mail came and found us still in bed. We each received three nice letters which immediately put us in a good humor. One was from you. How surprised I was. It was dated Wednesday night, from Hotel Stewart I guess. Perhaps I'll get one tomorrow too, but I'm afraid to hope for such a thing. Dear heart, you are quite right when you say that we should not wait until spring to be married; I feel as though we would be happier if we didn't put it off until spring. I am not, in any way, trying to hurry you up, you understand don't you, oh, that's not what I wanted to say at all. Please just know for yourself what I wanted to say. Without my knowing it first and saying it for you—that's a dear.

"Did you notice the new moon tonight, I wonder? Mary and I each sighed a little deep blue sigh, fretted with yearnings and wishes, at least mine was, when we saw that little, golden slip of a moon over the Endeavor hills.

"This afternoon our Beta friends asked us to attend a baseball game to be played between [Penn]State and Endeavor. It certainly was some game. The poor umpire was almost mobbed. After each inning there invariably ensured a young riot during which the score was always readjusted to suit the stronger party. Me and Mary had a good laugh at the ridiculous lines of talk which were exchanged across the diamond, talk not always elegant but invariably forcible. The game lasted until the little fire flies began their mighty promenade. The other night we went over and borrowed some music from Warden's. Just guess what was among the pieces which we drew. A song from *Little Boy Blue*, that opera that you raved so about for several weeks after you'd returned from 'dear, little, old New York'. *Love Never Dies* is the name of the composition and, of course, knowing how much that opera took your eye or ear I've set myself the pleasurable task of learning this little ditty for your special benefit. I shall probably have forgotten it however by the time you're near enough to hear me sing it! Love's labor lost, indeed. Tomorrow there are prospects of having a picnic out at the Eddy. I'm saving a place in my heart for you, but I'm afraid the place by my side will have to be filled by some inferior mortal. Tomorrow, some day, when I say tomorrow, how much it will mean!

"Herein endeth the second day - Thursday afternoon

"Yesterday was a long, long day because it began earlier than usual. At 4:15 a.m., Laura screamed at Mary and me that there was a fire, the lower mill was burning. I don't see yet how we slept through those terrible whistles. When I look back over the last four or five minutes of my slumber that morning I realize that their penetrating shrillness was steadily boring into my consciousness even before I was out of dreamland. I think I was dreaming of the cries of the eternally damned when Laura kindly came and released me from the dreadful nightmare to a not less dreadful reality. Well we snatched on some clothes and in less time that it takes to write it were rushing hot footed up the boardwalk toward the mill. But after all the fire didn't amount to much; the night watch had been able to give the signal soon enough to secure the necessary aid, so we were disappointed! I expected to see the lumber yards the mill and half the town go up in smoke and to just barely escape myself with a bundle of clothes under my arm—and after working myself up to such a pitch of expectation it certainly was a long drop down to the common place again. Mary was wise and went back to bed but I got a strange working fit yesterday and I tore around as if everything depended upon the work I could accomplish in eight hours. About the middle of the afternoon it began to look threatening, the big thunder clouds piled themselves solemnly up above the hills and stayed there in a deep, menacing silence. We gave up the picnic of course, we hadn't really definitely decided about it any way so nobody was very disappointed.

"In the evening the two wearers of the diamond and three stars trailed down to see us and another couple dropped in. Between showers we went after refreshments and just barely got home in time to save ourselves from getting soaked.

"Then the four of us packed ourselves into the corner swing, packed is the word, and crazy Mr. Bowman put up an umbrella and there we sat in the awfullest[sic] downpour you can imagine. My hair got pretty wet but for the most part, half of Mr. Bowman's raincoat and the umbrella doing reasonably well as protectors against the dampness, I kept dry.

"Heavens, I hadn't slept for so long that I grew lightheaded and got the hysterics in quite the way I had them once when we were walking past the high school in Wooster, after one of our drives through the mud. Mary seemed (word seemed too splashy, dripped over a bit) to catch a little of my idiocy so the boys had their own little troubles trying to make us sensible. I implored Mr. B. to be severe and stern, and he tried, bless his heart, but twas[*sic*] no use for a clown like him to try to impress me with his seriousness.

"You can understand now perhaps, why I didn't write last night, or rather this morning. I was too tired and should have made a worse mess of this letter writing business than I am doing now. For some reason or other I'm tired now too, but there are a hundred and one things to be done if we are going to the Eddy for supper, and they must be done before five o'clock. Oh, Billy how I wish you were going to be with us, but there is no use wishing for you. I've found that out by this time.

"Oh, two letters came from you yesterday, the last two you wrote. They were both very beautiful letters Billy and made my heart sing softly to itself all day. This separation is the best thing in the world for us; I love you now as I never loved you before, and my love is growing, and becoming more perfect hour by hour. Imperfect as it now is, it is all yours for you made it possible for me to love.

"Herein endeth the 3rd and 4th day.

"You have been sailing a whole week now, it seems much longer than that because I'm prone to think of you as being away ever since the last time I saw you in Canton. Today has been rather uneventful. Mr. Bracken, one of the boys who was here for our little house party…came to town today and stayed long enough to eat dinner with us.

"This afternoon I wanted to take a long walk up to the rocks, but Mary was afraid of rattlers. She said it was perfect folly to go up there without a man to protect me. I saw no chance of getting one at that hour of the day and I did want to take a walk so I went alone, armed to the teeth with a broom-handle and my revolver. I had a lovely time. When I came to a beautiful shady spot I sat me down upon a moss-covered rock and sang you a few songs. Did you hear me, I wonder? Of course not, how foolish of me to ask. The tones that came from my throat weren't much to listen to, but what came from my heart, I swear 'twas the best there was of me. The memories that crowded into my mind as I climbed that steep narrow path way! The last time I was there, we were together, but you were not so much to me then as you are now, yet you were a great deal, the best thing that had ever come into my life, only I didn't know it.

"I must tell you, because of course, you're interested, that the picnic last night was a decided success. The menu was duly appreciated which made the cooks quite happy to think they had taken such great pains to make everything appetizing.

"I heard from Philadelphia about the photographs. They were mailed to you on July 4th. I certainly am sorry that they missed you. Perhaps you'll get them in a month or so, they'll probably follow you around the world. When you see that dentifrice advertisement you will doubtless sing 'only the ghost of your smile, sweetheart,' with a new meaning. I do wish you hadn't asked me for those shadows of the past, but you went and done it, you did, so who could resist you! I wrote asking Miriam to see that they got forwarded to you, because I wasn't at all sure that packages were ever forwarded.

"Mary and I are the Beta twins tonight. She's in her pink and I in my blue dress", (referring to Beta Theta Pi's colors: light shades of pink and blue, while their flower was American Beauty rose). She has started out on a 'date' but you see I'm still writing to you so probably my own true has forsaken me. If he has, I certainly shan't speak to him again very soon! Oh, Billy I want to see you—I'm tired of this place already, tired because it reminds me so of you, of the sweet and bitter times we've had here. I know Mary would be offended if I should leave so soon, but really, I don't see how I am going to live through it and keep any sunshine in my heart at all. And that house party! And the invitation to the Corry Races at the end of this month! Of course, I know if I go that I'll have a grand time, and for the time being forget a lot of the heartaches which I am having now, but dear, I don't want to forget them, I want to remember every moment that you are not with me."

"Saturday afternoon

"This is the last installment to be added to this stupid daily chronicle of mine. Perhaps we'll change our tactics a little next week and give our subscriber something less monotonous. It always pays to hope for the best. So far, the day has been colorless except for a trip after the mail, then I met everybody worthwhile meeting in town and drew a letter from Helen into the bargain.

"Dearest, there are so many things I would like to say to you, but I can't write them. I doubt even if I could speak them if you were holding me in your arms, but then I would not have to voice the things which were in my heart, if you really love me you would know and feel what I could find no words to express. My Sir Galahad, and mine alone, is it not so? To have and to hold, for better, for worse, now and forever, till death do us part. I at least must believe and trust that your love is indeed the love that endures. And as I trust you so I must feel that I am trusted to be true to myself and to you, for truly I am one who loves you deeply, yet but little compared to what your wife shall love who is now your promised wife to be."

By July 21, It is a Sunday evening when she writes, "Last night several of us went to a little informal gathering. I suppose you would call it, at one of the girl's homes. We stayed until the party almost turned into a slumber party and then turned our weary, footsteps homeward only to find when we arrived that we were locked out. Well it was late, I'm bound to admit that and Laura just supposed that Mary and I had decided to stay all night, so calmly locked up. One of the boys, however, put his shoulder to the kitchen door and broke the thing open, making just enough noise to arouse Laura who straightway descended upon us! I retired while she and Mary had a few 'explanations'. Laura certainly was 'up in the air', but I guess she managed to get down again without any serious injuries. Mary and I maneuvered so as to be up by dinner time and were mighty glad that we did for the dinner was well worth getting up for. Most of the afternoon we loafed comfortably at a friend's and I indulged in a mental debaucle[*sic*] reading a perfectly trashy impossible book which was also perfectly harmless, 'O Clarite beloved! Tell me 'tis false'!' Tra, la, 'twas mush indeed and altogether hopeless. But my dear, he won her 'honest' he did; perhaps not altogether honestly but nevertheless, the dear brace, bad, hero was made madly, unspeakably happy when the ravishing Clarita percipatated[*sic*] herself gracefully into his strong arms! The humor which lies in a book of that sort is indescribable! If the author would only label it 'jokes' then one would know what to expect but he probably expected though public to take his magnum opus as seriously as he did himself.

"Mary and Gladys (Shaw) have gone for a stroll doubtless they will bring all the young men in town home with them. You see I stayed at home to write to you. Mr. Bowman will be here about eight-thirty, I suppose, so I have a good half-hour yet in which to talk to you. Oh, I dreamt[*sic*] about you last night, the most ridiculous dream, but it had a sad ending, only I didn't seem to care in the least. Billy, you fell in love with a chorus girl! Sir Galahad, imagine and you had the nerve to tell me so after you'd been my own true husband for a year! (Say, don't stop to count the exclamation points, I'd change the punctuation if the English language only offered a big enough variety to choose from!). So of course, after you told me calmly all about your affinity (I was eating shredded wheat with strawberries in it when you spoke them fatal words, them harsh, harsh words,) naturally it took my appetite away for that one meal and of course, we parted, but as I said before nobody seemed to care. Dear me, just look what's in store for us, life shall not be monotonous after all!"

"Seven guesses (I feel generous tonight) what sort of a mood I'm in. But then, I think you could guess in less for you've seen me this way before. If you were only here I'd make you just as miserable as I possibly could and then try to make it up just at the last moment when it would be entirely too late dearest and you think you love such a changeable undependable woman as I am? Well, having expressed yourself, please keep right on saying the same thing 'over and over again'. Oh, I'm the most irreverent creature under the sun. I know absolutely no respect for the fowls of the sea, the fishes of the air, or the creatures which dwell in the waters under the earth! I'll have a good time tonight, I feel it. I just hope I won't have a reaction and go down into the deep waters before dawn sufficient into the hour if the joy thereof, 'fig for the man who sits and frets, it isn't raining rain to me, it's raining violets.' Kuschke just came in and told me to give you his best, idiot. Of course, I told him 'my aunt' would be delighted to have a bunch of love thrown at her in that way but he didn't seem to be convinced at all as to the identity of my correspondent. The clans are gathering, two couples are here already and people are wondering why under the stars I don't come out and join the happy throng. We are going to have English Moloney coffee and the usual side dishes in a little while. You remember, the usual Sunday night lunches, I'd give a good piece of my lost youth to have you here, but I guess I can't, so I'll drown my sorrows in a shallow cup of black coffee and talk unceasingly world without end, Amen, and Amen!

Herein endeth the first installment to this sacred chronicle."
Monday night - Almost midnight

"This isn't going to be very long tonight because I want to go to bed and dream a few nice dreams before dinner time tomorrow. Last night the coffee which was served with the Welsh Rabbit[*sic*] was too much for me. I guess because I simply couldn't sleep. The party broke up about twelve and then I sat up and read a book until after four—the second book too that I'd read yesterday. Sleep was the most elusive thing. I chased it into a corner finally though and managed to get a few winks in before eight thirty. Dreams of you visited me pretty frequently, most of them were wide awake dreams but they were very vivid. I had a horrid one this afternoon when I took a nap, I won't tell you what it was though because you wouldn't like it.

"Mary and I washed our hair today. You should see us now. You'd certainly appreciate the vision. Mary got into a little rough house which resulted rather fatally for her because her hair came down and is now in 'charming dishevelment' a la George Barr McCutcheon's heroines in a railroad wreck! Mine is little better but it did manage to stay up to the end of the fray. Never again! A little of my last night's mood seemed to remain tonight because well, I've been on a disgraceful tear but I'll say this much it might have been much, much worse.

"In the gray hours before the dawn Billy I thought about you so intensely that it seemed as if you must know and come. But of course, it wasn't possible for you to know and yet I felt as if it might be as if no distance could really make any difference. I do not mind the days' dear heart, I am living them as best I can trying to get as much out of them without your being here as is possible but the nights, oh dearest, it is then that living seems unbearable, that doubts and fears crowd into my brain and make me a coward. You who say you love me, can you understand?

Tuesday night – Early

"I'd give anything in the world to have my mother take me in her arms tonight. I know I mustn't let myself get this way, but well I am deep down in the depths and the waters are way over my head. Perhaps it's because I've read too much Tennyson lately, not his hopeful poems, but the others. There hasn't been anything today to make it worth remembering except that I burnt my foot. That is constantly reminding me that I'm very much alive. Not much of a burn, about an inch square, but it hurts like everything. Please don't sympathize. I've been sympathizing with myself too much as it is and it hasn't done me the least bit of good." Elsie missed her mother although she didn't miss her lessons on life.

"The lumber mills were busy all day but the Penn State forestry students had the advantage of their vacancy at night, "The 'foresters' have to work all night at the mill, poor lads, measuring boards from seven p.m. until six a.m. with just an hour off at midnight for dinner. Consequently, we are deserted. I'm glad because I simply couldn't be decent tonight, or else I'd do something for which I'd be eternally sorry. I'm going to bed early, it's just about nine thirty now. I guess and see if tomorrow won't be as perfectly beautiful day! I shall think about you until I fall asleep but thinking about you dear only makes it worse. Oh, dearest, you have given too much to me who can never fully repay you. Goodnight!

"Much later…you see, I didn't go to bed after all and I'm glad because, well things are better already. I just finished writing to Mrs. Krichbaum, the letter wasn't much but I hope she'll understand that I meant to say a lot of nice things. In a few days, you will be in Japan. It's a shame that it's not cherry blossom time because you will certainly miss a lot. Perhaps the wisteria will be blooming though, and that will in a measure make up for the other. Mary is reduced to reading the Wooster 1912 index. It certainly is high time I was taking her up to bed, besides its late enough for us to go anyway and still keep our reputations as being 'night owls' of the first class. Helen in her last letter assured me that I could sleep all I wanted to after I came up there. Fancy sleeping at Lake George. Why I intend to be on the move every minute I'm up there, if I'm up there. You know, I couldn't very well tell Helen that I was quite sure I couldn't come because well, I thought perhaps I might be able to and then after I'd said 'no' absolutely I wouldn't have the face to just saunter in on her. However, I'm not at all sure that I'll get there, I'm hoping but there are so many things planned ahead now that I'm awfully afraid I'll never make it. Next week Mary and I are going to Corry to the races." Corry was a city outside of Erie and had horse and sulky racing at the Fairgrounds during the summer months. "We'll probably be there four or five days. Then the house party up at Tionesta begins." Tionesta is the largest city close to Endeavor with a business district and large lovely homes on the Allegheny River. "Really, I have a big notion not to go to that at all, only Mary would think I was backing out for certain reasons which you might guess but probably won't! You see we'll be up there most likely for ten days; the middle of August and neither my uncle nor Old Point Comfort will have been visited. I came within an ace today of packing up and going to Lake George but wouldn't Helen have been glad to see a person in my state of mind though! She wouldn't have known what to make of it, and certainly would have been disappointed to find me a perfect grouch instead of a sunbeam. Goodnight again and forgive my little deep blue moment please, it is buried now, deep down out of sight and will soon be lost in the flood of golden thoughts which must come when I think of you."

Wednesday afternoon

"A nice rainy day, so Laura, Mary and I are going to make calls on the first families of Endeavor; namely the Wheelers, Wardens and Scherer's. None of us care particularly about paying our respects but it seems the most propetous[*sic*] time to do so, and we owe the calls of course and do so want to be perfect ladies! Blix wrote me a twenty-page telling me all about the gay life in Canton, but her letter was not quite all sunshine because her mother is much worse. Her whole arm is infected now and has been cut in several places. Blix says there seems to be no end in sight at all and they are all pretty discouraged.

A letter from Hazel also came trailing in today in which she told me (in confidence) that she had broken off her engagement with Satan. She mentioned having received your letter full of its pleading for Satan's cause and asked me to thank you for it. She'll write to you herself, of course, as you probably gave her all your addresses. When I write to her she shall hear a few things stated pretty plainly and no mistake! Poor Satan, if he had only been a little more of a brute and not so much of an angel he could have kept her and she would have been perfectly content. But no, he must humor her every mood, give way to her every whim, so what can be expected from a girl who is spiritually nothing but a capricious child! Hazel doesn't know herself that her heart stopped growing years ago. Perhaps I'm altogether wrong in my judgment, but it seems as if her actions have shown that I'm not altogether. What would she say I wonder, if she could hear an infant like myself talking this way! Most likely she simply would smile a smile of superior wisdom and let me rave on. Now really it wasn't my intention to write all this to you, but then whom am I to write it to? Even if you're not at all interested, you will be polite enough to listen, of course, and not yawn in my face.

"Mary says not to forget to remind you of her pink kimono, pink or lavender, it matters not, she says. Sometimes I think I would rather have a pink one myself; but no, I guess I still lean a little more toward the yellow one. Slippers? Really, I don't know whether they go with kimonos out there or not. Suit yourself. I just love to patter around in my bare feet I guess I got the habit of doing that because my aunt always used to send me prickly little knitted slippers every Christmas. Beautiful to look upon, but too wooly to be comfortable. I scorned to wear them and now nothing but satin or silk will do, you know! This must catch the stage. I'm going to send you half a journal at a time now, a whole one I'm afraid is too much for you.

"Oh, I want a letter from you so. Will it be a whole month yet before I receive one? Of course, and perhaps longer! Mary gets a letter every day just like I used to and when I see her opening her mail, even if I get a half a dozen from my friends, I'm jealous, terribly jealous, because my dearest friend hasn't written to me; I know he can't, but still I long to hear from him so much that I grow unreasonably jealous of those who are fortunate enough to hear from those who love them. Give my love to your mother and father, and for yourself, take whatever you will, it is all yours."

Elsie is staying in a room at the Acme Milling Company at 236-242 Washington Street, Corry, Pennsylvania and writes to Billy on July 31. It is a Wednesday afternoon, early and her mind was on past events, "Several things have happened since last Saturday afternoon which you might be interested in hearing about. Saturday night the dance came off and was a great success. After the affair was over six of us adjourned to Gladys' (she lives in the apartments over Mr. Wheeler's office) and had another little party of our own. It came very nearly being a slumber party for everybody; Mary and I were going to spend the night anyway. However, the boys finally did go home, but of course we sat up and talked until very nearly day break. It was hard to get up and go to church but I'd promised myself that I would, so I managed with a great exertion of will power to drag myself out of bed, dress, trail down to McKean's, get on something suitable for church and trail back again. Jerry (Groves) also kept his promise and went to church too. We expressed our mutual surprise at seeing each other up so early in the morning!

"Sunday afternoon there was a 'gathering' and in the evening eight of us went to Gladys' for dinner. As the boys had to be back up at Corry by seven on Monday. This was, of course, to be the last little party at which this particular crowd would be present. Everybody seemed to realize this and did their best to make it a night to be remembered. I must tell you of an awful 'break' I made; Mary just screamed when she saw the point, but Jerry got in first. This Jerry, 'Elsie how are you going to treat me tonight?' Elsie, 'Well Jerry, dear, since it's the last night, I'll treat you white!' Could it have been worse, Billy? We are invited to go up to Camp Seven someday next week, nothing very definite has been planned as yet, but we know that we'll have a good time Monday night we struck this town."

"There was nothing very much doing Monday night. Mr. Merrick and Mr. Bracken had been down at Oil City all day and didn't get back until nearly nine, but we managed to take a car ride and some refreshments before morning. Last night (rained in afternoon, nothing much doing at the races) we took in the moving picture shows, went to Baeders for lunch and then took a short machine ride in the rain just to get up a little excitement. We didn't get home until pretty late and it was much later when we finally went to bed, consequently, we had breakfast and lunch in one when we got up. I wrote to you Monday but dear, the letter isn't fit to send. It's not a nice letter at all so I'll just tear it up and save you a great many unpleasant thoughts.

"Mary has been telling me in no very gentle tones that I won't be ready to go to the races if I don't stop this and get dressed.

So, I guess you'll have to excuse the shortness of this scrawl but there really isn't anything else to say anyway. If we made a fortune I shall take the next steamer to China and you can find me anytime you care to call at the old homestead in Fati, Canton. In the meantime, however, I am always, as ever."

It was August 5 when she wrote again, "Two letters came from you Sunday before I was up. Mary forwarded them to me in Corry and I was certainly glad to get them. The more so perhaps because I had forgotten about the possibility of receiving any mail from Honolulu and therefore did not expect to hear from you until the last of this month at the earliest.

"I'm proud of you for eating three meals a day during the voyage. Truly remarkable! But I'm horribly jealous of any of the lucky…serving people who have heard you sing, those 'old songs' which I never could manage to make you sing for me unless I used force. Someday young man, but threats sound quite foolish at this distance don't they? Therefore, we shall refrain from saying anything terrifying.

"Oh Billy, we are going to procure the most beautiful picture someday. I've quite made up my mind that we must have it. At least I must, so I do hope you'll like it too. It's one of Burne-Jones, you know his style, and one of his best I should say, *In the Depths of the Sea* is the name of this masterpiece. Have you ever seen it? If not, you've something really worthwhile to live for and if you have; of course, you couldn't forget it.

"Monday noon found me back in Endeavor again, so tired that I scarcely knew which way to turn. As soon as possible I went to bed to snatch a few hours before time to dress for the hay ride, the form of entertainment which the boys had arranged for the evening. Three of them came in for supper and as I wasn't up yet Jerry was commissioned to wake me, and he did. I was sleepy and cross so he got several choice names thrown at his curly head when I was aroused enough to talk! The boys took turns baking waffles for us and themselves; we had quite a time keeping them busy and out of mischief. After supper, we went to the ball game and after that was over started on our ride out to the Eddy. Only we went to West Hickory first and then over toward the picnic grounds. Do you remember last year Billy that night two men offered us their canoe and how we took it and paddled up the river in the moonlight? Well, one of those same young men, Bill is his name by the way, happened to be camping at the same place this year and last night the crowd was introduced, all that didn't know him already that is, and I discovered after the introduction that he was the poor chap that fell over the lantern. We didn't get home until very late and all the way home several of us simply had the worst sort of a rough house. There are some people I wouldn't think of rough housing with; but Jerry, well he's different.

"I guess none of the 'bunch' got up before noon today yet none of them look particularly pert for all that. Mary swears that I look as if I hadn't slept for a week but then she can't see herself or she wouldn't say a word. If you were here I'm quite sure you would never guess for a moment, I mean think for a moment that I was the least bit sleepy. Oh, I'm not dear no, and as I haven't got an engagement tonight I'll just prove it by going to bed in about twenty minutes.

"Next week I expect I'll strike Philadelphia. What a time I'll have making up with all my aunts and uncles. It will take a great deal of energy and soothing syrup and taffy and sugar coated pills and a whole bag of other sweet sticky things to win them back. Behold, I will arise and go to my relatives and say unto them, "Pray, slay the fatted calf which hath been fattening all these years 'gainst my return and for mike's sake don't keep me waiting! Then there will be a great clatter and cackling a mighty bristle of preparation and I shall find myself not robed in the festal garment of purple and seated at the groaning board but sprawled figuratively, of course, in the middle of the broad highway with naught save a peasecod in my hand! Please excuse this driveling nonsense because dearest it's the very best I can do tonight. Allegro! It shall always be, not Doloroso or even Largo. I am ashamed of my letters of what I write and of what I leave unwritten. Do you know, I wonder how much I love you?

Wednesday Afternoon

"The sky is a very beautiful blue today and the hills are quite the approved of green for a romantic setting; doubtless on such a day the whole world is happy. I received a letter today a rather unpleasant one to say the least which cut a little but as it wasn't intended to be any Balm-of-Gilead kind of communication. I must admit that it admirably fulfilled its purpose. Dear, I wish I could tell you some things you are that only a person might possibly tell them to and I couldn't even to you. Ali, truly this is a most beautiful world!

"Tonight, we are having company for supper the two Betas and Peter Bill Hiles who is a mighty nice sort of a chap. The more excitement the better. Last night several of the 'bunch' descended upon this place about 9:30 p.m. but I'd gone up stairs to bed and really couldn't think of coming down again. Crazy Peter Bill insisted that I should array myself in his mackinaw (a heavy dense water repellant woolen cloth used to make a short coat) and come down. But he really would not have wanted me to stay if I had suddenly appeared on the scene, I'm quite sure of that."

She starts a letter on August 21, continues writing on and off for three days before mailing it to Billy, "This is my usual time for beginning a letter to you and I never felt more like writing in my life. We've finished now midnight breakfast and the other

233

members of the party are scuttling off to bed—so I'll have you all to myself for as long a time as I want.

Mary thinks she is getting a colony of germs located in her somewhere, at any rate the creatures are making an awful fuss about settling down and consequently Redhead McKean feels pretty sick just at present. Well, it's her turn, but then we all sympathize just the same. She has been making the prettiest dress for Helen Moore's wedding, she's going to be a bridesmaid. It certainly is a dream and when finished will look something like this! You'd be quite crazy about it I'm sure. How absurd it seems to describe a dress to a man, but you do notice clothes, don't you, more than most people, and therefore should be interested in a perfectly good 'bon ton' creation.

"Billy, what wouldn't I give to have you here with me! Two more months before we shall see one another, it seems very long dear, when one counts the days!

"I certainly should like to see Mrs. Waterhouse, that was the name, I think of the attractive woman you said reminded you of what I may be some day. I didn't tell you, did I, that Mr. Kuschke reminded me so often of you, only he couldn't keep a tune, not even give you a hint of what a tune might be; only he had big, dreamy eyes, etc., but nevertheless, even with such drawbacks, he succeeded in impressing both Mary and me, that he was rather like you in a lot of ways…I'm quite sure now that I'll not get up to Lake George this summer, but next summer you know we are going to have a very beautiful little house party up there, aren't we? Oh! You hadn't decided about that? Well, there is plenty of time left yet to make your decision correspond with the one already made. Well I guess I'll do a little more embroidery before I go to bed. It's quite necessary that I get dead tired before I go because otherwise I won't sleep. Mary lectures me now instead of you or Peggy, and it does almost as much good! Sweet dreams to you."

A few days later, "I'm quite weak from laughing—and feel as if I'll laugh again in a minute and get still weaker. Mary and Gladys blame it all on me, this awful 'silly streak', but you know, don't you, that I never was silly in my whole life! You would have been amused though if you'd seen this giggling crowd attempt to eat lunch at 12:00 with decorum. One after the other they rushed away from the table to smother their confusion in a fine linen napkin. Really, it's a mercy that we are going to break my bachelor quarters Sunday and return to a more sensible even if not more exciting, mode of living. This has been great fun though, and none of us would have missed it for worlds. We shall 'suffer' for it in days to come, however, so saith the village gossips.

"It surprises me that Mary hasn't thrown me out long ago but she still tries to make me believe that I'm to stay all summer and as I've stopped to argue the point with her, I'm afraid she's almost right. This is just the right kind of a place in which to 'rest up' and you notice that we are taking advantage of all the opportunities offered. I wonder if you have had the nerve to carry out your threat about a mustache? It just occurred to me that in all probability you would spring something like that on the poor bewildered Orientals and fancy that you'd done something mightily clever! Have I misjudged you again? What a horrible mistake to make on a moonlight night, too…You just ought to hear this old mill buzzing away if you wanted something to sooth your nerves. I believe I hear its screeching saws in my dreams now. There may be music in them. 'The Song of the Saws' is beautifully illiterative[*sic*] at any rate, but to me their noise is nerve wracking.

"We were asked to go canoeing this evening, but of course, it would rain even with the moon turned on full blast in the sky, so Mary and I had to stay on the unromantic dry land. Tomorrow night there is to be a corn roast. Mr. Paterfield is to show me a good time, he is not a willing slave of mine at all, though, but has been quite enthusiastic about George Warden's sister. However, we shall have a good time just the same because both of us can get along with almost anybody that's not 'impossible'. Mary tried her hand at staying up half the night last night so she's all in now. I was awake until after 3 a.m. but she made it until 4:15 and at present holds the laurels. I was going to pull out of here to-morrow but Mary seemed to think it was outrageous and finally she made me promise to impose on the McKean's another week. Uncle Howard, you see, will get a little longer vacation for when I arrive his troubles will begin.

CHAPTER 11

The White's Travel to China

After a delay, the White's left San Francisco aboard the S.S. Tenyo Maru and arrived in Honolulu on July 18, 1912 on their way to Japan and China. Dr. White had been to China before, but this was their first trip to Japan as a family. Dr. and Mrs. W. W. White, along with his assistant, Miss Carolyn L. Palmer, were destined to Karuizawa for meetings with missionaries and their families from China and Korea. Karuizawa was a beautiful summer resort, 3200 feet above sea level, in sight of the active volcano Asama, 14 miles away. The agenda focused on classroom and speaking work in seventeen days and many interviews with individuals and groups from all denominations. The hopeful outcome was consideration of a Union Bible School on the lines that Dr. White proved to be effective in America. Billy, however, would assist his father with any request as needed. His focus, however, was on traveling down to Canton, China to meet Dr. and Mrs. Machle and ask Elsie's father to come back to America for their wedding, yet by the time they arrived back in America, life became complicated. Billy had corresponded previously with Jean and Edward Machle when he asked to marry Elsie. Months earlier, Elsie had a letter from her father outlining his plans for their future and encloses it in her letter to Billy, "the easiest way is to quote excerpts" from her father, 'I had a plan of having you come out to Japan this next summer where we expect to be and then go with us to Canton and stay until your other half wants you, but those I've consulted say that this country in its present condition is not a place for a young lady.' This plan of dad's would have been very nice wouldn't it and would have come at just the right time…the fates are against me…they have made plans for your welfare also…'if Wilbert would take up Y.M.C.A. work in Canton, it would be fine. We requested the Board last year to send such a man…I hope Wilbert will make application for the position and then prepare himself for it' (what a knock that last is, isn't it?) You can take up work in Y.W.C.A. and both of you groom these lines of work in China. Let me hear from you in regard to this matter.' Knowing how sick and tired you are of having people make suggestions as to what your 'Life Work' (Elsie capitalized this for emphasis) shall be…I thought you would find this last excerpt particularly entertaining and refreshing. Of course, dad never thought you'd hear about this excerpt, of course. He probably expected me to make the suggestion to you, never thinking for a moment that I might be endangering my precious, young life by so doing!"

Once again Billy's response to the suggestion added more hesitation to his career path, "It was mighty good of your father to think of me in connection with that Canton Y.M.C.A. position. There certainly are peculiar circumstances flying around you and me, aren't there? China seems to figure pretty prominently in those circumstances in every way. I know dear that you want to go back to China, and you know that I want to do what you wish. But that is about as far as the taugh[*sic*] will come apart. Indefinite again, I'm disgusted with myself." However, plans were being made to make the trip and he included some of the preplanning, "For father seems to think that it may be best for me to stay in New York and catch hold of some of the ropes during the summer, and I am under his orders to a certain extent after college closes. I wrote him a long letter yesterday, and will no doubt get an answer soon about it all. He is coming out into this vicinity again in a week...and we are going to get together." Up to now, Billy and Elsie seemed to be independent minded, an impression reflected by their impulsive actions, but when it comes down to it, both of them are dependent on their father's approval. Doubt arises when Elsie desires to return to China, and Billy is unable to decide what he wants to do with his life. In many ways, it is easier for him to give in to his father's plan that someday he may take over the administration of the school. At this point in their relationship, all Elsie can do is wait.

The White's arrive in Karuizawa on August 4, and Billy is able to catch up on his letter writing, "How hard it has been for the past month that I have had no word from you...father is turning more and more of his less important stuff over to me and consequently, even though it really shouldn't be very hard, it keeps my little brain humping to get it all in on scheduled time. I have just finished a rather exhaustive letter to your father...exhaustive I am afraid at more than one end of the line. He simply has got to come home this fall. I can't wait for you any longer dear. I love you, I trust you, and I want you for my wife just as soon as possible. Poor dad is tired to death, he has been having classes and conferences with people all day." Christian leaders came from all over Europe to attend the meetings. At the closing meeting, Dr. John L. Dearing, of the Baptist Mission and Chairman of the Committee spoke. Other speakers present were Dr. Sidney Gulick who promoted the possibility of the Union School with deliberation and prayer about the appointment of a strong committee which could be reported back to the Assembly. This proposal emulated the one in Kuling, China, where the movement started. "I hope that tomorrow won't be as strenuous...it seems like an age since we came to this joint, and it isn't a week yet, and we don't leave for two weeks." As important as this trip was to Dr. White in the development of a school in Japan, Billy seems bored with the meetings and his lack of interest in their content. "Two months more and we will be nearing San Francisco and home and you...I'm going to write your father again soon. The letter I wrote him was a masterpiece, I wish I had saved a copy of it. I never showed you the first one I wrote to him did I, the one in which I made the great request I've still got about the eleventh edition of that one put away somewhere among my sacred things. I showed you the first one I wrote to you. Someday, I'll show you that other one. I think that one of the reasons why your father gave his consent so readily was because that letter I wrote to him was so short. You will be surprised when you see it....no use in trying to write a whole lot of words about how much I loved you, and give him my full pedigree, and a whole lot of other things. I made it short and to the point."

There were dinners, luncheons and breakfasts to attend. His father gave him a stack of letters with instructions to reply as indicated. This was one assignment he didn't like as well as the social expectations, "The old students in the Bible School decided to have a banquet. There are about 30 of them up here, and 24 were present at the thing...we sat down at seven and arose at 15 minutes to eleven. I'd been sitting between a Miss Armstrong who has 'been in the field' some twenty-one years and a Mrs. Curtis who was almost as good...One of the missionary ladies was telling the other day of once when a congregation was singing *Work for the Night is Coming,* one of the Japanese women turned to her and said 'what is the use of hurrying anyway?' and that is the way they all seem to take it...poor old dad works his head off all the time, and I, well, I'm not very much of a help at any time and most of the time I fear that I am pretty much of a hindrance. Oh

Elsie, dear heart, I wish that you were here. You can do so much for me, even the thought of you trusting me and believing in me makes me feel that there must be something in me that may be worth something someday...father said this afternoon that if nothing else came up we could leave on Saturday...if anybody should ask me again to take this trip without you, no matter who or what he was, I'd be tempted to tell him to go to the devil, I surely would not think about it for a minute."

His vision of the Far East was confronted with reality as he describes to Elsie how things have changed, "the lure of that 'somewhere, east of Suez' doesn't call me nearly so much now as it did at one time. I think that you will find the place people and the entire countenance of the landscape changed from what you remember it to be...this country is no place for weaklings, I mean morally rather than physically...Elsie dear heart you don't know what a poor weak fool you are marrying...I've crawled down into my own little private shell and been as darned ashamed of myself for letting you think the things you do about me, when I know I don't deserve them, but sweetheart I'm trying every day to make myself more worthy of your love, to live a little more like that man lived whose name you give to me sometimes. Trust me dearest one, as I live I shall someday make you happy."

Billy's family left Karuizawa and arrived in Nikko for two days, before traveling to Seoul, Korea for ten days, and heading to Nanking, China, "Nikko is the religious center of Buddhism and Shintoism...there are a whole lot of temples in the city for people to see. We rested over Sunday, did nothing much more than sleep and eat. On Monday, mother, Miss Palmer, myself, and a native by the name of *Komona*, who was acting as our guide while we were there, went up over the mountains in rickshaws to Lake Chuzenji. It was a mighty interesting trip...and the riding in those little two wheeled, bumpy affairs got rather tiresome. We took some pictures along the road. Three weeks from yesterday we sail from Shanghai. On Tuesday, we started to see the temples and sights of Nikko, and they certainly were interesting…especially the taking pictures inside the gates which is strictly forbidden. I wielded the Kodak and we managed to get about a dozen pretty good photographs of the intentional workings. One of them was of one of the dancing women who does religious dances for the pilgrims…we got here to Seoul on Friday…the worst trip of any kind I have ever taken….soot, dirt, all the insects of the Orient, and the train moving along at the rate of about twenty miles an hour…we crossed over to Korea in a little dinky steamer…father and I stayed on deck most of the night…all day Friday on the train from Fusau to Seoul…I didn't realize that I was so homesick until I saw…Lera Avison… on the platform." Elsie knew Lera from Wooster. Lera was also a "mishkid" and a member of Quadrangle Club, "I guess that I must have appeared just about the same to her, not because it was me, but because I was from Wooster, and had seen Joe lately and could tell her a little bit about the things as they happened there lately…yesterday afternoon I went over and she fired questions at me for about five hours till dinner time. Poor kid she is literally starved for the sight of someone who can understand how she feels being way out here…we had a little sing after dinner…Wooster and Beta songs until we both felt that we couldn't sing." Billy was homesick, but he couldn't get over the feeling of trepidation when there were fewer letters arriving from Elsie. He would start to write, then tear them up unfinished, wondering through his despair about their relationship, "You seemed so very, very far away and well, I wondered for a while whether I had succeeded in making you love me…I had only gotten two letters since I left Wooster." Several days later, he feels obligated to explain his mood swings, "Forgive me if I seem a little bit grouchy in this letter...I have nobody to jump on and cussed out for not doing the right things...these letters from Seoul will be mighty interesting...the main topic of interest is tabooed from all letters...I've been spending a good bit of the time out here with Lera. Most of the time I've not been working...she is from Wooster and she knows you and understands what it means to be out here away from the person she loves most in the world and it is mighty nice to see her again...last night we cut a meeting... Lera and I, and a Mr. Widenward and Miss Brownlee, and went away out to the edge of town and beyond to the Queen's tomb. We went in rickshaws and didn't get back until after midnight... we had a mighty good time. Our bunch go over to Avison's to dinner this evening. I'm going over early so that Lera and I can write a letter apiece to you and Joe. We leave Seoul for Shanghai next Monday, then sail for home on the next Saturday...in less than two months I will be holding you in my arms...these days and months have seemed as long."

On the boat from Dairen to Shanghai in early September, he shares his previous day's experience, "I thought that I would have some time in Dairen to get a letter back across Siberia, but the boat sailed about four hours sooner than we had thought... last night on the train, I got to talking with a man whose name was Castle, an army officer, and he turned out to be a Beta from Ohio State University. He had been doing college duty in Grove City College for the last four years and knows Professor Kelso. Isn't it funny how we run into people in all parts of the world who know us or people we know. He is the first man who has been at all complimentary about my dignified appearance since we started on this trip. I told him that I had been in Wooster this past year." He thought Billy was an instructor, imagine that. "Last night when we were waiting in Mukdun and the Siberian Express pulled out, it was all I could do truly to keep from getting on and going home to you…I haven't heard from your father yet, I was hoping to get a letter…you are just about getting the letters I wrote from Yokohama and the first ones from Karuizawa. My, but I'd like to get a letter from you…I don't know when you will get this one…I wonder where you will be when I land. How about coming out to Wooster for a few days about the 10th of October?" The following Wednesday he wrote, "We are now on the Manchurian Express enroute to Dairen where we get the boat for Shanghai. We have only ten more days in his land. All of our mail has been examined and if there was anything that looked at all suspicious, the whole business was confiscated. It has been on account of this so-called Korean Conspiracy to kill the governor-general. I spoke this morning in the boy's school at Sen Sen where this conspiracy was supposed to have been started. It was my first attempt at public speaking, and of course, had to be done with an interpreter. It certainly was an experience for me. It was simply a chapel talk. I wrote to San Francisco yesterday engaging berths on the Overland Limited for Chicago, it makes it seem like we were getting a little nearer home. Don't forget that you are not to make any scenes by trying to keep me from kissing you when I see you, no matter where, I won't be able to wait."

"Sweetheart, I never wrote that word to you before, something new, I can't find any nice enough ones any more. I'm thinking of going into the manufacturing business myself and turn out some really quadruple, sugar coated names for you, not syrupy, just real, real sweet, the kind that you could take plenty of without winning your mental digestion…I can scarcely wait until I see you…and I just have to, you know…perhaps it will only be one week, Crazy Boy, until I'll have you to amuse me. Have you got a good store of witty things to spring on me. I insist on your having several fresh, cool jokes ready to serve up at a minute's notice." She didn't finish the letter, but wrote, "Dear, I'm not even as successful as you are when you have the blues in trying to look cheerful. Uncle Frank asked me the other night...if you had done anything to make me look so sad. I told him it was all imagination on his part, me look sad, you couldn't conceive of such a thing could you, just because I'm not one big, blooming sozodout[*sic*] advertisement, he fancied he saw traces of sorrow on my damask cheek, these same sentiments I conveyed to him with force and emphasis. He remarked he was glad to know everything was all right because if you had been responsible, he swore he'd take me away from you...if it could be accomplished, but it would take all the king's horses and all the king's men to say nothing of uncles, to drag me off. I doubt if it could be accomplished gracefully, and without bloodshed.

"The other night I had another crazy dream, not half as nice as my Broadway one, I was leading lady in some grand show, but you didn't seem to mind letting him make love to me a bit. Everything in the play was just getting to a lovely climax, I had just thrown myself into the leading man's arms and was preparing to make the speech of the evening when you, a supe[*sic*] you were, I'd never even noticed you before, came and spoiled everything. Oh, dear, I forgot my lines. The house rose in a rage of disappointment—grew nasty before my eyes, then melted out of sight, then you stopped and I awoke."

Finally, confirmation came from Billy that he met Elsie's father in Hong Kong. While his parents and Miss Palmer sailed from Shanghai, hoping to reach New York before the middle of October, "I saw the China division of the Machle family off on the train for Canton at about three," on September 14. "They had come down on Thursday to meet me and so we had almost two days together there. I was mighty sorry not to be able to get up to Canton but there was no possible way of doing it and of still catching this ship, so we had to content ourselves with a frightfully hot day in HgKg. We sailed last night at 6 o'clock…I just now got your letter so you haven't heard anything yet of my trip to Hong Kong to see my future father-in-law? Well, I was there and that was why I missed the boat. But I can't begin to think logically so I'll keep it to tell you."

Since letters often crossed paths, Billy didn't receive the letter telling him Elsie left Endeavor and arrived at her Uncle Howard Wood's home in Philadelphia. When he finally received Elsie's letters they sounded jubilant, "Billie Boy…I wish you would come and take a walk with me out into Eden Park…we could sit under an accommodating tree and read *Amar* or from the little divine sonnets of our friend, Elizabeth Barrett. As you won't come, I'll just stay at home and chat with you instead…I needed to go to church today…the old man who preached seemed to have such faith in everything that his sermon was quite convincing to a hardened sinner like myself. How amusing you can be dear. Do you look 'easy'? Of course not, but you do look perfectly kind and adorable and a dozen other things that are nice, so no wonder people want to ask you to do things for them! You know what I used to think, well maybe I never did tell you after all, but you know quite well now what an immense admiration society I have worked myself into all about you, Crazy Boy."

Billy was writing to Elsie from the Great Northern Hotel in Chicago. Elsie was now located in Haddon Heights, but he didn't know where she had gone. He wired Mary McKean to find out where she was and waited two days for an answer before pledging to head to Haddon Heights to see her. As excited as he was to see Elsie again, he had to stop in Wooster to pick up his belongings in the fraternity house and 'fix up my diploma tangle.' One can only imagine what that meant after he flunked chemistry and history. Was there still outstanding work to be done? His plan was to get to Wooster on Thursday night, then go to Philly and, "one thing is certain though, I'm coming through as fast as I can."

It was only six months earlier that Helen took a trip to Japan, via Honolulu. Everything appeared normal, but shortly after arriving home, Billy's sister, Helen had an undisclosed illness. On October 12, Elsie wrote a letter saying how disappointed she was because no letter came from him. Then, "the mystery was solved. Your letter had wandered joyously over New Jersey in search of a fair spot in which to rest, a la'Noah's dove of peace, and might be wandering yet, I suppose, if it were." But life for Billy had become more complicated because of Helen's illness and would shed some light on why their marriage plans changed.

"A letter came from Helen written by your father's secretary telling me why she hadn't written to me, I'm going to write to her just as soon as I finish this to you. I'm so sorry Billy that she's sick, you know that anyone who is dear to you, well, I know you understand without my saying; after all, I am really thinking of how you must feel, because I love you. Dear, I realize it more and more every day, how much you mean to me. Perhaps I do not show you always how much I do love you, but you must know that I do. You blame me so often for not telling you things; it has been a little hard for me in these last six months to have anything to tell which you would care to hear. There is not a secret of my heart that I would not gladly tell you; there is nothing that has ever influenced my life in any way that I could not tell you, looking straight into your eyes, no matter how hard it would be to do it. I'm not half the coward I was before your love came to strengthen me, to be with you, I would give anything I possess. Oh dearest, if you only knew…you were surprised to find that I hadn't telephoned to Aunt Bessie, well, I did telephone but could get no answer. Aunt Bessie told me afterwards that she had been out for about half an hour so that explains it. It's too early to go to bed but I'm afraid I'm doomed to go when the rest do. I'd like to stay up half the night in front of the fire and dream, and dream. That's all I've been doing all my life though, so it's high time I was waking up. Be good to yourself and write to me often, please if you can without taking too much time from more important things and believe me to be yours, always yours."

Helen was in a hospital at Garden City. His father took Helen to Long Island and stayed with her. The rest of the family visited as they could, while Billy became responsible for more duties at the school, "I've been downtown doing some stuff for Helen this morning and now have about twenty minutes before lunch."

Elsie had been writing to Helen, "I'm sure I'm going to love Helen, Billy; I wonder if she'll like me. It would be pretty hard on her if she didn't, you know, to have me staying around there for a month." At one point in their correspondence Helen invited Elsie to come up to the lake. "Helen hasn't answered the letter I wrote about two weeks ago and I'm anxious to hear from her. I'm almost sure that I shall not be able to go up there this summer at all, but then you wanted to show me Lake George yourself, you remember, and I would like to have you. When Helen goes back to New York, I'll walk in on her someday, if she asks me to."

Billy is concerned about his sister's condition, "I got home too late, of course, to see Helen before they left, but mother says it is pretty serious although she doesn't know yet what it is." A month later, "We just got in from Garden City where Helen and father are staying…Helen is quite a bit better. She can walk around a bit now if she hangs on to somebody. We, she and I, walked for almost an hour this afternoon through the most beautiful trees and walks. She is in such a state though that any little shock will put her clear off. Mother, Don, and I went out right after lunch and took dinner with them out there." By the 21st, Helen was back, but would be going to Montclair, New Jersey for several weeks. On October 24, Helen left New York for Montclair, "She couldn't make the bend today on account of the rain. She isn't sure yet how long she will have to stay away from the city; the doctors say a month or six weeks at the least, but she entertains some hopes of coming back soon."

Billy took Helen to Montclair one Thursday afternoon, "She is going to stay at the Jellerson's, maybe you have heard Marjorie speak of them. There are three girls in the family and she knows them all well...hope it fixes her up." By the end of the month, Mrs. White, "went out to Montclair to stay for the night...we haven't heard very much about how Helen is getting along except that one of my darn fool aunts went over...where she is staying, last Sunday, and entered into a violent dissertation on the darn foolishness of Helen's doctor's ideas on treating a case such as hers. Helen, of course, tried to defend Dr. Hale and this rested her brain cells so very much that she had to stay in bed the next day just to rest her body up a little so that her brain and body wouldn't get out of equilibrium. Another one of my aunts, bless her dear, loving, gentle hearts, wrote her and in the letter told her not only of the death of a very dear friend of hers, but what was the most thoughtful piece of all, of the very unhappy marriage of a man to whom Helen was engaged at one time, I don't mean of the marriage itself but of some nice juicy bits connected with his married life. And the worst of it is she still cares for him. I should like very much to take each one of my aunts...separately by the back of the neck...and cast them forth."

Billy goes out to Montclair in early November to meet some Wooster friends. By this time, Helen is improving as he describes, "I saw Helen for a few minutes just before dinner" at Jim Sander's house, "She seems to be getting along very nicely and I hope is going to get entirely well, although it is darn hard to know just how to get at her case."

249

The family crisis interfered with his plans to go to Philly to see Elsie. Billy was obligated to Helen and the family. Imagine the disappointment Elsie must have felt after all these months, with so few letters from Billy, now a family emergency postponing their meeting again and more time apart. Perhaps that was the hardest for Elsie. Being away from Billy for a long period of time and sensing some doubt. But, it was the waiting! And she would do a lot of that in the future.

CHAPTER 12

I'll Meet You in Arcady

The crisis with Helen's illness was past and they started to make plans for the wedding. It was early November and Elsie was staying with Aunt Elizabeth in Swarthmore while Billy was in New York. Their relationship was complex and planning a wedding with distance between them wasn't easy. Their love of the classics brought them together, but poetry brought them through their trials and tribulations. Elsie, who genuinely understood their differences, didn't always agree with Billy's cavalier attitude about life. Both of them loved Henry Bunner's poem, *The Way to Arcady*[5]. So, a dialogue developed using Arcady as a code word for their love conquering wisdom through the golden years ahead.

Billy wrote, "Arcady seems an awfully long way off just at present." Yet to them, Arcady was their symbol of love over adversity. "You and I were made for each other from the beginning. I know that I could never have loved another woman the way I love you, and I could never have believed in another woman's love the way I do in yours. I'm coming just as soon as I can to take you for myself and be myself for you." There were pitfalls along the way when he was confronted by his fraternity brothers with unpaid bills from the failed Minstrel Show fund raising stunt in the late spring, not to mention money he owed one of his college friends.

He was always trying to impress Elsie with his youthful creativity so it wasn't unusual for him to draw stick figure pictures with emphasized messages in capitals, "Come on over, The Call of the Wild". Sometimes he drew pictures of what their future home would look like with little comments added here and there. But with the upcoming presidential election, Elsie's desire to become active in the suffrage movement led her in another direction at the time when she was also planning her wedding. Although at the time she may not have seen herself as an activist, she was a supporter of Taft through her father's childhood connections with him, while having the type of personality which advocates for women's rights.

Elsie made a decision to leave Paulding and the teaching position and stay with her mother's family. She was in Swarthmore with her Aunt Elizabeth in early November when she received this letter from Billy, "I'm not going to write much tonight, for I'm tired and sleepy and blue, and I'm in no fit mood to talk to the dearest girl in all the world. Mother just got your special delivery a little while ago. I am mighty sorry that Aunt Bess is sick, hope that it isn't anything serious and that she will be over it soon…we were mightily disappointed that you couldn't come. I had a hunch all day that you would be here, and couldn't even give up hope after dinner, but answered the phone about two dozen times, each time with an extra little pull at my heart, in the hope that it would be a telegram summoning me to my reward… I have your last 'reluctant' offering here in front of me now, and oh Elsie it makes me jump, jump, jump around the heart. 'What can a fellow do?' Those triple quotation marks make me cuss. I'm all up in the air. I want so to see you, and be near you, and take you in my arms and kiss away whatever there is that is making you unhappy. It just makes me crazy to see you again. That doesn't mean that I haven't been, it is, well intensified…You don't know yet how I love you dear heart, it's way too much for me to be able to explain, all I know is that God is good to let me love you the way I do, and the way I shall always."

Elsie left Swarthmore and was in Haddon Heights at her Uncle Howard Wood's home, when she wrote, "It certainly seems a blue moon since I've seen you and it has been a rather blue half-moon in very truth, two weeks, nearly and two such hatefully long weeks too! I am reminded, now that I've really set out to write you a letter that I haven't told you anything for some time past...Sunday two couples came for dinner, also an extra young man, one of Bill's friends, and they all stayed until nearly church time. There was plenty to do, but Billy, your clever remark about my working myself to death was duly appreciated all right. Give me time, and you shall receive a cutting reply, no doubt. Wednesday was spent visiting my cousin who was married last spring to a Mr. White. You have a cordial invitation to come and see if you care to trace your relationship to them...Wanamaker's makes me realize more than any other store the inconvenience of being poor; it's a disagreeable feeling to endure unless one launches recklessly upon fried oysters and chicken salad.

"Today I went to see a great aunt of mine who is young, and ninety! It'd been twelve years since she'd seen me so she noticed some slight changes. The dear, old soul could scarcely believe her ears when I told her I was twenty-two. Why to her I was a child just yesterday. When she heard that I was going to marry you (you were not you to her, of course) she came up to me and drapped[*sic*] her hands upon my shoulders and looked up into my face with a sweet questioning look in her dimmed, blue eyes 'is he a good man?' she asked. I tried to make her understand without many words, and I know she did, for her kiss was almost a benediction.

"The letter Helen was supposed to receive in Garden City had the impertinence to come back to me. It's just as well because 'twould'[*sic*] have only made her worse to read such nonsense.

"By the way do not stop writing to me just because I have spared you the reading of a number of dank, drizzly, altogether foolish letters by not sending them. If no mail comes from you tomorrow I shall surely rave! Three days is more than I can stand to have my illustrated periodical delayed. Let me congratulate you on the stunning way in which you pictured our meeting. Last night when I was rereading some of your delightful manuscripts the picture supplements struck me with renewed force.

"If you would only come and just hold me in your arms for a while, I'd promise to make up some time before you became too tired and kiss you goodnight...Without a doubt I should have enjoyed reading June's remarks upon our latest plans. He is quite right about some people 'wondering', those special some have been expecting us to 'spring' something on them for the past year. Should they be disappointed?

"There seems nothing to say except what has been said until I hear from Mary, redhead. She must be thinking some thoughts about us just now.

"I'm not at all sure but that I'll let Thanksgiving pass without marrying you; it would really be easier to slip over to Endeavor about the tenth of December, instead. However, we will not argue that point just now for obvious reasons. Tomorrow I am going up to Swarthmore to see if I can lose my new hat some place. I hate it, hate it and simply refuse to think it's at all pretty, neither will anybody who sees it and my face together cause the latter will be sadly disfigured with anger, disgust and, wholesome loathing. Saturday I'll be back here again and more than likely with you. Please don't be too tired, when I come up, to talk a bit, because I'm not going to stay very long, two days or three at the most, so you see a great deal will have to be accomplished in that length of time.

"Perhaps there is another letter for me from you, at the post office. If there is, I'll write to you again tonight; if there isn't, of course, it will not be at all necessary to do more than send you all my love now."

Within a few days, Jean Machle dropped her a line, "I am posting your linen goods by this mail...one-half to E. Machle, and the other half to Mrs. W. W. White, Jr. (noting that Elsie and Billy were not married yet). We are waiting to hear if the wedding is truly to be on Thanksgiving Day. I hope you will get the goods safely and unharmed...I hope you will like them. They will be good for a life-time, and the embroiderers have done the work well. Only I'm so sorry they are late. We are well here, but your father's leg is very painful. I think he will go into the hospital during Christmas vacation and have some skin grafting done. With kindest regards to Mr. White and love to you from us both."

They often communicated by telephone about the plans but there was one thing missing. Not only her father's presence but the exclusion of the White family. Elsie was disappointed in her father. Perhaps she thought if he truly loved her, he'd come back for her wedding, but all that was based on her unresolved grief. Billy's family became a silent partner in their plans, perhaps because of Helen's illness or some unknown reason. It is imagined that Billy understood the reason and focused on Elsie's mood when he tried to sooth her, "Dear heart I do wish that you would tell me what in thunder it is, that has made you feel the way you have in the past week. Can't you let me know and feel the different ways you feel about things. It isn't merely curiosity you know that as well as I do. It isn't an altogether selfish idea of wishing to sooth my own heartache that I get at such times. It's because I think that it would make you happier if you did talk to someone, perhaps you do, about some things which you don't or won't or can't, talk to me about. The reason I think this, is because I feel that you too, know that you would be happier, and that you want to talk to me, as I want to talk to you, but you can't. And darn it all, I can't. What is there in me, or in us, that has made us be this way. Am I a fool in this respect about making confidants of each other, not only that but just telling things to each other? Tell me dear, are you coming up this week for over Sunday? If you are not, I'm coming down, for I can't stand it to be away from you much longer, and I'm not going to try to keep standing it. I want you and I'm going to have you. Tell me right away, will you, so I can plan to leave early. Of course, if Aunt Bess is sick and you are still in Swarthmore, I won't think of going to the house. There is some kind of a hotel there, I know. This is worse than being in China and not getting mail…nasty, forgive me, I love you so much. God, it hurts." Billy went to Philadelphia to see Elsie, where they planned their upcoming wedding, "I'm sore that we didn't meet where someone could see us. I had all my nerve up. However, it's up to stay. I must confess that this day is beginning to drag a little. I really am not tired though. This morning when I was coming through the Broad Street Station, I ran into Uncle Will and we talked. I think he was kind of peeved that we hadn't gone there to see the game, but I told him that I didn't get down till late.

"Monday seems to be kind of a slack day around here, and I think that I'll shut up shop and go look at some apartments for an hour or so. Don't forget dear heart that that wedding of ours is going to be on the 28th of this month. Don't think about anything else but that, I mean in the wedding line, and for Pete's sake, keep me informed as to the news of how the things are moving. Are you going to write to Peg and Clara? What do you think of my sending for Vic and Jack Loy? I know Jack would come, and he and Jim are the two fellows I'd rather have there from my friends. I want to have Vic there, too. Do you know I've never even written to him? It's a downright shame. Now for heaven's sake write me. I'll keep you posted...at this end."

Seventeen days from the wedding date, and they are still making plans. However, Elsie's mood is low when she hears from her father, "If only I had not yielded to an impulse to talk to you last night just because I wanted you to understand and comfort me a little, I would be a great deal happier today...Dear, my sarcastic remark about there being a letter from my father...proved not to be a bit of sarcasm after all. I guess he loves me a wee some bit after all, and I'm quite sure that I've been very, very foolish to feel the way I have for my short life time simply because he didn't have time to tell me he loved me only once or twice a year. But it hurt, I can't forget that, although I'm never going to let it hurt me anymore...If everything goes as I expect it to, I'll come up to New York Saturday or Monday. At any rate, it will be quite soon. Tonight, I'll write to Mary and the die will be cast. It makes my heart beat faster to think of the happiness which is really going to be ours so soon, then even it made my tears fall to think that it could never be ours. I am glad things have been as they were, except that I would have saved you all your heartaches if I could, for we have been brought closer to each other this way, haven't we... if some things had never happened. If I ever complain again against fate, just don't you pay any attention at all to my whimpering but bury your unsympathetic face behind a screaming Sunday newspaper supplement and smoke your pipe in silence. I won't deserve to be noticed at all if I haven't the sense to be perfectly happy with the dearest man in the world, so there!"

The next day Elsie received this letter, "I wish I knew for sure where you are at this moment and where you are going to be for an hour...but I'd send a telegram, I'm afraid that you wouldn't get it any sooner than you will this letter. I'm glad I didn't know the glad news last night…Now this bright, beautiful day seems infinitely more bright…since your letter came. I opened that letter with…trepidation for I wasn't…sure why the address on the envelope looked a trifle more excited than usual. We are so much closer together dear heart, than we ever could have been if we had been married without a single thing to make a few ruffles on the surface. Some of them went pretty deep truly but it won't be that way again…I am so glad that a letter from your father was there yesterday. I felt…sure that you would hear from him. I know that he loves you a whole lot more than you imagine."

"I wrote to Jumbo (Edward Chalfant) last night. I suppose that it might have been a little wiser if I had waited until you hear from Mary, but he is pledged to secrecy and won't even mention it to Mary until I tell him he can or until she mentions it to him. Just how far and who are we going to let know about this before it comes off. You know how things travel, and if we want people to think that it is more or less of a sudden decision at the time, why we have got to go kind of slow. Can't you come up sooner than Saturday? We ought to talk the whole thing through when we aren't clear, or rather almost, gone for a little sleep. When will you be going out to Endeavor, and when can I write to Mary? Those and thousands of other questions, I want to ask when I see you…don't wait until Monday to come up…I've got to go up to a meeting now, there wasn't enough gumption left in me yesterday to look for apartments, this afternoon, maybe." Their excitement is building as the time gets closer to November 28. "The time drags along in a most monotonously leisurely way until the next one meanders in. But it isn't going to be very much longer now that I will have to wait for letters. How queer it will seem and how perfect, to know that at the end of the day's work I can take you in my arms and be with you. Every day, I won't have to stick around and wonder what in thunderation I'm going to do to keep my mind off the fact that you are away off somewhere... I don't know what I've been saying in this letter...but you know dearest what I am trying to express." Mary's letter came, "Elsie is coming to Endeavor for Thanksgiving and I would be very glad if you could arrange to come at the same time. Endeavor is rather dull at this time of the year but perhaps we could manage a little excitement by ourselves. Jumbo will probably be here, and we can have a little Wooster reunion, which would certainly appeal to me...Let me know as soon as possible and I will order an extra turkey just to celebrate."

"Got a letter from Jumbo last night and he wanted to know if anything was certain yet. He talked foolishly of the crowds of people who would soon become nervous wrecks if we didn't break this suspense soon. Say, people are wondering aren't they, they have got to thank us for giving them something to help fill up the cavity in their top stories...It is pretty soon now darling, two weeks from tomorrow, for heaven's sake keep me posted, I can't write coherently anymore."

Jumbo's letter was sent on November 4, the day before the presidential election, from his home in Pittsburgh, "Hurrah for Roosevelt! Your good letter came several days ago, and I apologize for not answering sooner but my duties have been numerous and my energy lacking. Letters from Geo (George Hackett) and Ken (Johnson) arrived days ago and one from Satan (Gregg) this afternoon are the latest dope I have had. Satan is 'working' hard as usual though he did find time to come down to see Hazel at Cincinnati. Ken tells me that you and the Pennsylvania Railroad are having a great time between Philadelphia and New York but as yet nothing stirs, s'matter? How about that Thanksgiving stuff. Are we not to have something to be thankful for this year? Syl(vester Scovill) and I are still keeping Wooster in the lime light, and other lights. I suppose you noticed that Oberlin walloped Wooster 27-6 Saturday and also State beat Case 31-6. Syl and I took in the Notre Dame game against Pitt Saturday after which we both had exciting times. He got into a brutal fist fight with some friends (after I left, of course) and I almost got my 'konk' busted by a certain female's lover. You can get the particulars about her from my letter to her, she's the one Syl and I bet the quarter about. Syl surrendered his claim to the quarter without even trying while I have not accomplished anything yet, though I nearly got my head taken Saturday night. But enough of such ghoulish discourse. Syl was up for supper last night and we had a little session on the third floor looking over indexed, magazines and my scrapbook, smoking thousands of cigarettes and even drinking some of the medicinal whiskey in the house."

"Say by the way old knob don't forget that little bet you made on the train between the Union Station and East Liberty that Wilson would win 4-1 me taking two dollars and you paying eight. I am telling you this before the election so you can't crawl. Tomorrow I cast my ballot for Teddy like a loyal Moose, also have a job as clerk all day in our precinct here which means five dollars in my pocket and another ten extra votes for Roosevelt! Satan ended his letter with a violent plea that I vote for Taft 'Chal' he says, 'The country is going to its doom unless Taft is reelected so for – Kai vote for him'. He goes on to add 'any C.S. (I presume he means corkscrew) who could vote for Roosevelt might have his nuts cut off'. Notice he gives me credit for having two! But as we aren't rooming together this year this talk (about nuts) probably doesn't interest you as it used to (there's one that'll hold you).

"Say wouldn't you give a lot to be back in college again. If I have thought about it once I have ten thousand times. I have been back three times since commencement which is pretty good, but it isn't like the olden days. I'd be perfectly happy if I could be a freshman once more and flunk in the same old-fashioned way, only I wouldn't flunk this time, would you? Certainly, we would.

"Ken writes that they are having numerous 'tippling' bouts in their 'apartments'. I'll bet it's some apartment. If George hasn't got something keeping him warm these nights, I'm a liar. I hardly think he has because rubber is still expensive (quarter a piece, aren't they?) and he could buy a can of cube cut for that and it would last much longer unless he could get it done the way e wanted it now for nothing.

"I am still on the job here and the chances are that I will be for some time to come. It's about the toughest uphill fight I was ever mixed up in yet believe me I'm going to see it through. If my father can only keep his nerve and vitality up I think there is some chance but it seems that every time he begins to feel better some new complications turns up and spoils all the dope again. If it wasn't for the fact that Syl was here and I been around with him, I'd have gone crazy long ago. Gosh that fellow is a prince. Bill, I thought I knew him but I didn't. He hit the booze and the women but between you and me, there's only one person to blame for that and he is John K. Davis, damn him. I wrote Shepardson a letter dated from Wooster and Ralph signed it and sent it on but have not heard yet. You see Ralph wrote Brown and the latter said Syl would have to petition the National Convention and c. which is too much red tape. I hope Shep can suggest a remedy.

"Well, I must close. Give my very best to Elsie and tell her to quit holding the world in suspense and let us know the dope. Also, you wouldn't have to spend so much railroad fare. If you see Geo, Wil, Fritz, Ken, Packes or Ray, give them a hop in the ass and my best."

Elsie was shopping at Wanamaker's and by mid-November, "Surely you'll forgive me for not writing so long as my time was properly occupied. Mary will receive her letter tomorrow and I do hope she will answer right away. In regard to asking Jack Loy and Vic, I would suggest that you did not ask them. Vic, I know couldn't come and…it would be all right to ask Jack, of course, but I'm not going to ask Clara Louise or Peg simply because if I do, it would hurt Blix's feelings…to say nothing of several other people's. It is scarcely possible for me to come up to New York before Monday."

The excitement and anticipation was growing in Billy, "Two weeks from today close in your vicinity there is going to be one of the most gloriously, wondrously happy man that ever breathed the air of this blessed world, or saw the light of the burning sun. Dearest girl in the world, do you realize what wonderful happiness will be mine when you are really my wife…me Billy White, and you love me, and love me only that's what is so wonderful and almost incomprehensible to me. My prayer now is that someday I may be worthy to love you, and if I ever attain that, and God and I know I am not now, it will all be because of you and what you have done alone. I love you, sweetheart forever."

As it turned out, there was still uncertainty about the date but correspondence between the two of them continued with comments and directions, "I hope that before this note reaches you I will be with you in New York. I shall leave here Tuesday morning some time and doubtless arrive there some time also. You'll get a telegram giving you the details. Please don't be sleepy because we will have to talk things over and over again! I'm too sleepy to write anymore." Also, a quick note from Elsie to, "Dear Boy, in about two minutes Aunt May will have her eye to the key-hole to ascertain just why my light is burning at this hour, so I must hurry if this is to be finished before a 'halt' is called. Four rooms, let it be if it needs, must! What horrible, grasping personages New York landlords must be, to be sure! Indeed, I should like to come up Saturday…so that things can be settled as little more than they are now...I'm glad that your father appeared delighted. It might have been a trifle more exciting if he had not been pleased, but of course that wouldn't have really made any difference except perhaps that out of consideration for his feelings I might have failed to keep a rather important appointment...Be good to yourself and do not overwork...Who is and who is to be enroute to Philly and ever will be. You will have to forgive the writing and the pencil because this car runs anything but like the Lake Shore trains run. This is the only chance I'll have to write so I hope you won't mind very much. The dentist has been grinding my teeth to powder for the last hour with the unusual caressing tenderness! I wouldn't let him grind down to the nerve so he filled it without quite killing me. My mouth feels large enough to swallow the river Amazon; when I smile surely there must be a grotesque resemblance to the hyppopatamus[*sic*] easily noted."

By Friday, Billy created a quick note, "You said something about putting off going to Endeavor until December. Don't put it off dearest, let's go out on Thanksgiving. That's the date I do want to have it on...I'm tired tonight and want to see you so very much. Tomorrow afternoon is going to be put to the cause of apartments. I'm almost discouraged, the best one I saw yesterday was a five room for $45, and I don't see how we are going to live on the rest if we use that much for rent."

Elsie shared the news with her family about marriage plans on Thanksgiving Day in Endeavor, "This has been a terribly strenuous day. It seems weeks since I penned that letter to you at Gimbel's store. I broke the news to Uncle Howard today while we were having lunch at a restaurant downtown; that saved us from having a 'scene.' Of course, I told him that I had accepted an invitation from my friend, Mary McKean to spend Thanksgiving with her. Aunt Bert and he both went up into the air a little.

Uncle Howard was plainly disappointed, Aunt Bessie obviously disgusted. 'Yes, I am going', I said quite firmly, though my heart was beating hard and fast. Right out loud it seemed to me saying well as my heart spoke it need not be written…I explained to them that when Mary learned that my plans had been changed and that on Thanksgiving Day there would be no wedding after all, she (who) is, was, to be my maid-of-honor thought it would be lovely if I could visit her for a week or two! 'And what will Billy do in the meantime?' quoting Bessie, always thoughtful of your welfare, 'won't he be expecting you up there on that day, and won't Mrs. White probably ask you to come up and celebrate?' I replied ruthlessly that you probably had your own plans. It's getting harder every minute…you are more to me than the sum of all loves and friendship. I am trusting wholly in your love to fill my life so full of happiness that if there should be nothing offered from others, I would not miss it."

Apartment hunting was frustrating for Billy and often took his frustration out in his writing. He wrote this note to Elsie on the 17th of November about his search the day before, "I went forth again in quest of some place for us to call ours. It's very darn easy to say, 'pick out a house' but it is quite a different matter when it comes down to finding one…I'm in an awful pickle and want some help in several ways…I got a dandy letter from Jumbo on the same day as the one came from Mary. He says that he will be there if his father doesn't get worse…Have you gotten a letter from him? Next week, and you will be mine before men for always. Darling you know that I love you always and forever alone."

Billy received a letter from Jack Loy on November 13 recounting memories of their days at Wooster, "Yes sir, by gosh, just about the same time that you were thinking of it, I was also thinking of that song of ours, and couldn't help but believe that we said something that was true. Ain't it the truth, boy. I guess you did most of it, though. Doggone it, Bill, that Sunday night sing, just about got my goat. It brought things, people, and forgotten ideas that took me back into another and better life. That's rotten grammar, but good logic. You know I have a hell of a time expressing my sentiments, but I believe that I have the same things that others have.

"Bill, do you ever sit and try to be back there with the bunch, Jumbo, Bobby, Pal, Satan, Carrots, George, Hat, Ken, see them all around you, each making his customary remarks and each doing his habitual doings. Can't you hear Jumbo singing '*Cradle of the Deep*', or George belching, or Satan and Carrots quarreling over the messy floor, or Hat smoking a cigar, that's beyond, or Ken singing *Humm'Coon*, or Kil selling a sweater, or Fritz making a raw statement, or Bobby swearing fast and furious. Those names are all sacred, aren't they? But gosh wouldn't I like to sit down with you to a pipe of cube cut and talk about things that the rest don't always talk about." Perhaps Jack had a hard time visualizing Billy settling down.

"How about the wedding? It seems to me that it will be rather hard for you to get ready now for a big wedding Thanksgiving Day. That bunch about a justice of the peace wasn't all wrong either. But whenever it comes, boy, I'll do all in my power and prayers to show you that I want 'all that is true to be yours'. If it is in Ohio, I'll be there yet some of your happiness by assimilation. If it is in the east, all I can say is that I will try to be there, and if I can't why you know a wave of happiness and peace can travel over a big country without half trying, and my sincerest wish will be that my spirit, being with you, may help to make you the happiest man, the best husband, and the biggest friend in the world."

Jumbo was committed and planned to be there for the event, "Your communication regarding the Thanksgiving lunch came yesterday and I'll keep quiet about it in spite of all those endearing bonds you placed on me. Sounds good Bill and I shall certainly appreciate being there with both feet and arms shall I say? Of course, I can't tell this far ahead whether I'll be able to get away or not as father's condition is very uncertain, good one day and poor the next, so I'll have to wait. However, if there is any possible chance when the time comes Chal will be there…I'll be on hand when the whistle blows provided I'm not disqualified for some reason here…Old Chal with his right hand on high; broke to extend his very best wishes to Elsie and Bill for all kinds of luck in the plan shapes to be able to be an eye witness of the coupling of the best Beta and the best Kappa."

It wasn't indecision, but concern for Jumbo's father when Billy received another letter from Ed saying, "His father isn't so well as he has been, and Jum doesn't, can't, know for sure, whether he can get away or not. That would honestly be a calamity, if he couldn't come…I'll send down (the trunk) tomorrow or at the beginning of the week, so you had better let the Haddon Heights people know what to expect. You won't need the key until you have, and I think I'll be down, next Thursday afternoon… and I can bring it then…it is only two weeks now and that is an awful lot to be thankful for. The orders came from Satan last night…and I think I'll come down on Thanksgiving Day in the evening and stay over Friday, and we can get the stuff together… are you going to be very busy on that day? I'm coming anyway… Do you know how we'll have to economize in everything to be able to keep" the Godwin house. "My how I wish that there was something that we could do for that poor little lady…perhaps we have done something in taking the apartment off her hands… you know that I don't and never did know the value of money. But what do I care, I know what it means to love a girl with all my body, soul, and being and want always to be with her and loved by her alone."

The flurry of letter writing was a dialogue between the two of them about the plan, but it was the middle of November and still, nothing was firm, "This doesn't look as if I intended to write to you 'every hour', but really that was my intention...How Aunt's Bert and Bessie are going to take this stunt worries me a bit. You see there is bound to be some kind of stir made by this seemingly ungrateful behavior of mine. However, it is only you that I'm thinking about—your happiness and mine...A special delivery was waiting here for me from Mary. She is terribly disappointed because we can't come when we said we would. She told me several endearing things to say to my dressmaker and suggested a few alternative ways for her complete annihaliation[*sic*]. However, if it must be the week after, she wants us just the same, only more so. Dear, you know how much I hated to leave this morning. It is always that way. I felt last night as if I really was yours; I knew I was, body and soul. I love you with a love that believeth and hopeth all things, so long, as you love me as I feel that you must love me now (or I could never feel that I belong to you) so long, let me be all yours." By November 22, she writes another quick note to Billy, "If I really live through the next two weeks without telling a few people to attend to their own affairs or else shouting everything I know right into their ears, I'll surprise myself. Today has been spent sewing. I didn't do much of the sewing because my thimble got lost and one hates to spoil one's hands by sewing without one! (a la' Helen Stafford)...Tonight or tomorrow I'm going out to Oak Lane and then back to Haddon Heights on Thursday. I do hope you'll be able to come down when you said you would. From your last letter, I gleaned that you thought perhaps we might not be married on the 6th after all. When did you get the idea? Yesterday my dressmaker and myself had an interesting conversation and she understands several little things now, I fancy, which perhaps she didn't before! Be sure and explain carefully everything you want me to do in your next letter so that my stupid mind will be able to grasp it.

"I must tell you right away what I think about turning over was-to-be guest room into that 'other room' of yours. Certainly, we'll do it. I have seen too many poor men left with nary a corner in which to stow away their own, peculiar, precious things ever to want you to be treated as they have been. After all, it's vastly nicer to have a place for things of that sort than to have them all over the place, isn't it? I am not sure you know, of course, but how could anybody be expected to know just where to put any articles if there was no place for them. I have visions of them being draped from the last Chen silk to the chiffonier! If you have no objection to using a room in which the paper is a trifle pale and characterless for your ali 'study' shall we say, it certainly shall be yours (nice of me, isn't it) when this' yours already. No use trying to frighten me out by saying we will have to live on nothing. Doubtless we shall have champagne with our Christmas dinner just the same, and a fresh egg once in a while on just ordinary days!"

Anxiety was building in Billy's letters about the unconfirmed plans, "I just got the letter you wrote Sunday on the way to the suffragist-gest-or jester meeting whichever it turned out to be. How under the shining sun did you ever get the idea that I had any notion of not being married on the 6th of December. If there was a hint of such a fear away back in the back part of my brain it was only because I didn't know for sure whether Mary was going to be able to have us there or not. However, I surely am glad that that dressmaker knows more now than she did before. I'm coming down to Haddon Heights…on Thanksgiving afternoon just as soon as I can legitimately release myself from the bonds of a family dinner, to which the Whites' are going from all over this corner of New Jersey and New York to be held in New Brunswick. I wish that you were going to be there, but I know the chances of taking you away from Haddon Heights on Thanksgiving Day. Tell me, do Strawbridge & Clothiers have any furniture, or are they simply carpets, draperies, etc.? If they have furniture we might as well get as much as possible from them and have it all shipped together at once. If they do not have it, I can get enough here to get along on until you come and we can pick it out together. We can look at some stuff down there on Friday though and get an idea of what we want...My, that will be some fun, going around buying stuff with you for you, for me, for us."

His inexperience with weddings became obvious and maybe a little silly, "Tell me too, dear heart, when I ought to arrive in Endeavor? You will get this Wednesday...Then, what kind of flowers do you want for a bouquet, and Mary's? Ye gods, I don't know nothin'! But what the deuce is a fellow to do? I've only been to three weddings in my brief journey so far. No; one, I got sick eating bananas; no, two, I was too young to remember no; three, (Miriam's). I was too much in love with the girl by my side to pay much attention to the details of the ceremony. So you see I'm green, and I want this to go off right. Now, what kind of flowers shall it be. I can get them in Pittsburgh...so that they will be fresh; roses, orchids, lilies, or what? To see about the orange blossoms today or tomorrow and will let you know right away."

Elsie was getting ready to leave Haddon Heights and jotted down final details for Billy on November 25th, "I just finished writing to Mary so she will expect me there on Wednesday, December 4th." My cousin, "Betty (Elliot) and I have just finished breakfast and in a few minutes, we must get ready to go to the great Suffrage Mass Meeting[6] at the Metropolitan Opera House. Heaven only knows if we'll ever get in, but there is nothing like trying in order to satisfy our vulgar curiosity; afterwards we'll probably go to Vesper Service at Holy Trinity – there is always beautiful music there."

Days later she briefly described the meeting to Billy in a quick note finalizing the wedding details, "It's getting nearer every day, isn't it and there seems so much to be done. The Suffragist Mass Meeting from all accounts was a great success…we couldn't get into the Opera House so had to content ourselves with listening to the speeches of several rather inferior speakers, inferior only that is, compared to Dr. Anna Shaw and Miss Jane Addams." While she was energized by what she heard, Billy appears to be oblivious to the cause by skimming over the episode as if it was nothing. To him, the only important event was being with Elsie forever, for if he was aware of her unrest, he dismissed it.

One week from Tuesday, November 26, Billy and Elsie will be together in Endeavor for the wedding. Most of the preparation for the wedding is complete but they are still unsettled about the apartment and furnishings, "What do you think I want to throw around in that spare room. We will settle that at some later date though when we both know more about it. All I want is some place to put my desk. I'm going to have it sent up and if there is no other place, we can put it out on the fire escape, or use it as a kitchen table. I wrote Satan about the possible chance of getting furniture, for there is a tremendous profit in that you know. Something like 100% or above. He said that all the houses were rushed like the deuce just now, and if he ordered for us he would have to get it direct from the factory, and it can't be sent until after the new year. One week from today you start for Endeavor? Will Thursday morning be too early for me to get there?"

One final letter before he left for Endeavor, "Believe me, that trip from Philadelphia to New York was some long journey, every minute I got farther away from the place I wanted to be, and the person I wanted to be with. The train was forty minutes late too, chiefly on account of the crowd coming home from the game. The train was jammed to the vestibules. I got a seat at one end of the car, and almost froze to death for the three hours it took to get home. As a result, I have had a slight sore throat today. If I get pneumonia and die, you wreak vengeance on Jay E. Kilpatrick for not sending in my winter clothes to me in time for the cold weather.

"Darn it all anyway, why was it necessary that we should have to be parted just when we wanted to be together. Not for long now—five days more.

"Say, for Heaven's sake, don't forget about that dining room furniture. I know that it seems like adding insult to injury to ask you to see about anything more, and I just happen to remember that you may not remember that salesman's name. I have his card here and will enclose it so there won't be any mistake. If you happen to go in there, it might be wise to jog him up about sending that stuff up right away because I'm beginning to fear that we may have to live in empty rooms for a while unless they get busy right away. I darn near get busy when I think about how absolutely heavenly that place is going to be when we get it finished. And that living room, too much for mere words, and with you in it, well it unbalances my thinking ability, questionable quantity though that may be.

"Goodnight dear heart, my own true love, and my wife-to-be, you know that there is only one person in this world I love and that person is you. Elsie, and I am yours alone forever."

On November 28, Elsie's father wrote this letter:

"My dear daughter,

This, the hour and perhaps the moment when you are changing your name and entering into a new relationship that shall either beautify and sweeten your life or mar it. This relationship to be sweet and in harmony depends on unselfishness on your part as much as on Wilbert's.

This union, my dear, is not a union merely between two creatures but between two spirits. The intention of this bond is to perfect the nature of you both, to the one strength of character and firmness of moral will to the other sympathy, meekness, tenderness.

There is no earthly relationship which has so much power to ennoble and exalt.

How happy you both will be for Christ will be at your wedding, for I know you both have found favor of the Lord.

I am picturing you in my mind going to the altar. Your robes are white, your heart is all a flutter, your thoughts are of the great change in life which is just about to begin, you wish for God's blessings and you know down deep in your heart that the future will be bright. I think so too, for Wilbert seems to me a fine fellow, and will make you happy and give you the home life for which you seem to crave and have had so little in your life thus far.

Mother Jean and I went out to the ivory shops on Saturday just after Thanksgiving day and bought a few pieces of ivory.

We are sending two ivory napkin rings for a New Year's gift.

Let me hear about your new home, etc.

With much love,"

The wedding announcement appeared in The Forest Republican, Tionesta, Pennsylvania, "The home of Mr. H. M. McKean, Endeavor, Pa., was the scene of a very pretty wedding on Friday evening, December 6, 1912. The bride was Miss Elsie Machle, the daughter of Dr. Machle, a medical missionary in China, and the groom was Mr. W. W. White, Jr., of New York City, whose father is president of the Bible Teachers' Training in New York. Both the bride and groom are graduates of Wooster University, class of 1912. The bride's gown was white satin trimmed with real lace and her tulle veil was caught up with lilies-of-the valley and maiden-hair. She carried a shower bouquet of white roses, lilies-of-the-valley and maiden-hair. Her only attendant was Miss Mary McKean, who wore a gown of yellow satin veiled with bordered chiffon, and carried a bouquet of Miss Taft roses tied with pink chiffon. Mr. White was attended by Mr. E. N. Chalfant, of Pittsburgh. The minister officiating was Dr. J. W. Smith, of Warren, Pa. After the ceremony dinner was served, covers being laid for eight persons. The table was decorated with pink roses and ferns. The menu was as follows:

Grape Fruit.

Cream Tomato Soup, Crouton.

Fried Chicken.   Mashed Potatoes,

Creamed Mushrooms in Patty Shells,

Rolls, Jelly, Olives.

Fruit Salad,　Saltines.
Sponge Cake with Whipped Cream.
Coffee.　Salted Almonds.

Mr. and Mrs. White left for Pittsburgh immediately after-wards. They will live in New York City."

It was a quiet ceremony for a small group in a private setting. Just what Elsie wanted. Billy changed into traveling clothes, a dress overcoat with a derby hat and cane, while Elsie changed into a traveling dress and hat. They stood together outside of the McKean's home while their picture was taken. She, holding one rose, the symbol of their union; and he, with his derby and cane before leaving Endeavor for Pittsburgh, then on to New York City where they rented a small apartment.

The presidential election was history, yet it ignited an inter-est not only in politics, but in the idea of a "new woman". Elsie had arrived in that much desired spot of Arcady, longing to be with Billy, but with a new perspective on the new movement for women and woman's place in the home.

CHAPTER 13

It Was Not Shangri la in 1913

They called it home. A five-room apartment at 390 Wadsworth Avenue in an area known as Washington Heights in New York City. Notes of wedding congratulations began arriving, along with a note from Cara Lehman sharing her disappointment that she wasn't invited to the wedding, "Elsie darling, I'm so glad! You and Billy could not have done a better thing than to up and go to Endeavor and get married...I wish I'd been there." "I often think of you both" wrote Hannah Johnston, "And in my mind I see you in your wedding dress and think how pretty you must have looked...I see you in your home...putting things in order... Perhaps getting up some pleasant surprise for Wilfrid. You see I don't call him Billy. You know that was my donkey's name." Elsie was known to have a pet donkey named Billy, or were the two connected? Jumbo forwarded this letter from Jack Loy, "Your description of Billy's wedding brought tears to my eyes. It is hard to believe that he is single no more as I thought he was scheduled for future heart breakings, but from a letter that came from him not long ago he seems to be very happy. Is he going to stick to the Bible School or what in the devil is he going to do? From his letter it seemed as if he was going to pull out. But he will get by all right if he will be given a chance to figure out his own future and be allowed to down a cigarette now and then." Tempered with sarcasm, Jack posed the question about what he was going to do with his life.

In May, 1913 Billy spent three days in Cincinnati meeting Elsie's relatives and, "called Uncle Harry. Here was the conversation on the phone. 'Hello, Mr. Machle?' 'Yes.' 'This is your latest acquisition in the nephew line.' 'Well' 'This is Billy White' 'Oh, oh, I beg your pardon', then it was very smooth sailing, I went out about 7:30 p.m. I had to laugh when he asked me if I knew Helen's cousin in New York, Elsie Machle. Met the whole bunch at Uncle Harry's. Vic came over about 8:00. Then we went over to Uncle Frank's and met the people over there."

Shortly after arriving in New York, Elsie attended one of the Suffragist Progressive Dinners. Women didn't have the right to vote in every state in America, although the movement in Europe was successful as early as 1881. The Suffragettes were members advocating the right to vote in every state of the union, "It didn't progress fast enough as far as the speakers were concerned so all of us left before the celebrities had finished telling us just how the world was to be reformed by their particular party in the year of grace nineteen hundred and sixteen!" By December 1912, Alice Paul was appointed chairman of NAWSA's Congressional Committee at the convention with the support of Harriot Stanton Blatch and Jane Addams. Other members were added with a minimum of funds to support the effort. Eventually she would become more active, but she had other interests to keep her busy. She began by taking a course on Psalms at the Bible Teachers Training School. Before long she was associating with friends of the White's and attending various social engagements. Many invitations came from the families who had cottages at Lake George.

Billy found himself alone after Elsie left on July 8 for Lake George. Returning to an empty house, he begins to think, "If

I could only let you know...how I feel...you would never doubt my love again in the whole long eternity...you being away, your onetime presence here, your love, your kisses, yourself, just came over me with a rush." He can't help but wonder how she is perceiving the place, "Well, how does Lake George and Silver Bay come up to your expectations? I'll bet a hat that you had a paradise pictured, and while I think that place physically is almost a paradise, still I can't, of course, know what you had pictured in your mind." She was a chaperone at Lake George for the Y.M.C.A. youth when they went on tramp. "Father said that you were making heroic efforts and great progress learning to swim."

However, this was the beginning of a theme that developed in their relationship. Elsie was away visiting while Billy stayed and worked, usually at something that he either didn't like or the details bored him. It was a restlessness that could not be satisfied. He wanted to be with Elsie, yet he desired to be young and carefree, never sure about what he wanted to do. Jumbo called his attention to a *Collier Magazine* advertisement that paid $1000 for articles, "Get busy hon and we'll make money yet on our Dunnorian style...I hope you keep on the lookout for story material, settings, etc." During this time, he also began to borrow money from friends to keep up his lifestyle. But there was always a question about what he did with their money.

He kept busy at the Bible Teachers Training School. Dr. White was planning to enlarge it and rename it Biblical Seminary of New York but his dedication was as long as his ability to concentrate on why he was there. While Billy was expected to set up exhibits for recruitment for the school, there were times when he felt like a handyman and would decide to leave for a while in the middle of the day. Essentially, he was a secretary until his father put him in charge of the Practical Work Department. As Elsie reflects on the assignment, "Father...needs a rest...I know you are going to be the biggest success…he thinks so, and I know so. I am backing you with every bit of good that there is in me; every bit of love, every bit of faith." His father traveled to speaking engagements but was tireless in his pursuit of contributors. Occasionally, he took Billy with him. It was after they relocated to 130 E. 50th Street that they met Florence Thompson, a missionary. According to the census, there were six families living at that address, most of them associated with the seminary, either as missionaries, teachers, or custodians.

The pattern of their future was set that summer. Billy wrote to Elsie every day becoming more frustrated when he didn't receive a letter from her, "What's the matter anyway hon. Did the tramp do you up so that you decided to take a day off and go to bed, or aren't you back yet?" Often, he would rush to judgment about where she was, what she was doing, or how she was doing it. There was frustration at being separated even though he suggested to Elsie that she go to Lake George. It wasn't unusual for him to suggest that she visit her relatives as well. By mid-July, he voiced some of his insecurities, "I want you to help me, oh I know you will, and I know very well that you have worried and had so much trouble just because of me, and I know that I have known the cause. Take it from me honey I'm going to be very, very darn sensible…as insensible whichever you want to call it… from now on. Please forgive me sweetheart for all the pain and worry I've caused you, forgive me for having been such a brute, and help me to be worthy to love you." They were burdened by money troubles. Billy gave Elsie $5 to last until he saw her, but she worried that he didn't have enough to eat and sent him $2 of her money. Then they had to give up their nice five room apartment. It seemed logical that they move to the school at 541 Lexington Avenue in three rooms which was more like student housing than an apartment, but sacrifices needed to be made since Billy didn't have a sufficient income to support them. Of course, it didn't help when Elsie received a letter from Mother Jean sharing her concern about the decision and writing, "You ought to have known better."

Often Elsie wrote to Billy encouraging him, "Please don't be blue any more just because I'm not there." She was away for four months and hoped he would come up to the lake, but as time went on he stayed in New York and didn't arrive until August 6. She needed extra clothing for hiking to Black Mountain, one of the scenic places in the Adirondacks, and asked Billy to buy some for her, "When you come, there are several things you had better bring…If you could send me two suits of that knitted what-have-you-got-on-under immediately so I'll have some substantial to wear on that long tramps, I will be eternally grateful." While he promises to shop for the 'honorable underwear', it is a new experience for him that leaves him embarrassed at the thought.

An outbreak of typhoid fever in New York City in 1907 led to the development of a vaccine. Dr. Henry E. Hale, the family physician and a regular resident at the lake suggests that Elsie should be vaccinated. While it was unlikely that typhoid would exist at Silver Bay, the recent outbreak was enough to convince Elsie to proceed with the inoculation. Billy had some concerns, "I was somewhat surprised to hear that you're going to have a typhoid germ shot into you. Hope that you don't get very groggy, and that it is all over by the end of the week. I don't suppose there is any use in me having it done. You can't have the stuff twice can you? I had it out in India, so I suppose that I'm sufficiently inoculated." Billy had not been in India since he was a child. Since the vaccine is only good for seven years, he wasn't protected from the disease. Several days later he was concerned, "Your letter didn't say anything about the effects of that inoculation." A statement that makes one wonder if she was experiencing some ill effects.

Beta Theta Pi Club was located at One Gramercy Park. Billy and his Beta brothers met regularly during their visits to New York. Since Elsie left for the lake, friends had been dropping in on Billy at their apartment. Most of them were fraternity brothers looking for jobs. To Billy, it was like old times at the fraternity house. It could be crazy. Some of the guests didn't carry their load of responsibility, except one. Jumbo stayed with Billy while he walked the streets of New York looking for a job, "Jumbo and I are on the trail of a job. It looks fine from where we stand now. He has seen the man and has a date with him for Tuesday lunch. I haven't talked to him yet but will soon. He wants four or five college men, and prefers them without experience, he has been hired to handle the advertising of four large fashion magazines and wants to train his men in his own way." Elsie's friend, Mary McKean and Jumbo developed a romantic relationship since commencement and were engaged. Mary was also in New York and occasionally cooked meals for them at the apartment. The guys kept the apartment clean. When Elsie received the news, she wrote a note to Jumbo, "Your very charming little note of congratulations regarding the latest victory of our demuriative[*sic*] cherub of the bow and arrow faire was received yesterday with much facilitation amid loud curses and protests on the part of Bill. He still wants to know what the note contained, declaring that you were overstepping your woman's privileges, but I told him that it was none of his 'damned business' and he very promptly closed his fly trap."

It was common to find Billy with the opposite sex during Elsie's absence. He liked being a flirt, "I just got in this morning from Mr. Tjader's country home in Connecticut. I didn't know I was to go along until yesterday noon. We had a fine trip in the auto out to the place, it is on the Sound. After supper, I took the three daughters out in a canoe for a short paddle while the older folks sat on the porch and chewed the rag. One rather funny thing happened when father told Mr. Tjader that his son was staying here with him, they thought it was Donald, so when I came out and got into the auto, he was very much surprised, as were the rest of the family when we arrived at Darien. Well, the talk was all of the weather, and such topics, and I found no opportunity to ring in the glad chorus that I was married, and that I had the most wonderful wife in the world, and end with the sad refrain that she was in the country just at present. There were three rather attractive daughters between the ages of 18 and 23 or four, I should judge, and in my usual foolish way, I looked about 20. I had on my black Norfolk by the way, they first wondered where I was in college, so you can see how woefully underrated I was. During supper, I felt no inclination to break up the Billy Sunday conversation by arising and announcing, 'keep off! I'm married.' Uncomfortable as I felt, with those three pair of eyes watching me choke down a couple of vile claws (I hate claws worse than parsnips or liver). After supper, they asked me to take them out in the canoe, as they very seldom got a chance to go out in the evening because they had no brother, and there was such a scarcity of men. No chance there to break the news. When we got into the boat, I was afraid to say anything for fear of the boat capsizing for I swear they still thought I was the weirdest kid. Well, when we got back to the house, father had broken the news to the older folks. It all came out all right. They wouldn't believe it at first. Darn it all, why don't they have some kind of a sign whereby a person can tell when he is introduced to a man whether he is married or not." Billy Sunday was the ultimate showman. He was a Presbyterian minister and evangelist who drew big crowds to his events.

It didn't take much to bring his passion to a pitch, "I got your letter, written Wednesday afternoon 'upstairs'. Had to go downtown to see a man about some stuff so I couldn't answer it right away," says Billy, "You surely can get me up in the air when you want to, as for instance—after I've been longing and aching to see you for almost four months, then after a night when I lay awake most of the time thinking of you, and wondering how you are, and sending love messages to you on the wind, and wanting to be with you, and while I was asleep dreaming of you…beautiful dreams…then to come down here to the office in kind of a haze for I seemed to be still dreaming of you, to find out then that I can't possibly be up at the lake before next week, then to read your letter, and to know that you were writing that letter with nothing on but one of your sweetest dearest things…words fail. I am still up. My, how I hope that a page of that letter dropped from your hand and rested for a moment just where I would like more than any place to rest my head. I know that it did, I kissed those pages and felt your body near. Oh sweetheart, I want to be with you."

The following summer of 1914, Billy urged Elsie to take a break from her course at the school to visit his aunt and uncle Kate and J. Campbell White in New Brunswick and Princeton where she would enjoy the "stroll about Princeton's beautiful campus."

There was a sense of frustration in her letters, "What I wrote about the box of candy was foolish. Don't bother about it now, the book either. I would rather send it back myself for I know you are busy, not only with the telephone and 'hopping' about all day but also with interviewing sleek bondholders and magnates to say nothing of Bitter Almond. You know I am hoping and praying for the success of the plan, or rather, 'The Plan', that is if it doesn't spoil us both for life. Do not bother to write. Of course, I understand that silence is a delightful and refreshing virtue, but you need never hope to see it very well developed in your loving wife." There was also an invitation from Mary McKean to come to Endeavor to camp on the Allegheny since she couldn't come up to Lake George. However, Elsie was still dealing with the ramifications of the inoculation and drops a note to Billy from Swarthmore during a visit to her Aunt Bert, "I am feeling very well although no change has taken place in my condition since I left you. I am anxious to hear your plans about the rest of the summer and next year."

But Elsie also discovered that she was pregnant. She had been tired. Sometimes she couldn't keep her food down. Imagine her disappointment when Billy writes, "Sweetheart, I don't want you to come home this week. It is going to be a tough week for me, and I'll have to be working until 10 o'clock at night...Then, there is another reason, I don't think I need to mention it, but it won't help matters a bit for you to be here, it will only make it harder for me. That same reason will be a reason all through this conference, until the 15ᵗʰ or 16ᵗʰ...Do anything you think best, stay at Princeton, go to Philly, or New Brunswick, or anything. God knows I want you badly enough, but I do think it would be better if you didn't come home now...I know it sounds terribly mysterious, but I think you know what I mean, if you don't, I suppose you'll come home to find out." Billy's encouragement to stay away was still difficult no matter how she coped with it. While at Uncle Cam's, she attended Rutgers' Commencement with the family, "It probably will be dull as a class social, but there may be one thing that will make the whole morning worthwhile." It was June 17, 1914, when Elsie described her experience while visiting, "We went to Rutger's commencement, and enjoyed it a great deal. It really wasn't tiresome at all. The three orations were good, and well delivered. Several celebrities and numerous high-brows were given honorary degrees. Among the former, Governor Fielder of New Jersey. He seemed not at all confused at the unusual bonnet the President draped on him; evidently the man had gone through worse ordeals and had also become accustomed to being fussed over...There is a good joke on Aunt Kate and Uncle Cam. Last Wednesday Uncle Cam came in early from town, having first visited a tonsorial parlor and a haberdasher...they departed into New Brunswick...Aunt Kate and he drove their vehicle down the most prominent street and eventually hitched in front of a fraternity house! From that point they proceeded, in full sight of all the young gallants draped upon the porch to the alumni hall where the reception was to be held. To their either amazement not a living soul greeted them, no white gloved hand grasped theirs in cordial welcome; no liveried negro passed them salad and drinks. Only ghastly signs blatantly screaming, 'Fresh Paint' stared coldly and unappreciatively at them! They were a week early! Need I go into details concerning the immediate sensations that must have coursed through the sensitive minds of our two well-loved aunt and uncle?"

Billy was in charge while she was away visiting which meant Elsie had to rely on him for clean clothes which were mailed back and forth. Of course, a housekeeper at the school did the laundry. Wherever she went, she took her embroidery. Now, she was busy making baby clothes. While at Battlefield Farm, Kate taught her how to put up vegetables from their garden. Whether it was grape juice, tomatoes or pickles, she would return home in the fall with a supply for the winter. The winters were long for the couple, they argued and their relationship suffered.

"Now that I am away, he begins to talk about my charms and beauty, and when I am there with him, he doesn't see, or care for them at all," says Elsie. His response to her was, "Now that is where you are dead wrong sweetheart. Every time I see you, I can't help saying to myself, 'You lucky fool, how under the shrinking sun, did you ever get her?...Darling, I love you now, this moment more than I can ever tell you, more than I ever did before, more than all else in life, and death, and eternity, and the wonder of it all, is that I have you, you the fairest of all, the dearest, the sweetest, the bravest, the purest, the most tender. Oh Elsie, my darling wife, how I want to prove to you, and to the rest of the world that I am as near worthy of you than ever before. It can never be, of course, but I'm going to be as near worthy as possible."

While Elsie is visiting Aunt Bert in Philadelphia she begins to develop a feeling of abandonment, but most of all, loneliness, "I can't say how much I loothe[*sic*] this life of living alone. I'd like to curse but have foresworn all of that kind of stuff. Have a plan that will, I think meet with your approval when I spring it in the near future. Talked to father about it a little this a.m. and he thought it pretty good. It embraces our canoe trip and the time when you are going along to act simply as your 'squaw. I suppose you remember having said that."

"Visiting is getting to be a nuisance," cries Elsie in a letter to Billy, "Aunt Mary said I could come down anytime, but really she didn't seem as cordial as usual...I think I'll just come and stay with you and not go visiting any place after I leave here...but for the most part, it is about as restful a pastime as going to battle." Yet, they continue to be apart and lament about their separation. While at Aunt Bert's there was a plea, "Wish you and I were together somewhere also, I wish I had never come down here at all." Her visit to Haddon Heights was extended but the pressure is growing, mainly from the family, that there must be a reason for their separate lives, "So Aunt Bert thinks that my ardor has completely cooled does she...well I'll show her how much by coming down there one of these days pretty soon and bringing you back with me," writes Billy on July 25." Several months later, while visiting Kate White, she asks him, "When are you going to let me come home?"

By this time, he has decided to stay at the school with his, "father for another year and put all the other things that have attracted me from my giving my whole self with the work to the side for the time…it is all going to be different, we are going to… be together…You are really going to have hands on the purse strings, and they are going to be the only hands that have anything to do with them…don't get entirely discouraged over me, for I am still your adoring husband." All along Elsie urged Billy to be more careful with their money. He had borrowed money from Jim Sanders, "Well, I saw Jim this morning and gave him $25 on the total $75 and told him that I would try very, very hard to get the rest before the end of the month…father left me some money and that is the way I happened to be able to give it back." Elsie questioned him about it, "It was fortunate you could give Jim that much, but I thought from the list that father sent me when I was at Haddon Heights that you had already given some of it?"

There were times when they were together, "I am so ashamed of myself that I feel like crawling into your big, roomy shoe and dying. You see I had to wait until you were away to apologize and ask your forgiveness for my sins. The idea of a sensible woman shedding tears and seeing big, white horses when she seems to be sound asleep! It isn't to be, suppose that you'll really forgive but you must know that this foolish woman is sorry for doing the things she did last night. If she didn't love you past all reason, you wouldn't be able to hurt her just by going directly to sleep when she just longed to be cuddled and babied, not by a big, hungry bear either, but by a strong, tender man who understands." Before leaving he asks for Gertrude Haupert's address and phone number. Gertrude was a graduate from Wooster who found herself in New York where her brother lived. He assumes that while his father and sister, Helen will be away, he can, "Take Gertrude out to dinner somewhere without them interfering, not that they would say anything, but they might look over their glasses in a peculiar way", and follows it up by saying, "wish like thunder that I could come out there again tonight, but it can't be." His plans went awry with Gertrude, but, "I went to the Roof Tree Inn for supper last night with Paul Harvey...he has some very thrilling tales of the war, outside of a fight in the air, he saw between an aeroplane and a zeppelin." Perhaps this account was the beginning of a dream. "A letter came from Gertrude Haupert this morning, and I read it. Hope you don't mind. I thought that perhaps she was coming down and had asked you to call her up, or something like that, perhaps go to tea, and I was going to try to fill your shoes, however, there was no such chance for me to be a hero as you can see from the letter which I am enclosing."

Elsie read the letter about Paul Harvey and exclaimed, "Babe" Harvey! Paris would be no place for such as he...but tell him that you can't squander money showing him New York." But their money problems were developing. He gambled in the 'Chapman' affair which put him in debt, borrowed from his friend Jim and slowly repaid him, but is extravagant when he entertained friends. It was discouraging and she tries to explain how she feels about their life, "It would be wonderful to get away from everybody for a while; just you and I and start our life all over again, and start it right. Of course, when I look over the last year, I realize that most of it has been my fault, because I did not and could not make you love me the way I have dreamed of being loved. Sometimes, I have felt bitter because there seemed no more romance left in life, no glamour or illusion. People of experience, of course, would say that as long as I deluded myself into believing such things really could be, I wasn't living. Pooh, pooh and fiddlesticks! I can't live without being deluded; it's meat and drinks to me. So, you see, we will just have to weave another fabric of life as magical as the web of the Lady of Shallot, and we must keep our dreams, for the hard realities. Ali! I may end up in some asylum…very likely such an arrangement would prove most satisfactory; my brain cells could go on a grand debaucle and think the'darndest' things without causing the least irritation to my amiable, half-witted companions…please do not expect too much from a mere woman."

It seems as though Billy didn't have a clue why Elsie was upset with him. Yet, "I think that I would have gone clear luny and hopped a train and blown in out there if I could have gotten one…I don't think you had better come back before Friday, or Saturday morning, and if it wasn't for that darn choir, I'd come out Saturday afternoon. But I've got to be on hand here for Friday night, and now that you are there, I think that you ought to stay and get to feeling all right again…Have got to go over to the Singer's Club tonight. Worse luck, but it won't be for many more weeks now, two more is all…Gad but it's lonesome without you, but I mustn't get on that strain for I want you to stay until Saturday. Them's[*sic*] orders! Give my love to the folks, and for yourself—oh just hug yourself, and kiss yourself for me, and oh dearest remember that I love, love, love you."

Early in 1915, Billy went out west, stopping in Pittsburgh to visit Syl Scovel. While there, he borrowed $30. He made an attempt to convince Elsie that he was working hard, with brief accounts of his day, but the letters were less and less with nothing to show for it, and no indication of why he needed the money. His notes were to the point, "Don't desert me darling during these days when I need you most…just a line is all I want." Again, the money wasn't coming in because his sales were lagging behind. Without explanation, "Say honey, I think that if you would forward all of my mail right away to me, it would solve a lot of bother and worry. Don't you? Better do it after this". But there were indications that their relationship wasn't going well. In March, "He had quite a time at the 'Woman's Ball' asking different ladies I danced with if they wrote for 'Snappy Stories' or 'Youngs'. They picked the former." But there was always a reason why sales were down. Occasionally, the two of them stayed at The St. James in Philadelphia. Other times he spoke about the luxury of the hotels with promises to bring her along on a future trip.

On March 26, 1915, Elsie gave birth to Elizabeth Worthington White[7] in New York's Nursery & Child's Hospital at 161 West 61st Street. Helen was especially happy with the nine pound bundle of joy, "Just how I am going to manage to wait until Thursday until I can see my sister mother and little Elizabeth...Bless her heart, I am glad she has arrived safely and that you are getting along so well." Edward and Jean Machle were expected to arrive home and were going to be staying outside Atlantic City in Ventnor, New Jersey. "I presume ere this you have hugged baby a thousand times and feed it about 12 times a day...Kiss the baby for her truly grandpa and her adopted grandma." A note from Jean, "if all goes well, we shall be able to come on by the end of the month."

It was a welcomed reunion for Elsie. She took a train to Atlantic City and stopped at The Breakers to use their stationery to pen a note to Billy. The Breakers was one of the large hotels built on the boardwalk to accommodate the tourist population. "You would have enjoyed following Elizabeth and your wife from Twenty-third Street to Atlantic City...our journey was one progressive reception, as it were, by porters, conductors, old ladies and good-natured gentlemen." She spent several weeks in Ventnor with Edward and Jean in their rented bungalow at 24 North Portland Avenue in May 1915. They were on furlough so it couldn't have come at a better time. They kept late hours, but, "I want to talk to you" Billy, "for I should be in bed this minute instead of scrawling sweet nothings to my silent partner. That last was not meant for a slam because I know you wrote as frequently as you could." She continued to write about Elizabeth as she describes how she didn't like the ride in a chair and how she, "protested for nearly the whole hour while we were riding on the Boardwalk." The Boardwalk meant only one thing, enjoying the beach and social life in Atlantic City. "We came home in a jitney and she showed her dislike for such plebeian vehicles by screaming lustily all the way home. As soon as I took her into the house, however, she looked up into my face and smiling the most adorable smile said, '*y-u-eh*'. There was not the sign of a tear in our darling rascals' eyes! She gets sweeter every day, Billy: I could just squeeze her plump, pink little body to death!" There must have been moments when Elsie felt there was incongruity in their relationship, because there was no other way to explain it. They spent several days at Atlantic City strolling the Boardwalk with Elizabeth in her arms. While Jean and Elsie became acquainted, Billy stayed in New York preparing to take a group of 400 to hear Billy Sunday. "Really, you have no idea how much I appreciate your letting me come down here when I ought to be at home doing the few things I do do occasionally for you." However, she notes in his letter, "I shall love thee better after death."

The Whites were members of Fifth Avenue Presbyterian Church, known as the 'Church of the Patriots' because the pews were filled with passionate voices that paralled[*sic*] the nation's growth. It was one of the most prestigious churches in Manhattan located at Fifth Avenue and Fifty-Fifth Street. One Sunday, Billy heard Dr. John Henry Jowett[8], a renowned British preacher and writer from Birmingham, England, who assumed the pastorate in January 1911. By 1916, the church membership was at an all-time high. It was on May 23 when Billy heard him, "It was a fine sermon. One of the best I've ever heard him preach…What do you say Elsie to having Elizabeth baptized next Sunday afternoon? That will be Dr. Jowett's last service before he goes to Europe." She was baptized in Fifth Avenue Presbyterian Church with both families present. Dr. Jowett was called, "The greatest preacher in America". He had a philosophy that a preacher, though called by various names in the Bible, has several key roles in the ministry.

Elsie sent her regrets that she would miss the Rally but, "it seems better to stay here in this lovely place as long as possible." It was shortly after the Practical Work Rally, when Billy announced, "I'm thinking of taking up shorthand with Miss (Nina) Quinn and learning typewriting." Nina was a secretary at the school. "It might help sometime in the future."

By August 4, Crowe wrote Chal with this information, "I have just written White. Lake resigns on September 1ˢᵗ. Is White, in your opinion, up to handling his territory?

"This whole matter is confidential at present...particularly glad to be able to give White a real chance.

"If you can meet it, he is fixed and ought to progress very steadily. If he falls down, of course, I will have to let him go...I am very sure that White has it in him to succeed, but he had got to work a great deal harder and a great deal more earnestly than he has."

Billy finds a job with SYSTEM, the magazine of business. Jumbo had been working for the magazine for some time and interceded for him. "I have hooked up with the advertising department of SYSTEM magazine, and I really do not think that I could be connected with anything that would give me a better training and foundation for any line of business. It is really a wonderful organization, the bunch of men connected with the magazine is exceptionally fine, and altogether I am very well satisfied. While the salary is not everything that could be desired to begin with, I realize that I have very little experience in the advertising line, and then it is large enough to get along on until I can prove of greater worth to them than I now am." The letters that followed were from Philadelphia, Baltimore, Pittsburgh and Scranton. He travelled most of the time, leaving Elsie and Elizabeth alone. Then Elsie found out she was pregnant with their second child. The days were strenuous so Billy suggested that she, "make some arrangements with Rosie as soon as possible. You must get some relief from the baby, even if she is the cutest in the world" and "asked Dr. Hale to drop in and see you…you must be put in better condition."

Ever since May, Billy kept secrets from Elsie. He started to feel ill, "Feeling kind of weak…took a large dose of castor oil last night, forced down my throat by father, but I've lost eight pounds since Wednesday evening." It was Chal, his best man at their wedding, who presented Billy with the ultimatum after receiving Mary Scovel's letter. "I received a letter from Syl's wife and for God's sake do something. Go out and rob a bank if necessary but send her that money. Understand that she's going to have a baby in a few days and she must need the money darn bad." Chal forwards the letter from Mary Meeks Scovel to Billy, 'Can you see Billy White and tell him I could use the twenty dollars now, (that is the balance, he paid ten of it). I had to borrow the money from the firm to lend him at the time and of course, had to pay it back. Just at this time I could use it, in fact I need it.'

Mary and Chal returned from their honeymoon on August 6. Then sends Billy a letter he received from Crowe, "Well we are back at home and starting housekeeping…I found attached [letter] from Crowe and it ought to look pretty good to you. In spite of the fact that I am not supposed to send this letter to you it is so much to the point that I can't help…please don't say a word to Crowe about my sending it. Read the letter about five times and get the full impact of it and then Monday when you see him go right after this. It is your big chance and you can handle that territory yourself better than Lake did. You have done some mighty good work and you can get the business but darn it you don't work more than half the time. Now give yourself a kick in the pants and work from 8:30 till 5:30 for a few months and you'll see it coming. We're all rooting for you Bill and if you'll only get busy and land this territory and get a little confidence on it, perhaps someday you and I will be running System in the East and putting down some real money. Your salary will increase as fast as you make it."

"Had lunch with E. R. Crowe and he began discussing you and asking me a lot of questions. Bill, he's sized things up pretty clearly and I had to agree with him on several things that I'd prefer not to, but what's the use of beating around the bush in a really serious matter...he thinks you've got a lot of good stuff in you but you've got to jar yourself loose from some of your 'collegiate habits'...he spoke of petty indulgences such as Pullman ride to Philadelphia, large expense accounts, losing traveling money...darn it Bill, it isn't the idea of expense that seems to bother him but the fact that you should be pulling these little things so early in the game. After a person has made good and carved his berth...he can get away with little things like that, and even irregularity in schedules but at the beginning it simply can't be done." In the words of Harry Emerson Fosdick, "Sin is treachery to the cause of human welfare; it is going over to the race's enemies in the spirit of Benedict Arnold. Righteousness is loyalty to the cause of the world's salvation."

"You've had a pretty soft time all your life and things have always came out all right in the end, so you don't worry against the future, but now it is different. You are in business for yourself, for Elsie, the kid, for your reputation and theirs, your father's and mother's and your friends and you've got to start building. The

SYSTEM job is your future. That Philadelphia territory is your territory, there's just as much money and advancement there as you care to make it. Of course, it's hard sledding at first. No one expects you to go out and tear off a twelve-page contract each week or each ninth for that matter, but you do have to master your territory and begin to show advertisers and agents that you know your business better than they do. The sooner you go in to see a man with the idea that you're better than he is, that you can tell him something he doesn't...the sooner you'll be betting the orders. There isn't a squarer boss in the game than Crowe. He'll treat you better than you've ever been treated, and he'll give you every chance in the world but he's no damn fool and when he wants something done he means it and he hates like hell to tell a person twice and he hates worse to have you say you have done this and that and then find you haven't. I don't know what help I can be to you...if there is anything I can do I'll gladly do it, but you've got to ask me. I can't just sit down and deliver a lecture. If you will sit down and make out lists of things you have come up against and ask me or George Suadl will do our best help and if we can't Crowe will, but you've got to do the asking.

"It's awfully hard to write this kind of stuff because I've no license to begin to pose as one who knows more than you, because I don't but you've got to show a poker up your spine and straighten up, Bill. Don't look as though you've been licked every time you come in the office or see an advertiser. There's nothing in the world easier or more pleasant than calling System if you'll really get self-confidence and know your proposition. Now let's get together and plug like hell. Put in a little work around the office in the evening, dream about your work a while and pretty soon it'll be a cinch."

It was early December when Billy wrote, "Don't know when I've worked so hard...from 8 a.m. until midnight every day...Mr.

Crowe has been over here all day working on some of the larger accounts…have a terrible day ahead of me tomorrow, but will get through, and be home tomorrow night."

Billy was in Pittsburgh when he dropped a note to Elsie from the Fort Pitt Hotel, "I got to Wooster on Saturday…went to Uncle Cam's. I sat in the presidential pew and thought longingly of 'Rother's Row' and a certain seat in the chair loft…But, Compy was right behind and I couldn't think of them too hard or he would surely have read them all off the back of my head."

A Wooster College friend, Jack Loy, is working for a stone company in Piqua, Ohio and writes, "If I ever for one single moment thought that a little stinking bit of rotten money could in any way affect the friendship I feel for you, I would have sued the account…You see Billy, I am looking for big things from you. You are bound to live up to what I expect, aren't you? One naturally looks for big things from a big man, and that's why I am looking up to you for them."

CHAPTER 14

World War I 1916-1918

B uster was a 9 lb. 2 oz. bundle of joy. It was the nickname Elsie and Billy gave Wilbert Wallace White III when he was born on August 6, 1916. They started a diary and tucked inside one page was a lock of Buster's hair. She recorded short snippets of activities until it suddenly stopped seven months later on March 6. That was the day they found out Betsey was deaf. They thought she was developing normally, until Aunt Helen observed her lack of response to certain sounds. At first, Elsie and Billy didn't think it was unusual, but decided to have their physician, Dr. Henry E. Hale, examine her. He referred them to a doctor in Philadelphia where it was verified. In 1917, there were few schools for the deaf, but Helen and Elsie would search for one. But that heartbreak didn't compare to those lying ahead.

Edward and Jean received the news, "I send my greetings to the youngster and hope he will thrive like Elizabeth...shall be glad to get a picture of the baby boy named after his father as soon as he is presentable."

Feelings of romance filled Elsie's soul, "I have been thinking of you all day, of a moonlit and a cushioned swing, of a sweet gray down which stole upon a pair of lovers, unawares, and most of all, of a song that you sang in your heart, and have been teaching me to sing these years. Do you not think I have learned it well? The song, the words, I love you, I love you, I love you... your sweetheart, a thousand times more than on that night when you clasped her to your heart as yours." With a new baby, Billy's issues caused Elsie to reach out to Aunt Kate. Elsie received a letter from Kate White on October 3, "You surely have a generous heart. Here I have been feeling I must be in bad with you because I have not written for long. Yes, and in blows your letter just full of love. Thank you, dear heart for I never deserve it and least of all now...we are feeling a bit settled. I'll tell you of the house again...The girls are liking it and making friends fast... You do not say what Wilbert's doing. However, I hope he has found congenial work and that all your anxieties in that score are over. And as far as other difficulties which still come in your day's work just tell Jesus and get his comfort and as often as I am in the Station and get a wireless message. I will intercede for you against the adversary.

In mid-March, Elsie's father, 51 year old Edward Machle made an announcement, "for unto us a child is born and unto us a daughter is given, and her name is Mary Ida Jean. Mary for your Grandma Machle, Ida for Harry's wife, and Jean for the baby's mother. She weighed when born 7 lbs. 2 oz. (rather light weight compared with your son, 9 lbs. 2 oz.), she is thriving and will be 3 weeks old tomorrow at 3 p.m. Pray for her welfare."

On Elsie's birthday, Billy was at The Emerson in Baltimore, Maryland, "This is your birthday and I'm not home to celebrate it with you. I wonder if you actually realize how much I should like to be there now with you. If I were---well, there wouldn't be very much left of you I can tell you." In a worn leather bound book, Elsie underlined passages from Woodrow Wilson's book, *On Being Human*, "Let us remind ourselves that to be human is, for one thing, to speak and act with a certain note of genuineness...we expect what we call genuine to have pith and strength of fiber…individuality is lost the moment you submit to passing modes or fashions, the creations of an artificial society; and so is genuineness…genuineness we conceive to be always wholesome, balanced, and touched with dignity. Laughter is genuine, speech is genuine, character is genuine, …the art of being human begins with the practice of being genuine and following standards of conduct which the world has tested." Wilbert continued to travel for his job as a saleman for Systems Magazine while Elsie stayed in New York caring for the children, occasionally meeting him at one of the hotels where he was staying.

It was April 6, 1917 when President Woodrow Wilson signed the decree to go to war to help France against Germany, but didn't deliver a message to Congress until December 4, 1917, adding, "Let there be no misunderstanding. Our present and immediate task is to win the war, and nothing shall turn us aside from it until it is accomplished." General Pershing and the American Expeditionary Forces landed in France on June 13. There became a flurry of advertising in movie theatres and Liberty Bonds were on the market to finance the troops. France sold 4,500 airplanes to the U.S. and by July 31, the offensive began. The U.S. troops were popular everywhere they went, and the black soldiers were welcomed by the French. The newspapers featured articles about the threat since the death of Archduke Ferdinand. Yet the newspapers were also advertising for student fliers. One headline in the New York Times on June 25, 1917, "Government Calls for Student fliers: Expects to Graduate 200 a Week in Advanced Aviation Fields After August 25. 800 are in Training now: Twenty-four Camps Will Be Established to Accommodate Thousands of Students." And continued on page 6, Among the… current places in the U.S. to apply, was the "Mineola Field, at Mineola, Long Island." On July 5, Billy[9] signed up at the 68th Precinct, Bronx City. Then went home to 62 East 190th Street, a short distance from Fordham University, and told Elsie. They got into a heated argument. One account says that Elsie was hysterical but there is no indication that it was about signing up. After all, they had two children, one who needed special care leaving Elsie to manage the responsibility alone. By September, he was on his way to Toronto, Canada, "Got leave tonight and dropped in here to write you a note. Have to be back out in bed at 10:00 and it is an hour and 30-minute ride, so you can see how much of a letter it is going to be as it is now after eight. They work us out here like the very devil. Up at 5:30 for two-hour drill before breakfast and then drill again from nine till 11:45. In the p.m., classes and some more drill, with some inoculations and vaccinations mixed in. 'T' at 5:30, study, write letters, etc. from there till lights out. This blooming drill (English) surely gets our goat with the English sergeants giving us orders and swearing at us in a vocabulary that would back Pen Alcock clear off the map. I hope never to be so proficient as they, but don't be surprised when I get home or rather 'owe' I should 'sye' 'you '-bloody - blightess."

It was Sunday, September 23 when Billy wrote, "Have just finished a letter to mother...The reasons I haven't written in the past two days is because of the cold. The camp is of course cold as blixen and if I'd write from there you couldn't read it because of the shivers. Came in today to get these two off: yours and mothers."

"My how I'd like to be down there with you for a while at least. Do you think you could get me good and warm just once? We don't know just how long we're going to have to stay here but may be moved in to barracks in town any day. There is a probability that we'll all go to Texas very soon too. It is too cold up here to practice flying."

Three days later, "Will just give you my schedule for today and you can see 5:30 reveille, 6-7 drill, 7-8 shave, clean 'boots', tent and straighten up for inspection; 8-9 breakfast and half an hour drill. 9 o'clock inspection on the parade grounds, and drill till 10:30, 10:30-11 bathing parade; 11-12 lecture and wireless practice, 12-12:30 talk from our own officers, 12:30-1 lunch; 1-1:30 standing in line for mail, 1:30-2 study for gunnery, 2-3 lecture from medical doctor, 3-4 gunnery class; 4-5 map reading; 5-6 supper and some study; 6-7 practice in stripping a Lewis Machine Gun, 7-8 recite in wireless, 8-9 study and I'm now waiting for 'lights out'. Every one of these things are required except standing in line for the mail and as I haven't received any mail from home at all, I'm rather anxious to hear."

Within the week, "I am sitting here in the tent in an overcoat with all my blankets wrapped around me trying to keep warm. The wind is blowing a gale and my hands are about freezing, so if they get too stiff I'll have to quit. Have been studying radio most of the day. We have an exam on Thursday and have to be able to take ten words a minute—I can now take six without a great many mistakes but will have to push like thunder to get the ten. Each word is five letters long, and they're not real words, just a senseless conglomeration of letters...A big bunch of us were inoculated for the third time and vaccinated yesterday and I am feeling pretty much under the weather today. They inoculate up here over the left breast and I think that it 'takes' a whole lot more and better than down home.

"One of the fellows brought out the fudge Ann made for me about two weeks ago. It had been in the headquarters office at Toronto (we're about 20 miles out) all the time. He said that there wasn't any other mail in there for me, so I am still expecting a whole bunch one of these days. Have heard only once from you and know that you've written me oftener. Will have to write a note to Ann and thank her. The fudge was good even if it was two weeks old. Too stiff to write more now." Billy never mentioned

Ann Thompson before, but it is assumed Elsie knows who Ann is. The 1915 U.S. Census lists a Florence Thompson, missionary living at 130 E. 50th Street, as a missionary, the same address as Billy and Elsie, however, there is no way to verify whether Ann and Florence are the same person since his advertising job was located in the Philadelphia area.

On October 15 "Just a line before lights out. We are now at the University of Toronto working harder than ever." Elsie shows her compassion for Billy's situation when she shares what little money she has with him. "Your letter with the dollar and a half came Friday. I couldn't cash the order till Saturday night. It was mighty good of you to send it for I know you need every cent. I'll make it go a long long way…We came in here on Friday in all the rain and wind and were a terribly bedraggled bunch when we hit the city. Will probably have to stay here for about six weeks, and it is a thousand times better than camp anyway. How I wish I could come in on you all for a little while, and yet it isn't 'you all' it is just you. I'd give a whole lot just to be with you for a few days. Just us two. If we can arrange it, and I get a furlough, let's go off somewhere together."

It was November 4, "We are all studying to beat the band. Yesterday in one of our classes they announced that we would have our exams on Monday and go direct to Texas on Wednesday morning. We ought to arrive about Saturday. I will wire you my address in Texas as soon as we know what it will be. What I'm writing this letter for is to make a confession. There were a lot of things entered into it as a cause, but of course that doesn't excuse me. The long and short of the thing is just this. You know (perhaps you know everything) but at least, that Ann Thompson and I were terribly thick last summer. I told her a lot of stuff I shouldn't have and said a lot of foolish things I didn't mean or at least I felt way down in my heart were not true. And – well now I don't like to think how close I, or rather we, came to doing something disastrous. I've written her today that we were all wrong, that there is only one woman on earth for me, and as soon as I can I'm coming to you to tell you all about it myself personally, and to let you know that there can't ever be anyone else but just you in my life ever again for a single moment. I don't know whether you can ever love me again but for me, you can bank absolutely on my faithfulness. I love you as I never have loved before, stronger, deeper, truer, purer, and if you'll forgive me, no you must forgive, it's everything to me. I'm sorry, sorry. We may go direct to France from Texas but I'm going to try to get leave to come at least part way home and have you meet me for a day or so at least. We will probably be in France by New Years. Must close now and get back to work. Ever, more than ever, always and all ways your husband." Then she received a telegram that he arrived in Texas and his address would be, Talliaferro Benbrook Wing Eighty Fourth Aero Squadron Fort Worth, Texas, Cadet Barracks." It was known as the Flying Triangle: Hicks Field, Barron Field and Benbrook Field because of their locations.

By November 30 he was at Huckins Hotel in Fort Worth, "Two of us ran away from camp this morning after the inspection parade and came in to town. It is about 15 miles in and the only way to get in is by either foot or auto. We were lucky and bummed a ride in. Hope it is as easy going out. We have to get out there by 2:30 for the next roll call so haven't such an awful lot of time...We got here yesterday shortly after noon and were all dumped down into a brand new camp that is about half finished. The planes are here and all assembled except the engines which haven't arrived yet. But I expect we'll be flying in a few days again. The trip down was rather tiresome especially the start. We got down to the station about 3 o'clock Thursday morning and didn't leave until 3:00 o'clock in the afternoon. The troop train from the north was delayed. There were 500 on the train. About 25 Americans. It is great to be back among real people again but wish I could have stopped off for a few days and seen you. You don't know how much I wish I could have. I am going to try to find out very soon just what our program is going to be from now on so that I can arrange some kind of a way to see you. We 25 fellows are going to be a U.S. Unit attached to the Royal Flying Corps in France so we may have a different schedule than some of the others...Sweetheart please don't forget that there is only one woman on earth for me and that is you and I know that more truly now than ever before." As near as I can figure the best way to reach me is Camp Talliaferro, Benbrook Wing, Fort Worth Texas. 84th Aero Squadron R.F.C. Cadet Barracks."

Later that same day, "This letter is being written with a suitcase as a desk, and one candle about six feet away for a light. I hope that you'll be able to read it. I started on my solo flying, that is alone on Tuesday morning and got away very well. Vernon Castle started me off." It was the same Vernon Castle of "the premier dance team of the time, Briton Irene and Vernon led the way. The Castle's managed to combine a trend-setting image as liberalizers of behavior with an air of middle-class moral respectability" (Maltby, 1989 p. 44) in their dance routine. Before we started...took me off in a good field about five miles from the aerodrome and gave me a flock of landings till he thought I was good enough to go alone. The landings are the hardest to do right. Of course, anyone can get down to earth, but it is an art to get downright without bouncing all over the lot and crashing up the machine. Well, on Tuesday, I got away all right and did about an hour solo with about ten landings. On Wednesday, it rained most of the day and we had to clean up the inside of the hangard[*sic*]. Thursday morn about ten o'clock I had my first crash, and I feel a whole lot better about it now that it's over. I just about 'washed out' the machine that in air language means junked it, put it completely out of business, ruined it. I came down and thought I was about right to straighten out, but was too high off the ground, and did what we call a 'pancake'. That means instead of gliding onto the ground, you lose your speed and drop flat. Well, after the pancake, I bounced about fifty feet in the air came down on one wing, tilted over on my nose, broke my 'prop' (propeller) one wing, the undercarriage, the main street, and one longerou[*sic*]. It was a wonder. And I stepped out of the wreck as whole as I have ever been. The system we follow down here is to go up again as soon as possible after you crash a machine. So, I went up again right away and was all fine and dandy. Today I was up for about an hour and twenty minutes and have got about three hours in altogether. I have three more to do before I go to the advanced squadron. There have been four different fellows come and sit on my bed since I started this letter so don't laugh if it is a little bit disjointed...I've taken out my $10,000 insurance[10], took it before I went on my first solo. Will write father about it as soon as possible. Speaking of writing, you have no idea how tired we get just sitting around waiting for machines. The nervous strain is something terrible, and if you're up for an hour or more it is really hard on your nerves. By night you're perfectly ready to crawl into your blankets and go to sleep...Am afraid that we are not going to get through this course here before the middle of January at the very earliest. We will get our commissions down here after we finish the course. Then the news is that we get two weeks leave before going to France. I surely hope it's true. Two weeks is an awfully short time for me to tell you everything and show you everything I want to, but we'll have to make the very best of it, if you'll only let me, that is what I'm wondering all the time. Can you love me again, can you ever love me again as you have. Oh, sweetheart if you only realize how much I want you to just let me, give me one more chance to show you how I love you, one more chance to make you love me. It means everything to me dearest, everything. If you can't, or you won't, I want to know. I want to know before I go over. You're all in all to me—everything, it has taken me a long time to realize it fully, but now I know, I know, that you are the one, the only woman in the world. If I've lost you, there is no one to blame but myself, but oh Darling, Elsie, tell me that you'll give me a chance again, for I love you, love you, always and forever."

He wrote a letter on Sunday, December 1 about, "his 'joy ride', It was very bumpy up to about 1500 feet, then it got just as smoothe as glass. I went up to about 3800 feet and just drifted around and looked the country over. I was up from 4:00 o-clock till sunset---about 5:30 and it surely was beautiful. You would be very much surprised at how much you can see, and how plainly, from that height, roads, railroad tracks, autos, everything. When I was coming back down I had about a ten-mile run with a train. Of course, I could run away from it any time, but it made the passengers very much excited, and they leaned out the windows and waved and pointed. It really is a wonderful lot of fun. Wish I could give you a ride. Maybe I can when I get back...We are quarantined here for fourteen days...because of the measles in Fort Worth...I'm sorry I can't be there...these five years have been mighty hard one's for you I know, but if I am to have anything to do with the rest of the years of your life, they are going to be happier and happier as they go by. You'll only know this after some of them have passed, but Darling Girl of Mine, please try to anticipate them a little bit. I want you to know that I love you, love you, love you, as you have never been loved. All I can hope for is that you will someday learn to love me again."

Several weeks later, "Have just returned from a general call for the men to turn out for fire. The houses here are so frail and dry, and the water supply so scarce that we turn out at the slightest alarm. The fire tonight proved to be a little blaze in the pumping station and was put out before most of us got there. That is the second time tonight, the first was a false alarm. I told you in my last letter that I had been made senior cadet of the U.S. men in camp, and today I've been helping a lot of the fellows write up their insurance papers. Lieutenant Peters, the man commanding us is a good scout, but has not had an awful lot of experience, so between the two of us we have quite a time. I've transferred to the 83rd Squadron, that is the last one I have here in this camp. From it I got to the gunnery school (aerial) at Camp Hicks about 30 miles away. It will take me about 10 days in 83 and I'm hoping to make the gunnery class that starts on the 31st of December. If I can do that I ought to be through over there by the 13th or 14th. After that I'm not sure about the time it will take to get my commission, but don't think it will be long, then you won't be able to see me for the trail I make for home. I know how you must feel sweetheart about me. You can't help doubting my love, and I certainly can't blame you for a minute...how I wish I could be at home with you and the babes for Christmas, but here I am in a quarantined camp, without a chance of seeing you all, without even a chance of going to town to buy a few little things I'd like to send you and the rest, especially Betsey and Buster...that is the quarantine won't be lifted, so I'm afraid there isn't a chance of sending anything. I suppose you'll all be together there at 541. Well, I'm not going to enlarge on that, or I'll be boo-hooing... Your letter from Haddon Heights was a wonder. I don't know what to say or think about your plans. Of course, I know that you will be successful in them if you go after them the way you can. I've always said you would be successful if you tried. Perhaps this whole thing is just working out so that you can find your real self, or rather find the self-confidence for that is all that is really needed. I know you can do it, do anything you want to, and I'm 'cheering' all the way." Elsie made a decision to move to Philadelphia and take post-graduate work in bacteriology at the University of Pennsylvania. She found an apartment at 1912 Pine Street, close to Philadelphia General Hospital. She quickly became the laboratory assistant to Dr. Randle Rosenberger who was researching syphilis and assisted in the publication of a lab guide. By December 24, Billy sent a telegram wishing her a Merry Christmas and Happy New Year with instructions to write him at School of Aerial Gunnery AMP Hicks at Fort Worth. Then this letter on January 3, 1918 from Camp Taliaferro[11], "We came over here yesterday morning, are living in tents, have to walk a mile each way for meals to wash…and we don't care much for it. Am afraid I won't be home as soon as I thought. There have been fellows here who have been through the course for four or six weeks and are still waiting here for their commissions. They can't leave or even get away from camp. This American system is very poor all the way through. I can't tell you how big a disappointment the prospect of this delay is to me. Oh, how I want to get home, and how I want to see you. I'll be running away from this army one of these days and coming straight to you."

"In the tent, all alone", he writes on January 4, "Which is a wonder for as a rule when we are off duty, we're pretty well crowded in here. Tonight however, the rest of the fellows are exploring some of the would-be pleasure halls of the new camp. There is a large canteen here where they sell soft drinks, and sandwiches, and smokes, also there is a barber there, and oh yes, a victrola. It really is quite a place and lots of the fellows like to spend a good bit of their time off over there. Tomorrow night they are going to stage a couple of flights, and I think I'll take the show in. It will be a little bit exciting anyway. We're in the last stage now of our training in this country. According to schedule, we should get our commissions in about two weeks—we'll finish up in about ten days—then be assigned to squadrons for overseas, go to England where we have about a month more training in fast scout machines, then go on over to France. But the way they are holding the fellows up here after they've finished their training before they get their orders, it looks as if I would not be home for some time yet. Things may change though and they may rush us on through. They're needing men at the front now and for the Spring Drive more than ever before and they may come across for us. Well, we'll just have to wait and see what they will do with us. I haven't told you much about the friends I've made and am running around with here. It would take forever, and I'd hardly begin. The fellows in the tent are all college men, except one from Plainfield, New Jersey and he is one prince of a fellow, Bill Taylor by name. He has recently become engaged lately to a girl in New York, and we, you and I and Bill and his girl are going to have some parties together when we get home. Ed Bogart one of the other fellows just came in from the Squadron Office and says that we are booked to go over on the 15th of February, and that we'll get a 10 day leave after we finish here maybe. That means that we'll have to report back here before we start for New York. If that is true, I'm going to try to go home then meet the squadron in New York, but I'm afraid it will be mighty hard to work. I don't want to come home without my commission, but I want to get home worse than anything I know, and I'll go as a clown if I have to, to get there...You know sweetheart how and why I want to get home. You are the only reason, and I want to see you and talk to you more than anything...Goodnight Darling. The gang is here and there's no more letter writing possible. The tent is packed." But by January 16, he was waiting for his commission. There were three cases of scarlet fever in camp and he didn't think he would get home before February.

"This has been, and still is, an awfully long day". On Sunday January 6, "I had two exams to get off on the Vicars gun and have had to stand in line most of the morning for one—they were both oral, and practically all afternoon for the other. I got 95% in the first and 90% in the second. The latter mark was the highest the instructor gave during the afternoon, so I'm quite 'set up'...This is no idle dream, playing around here in the air, especially when you are fellows out of your own bunch dropping out for one reason or other. There are only about sixty of our original hundred left in the Flying Corps now, and a whole lot of them are more anxious to stay on the ground than fly. Two of the fellows have been killed, some have been scared completely out, and others have had to be dropped because their health wouldn't stand it. There are about 15 who have come as far as I am. Don't think I'm telling you this to scare you or get a lot of sympathy or anything else dark in motive. It's simply to let you know the facts. I'm forecasting nothing. My health and nerves couldn't be better for this game. I'll never stop because of fright, and I'd rather fly than eat. In fact, nothing on earth could take me away from camp, if I thought there would be a chance to fly except the possibility of seeing you but I want you to know Darling that if an accident should ever occur, every beat of my heart up to the last moment will be of you and of you alone. It comes quickly in this game when it comes, and oh how did I ever get on this strain at all...How are Betsey and Buster? Father said something in one of his letters about you taking Betsey down to Philadelphia to see some expert and I've heard nothing more of it...Has Buster started to say anything yet?"

It is 1918, a week after New Year's Eve and, "Two of the fellows have gone in to Fort Worth, one of the others is reading a story and making side remarks, and one of the others is reading an article on aviation aloud to the other, and it certainly is a joke.

Perhaps the author visited an aviation field at one time in his life, but in all probability he got most of his information from a book. It is a lot of fun to read the different articles and see just how gullible the public is, but of course they know nothing about it and have been fed up on so many stories, that no one knows just what to believe. I'll give you some real stories soon, and I suppose lots of them you won't believe. One of the Lieutenants who was giving us a lecture yesterday on some necessary stunts we will have to know how to do, and who is an excellent stunter[*sic*] himself, was hurt badly today. He came down doing a spinning nose dive but didn't start to come out of it until about 25 feet from the ground, and he didn't get all the way out. He broke both his legs, one in three places, and in all probability won't fly again for a year at least."

"So, you sent me some cigarettes in a package along with a bel...excuse me...stomach protectors" he chides in a January 9 letter to Elsie, "Well, I never got them. That is, I haven't received them yet, but will keep on looking until they arrive. As for the protectors of my abdominal regions, will tell you on the Q.T. that we don't wear them. The fellows who were down on the border last summer found them to be very impractical, insomuch that if you once wore one, you always had to keep one on and as I have not been cold in that particular spot since coming down here, I don't want to humor any part of my anatomy that doesn't need it very much. If anyone should ask you what I want most in the knitted line, tell them socks, socks, and again socks, after socks come sweaters, but when mother's and Helen's come, I'll be pretty well outfitted even in those...When are you planning to go down to Philadelphia permanently? So, do I hope that it won't be before I get home, although on second thought it might be just as comfortable for all concerned if we were not up at 62. I'm sorrier than I can ever tell you sweetheart about that rotten thing that happened there. Oh, how I wish I could live over those last few weeks at home. Oh, how very very different they would be, and how much happier would your last memories of me be…We've been over here at Hicks just one week now, in the School of Aerial Gunnery. The first week is spent on what they call 'ground tests' I got all of them finished up yesterday and was transferred last night to the Aerial Section. In the section I'm in now we have to do a lot of shooting from machines. I did most of my camera gun work today, that consists of going up in a machine with a machine gun mounted on the upper wing right over your head, and we have to go out and bring down a whole flock of 'enemy' machines. The only difference between the guns we use and the guns we will use on the front is that these are fitted as cameras, and we take pictures of each other. We have to allow for the speed of the other machine—whether it is climbing or diving, etc. etc. It is great maneuvering for position and drawing heads and shooting. There the pictures are developed, and we can see just whether we would have been got or would have gotten. The other tests are firing real ammunition at silhouette targets on the ground and floating on Lake Worth. We fire about 5000 rounds of ammunition apiece. I fought a little over an hour and a half today. Am the first one of our crowd to get my ground tests off and hope I can keep it up and get through first, and get leave first, and a whole lot of firsts…How I wish I were home tonight. I'd hold you close, oh so close sweetheart of mine. You wouldn't be able to get away from me if you wanted to. I'm crazy, absolutely crazy, to see you and kiss you just once more. I love you, love you Darling wife with my whole heart, soul and body, and I'm holding you close in my arms tight, so you can never get away from me, never. I'm always your own, through life, through death, through eternity."

By mid-January, he thinks he'll get his commission before he gets home, "They have given some of the more advanced fellows theirs, so they may hand ours out earlier than we have been expecting" but by the 18th, he wanted Elsie to tell him "some of the things Betsey and Buster do. You have no idea how I'd love to hear more about what you all do. I know it must be hard to find time to write very voluminous letters, but when you can find time, please do it…don't know when we are going to start north, but it won't be for a few weeks yet anyway. Am going to see someone soon about leave. Just to start the ball rolling…Got a good letter from father today." It was January 22 when there was a mix up with his father and mother's birthdays. First Elsie forgot Dr. White's birthday and then, he wrote both his father and mother on their respective days but got them twisted around and sent them. "Darn it all I'm sorry as the dickens about it but suppose they won't take terrible offense…If God is good enough to let me live through what is before me, my one object in life is going to be to make the rest of your life my Dearest the happiest in the world. Every energy I have will be thrown into that one thing. I'm selfish I admit, because in so doing I'll be giving myself the greatest amount of pleasure possible." It was January 26 when he wrote a letter to his father, Wilbert W. White, "Life is to me is a whole lot more serious matter than it has ever been before. I realize that I have something to live for, and if necessary to die for, and I'm fully prepared to do either. If God wills that I come through this war with my senses, I'm going to do a lot of things I was never thinking of before, and if I am not to get back – well, I will at least have given my life for the right. It is a great war we are in, father, a wonderful war; a war between right and wrong, and I'm in it heart and soul to the end."

"Your letter with the illustration of the inmates of 190th Street sleigh riding came today", on January 30, "you surely are some artist. I liked particularly the 'chin-up—look straight-ahead' atmosphere of you all except Buster when I was supposed to be coming down the street. Please don't let that atmosphere prevail when I do come marching home. Glory! How good that word 'home' sounds. I'll never want to leave when I do get there let me tell you that…say Sweetheart how much and what, or have you told father anything about what happened up at 62 before I left. The reason I ask is because he has hinted in a couple of letters that he wants to have a talk about some things that he doesn't want to write about. He makes a lot of references about how much he wishes we were out of 62 (and I agree with him there) but I do want to know how things stand. You understand, don't you." The reference to 62 is unclear but indicates that he has remorse about it and may not have had anything to do with signing up for the air corp.

He was assigned to the 147th Aero Squadron, a Day Pursuit (Fighter) Squadron whose mission was to engage and clear enemy aircraft from the skies and provide escort to reconnaissance and bombardment squadrons over enemy territory, as well as attack enemy observation balloons and perform close air support and tactical bombing attacks of enemy forces along the front lines. "Have a few minutes before I go to the squadron meeting… I find out that I can be more sure of getting my mail if you send it care of the 147th Aero Squadron at this camp…you had better burn these letters just to be on the safe side…when I get my commission which by now has been fully decided will be a Second Lieutenancy. I'll get between $175 and $180 a month. In about three months I'm hoping for a first, then go on up as fast as possible after that, but it will be impossible to go up a rank inside of three months. The first Lieutenant's pay is only about $25 a month more, but the next step is considerable. I will allot—that's what they call it—50% of whatever my pay is to be sent directly to you from Washington. Am hoping that will commence with next month's pay. I may be able to make it more when I get over there and see what the conditions are...wish you'd tell me more of your plans about Philadelphia...you told me about your being in Philadelphia and going to see some man down there and your plans about going to some school. Then in the next letter I got, you said the rooms in Philadelphia were almost ready."

By January 26, he passed his R.M.A. and will get his commission. He has a new Commanding Officer, a former Montclair boy, Bonnell...he came about a year or two after me in high school. Have only seen him once closely but am perfectly sure he is the same. He played the M.H.S. hockey team with Ken Johnson, and we knew him as Jeff Bonnell. He was in the R.F.C. over in France and brought down Von Bolke, the great German aviator. He was then made a Captain and when he transferred to the U.S. Aviation Service became a Major. He is about 27 years old. Am positive he is the same fellow. I have not said anything to him yet for I don't want him to think I'm looking for favors, for that doesn't go in the army. I'd like to go over in his squadron, but the fellows I've been going with and have trained all the way through with are in the 182nd and are after me to try to get transferred to that one. I don't know whether Major Bonnell will let me or not, but I think I'll try to do it, for that bunch of the fellows are the very best flyers in camp. A rather nice pat on the back, but it is true. Am enclosing a picture of nine of us, the tenth was not around when this was taken, also a picture of our tent the morning after the big blizzard...the moon down here sweetheart, it is perfectly wonderful, last night and the night before, it was calm and clear, and the sight of that old moon hanging up there, just about tore the heart right out of me. I was thinking all of you, longing only for you and praying that someday I'll be worthy of you. That old moon can tell so many, many things, can remind me of so many wonderful times with you. And it doesn't have to be a beautiful night either darling, oh it is all the time. No matter where I am, no matter what I'm doing, I'm thinking constantly of you, always of you. Will I ever be able to win that love which I know is in you for someone or will I have to go away without knowing. I…must know before I have to leave New York."

By February 6, "From now on you can send my letters addressed to Lieutenant W.W.W. that is, of course, unless you get a wire before you write, telling you I'm on my way to you. I have not yet received my commission but have seen it and am to be sworn in tomorrow a.m. at 10 o'clock…Can't tell for sure yet about when we leave but it will be within the next ten or twelve days. No one is going to be allowed leave before the squadron leaves, but we'll be able to get it while we're waiting in New York. That is the best way anyway I think for if I got leave I would have to spend between $50 and $75 to get home and by going with the squadron, our way will, of course, be paid…That birthday party of Ann's must have been a great success, no men about and all the stories you could think of…suppose I could use an adjective in front of 'stories'. But say, the next time you address one of Ann's letters for her. I'll well, I'll do something terrible to you when I get you. That's a warning. It was a mighty nice letter she wrote me and I'm going to write her very soon. Also, Harry. I know I've acted like an awful cad in not writing before this but well I just didn't want to think anything more about that chapter in my life, than I have. Oh, darn it all, what a fool I've been, and what a general mess of things I've made…Your letters have been wonderful, and how I do hope you really, really, way down deep in your heart, want to see me as badly as you say you do. If you only knew how much. How very much I love you, and how much I want to see you and hear you tell me that you love me. Oh you'd write it to me all the time. But Darling, I'm going to see you soon, going to hold you in my arms, and feel your arms about me, I know it, I know it. You're mine, all mine, and nothing on earth can change that fact."

By March, the squadron was at Camp Mills Aviation Concentration Center in Garden City, established to facilitate Air Service units for the purpose of embarkation to Europe. He was at the Garden City Hotel one afternoon, "Perhaps I should have come in this afternoon, but I know how things are. It would have been one mad rush to get in, a few minutes together and then another goodbye, so I didn't do it. I'm sure you will understand. Don't think I didn't want to see you and the rest again, but you've all been on a pretty big strain during the past few days and I didn't want to make it any harder. I have been made 2nd in Command of "A" Flight. Frank Ennis is the Flight Commander and we should work together pretty well. By the way. Tell father that if the boots come for A.H. Jones, and the coat for E.A. Bogert, hold them until called for. Am writing Bill Taylor and when he comes through he can get them and bring them on over for them. Well sweetheart we are going to be separated for some time now, and I surely hope that you're going to be happy while I'm gone, and when I come back. When I come back, we're going to have a perfectly wonderful home, and a perfectly wonderful time 'until death us do part'. Just remember that no matter what happens there is and always will be only one woman in my life."

He sailed on March 4, 1918 and scribbled a note to his mother, "Just know mother dear, that no matter what happens, I'm thinking of you always, and will be back as soon as I can." And to Elsie, "May not have another chance to write so just want to tell you that everything is fine and dandy. Will have to leave this open if I want you to get any word before we land over there... Hope things went along well and that Dr. Wright is going to take

Betsey. For goodness sake don't exclude any details when you write. I'm longing for news already."

Elsie began writing poetry in March. Arbutus grew in China and perhaps the memory of her early childhood became more distinct.

"Arbutus
I know a sunny slope to the South
Where the earliest spring flowers blow,
A sunny slope where the delicate buds
Of the trailing arbutus grow.
What scents wafted from the tropic breeze!
Can equal the scent on that sunny slope,
Of arbutus among the leaves?
Glorious blue skies and blustery winds
The lamb and the lion together,
Eager, I seek that sunny slope,
For this is arbutus weather.
Surely some frolicsome elves danced here,
Joyous and light of wing
With rosy tipped censers of fairy land,
Exhaling attar of spring.
And then some prying mortal came
Disturbing their fairy glee,
And they scattered in haste from the sunny slope
Leaving their censers to me.
I gather you tenderly, fragrant things,
Rich glossy leaves and all,
I love you, I love you, frail beautiful buds
And the fairies who let you fall."

CHAPTER 15

The Skylark

Billy arrived in Liverpool on March 18 after boarding the S.S. Cedric on March 5 in Hoboken, New Jersey. The next day the S.S. Cedric left port at 10:00 a.m. It was March 23 before the 147th Aero Squadron received their orders from the American Expeditionary Headquarters in London to proceed to France as a unit. On May 23, he sent Elsie this message, "I am now a Flight Commander and am giving everything I've got to that work in the hope of learning a lot and getting something better. We are in a wonderfully beautiful spot, not right up to the lines, but close enough to get there in a few minutes by air. It is a rolling country, and just at this time of year needs only you to make it the only place on earth. Am taking a number of pictures and can show you some wonders when I get back. This afternoon about 3:30, I quit, left everything in the hands of my sergeant and came down here to the barracks to write you. Am sitting now just outside the quarters in a wonderful woods, and am expecting to be driven inside almost any minute by a shower, for by the sound of thunder off in the west, we will surely have one before long. The thunder showers are very severe breakouts. Only last week one of the men in the Squadron was killed. He was standing in the doorway in a little pool of water with his hand on an electric light switch, so he made a perfect circuit. It was surely too bad.

"When we got here, found a whole lot of mail, Lordy, it was good to hear from you again. But I cannot understand why up until the 20th of April you had had no word from me. It is very peculiar. I had written often, and unless the letters were either held up by the censor, which I think unlikely, for I've been very careful, they have either reached you by now or were on one of the ships that was subbed. I'm sorry dearest but know that you were not out of my mind a minute at least. How about the allotment, have you received any of that yet? I haven't been getting my flying pay yet, so will have quite a bundle coming in one of these days—it is due home the 5th of February. Here comes the rain, so I'll have to go in...Just a little addition to what I was writing the other day. We had to scurry around and put pans, buckets, and anything else we could lay our hands on, on top of our beds to keep them from floating away. After I had waterproofed our room pretty well, I was going into one of the others when the lightning struck our trunk line and illuminated the whole barracks for a moment. After the fuse had burnt out, we were in darkness. These French thunderstorms are like a lot of other things Francois, very intense, but not terribly lasting. Perhaps I'm slandering a wonderful people by saying that, for the way they have stood up under this war is truly marvelous. And, the punishment, they have received is stupendous, but there is a lot of superficiality in a great deal of what they do and say. Not that they are not sincere at the time, but they are a passionate, impulsive, nation, and in many ways childlike. So, unlike the British...Am writing this letter 'catch-as-catch-can'...We have moved again, a little farther up and closer to the real thing. In fact, we are really a part of it now, and it is all intensely interesting. I am just at present lying in bed—the doctor ordered it, so there is no other way out. Not a thing wrong with me except a little lumbago and stomach trouble, and I'll be up tomorrow for sure. I guess that my wooden bed must have gotten damp and the muscles of my back and abdomen absorbed it. I got a letter from John [Mott] yesterday and am hoping to be able to locate him sometime soon. Don't know just what part of the lines he is on yet but think I can probably find out in some way. Also, I got a letter from Quinnie about a week ago, and that was the saddest blow of all for she was in Paris when I came through. I inquired at the Y.M. and Y.W. but did not at the Red Cross. Whew, but I would like to have seen her. Maybe, I'll get a chance later on. Here's hoping. I saw Nancy (Hawthorne) the other day, too, she is stationed in this same section, and I'll probably get to see her quite often. Savvy...The doc was just in and I read him that last sentence, and he says there is too much mental work going into this letter and I'll have to stop." The author Samuel Hynes in his book, The *Unsubstantiated Air* addresses these reactions to flying, "fatalism, dizziness, staleness, loss of nerve—to the doctors of the American Air Medical Service these reactions to flying seemed to constitute a moral problem that was endemic wherever men flew. In August 1918 a party of thirty-three doctors and fifteen laboratory personnel went to France and England to examine the condition of American fliers there and to write a report of their conclusions." Medical doctors were assigned to the units to monitor the health of the flyers for combat readiness. They had the authority to tell the commander if the pilot wasn't mentally capable of making decisions in combat. If they weren't ready, they would receive orders to go home. Billy didn't always share his true feelings with Elsie or how the losses impacted him. After arriving in France, men in the squadron began to call him "Whitey". There was one instance when Lt. Ray Brooks, a friend in the 139th Aero Squadron, described one of his issues, "My most vivid memory of Whitey was when we were at Issoudun at the acrobatic field. He told me that he just couldn't seem to get the hang of it when it came to spirals, reversements and loops. He always over-controlled and fell out into a spin. He spent at least a day with 'Casey' before he finally got the idea... until Whitey mastered the techniques...but then Whitey was a valuable leader and 'Casey' an excellent instructor" (Ballad and Parker, 2013, p. 84). One day in September, Frank Luke lost his wing man on a mission. Joe F. Wehner and Frank were with the 27th squadron and "missed the 95[th.] Wehner was shot down... that night drinking was heavy. When Luke climbed up onto a table, words again failed him, but he was clearly moved by his comrade's thunderous approval. Eddie, Hartney, Wilbert White "Whitey", and Peterson gave speeches...it would mark the high point of the war" (Ross, 1917, pg. 244).

Then Elsie received a letter from his cousins, Pvt. John L. Mott and Basil Elmer, 1st Lieutenant, U.S.R. on June 5. They were in the H.Q. Company, 165th Infantry, A.E.F., "I'm celebrating today by writing you. I hope you will too. It's a great event. You're a peach, Elsie, to write to your delinquent cousin...I love to hear from you, and incidentally, I love you far more than I've shown by my actions this year over here! I've had a couple of notes from Billy telling me he's over here. I'm hoping to have him fly over me someday soon, and we'll get together somehow if I have to walk all over France to find him. I'm so glad he's over, and he certainly is in a wonderful branch of the service, and I hope he'll make awfully good at it over here as he has at home. Please don't worry about Billy over here. I wish you could be here for a while to see how much more natural and sane and easy to bear our life is than what is imagined at home. And Billy is in the branch of the service that is best taken care of, of them all. I almost envy him sometimes when I think of the pack I carry and the way they take care of us! And, I'm having a great time as an infantry private, so I'm not worrying about him at all, at all! I certainly would like to be up in the air today. I'm taking life easy just now after our last trick in the trenches."

By mid-June Elsie was living at 5148 Hazel Avenue, Philadelphia, and received a letter from Billy, "No. 10 just came in, and here at the end of a perfectly wonderful day. I can't tell you how much that letter means to me, the pansy and the poem, and the news in the letter about Betsy, and most of all you. You in the letter, wonderful you. Oh, sweetheart, I love you. Isn't it fine about Betsy. Am surely glad now that I made that call on Mrs. Borden and met her daughter that day. It may have had some little influence on the decision. I'm more than happy honey at the news. Not only because it is a wonderful opportunity for Betsy, but too, because it relieves you of the worry about what was to happen to our little girl. Hasn't everybody been good to us darling, and now if God will only let us all be reunited and stop all this terrible slaughter—oh won't it be perfect...Five other letters came" in the mail with yours, "Mother, Don, Leila Compton, Miss Conover in Honolulu, and Ann Thompson. That is the fourth letter I've received from Ann, and I hope to God she stops writing. I've written many a line to her. She told me of her mother's death, of her operation and of your visit. Have not decided yet whether she was enumerating calamities or not, if so, when she wants to, she may transfer the last to me any old time she likes. The other letters were all fine, characteristics of each one. Mother's sweet and well-wishing with the news of the New York contingent and school, Dave full of school athletics, etc. Miss C's just a note with a sky pilotish theme (that's not meant to be blasphemous) and Leila's all the gossip that could be crowded into two sheets. What more could a man want—in the line of letters. I don't know when on earth I'll ever be able to write them all an answer but must crowd them in somewhere or I'll lose a lot of friends...Being a Flight Commander in a Squadron on active duty at the front under Major Bonnell is a busy, busy job and one not to be taken lightly." As Commander of Flight "C", he had 15-1st and 2nd Lieutenants in his command, "I've got a wonderful flight by the way, Steve, you met him, is my standby, and really the best man in the Squadron. I'm only hoping that some accidental Archie shot (Anti Aircraft Guru) doesn't get him. He is as reckless as the old proverbial hot place and is being bet on to get the first Hun. No, we haven't gotten any yet, they won't come up and fight, and are terribly cowardly skunks. We no sooner sight one in the sky than they scuttle for home like scared geese. We can't follow them very far down, but one of these days are going to catch one or some unawares, then maybe you'll see our name in the papers, although that is unlikely…you don't know what an inspiration you are to me."

It was July when he saw action in the sky. He was in his Number 13 Spad S.XIII, a plane that was a superb fighter, an insignia of Mickey the rat terrier, and the words, 'Just Say Rats'. "You may have read about the one on the 2nd of July, when eight of our boys attacked nine Huns and got six of them. We were surely a happy crowd that day. Steve got one. The first of the bunch. I was leading the patrol but had to leave and come home on account of engine trouble, about 15 minutes before they sighted the Huns. It's too bad for I feel sure I would have got one too if I'd been able to stay, however, there are still plenty. We have sighted several since then but usually they beat it right away. The other day three of us chased twelve of them about 20 kilos back of their lines but they wouldn't let us get close enough to fight. Two of the fellows got three on the 9th, but outside of having a few holes shot in our planes at other times when they can sneak on us out of the sun there has been no damage and nothing doing."

He drove in to town looking for "Quinnie, but she has been sent away. "It sure is tough. It takes about an hour to drive in…

God, how I'd like to see you and the kiddies. Buster must be a scream in his B.V.D.'s. I'd give my right arm to be able to hold you all in my arms for a while just once more, but let's keep on praying that it won't be long now...We're going on a patrol in a few minutes so I'll have to close."

Elsie finally heard from Quinnie. She was located at the U.S. Base Hospital No. 1, American E.F., France, "I suppose if you have thought of it at all during your busy days, you have come to the conclusion that I am not going to write to you, but have just been waiting until I could write you a half-way interesting letter, but have given up trying to do it, so here goes—come what may, goodness only knows what may come. It is a case of uncertainty like a good many other things in life, n'est pas? That is one reason. Another is that I haven't had so beaucoup time, and now as the time seems to be dwindling am afraid if I don't catch it by the forelock or the heel, it might be gone...It is now ten minutes of ten, so part of this letter may have to wait until tomorrow or it might disturb some of the natives, and incidentally some of the boys who are in the wards just across the street. My window looks out upon one of the big hospitals and one of them particularly has been much interested in my writing today. My machine is up near the window, and his bed is right near his window and so when he hears me writing, he lifts up his head and if I see him, I wave. Then he waves and we both smile. Suppose you think I have lost all sense of the propriety of things; perhaps so. It gives him a lot of pleasure though I'm thinking, because he doubtless takes me for a French girl and I dare not disillusion him. If he thought me an American, there would be no more pleasure attached to it. Just at this minute he has called the boy in the next cot, and they are having a great time discussing the matter. Anyway, they are all the dearest lot of boys, and I'm getting to love the boys as I never even dreamed of doing in the days of my balmiest youth, but perhaps in a more maternal way… I went to church…in the courtyard of the hospital right near my hotel…some of them came in their pajamas, some hobbling on crutches, and two of the dearest blind chaps—one 22 and the other only 18. Miss Winifred Holt, the noted lady who has done so much for the blind, was with them and I met her. She is charming. There are three blind American chaps here—they say there are only six in the American army, which does very well compared to the very many the French have. They claim it is due to the different method of warfare…they joke most cruelly with each other either about their one leg, one eye…Have been trying to get in touch with Billy, and at last received a note from him the other day. I missed him in Paris. He says he is close to Paris, and inasmuch as he thought I was there said he was going to try to get in…I have left, I went out to one of the aviation camps near Paris and thought maybe he might be there…two of the aviators showed another girl and me around. We sat in a machine, worked the stick, lifted the tail, the wing, etc. It was lots of fun sitting there, even if we couldn't go up…With ever so much love, and a hug and kiss both for you and Buster and Betsy, if she is with you."

By August 15 Billy admits to Elsie that he, "has not been very well for the last few days…Perhaps my nerves are going back on me. Headaches, and a lot of other things. Don't worry. What I need is a few day's rest. Maybe I can get away and go down to the town where Quinnie is, for three or four days…Will be able to get away after this next move. Don't know where we're going, but we are soon…Saw Miss Hawthorne for a few minutes about a week ago. She says I'm looking well but getting thin! How about you? I'll be willing to lay a slight bet. I have your letters all but three, up to 19. Have received no mail for three weeks. Some will come one of these days. Oh yes, I did: The Wooster Daily Republican. Don't know who is sending it, but six copies came in yesterday.

"Here it is the 19th, and we are no nearer a move than we were a week ago. It seems that somebody got their orders mixed. But we're going to move and no more leaves are granted until after we move. Hope we don't go too far away. I want to be somewhere where I can at least get to the town where Quinnie is in the three days allotted me...The headaches I told you of, have largely disappeared. I guess they were due to a tooth I am still having treated...The moon is, well you can see the moon there, and it is 'just the same old moon', and it gives you a message from me every time you look at it, if it does what I tell it to, and if it doesn't give you the message, you must get it anyway, because I'm sending you messages all of the time."

Then on the 28th of August, "Am down here at Vichy with Quinnie for a two-day visit. I got three days' leave beginning night before last and thought this would be about as nice a way to spend them as any. Besides, I wanted to be convinced that there are some decent people in France. Don't take me too literally, but between you and me. This positively goes no farther. I'm sick of this country. More of this when I see you again. When I see you again! God, what a moment that will be. What a deliciously long moment. It is going to be stretched clean on through eternity...Quinnie is the same old impulsive, lovable girl she always has been. Tickled to death, so it appears, because I came down. Am leaving tomorrow early to get back to work. These two days here have been wonderful, but I wish for a few more...have not received any mail since the 2nd of August. Don't know where it all is, but we're bound to get some soon. The last I got from you was No. 21. You wrote it at the College Club when you had drops in your eyes. Please take care of those eyes dear heart. They're the most precious in the world, and I'm counting on seeing all the love of your heart of hearts coming through them when next I look into them…must go now to dinner with Quinnie. When you get time, write her a note. She's working awfully hard and is mighty lonesome down here."

Quinnie saw Billy once more in September when he was on leave in Paris, "I have intended writing you ever since Billy was here in September. He had a few days leave and ran down here for two of them. It was certainly good to see him pop his head in the room one morning and you couldn't imagine a more surprised woman than I was. He was absolutely unheralded. I gave him a real sisterly welcome, I assure you. You don't know how fine it is to see someone from home. We talked about you folks there most of the time. I think he realizes more than ever what you and the kiddies mean to him and is as proud of the little pictures he has as punch. The last day I took him up to Clermont about thirty-five miles away in our little Ford. It was an all-day trip. I bought a lot of things for our canteen and the hospitals— have been having to go up about once a week. He is a dear boy, and he loves you dearly."

While at the Hotel Meurice at the Rue de Rivoli, Paris on the 30th of August, he makes a copy of his insurance application on hotel letterhead and sends it home. The registered number was 18060, "This paper I picked up last night as I was coming through Paris on my way back to camp. There wasn't such an awful lot or I would have taken more…Left Vichy yesterday morning feeling a whole lot better for the two-day rest…there was mail here from Aunt Clara, Ann Thompson and yourself. Yours was numbered 26 and was written July 29, so I can still hope for 22, 23, 24, and 25 not to speak of several teens that have not arrived yet. This one had the letter from Miss Leonard telling of Betsy's thumb. What a darling that child must be, and what wouldn't I give to see her. Sweetheart, haven't you any more snapshots that have been taken there of you all, or any part of you. Pictures help to beat the band, and while I'm on the subject when are you going to send that picture of yourself that I ordered? Don't trust it to anyone to bring over but wrap it up securely and send it 1st class mail. I'll be more liable to get it that way than any other. Now, I honestly want it badly, want to put it in a nice frame and have it in my room where all can see it...The last meal I had in Vichy was with Quinnie and Mr. Bailey, the chap who used to be bookkeeper at the school, you remember him, no doubt. He is in the Base Hospital No. 1 Unit but expects to be sent up nearer the front with a surgical team pretty soon. He is a corporal and has taken on quite a bit of weight...This last letter from Ann Thompson enclosed a little clipping from some New York paper about my scrap. I do wish she'd quit writing. I don't know what to do about it though. When I think of what a fool I've been in my time, I wish sometimes that I'd have some kind of an accident that would make me forget those years, but it is best I know that I remember them. Not an accident that would allow me to forget what you have gone through for me, for sweetheart, I marvel every time I think of it, how you could ever stand it and me. I'm so darn unworthy darling and I do love you so much, oh so much. My heart just cries out for you all of the time. I want you, I want you. I want to see you, to feel you to be sure you're near me, to never let you go. I want to hold you close in my arms, to hear you say you love me and forgive me for all of those years of pain I caused you. I want to kiss you, kiss you, and feel the response in your kisses, I want to kiss your hair, your eyes, your cheeks, your lips, your hands, anus, breasts. Gawd I want you all. My heart is throbbing now so that I can scarcely write, with the thought of you my darling, my sweetheart, my love, my life, my all, my wife. Your husband loves you with a love that knows no bounds, you are his very life, his all. Help me, dearest one of all, to be more worthy, to be more as you would have me always, adoring you forever. With all adoration that is not only from the mind, or from the soul, or the body, but from all. From my whole being, worshipping you alone with each atone of me, I am eternally yours, yours, yours."

Putting censorship aside, it isn't what he writes in his letters to Elsie, it's what he doesn't say. For instance, the pressure he is dealing with, the unknown outcome of aerial combat, and the mystery about where he is moving to, "Things have been all topsy turvy here for the past two days and we've been in the throes of another move, as I found out as soon as I got back from my 'long' leave. We are now in our new location, partially settled, and all praying for a few days of good weather so that we can get entirely fixed before our real work begins. If things should start now, we would be in no mood to fight, for we've been soaked over and over again for the past week. Our tents make a fair wind break, but the water hesitates only a moment before it comes sprinkling on through on our upturned faces. We've got quite used to sleeping with the rain playing a tac toe on our noses. In fact, I woke up twice last night, because the rain had stopped temporarily, believe me, if you want to. We are promised barracks soon, but promises are the best thing the army makes...One good thing that happened in this move, was that a bit of our mail was delivered. I got your 23rd epistle, one from mother, father, Don, Miss Palmer, Quinnie, Helen and Anne Thompson, say honey, if you are still writing to her, won't you please let your letters get less frequent and more so, till they are no more. Perhaps I'm silly, but I somehow do not care for the idea. I don't like to receive her letters. I have not written her any, and don't intend to. What do you think, should I?" The real question isn't whether he wants to receive her letters, but who gave her his address to begin with. "I suppose the children are both back home again, and when you get this. Betsy may have gone away to school. Darn it all, it seems a shame that we have to be so broken up. That dear kiddie away, in good hands truly but away from both of us so long. And Billy Boy, oh do keep him close to you as much as you can sweetheart, and if anything should happen, do, oh do, keep him clean. I know this is all needless, but there is so much bad in this world, and I've seen so much of the effects of it lately, even where you would least expect it, that I'm perhaps overanxious for all of my loved ones. You, my dearest one, are continually in my thoughts. Through the day, all of the night, last night I had such a perfect dream. We were together, you and I, alone with our babies, in our own home, and what a wonderful little paradise it was, and oh how happy and contented we all were. It was the only complete dream I have ever had. I did not wake up until we were both fast asleep in each other's arms, and darling, I lay there in my cot and kept you close to me, holding you always in reality, all through the rest of the night. But that is not the only time I've held you close. It is a big comfort for I know that you must be thinking of me in the same way and at the same time, else it could not be so real, but sweetheart of mine, I want you, really, bodily, so. The spiritual communion of two who love is wonderful and I thank God for it, for I know how much it means, and will mean to us. But oh, to be able to see you, to hear you, to touch you—I'd cheerfully give ten years of my life if I could. I love you Elsie with all my life, with the purity of my body, as well as my soul. I am, I have always been, and will always be your husband, yours alone, not only in words, but in truth, not only through life, but through eternity." She finally received a letter written on September 15 with a notation at the end, "Got a Hun and a balloon yesterday."

The squadron is seeing a lot of action and on September 24, "You have no idea how darn clean I feel, this is the first time

I've felt that way this month. Had a chance yesterday to go get a bath. Now don't get sarcastic and say something about feeling natural...Well, we have been through another big American drive and I wouldn't be surprised if it would be three by the time this reaches you. Can't say more. The weather is poor for flying, clouds bad, and rains most every day. We are still in tents but expect to get under a roof sometime before Xmas. Got the pictures from Bill Taylor (by mail) yesterday. They are pretty good, but why so many of myself."

"You ask if I ever dream of you. It's a coincidence that in my last letter, I told you of one dream. Ever? Most assuredly ever, almost always, as I told you, some of the days when the work is particularly heavy, I sleep a heavy dreamless sleep, but the last thoughts I have at night are of you and the first in the morning. You cannot imagine, I think, how you pervade, inhabit, fill, my being. It is the most blessed thing in this whole war, the thing that holds me up more than any one other."

On the morning of October 10, Kenneth Porter returns to quarters to find White writing a letter to his wife. Seeing Porter gearing up for a flight, White inquires about his hurry. Porter says Hartney has detailed Flight "A" to take out a balloon over Dun-sur-Meuse but, as that flight has no operative balloon gun, Flight "C" now gets the assignment. White asks who is going. Porter says he, Herron and the new man, Charley Cox, will do it. White begins to gear-up and Porter objects telling him he doesn't have to go. White tells him, "I got the kid up here, and I want to see him over the lines for the first time. I promised his people that." On the flight line, Meissner and Rickenbacker object but give in. Putting all caution to the wind, White meets Cox on the field and they stand aside talking.

The flight now appears more complex, calling for simultaneous attacks on a balloon at Dun-sur-Meuse and one near

Bantheville. White's Flight "C" is to protect flight, will take out the other balloon. Both flights are to be covered by Rickenbacker's 94th flight flying high cover.

Nearing takeoff, Rickenbacker tries one last time without success to convince White to stay behind. Flight "C" takes off with Squadron Commander Meissner also along. Porter immediately drops out with mechanical problems. He tries another plane but does a nose-up on the muddy field. In a third he overheats the engine and never gets up, showing the frailty of even the newest aircraft of the day. Flight "C" leaves him behind and heads over the lines for the rendezvous with the flight from the 94th.

Without Porter the others cross the lines. Brotherton flies at 400 meters to take the balloon with his 11 mm guns. Slightly back at 700 meters high, White comes on with Cox to his rear between Meissner and Herron. At high cover, flying wide of his own flight, Rickenbacker sees the first of eleven yellow-nosed Fokkers from Jasta 10 of the Flying Circus coming out of the late afternoon sun to meet them. Rickenbacker maneuvers to attack the rear of the German formation as Brotherton dives on the balloon. White now sees the Fokkers ahead and above and he turns his flight towards them. Five Fokkers swing out to attack the rear of White's approaching formation. Meissner rolls out to avoid one. Herron engages two others. White rolls out also and gets on a German's tail, fires a short burst but his Vickers jam. Maintaining position and struggling to clear his guns, White sees a Spad with a Fokker on his tail speed by. It is Cox. White gives up on his opponent and turning on a wing-tip climbs into the path of the pursuing German to meet him head-on. The two planes now close at nearly 250 mph. Rickenbacker recalled that White always said, "Make them turn out...they'll turn." There seems to be controversy about whether Whitey's guns were ever fired. Several eye witnesses said he never fired his guns but rammed the German head-on.

147th Aero Squadron
1st Pursuit Group
American F.F.
France

My Dear Mrs. White:

It is ten days since your husband has been missing over the lines and while knowing you would be very anxious to hear details of his last trip, I've waited in hopes our troops might advance over the region where he fell, and I could send full particulars. You may be sure I shall do so when the time comes.

Your husband was the bravest flyer I've ever seen, in all his combats his last thought was of himself, it was to beat the Hun that he had come here for, and he usually out nerved him. You know he had six official enemy planes to his credit, yet he fought harder every day. He was flight commander of C Flight, flew more than any one else in the Squadron, and set a wonderful example to us all.

October 10, he led a patrol out as protection for Lieutenant Brotherton, who was to attack a balloon. The designated balloon wasn't up, so Brotherton attacked one near it, on the ground. We saw him dive and for a moment lost him in the heavy haze. Just then, five strange planes appeared over us and we saw they were Fokkers (the German equivalent of our Spads) as their leader dove on a new pilot in our formation of 3. "Whitey", leading, instantly turned in his tracks to dive the Hun off and save the new pilot, naturally excited and apt to lose his head when he heard bullets crack around him. The Fokker kept diving and "Whitey" raced back at home, shooting. But the Hun never turned, and it was not in your husband's creed to turn first in a head-on attack like that. I was racing in to help, still too far away to shoot, and watched the inevitable happen as they met, and fell out of control from 500 meters altitude. It was the most terrible, and yet inspiring sight I've ever seen, to realize why he had done it and what magnificent heroism he had shown.

It was a true Spartan's end, that must be your comfort; my deepest sympathy goes out to you and your children (whose pictures he had proudly shown us), but how little all the sympathy in the world can help ease the loneliness of such a loved ones loss! It is a blessing to have children to help comfort you, none could have a prouder memory of father than they. You have given everything to your country, and it is because you have sent the spirit of your patriotism across to him that he has been the fighter we all so respected and loved. His record must be your comfort, and your love of country.

Anything in the world that I could do, anything you think of or desire from his Squadron, please let me know without reserve, for I feel that we all owe him a debt we can only repay to you, a debt of he volunteered to replace "Lieutenant Brotherton, who was to attack a balloon. The designated balloon wasn't up, so Brotherton attacked one near it, on the ground. We saw him dive and for a moment lost him in the heavy haze. Just then, five strange planes appeared over us and we saw they were Fokkers (the German equivalent of our Spads) as their leader dove on a new pilot in our formation of 3. 'Whitey', leading, instantly turned in his tracks to drive the Hun off and save the new pilot, naturally excited and apt to lose his head when he heard bullets crack around. The Fokker kept diving and 'Whitey' raced back at him, shooting. But the Hun never turned, and it was not in your husband's creed to turn first in a head-on attack like that. I was racing in to help, still too far away to shoot, and watched the inevitable happen as they met, and fell out of control from 500 meter's altitude. It was the most terrible, and yet inspiring sight I've ever seen, to realize why he had done it and what magnificent heroism he had shown. It was a true Spartain's end, that must be your comfort, my deepest sympathy goes out to you and your children (whose pictures he had proudly shown us), but how little all the sympathy in the world can help ease the loneliness of such a loved one's loss! It is a blessing to have children to help comfort you, none could have a prouder memory of father than they. You have given everything to your country, and it is because you have sent the spirit of your patriotism across to him that he has been the fighter we all so respected and loved. His record must be your comfort, and your love of country.

Anything in the world that I could do, anything you think of or desire from his Squadron, please let me know without reserve, for I feel that we all owe him a debt we can only repay to you, a debt of deepest friendship for a man.

*Please convey my sympathy to his mother and father, they
may well be proud to have reared such a son.*

Again, in sincerest sympathy,

*James A. Meissner, Commanding,
147ʰ Aero Squadron, 1ˢᵗ Pursuit Group"*

Lt. Charles E. Cox was assigned to the 147st Aero Pursuit
Group in October 1918 after training in Issoudon, France.

Friends and fellow pilots wrote notes of condolences to the
family, each sharing his feelings about "Wilbur" or "Whitey", "he
wasn't afraid to take chances and often did so." Yet, another
explanation, "Fascination, the individual may perceive all of the
significant aspects of the total situation, but still be unwilling or
unable to make the proper response...it is a repeat of White's
fight forte developed since he first entered combat...he flies as he
has lived. He 'is in it to the end, no matter what it may be.' He is
unwilling to give the fight to the enemy." "Back at Rembercourt
Rickenbacker seeks out Hartney. Barely able to talk, he chokes
out the sad news about 'Whitey' then steps outside to get sick...
nineteen years later Rickenbacker recalls White's act as the war
memory that haunts him the most" (untitled newspaper clipping, September 15, 1937).

Samuel E. West shared a memory from the summer of 1907,
"A week that was devoted largely to singing and swimming. Billy
had his banjo and every evening was filled with music. There
was a humorous side to that outing, too. By the time we arrived
in Sandusky on our return trip, there was not a penny left in the
pockets of any of us, and I think the banjo had to be pawned.

Billy too had a soaring spirit and a pure heart. Doubtless the
two go together. I for one was not surprised to learn that he had

gone into the air service, and it was not unlike him to give his life for a friend. "Greater love hath no man than this."

New York Newspaper Headlines

Newspaper accounts of his gallantry, decorations for heroic efforts when he attacked three Halberstadt fighters, felled a balloon, and received the Distinguished Service Cross from General Pershing for his exploit on September 14. Elsie read the article in The Evening World, on Thursday, November 7, 1918, cut it out, and kept it with her other clippings, "Aviator Who Won American Cross, and His Wife and Two Children...With the terrible news that the Family of Lieut. White Rejoice in Honor He Won, but Wait News of Fate." The article, "Wilbert W. White, the Lieutenant's father, laid two newspaper clippings of last week on the table. "Our joy over the news in the dispatch you brought would be unbounded," said he, "If we had received confirmation that neither of these clippings was true." One of the clippings reported that Lieut. White, in a daring and self-sacrificing effort to save a fellow aviator, had crashed into a German machine and had fallen behind the German lines. The other reported him dead.

Lieut. White's father is making every effort to obtain details information about his son and is awaiting a cablegram sent to the Red Cross by way of Switzerland." Lieut. White was credited with eight kills, making him a Flying Ace.

One explanation about why Whitey rammed the German can be explained in an article, "Meissner's method of fighting is said to be both picturesque and dangerous. It has been used as a model by Eddie Rickenbacker, his team mate, with the result that the squadron has been christened the First Aerial Ramming Squadron. Meissner has on several occasions collided with enemy planes, doing considerable damage to his own wings but putting the enemy permanently out of repair" (Cornell Alumni News, 1918 p. 463).

Col. Hartney described some of the flyers aerial combats in his book, *Up and At Em*, "I heard of fliers ramming the enemy, Wilbur White, one of the best pilots that ever flew for the U.S.A., actually did so later in the war in my outfit and died knocking a Hun off a comrade's tail. I have heard plenty of people say it is impossible and incredible. Nonsense! In desperation, it is a natural instinct...Some say he fired his gun but it jammed, yet some think he flew right into him ramming the plane so hard the two planes telescoped one another and pieces of the planes went everywhere in a downward spiral". Lt. White's plane fell earthward while the German pilot Wilhelm Kohlbach of Jasta 10, used his parachute and bailed out of the plane and survived. It was December 26 when Quinnie contacted Norbert D. Gorman, 2nd Lieutenant Air Service, for information. It didn't provide anything additional. So, they waited.

Months went by with no word from the Army about Wilbur until Dr. Wilbert W. White went to France. It was Easter when Col. Frank P. Lahm, Commander, Air Service, American Second Army noted in his diary, "Dr. Wilbert W. White...came in today. I am sending Carter with him to Grandpre in the Argonne where he will look for grave of his son who was killed on October 10." By Sunday, April 27, "At Toul airdrome, found Major Reed Chambers of the 94th...who returned today from his trip to Dun-sur-Meuse with Dr. White---they found his son's body buried about 18 inches underground, grave unmarked—and located some distance from the remains of his plane. His watch, identification tags etc. had been stripped from him. In his hip pocket, they found a letter from his mother and a leave order by which they positively identified him." The order to return home was signed by H. E. Hartney, CO, "To Lieutenant W. W. White:

Embarkation orders await you at Colombey les Belles. They need you back in the United States to advise there in staff and school. This is a great honor and you deserve everyone's congratulations. Turn your command over to Ralph O'Neil and come by group headquarters soon as you can." (Hartney, p. 192).

As Dr. White recorded, "At last after many delays, I was off from Paris with the splendid aid of General Patrick's Air Service Headquarters, and that also of the Graves Registration Department in charge of Colonel Pierce...We went to Toul and then to Grand Pre, and then to Dunsur-Meuse. Our lost boy's Major had reported that he fell north of Dun, west of the river. Others had been over the ground in loving but vain search. I felt that possibly it was reserved for me to find the grave. I rose with the morning sun and walked up through the shell-torn field west of the river, looking for any clue of grave or broken airplane. One sliver of wood I carried back, forcing myself to imagine it might be a part of his "bus," as he used to call it in his letters home. I pushed on to where the river turns around the bend of the hill at the northeast edge of the "punch bowl." Seeing it would be useless to go farther, I turned to the left, crossed the railroad near a small stone house, climbed the steep side of the hill and gained the road for my return to breakfast with Major Patch and his men. Down the road I slowly walked continuing to look in the fields alongside for the grave. There were shell holes, cartridges, muskets, helmets and all the other cast-off implements of war along the path. When about half-way back I heard and at the same instant saw my second skylark. My first, at Didcot, England, was already poised at its highest point in air when I first saw it. My second, in France, was ascending in a spiral and singing as it went. It was that same sweet song which I had heard before. I cannot describe how it sounds. Professor DeMille tells us that 'describing the song of a skylark may be compared to an artist's attempt to paint a rainbow.' I shall not try to tell you how that bird's flight and song affected me. It is impossible. Our boy sang. His wife sang. I trust her song will return. I have heard them sing together. I can hear them singing now as I write. He sang. He flew. He, too, was a denizen of the air. This lark had doubtless seen him fly over that very field. I watched that messenger as it hung there in the air, a mere speck in the sky, and hurled at me 'hopes of such strange things as joy, and home, and love and peace,' while my heart was aching and my tears were flowing...About four feet from the ground, when it folded its wings and shot down in silence like an arrow. About four feet from the ground it opened its wings and glided off in safety to its nest, I saw our Wilbert fall with that bird. Not ten seconds later, on the other side of the road toward the sun which was now fast driving away the slight mist along the river and filling all things with radiance, another lark did precisely what the first had done, only it was more difficult to follow its flight and fall and glide, with the eye. It had 'privacy of light' indeed for its song, because the sun's ray confused me as I looked...We found the ragged remnants of his machine the next day on the other side of the river along the road toward Milly near Dun. Four days later, with Captain Reed Chambers of the 94th Aero Squadron, a fellow flyer that fatal day, led near to the spot by a shining substance which proved to be an aluminum part of the fuselage, far across the plowed field from the road where the machine lay, we found the unidentified grave under a heap of wire. Five days later, on May 1, which was his birthday, we placed his body in the great National Cemetery at Romagne. That was a lonely funeral. Lieutenant Lester Martin and I followed the liberty truck which was his hearse to the last resting place. Rain was falling. Six American colored men of the 3,500 who were on duty at the place under direction of the Graves Registration

Department bore the body across the uneven, muddy, desolate yard of graves, winding in and out between the trenches, up, over the around, placing it at last as gently as they could in the assigned place...A few broken words of appreciation were uttered as the six bearers reverently stood by, after which the two of us turned to walk away...We had gone but a few yards from the grave when lo! A fourth lark and its song! The quartette was now complete. Didcot and Dun and now Romagne!...My heart was soothed. It was almost glad. Why should I not frankly say that my soul was filled with resurrection cheer?" He is buried in Grave 17, Row 37, Block F, Meuse-Argonne American Cemetery, Romagne-sous-Montfaucon (Meuse), France."

While Dr. White was in France searching for his son, Elsie attended the lectures of fellow aviators, hoping for word about Billy. One evening Eddie Rickenbacker was lecturing at the Academy of Music. She went hoping to hear something about Billy but, "I was startled when I saw my husband's picture thrown up on the screen and to hear his name mentioned. When my husband went overseas that he would do wonders of course but to have the praise come from a man I do not know...about his bravery." She went on to say, "Captain Rickenbacker is different from most of the hero speakers that I have heard. He didn't seem to want to take any credit himself." Captain Rickenbacker went on to say he was reported missing after securing a six-month furlough. This was confusing since a previous report stated that he was sent home to be an instructor, and another to visit his wife and children.

After returning to America, there was a memorial service in New York City for Wilbur. An ancient Chinese gong ended the service. A monument was erected at Mt. Hebron Cemetery in Upper Montclair, Essex County, New Jersey which is inscribed, "Gave his life for a friend at Dun sur Meuse, "Greater love hath no man."

WEDDING PICTURE OF WILBERT W. WHITE AND ELSIE MACHLE
AT ENDEAVOR, PA ON DECEMBER 5, 1912

ELSIE AND BILLY WHITE ON BOARD SHIP TO FRANCE BEFORE HE LEFT NEW JERSEY

ELSIE MACHLE WHITE IN 1945 TAKEN AS PROMOTION
FOR BOOK, OUR NEIGHBORS, THE CHINESE

FAMILY PHOTO OF DR. WILBERT WHITE, ELLA HENDERSON WHITE,
ELSIE M. WHITE, GRANDMA WHITE AND BETSEY WHITE

VICTOR H. MACHLE, UNKNOWN WOMAN, ELSIE MACHLE
WHITE AND UNKNOWN CHILD IN 1957

CHAPTER 16

Lien Chow Revisited

It seemed as though time stood still for the White Family after Billy's death. There was hope that Wilbur would take over the school some day and now that was gone. Grief tends to make martyrs out of common folk. When Billy's personal effects were sent to 541, the letters to the family, except Elsie's, were re-typed by his secretary, but not always verbatim. Most noted was the absence of Elsie's letters to Billy of which there were many. Dr. White began to put his energy into a project for a memorial house. He worked unsuccessfully to get the Congressional Medal of Honor for Wilbur through the alumni of Mercersburg Academy. The efforts and failures became a burden.

Elsie's move to Philadelphia was two-fold, she would be closer to family and gain employment and experience in the field of biology. Securing a special school for Betsey eliminated some of the worry, but there were moments of despair when the memory of his indiscretion raised its ugly head, "Forgiving someone fosters your own well-being. As you begin to let go of the resentment and punishing scenarios, you gain energy that was frozen by vindictiveness and pain" (Glass, 2003). For Elsie, there were other unresolved questions. What was in the American Army doctor's report? Did he pick up Whitey's mental wish for "a small accident"? When so much was going on in the air war at that time, why was he being sent home for a visit? It seemed as though he was the only one sent home since no other pilot received papers to go home. The armistice was signed about a month later.

Relocating to Philadelphia and attending the University of Pennsylvania was the beginning of her metamorphosis. She began a life that could be called free-spirited. If she fulfilled her wish to return to China, what would happen to Betsey and Buster? Friends believed that the little girl was getting the best schooling and was intelligent enough to learn quickly, but would she adjust to her mother's absence at such a young age. It seemed to be the right time to go back to China. Her father was scheduled to go home on furlough within the next two years, and she had the blessing of the White family. But, she needed closure in the one area of her life, the death of her mother and sister. She had a lot to think about now that Billy was gone.

Lieutenant Kenneth L. Porter was placed in charge of "Whitey's" personal effects. His possessions were few; except for some photographs, a fountain pen, as well as letters from home in a leather suitcase with the Star of David on the lid. There was also a copy of Tennyson's Poetical Works showing signs of damage from the heavy rains. Elsie gave her book of poetry to Wilbert on July 2, 1912 with the notation, "Elsie E. Machle transferred to Wilbert W. White, 1912. Follow the gleam! *Millnum contempt mortis telum ad vincendum homini ab dis immortabibus acrius datum est*" and marked passages from poems fitting her emotions.

These items were given to the family, but his flight gear, a comfortable cot, and bedding, was shared among the other pilots.

After his return from France, Dr. White devoted his time to establishing a Lieutenant White Memorial Neighborhood House and Religious Education Center at the Biblical Seminary in New York. It would benefit the boys and girl's clubs at the neighborhood house. He solicited 600 former students and other friends of the Seminary, including 115 foreign missionaries to agree to pray and work for $1000 for the permanent assets of the institution. In response to his request came a letter from a former student, Norman L. Hummel, "Several months ago I received a communication from you to which I have thus far made no reply. There are several reasons for the delay, chiefly among which is the fact that your letter announced the going out of a life that was very dear to me – and somehow at that time I could not disclose my feelings to anyone. Excepting in a general way, I even knew the heart of Wilbert better than any student during the year he was Head of the Practical Work's Department. During that and the preceding year we were having very similar experiences, and on one occasion we had reason to speak of a matter that was extremely personal to both of us. And had it not been for the warm and kindly interest of him—no doubtless I would have left the school about two months after we entered. In the warmth of his personal touch, he was more than an ordinary man—and now to think of the manner of his 'going home' – what could be more fitting than to dedicate this community center and a memorial to this splendid life." Norman Hummel[12] was a graduate of Albright College and The Biblical Seminary of New York City. At the time he was serving a Methodist Church in State College, Pennsylvania on Beaver Avenue but would later serve as a Conference Superintendent for 20 years before his retirement.

Elsie expressed her feelings of loss by writing this poem,

"Wings.
Bright bayonets of light stab the night
Piercing the gloom which hides the wings
And seeking guns breathe forth their

Sulphurous breath
In gallant challenge till the last one
Dies.
White in a darkened hut, a mother's
To her new born, a simple lullaby.
She hears not doom but only her son!
Death flies abroad, but love hath
Stronger wings."

There was "a recommendation for the Medal of Honor, but this was down-graded to a mere Oak Leaf Cluster to his DSC". Later, Mercersburg Academy placed a bronze tablet in the narthex of the chapel to the memory of the fifty-six Mercersburg Alumni who died in the service. Wilbert was one of them.

Elsie kept busy planning to join her father, so she didn't have much time to think about Billy's death. For the moment, her devotion to her work at Philadelphia General Hospital assisting Randle Rosenberger, her Chief at the hospital, with lab work on syphilis was a priority. There, she edited and published a lab manual on syphilis under his direction. Philadelphia General Hospital, once known as the Blockley Almshouse, a benevolent hospital to the poor opened in 1732 and became a training hospital for many physicians. One of those physicians was Amelia T. Wood who left the University of Michigan Medical School to continue her training in Philadelphia in 1919. Her association with Amelia would last a life time and Amelia would be the friend she could count on. There were other interests, too. Because of her father's connection to President Taft, she was loyal to the Republican party and became active in the Women's Republican Club of Eighth Ward in Philadelphia.

While in China, Elsie planned to join her father in Canton, China. She resigned her position at the hospital and applied for her passport on August 11, 1920 with an inscription that she would join her father. She would fulfill her longing to go back to China. She had not been back since her mother and sister were killed, so it was an opportunity to bring closure to her mother and sister's deaths. Her step sister Mary was 4 years old. Edward Johnstone Machle was born on September 29, 1918. It was an opportunity to become acquainted with her step sister and step brother. Her own children would be staying with the White family. Betsey needed special schooling and Wilbert was enrolled at a local private kindergarten. Aunt Helen emphasized that it was important not to disrupt this education.

She would be working at Hackett Medical College organizing the laboratory, teaching medical interns English, and translating laboratory manuals into Chinese. Much of this was the early influence of the missions after the Boxer Uprising, "The mission schools have...furnished inspiration, example, and the stimulus of competition both to governments and to private schools. Text books have been translated, curricula worked out, methods formulated, leaders trained, though too few. In every phase of educational work the mission schools have contributed, oftentimes as pioneers" (Monroe, 1928). This was also the time of the woman's movement in our country, inspired by women like Margaret Sanger, a nurse promoting birth control and applauding the Y.M.C.A. and Y.W.C.A. for its movement away from the puritanical ideas by promoting women's rights through pamphlets distributed to women.

As she prepared to leave, she wrote to Helen, "If this letter is incoherent you must blame it on the two little red-headed imps, six and four years of age respectively, who are romping in and out of this, my boudoir. They are sweet enough, God knows, but even sweet things pall on one when letters must be written. However, there is a chance that they will leave me alone now...

(two sticky sugar-coated kisses (to be taken literally!) were just delivered by the red-headed cherubim!)." She left August 26, 1920 for China and would be gone for at least a year although she implied on her passport that it would be for three. Her plans were fluid. She left later than planned and returned home prior to her two year commitment.

Betsey and Billy and Aunt Helen

Helen wrote Elsie about the children's activities with a noticeable change. Perhaps this was intuition, or a sense that she should be concerned. Her friend, Cara Lehman was teaching in Northampton and was close enough to visit the White's and assess the situation. When Helen began to refer to Buster as Wilbert, Elsie wrote to Cara which generated a change of agenda from the two years to eighteen months. Betsey returned to Northampton when a letter arrived from Helen, "just a month ago...mother, father, the two children...went to Bolton on boat... we spent that p.m. in N. Adams, then Tuesday a.m. went over Mohawk Trail. Twas beautiful. The children were good as could be. Betsey understood she was on her way to school but couldn't seem to understand why she wasn't going in a car...after returning from auto trip and had to go pretty slowly for several days, so we took our time doing things. The weather was glorious – and Wilbert and I had a fine time. We came down Friday, the 8th and on Monday Wilbert started to kindergarden[*sic*] down at Friends Sem. 16th and Stuyvesant[*sic*] Square opposite St. George's Church. It's where Donald went when he was a lad. The lower grades are very good we find on investigation. Think it will be O.K. for this year anyway, then perhaps next year he can go where E. Curry goes. They have no kindergarden[*sic*] up there and take no one under 5 years. Wilbert likes it muchly...It seems splendid the way things have worked out, so that again we have Miss Seaman to help. She is taking some business training work, but we have 'fitted in' and she helps much with Wilbert. Takes him in a.m., etc. Then I can help more in apartment and do some things for mother and father...please remember me most kindly to your father and Mother Jean and also Martha Hackett." The White's knew many of the missionaries associated with Hackett from previous trips to China and Japan so it was with their encouragement and good will that Elsie left New York. However, it was becoming clear to Elsie that Helen was planning "Wilbert's" future without guidance from Elsie.

Although China was still not a safe place to travel alone, she traveled extensively with a group of fellow workers. Not only did she travel to Lien Chow and White Cloud Temple, but she also visited the City of the thousand boats, where junks and sampans so tightly fit together, they looked like logs from a distance. The peasants on the boats, lived, slept, gave birth, and died never knowing what it was like to live on land.

One experience in Central China she claimed she would never forget, "A group of us were spending the summer at Kuliang, a mountain resort near Foochow. Suddenly from a copper-colored sky the typhoon struck with awful fury. No sounds-affect man could do justice to the tremendous reverberations the wind made among the mountain, and no one could stand upright before the force of it. A fool hardy friend and I crawled on our hands and knees along an embankment, pulled ourselves up and crept to a grove of trees. Gasping we each clasped a trunk, wrapped our arms and legs around it and peered down into the valley. Breathlessly, we watched eight villages, one after the other burn as the wind swept flaming roofs off one village and dropped fire onto the next. Mountain mists caught the glare and the entire sky glowed red. Beyond the villages junks lay lashed together in the Min River. Suddenly we saw flames leap from one of them.

As they had been lashed together for protection none were able to pull away and all were burned. No one from the colony could give any help for it would have been impossible for a human being to reach the valley alive. Remembering this a faked movie storm doesn't impress me much!

One visit to Ku Shan near Foochow, "Is famous for its paintings, its great pool where hundreds of sacred carp, many of them incredibly old, are cared for by the Buddhist monks. Also, at Ku Shan is an ancient waterclock. Time is measured by a series of buckets which fill and empty into a pool, and as the water in the pool rises a mechanism is released that moves a huge wooden fish which is suspended horizontally from the temple roof, sheltering the pool. The fish swings forward until its nose hits a bronze gong. What is the hour when it strikes? That I was never able to learn."

She was present when the Civil War broke out and witnessed the last Viceroy of Kwangtung Province entering his sedan chair just before the fall of the Empire. She saw "The Monastery of the Four Winds, some distance north of Canton, is not so well known as Ku Shan, and much more difficult to reach. One must travel inland on a ridiculous narrow gage railroad with 'coaches' which are nothing more than two park benches set back to back and mounted on wheels. Ones feet hang over the side and are brushed by tropical vegetation as the train moves along. If one survives this, then there is an eleven-mile trek to the foot of the mountain and an interminable climb up a steep winding path, broken by series of stone steps, to the monastery. Guests are assigned rooms but must supply everything else themselves – beds, bedding, washbowls, food etc. No meat nor butter can be taken into the monastery as the eating of meat is prohibited by the Buddhist religion. The woodwork in the rooms I saw was richly carved. An occasional scroll hung on the walls. Spiders were plentiful. At the end of the cluster of buildings was an exquisite white marble pavilion from which one could look down into the valley filled with olive, lichee, plum and orange trees. Worship went on continuously, day and night, before the great god Buddha."

The idols in the Temple of the Five Hundred Qenii, the Pagoda in Empress Dowager's Hunting Park Western Hill, and visited the remains of the façade of the old Jesuit church in Macao. The church had been destroyed years earlier but the cross remained, and inspired the writing of the beautiful hymn, *In the Cross of Christ, I glory*. But her visit to Lien Chow was the most difficult. As she stood on the edge of the river where her sister and Eleanor Chesnut were murdered, is it possible that she visualized the event just as she recaptured it in conversation years later. Although we will never know how she perceived the setting 17 years later, it was an opportunity for her to bring closure to the devastating memory. There was so much to see and Elsie made every effort to visit all the places not only of interest, but places she remembered as a child, and be part of the life as it existed in this changing country.

The White Family Letters

Always close to her heart was the correspondence from Grandmother White, Helen, and Dr. White. There was a sweet note from Grandmother White on April 7 with a statement that she, "is in her 89th year, Somehow, I heard of a birthday in May, so I am writing you on this April day...you are like all of the family that go to Foreign field find so much to do that it is hard to decide on what to do first...John Mott is so busy and interested in his work and so delighted in being able to help those poor fellows in India. He thinks he was just providentially sent."

Helen's letters were often written in haste and somewhat incoherent, putting words on paper with dashes of statements about life. One of the letters of April 30 was, "Mr. Elkinton, delivered a package. In the package was linen, "tis lovely, and will be most useful...some time when you think of it, do please tell me how best to wash and iron it to preserve it...the little silk coat is so beautiful and how Elizabeth will love it. Am keen to see her in it...And the furs, my, are they beautiful, the white one would make such a lovely cover for baby carriage, told mother guess I'd adopt a wee baby, to use the cover! Hope we can have them fixed for the kiddies, how warm they will be, will have mother's and father's gifts for them to care for." And always a report on the children, "both so well—couldn't be better as far as we can tell... we let Miss Seaman take Wilbert to her house on a farm over in Sullivan Co, N.Y. for a few days. They all know much about children and then Miss S. has lived right here and knows how I want things done." Furthermore, is a report how well Elizabeth is doing at school and the possibility of going to Clarke School next year, "the consensus of opinion of those who know best seems to be that it would be better for her to be in the school." Then, an old friend from Endeavor made an appearance, "The Board is happy to announce that during the year it has added two well-qualified furloughed missionaries to its Executive Staff, Rev. W. Reginald Wheeler[13], formerly committed with the Central China Mission and more recently with the North China Mission."

In the spring, she sang in a concert for famine relief. Helen made the comment earlier, "You surely have a gift in your voice, and I keep hoping you will sing more. It does give such pleasure to folks." On June 7, Elsie sang *O, Promise* Me at the wedding of Dr. Mildred Jenks and Reverend Samuel McKee at Hackett Medical College. And, Elsie, true to her nature, couldn't resist writing her version of the wedding, "A wedding which was a great relief to the Hackett Medical College and inmates of the allied institutions was precipitated by 400 guests – 200 invited by the bride and 200 which slipped in through the fingers of the Religious Department, when Jinks and Sam McKee were united in marriage...Preceding the ceremony Mrs. White, generously exuding cold-cream, murdered Oh Promise Me after which Miss Marx' rendering of the wedding march jarred on the nerves of the restless listeners...Six phlegmatic brides maids were plucked from Miss Smith's darlings, Dr. Allyn's pets, and the N.D.'s right hands. Their limp blue shams clung to their moist necks, and they clutched wilted pink lotus. They started the parade – and toddling after them came little Herbert Thompson carrying the (Mc)Key ring on a dead powder puff. Miss Lulu Patton, maid-of-all-work, stalked in wearing a barnacle-trimmed dress of blue fish-net over lobster silk – carrying a bucket of seaweed. Scrambling after her came little Christine Smith and Margaret Laird in pink and blue rompers, strangled with ivory – the gift of the bride. They scattered bird-seed on which the bride slipped... The bride was raving in crudely embroidered *to-pc de soit*, with tatting. Her veil was of mosquito net – held in place with thumb-tacks – her train was caught with a fine-tooth comb. She carried a lovely shower-bath. Besides the pearly drops of perspiration she wore rakishly her aunts' gift – a crescent of opalescent shoe-buttons, and her pearl chandelier, the gift of the groom...Dr. Martha Hackett – coquettishly gave the bride to the groom. She staggered under the weight of a frock of Kobe flannel, and pushed the bride into the trap where she was pounced upon by the groom, in conventional pongee, incensed by the best man, Dr. Stephe Lewis of Central Africa. The Reverend E. C. Howe of Canton spoiled the ceremony; which took place under odorous tepee of fresh green onions. On the heels of this tragedy the bride vehemently kissed the groom – after which they wheeled around to receive the condolences of the 200 guests, the family having bolted for the food. The remainder of the refreshments consisting of a sustaining catsup punch, chicken sandwiches and crumbs of cake, were served to the guests…the most deplorable incident of this delightful occasion occurred when the maid-of-all-work, smiling courageously broke her bicuspid on the shoe-horn concealed in the wedding cake…Reverend and Mrs. McKee are spending their honey-moon on a raft – after which they will be at home to pedlars[*sic*] and book agents at their winter home, The Honey Pot."

There was always news about Uncle Cam and Quinnie. Quinnie spent four months' fund raising in Ohio and Pennsylvania for the school. A statement of success from Dr. White as he writes, "We are closing our best year, the 21st…considering the hard times, it is amazing how well we have gotten on…one hundred and sixty odd students are signed up for next year."

By late June, Dr. White informs Elsie that, "We are starting this afternoon to pick up Betsy at Northampton, and then go on to the Bay…The children are wonderfully fine…Oh, how I wish I had money enough to start a new school for boys, and study how to develop it in terms of Wilbert, I thought of this when Donald was about Wilbert's age. Maybe some windfall will bring to us the means of carrying it out now."

They spent the summer at Silver Bay, "They are both swimming," says Dr. White in his July 26st letter, "You should see them dive under a rope lying on the level of the water. Wilbert has been picking up fast in the last two or three weeks. He swims four or five strokes…You must forgive me for not writing oftener. The demands are so constant and so imperious."

Quinnie kept her apprised of the day-to-day events from her office at 541, "Today I received for the first time your letter of January 3rd—do not know whose fault it was…you were a dear to remember my birthday and to send the embroidery...You know I was in Ohio and succeeded in getting something like $3,500 and then quit the financial field...In June I sat around here---clear deep down in the bottom of that dark well you wrote about some time ago. Not even the least squint of light...Then the 1ˢᵗ of July our Registrar left and they have let me substitute until we can get someone else. I go to Minneapolis ...closely followed by Miss [Iris] Bolin to start a tea room or some sort of eating joint of my own. Never owned a thousand dollars before in my life and hope to have a good deal more by that time...you must come by and see us when you return next year. Just a month ago tomorrow I went up to Silver Bay with Dr. and Mrs. White in the car. We went by Northampton for Betsy on the way. I was supposed to get in touch with her teacher and get her summer lessons, which I did, and which meant only twenty minutes. My dear, if there ever was an angel on this globe, it is that little daughter of yours. It is just impossible to describe her."

Toward the end of summer, "I am very much ashamed for not having written you oftener" says Mother White, "and now I am alone with the two children and Lillian, our maid, who is a jewel in many ways. I am standing the real, hop, skip, and jump, life quite well, much better than thought I could...Wilbert had a happy birthday. We did not have any children. He gets so wild and Helen being away, I could not. We had all the people from the other house down for ice cream and cake. We had a nice cake with candles and he received several presents and quite a few cards. He was very happy and all went off smoothly...The children have just come to me and they want to write or send you something and Betsey had this written. 'I do not know what the first is but prob. Of it you can read. I am sure. Wilbert's is a house canor[*sic*]. The little red arches are waves. I must stop now.'"

"Elizabeth was learning to talk and act out things beautifully and is very interesting," according to Grandmother White, "Wilbert talks to her and has a way of making her understand so well what she wants to know. They have their little differences occasionally...Wilbert likes to be out with his grandfather fixing the car and things and talking like all big folks."

Helen went to Northampton in November and stayed at the Plymouth Inn, "Came up to see Betsey! Am waiting here in hotel now...just arrived last 5:00 p.m....am going back on 10:07. Elizabeth well and happy and growing in every way. She is so sweet and dear and pretty—where there were two upper teeth, that do leave a hole!.. I have been a bit anxious to see about her winter clothes for it is a bit puzzling to keep all going well at a distance... It's the first time I've been up since Elizabeth came to live in Dudley Hall...Mr. Elkinton finally returned to see us. We didn't take seriously his saying he would take a package to you...all was wrapped and on hall table a couple of days but no Mr. Elkinton has turned up and we have decided to trust the port with our bundle...Wilbert was sure—mother would want candy first of all...so extra candy we put in. How Wilbert is growing and what we have done...for he is a boy now, no mistake, no curly locks, for last Tuesday I had his photo taken which will reach you soon, then, before my courage gave out went over to Bert's and had his hair cut. He is a handsome laddie now...'Now, Aunt Helen, people won't say to me, are you a little girl!' He was the only boy in school with Dutch cut...He is growing so fast, in height, solid, yes, but not fat, is very well.

"Elizabeth is growing too. She seems well, has a little cough which they are watching up there, but say that generally after whooping cough, if a child gets a little cold, it develops into a cough. I was sorry to hear her, but she is being carefully watched, oh yes, out and all, but sick. It truly is wonderfully homelike and as little like an institution as any could possibly be. She was so funny about Wilbert's hair, when I talked with her about it.

"Oh, yes, about the clothes for the children...I have wondered all fall but wasn't sure whether the Spencer's were coming directly home or put off writing, thinking would surely hear from them. Well, the dear little dresses and suits have come and are pretty... Wilbert's can be fixed quite easily. The dresses for Elizabeth are fine but bloomers or panties are very snug. It is hard to fit them at this distance, but I think you did remarkably well.

"I took Wilbert to Montclair...He went over to Central Church to Sunday school and had such a good time. We stayed at Jellerson's but went down on Sunday after to see Ethel and her baby. Wilbert and I had supper with Aunt Leila, who is alone... Aunt Leila is kind of lost. It looks as though she may go to your part of the country with Uncle John early in the year. So rather think you may meet out there." She finishes her letter with, "Wilbert had just wakened. I had slipped out of bed and had started dressing. He woke up and after kissing me, lay quite still for a minute. I wondered what was up. When he said, Aunt Helen, today I'm going to try to be the best boy I've ever been in my life. It's quite a lot of trouble to do it that way, though, isn't that great!"

Always close to her heart were the "best sellers" on the market. She kept in touch with a former teacher of French at the College of Wooster, Emeline McSweeney, who writes, "Your 'little gift' as you so modestly called it, arrived in plenty of time for the celebration" of Christmas, Elsie dear, to think of your sending me all that lovely, real filet lace. It is simply exquisite...Do you know I have longed for a rose pink summer frock for five years, voile or dotted swiss, and now I am going to get one and trim it with this lovely lace...Are you really coming back in July? I thought you went for a three-year period...I hope you and your father can come home by way of Europe. How you will enjoy all that the Old World offer!..like you, I liked the *Brimming Cup* immensely. *Main Street,* I thought vastly clever, but so unfair. I have no doubt that I'll receive some gems in French quite equal to those you get in English."

Elsie's close friend, Cara Lehman kept in touch while she was in China with description of life in general but ready to do what she could to help Elsie. Elsie sent a request to Cara to stop by and check on the children. Helen describes Cara's visit, "Wilbert wakened…mother came over to 'our apartment' at 902/3 when whom should they say was calling, but Cara Lehman. Wasn't that nice, we have not seen her for well, I think, not since long before you sailed. And then she…stayed and chatted. Isn't she interesting and fine. We are going to have her down for dinner soon and her sister. Cara and I agree that you really should write some things for print, for your letters are most interesting. You have a gift there too, Elsie!" It was February, but her Christmas packages arrived just a few weeks earlier, "I want very soon now to get the letter to you I promised, telling more in detail about Christmas. We have been short on stenographers and I wanted to dictate, for do get so little time for writing…The last two Christmas packages, of your very generous lot, came a couple of weeks ago, and pleased the children immensely. The kimonos, they are so pretty! Just beauties, Wilbert is a picture in his and am sure Elizabeth is in hers. I let the convenient big tuck out of hers, as did Wilbert's also and sent on to her. You really can't imagine how these kiddies grow! The kimonos are fine, but 3 or 4, no, 5 or 6 inches from ground (on Wilbert) with tuck all out! By the way, the kiddies were only things had duty to pay on, was glad to do that…Do let me tell you again how grateful and pleased I am with my lovely gifts from China. The dear little frame is right here on my desk with a wee Kodak picture of the children in it...Five words from Elizabeth, though not much of it. Both children are well as can be. I hope all is fine with you. Summer is coming, isn't it." The Rawleigh's almanac predicted dull, damp and cloudy weather for the area east to New York with temperatures below the July average, putting a damp spirit on their summer at Silver Bay.

She notifies everyone that she is leaving for home on July 5... Keeping in touch with Elsie was important, especially to her old friend from 451 Lexington. Quinnie kept in touch, "Anyway here I am at 1:30 p.m. on the Sabbath Day sitting up in bed with my typewriter on my knees at last trying to do justice to your wonderful letter of November 20th. First, let me say I love you very very much and never shall you be forgotten – any neglect is not for lack of love but lack of time...sometimes for lack of spirit... What a great old letter you write – it is a poem from beginning to end, if a bit tragic at times. I loved your letter, what a picture it gave me...both the lines and in-between. Thank you muchly for it. Have intended ever since...before Christmas writing you... Thanks, child, for the beautiful pin. It was dear of you to send it, and I am getting much joy out of the wearing of it...Frankly I am more puzzled about everything every day I live – have been sitting in the shadows for months. Whether I will ever let the sunshine come in again I don't know – remember a letter you wrote some time ago about sitting in the bottom of the well refusing to look up. No doubt it will all work out somehow someday. Now you are sorry you are hearing from me, aren't you?

"I have a great little tea room – can seat about 96 and they mob us at noon. The University students – mostly girls – and the best type too...am doing my own cooking and baking – yes, have come to that – was losing every day the other way, and not making any money...never dreamed I'd ever really be a cook." She begins referring to Iris Bollin as "Bollie has helped me with the baking, but she is all upset and leaves us this next week for parts unknown…I know how happy you will be when you head home- wards – at least I imagine you will be. How happy to see your kiddies – they surely are most adorable, and I don't see how you can help but stay with them from now on – but what problems we have, and how helpless we are in working out the problems of others. I, frankly, have never felt I could share the children like you let me do at Fordham. Don't ever mention this – know you won't. They are truly part of Helen's life and tissue now…that is a puzzler too, isn't it?" This was enough confirmation that Elsie was needed at home to regain her role as mother to Betsey and Billy.

She left Minneapolis and returned to New York, "Have sold my tea room, and Dr. White took pity on me so I am here for a few weeks – just now playing around up here at the Bay. The kid- dies are more than adorable, and how I would love to be around when you get your first glimpse of them. Helen is sending you some pictures. News about Grandma White" who fell and broke her hip, "trusting your journey home will be a wonderful experi- ence for you." Although Quinnie is in New York for a few weeks, she made plans to return to Minneapolis.

There is confusion at the bottom of the letter when Dr. White realizes it isn't his letter to sign, but Quinnie's he is signing. He jots a note to Elsie, "Give my love to your father. We are changing maids today – A colored cook comes on board tonight. We hope she will be able to boil the water while she brings my postum in the morning. Won't we have a cup of coffee each the day after you reach American" soil.

I hear from New York occasionally…understand the year has been a hard one financially. Now I wish that relief could come… please forgive this letter, am sure all will be brighter soon."

By September 27, Elsie was on the SS <u>Majestic</u> headed to Southampton, England and home to New York. In December, she wrote a letter to Kappa Kappa Gamma at Wooster, "When one is studying Chinese 10 hours a week, teaching English 9 hours, bacteriology 2 hours, training internes in lab. Technic, and running the laboratory the rest of the time, there is not much time left for introspection. But it was not all work by any means, so I burnt the candle at both ends, and played as well, often until the Southern Cross set below a tinted horizon.

"The social life was exceedingly gay in the English and American colonies, so we had countless good times.

'Two months after my arrival a robust, little revolution broke out which proved diverting and exciting. An ex-bandit, *Mok* had control of the government, and the legitimate governor was trying to persuade him to leave like a gentleman. However, they couldn't agree on that point so the forces gathered. I'd never before had a whiff of powder except at Fourth of July celebrations, nor heard the whizz of bullets outside of target practice. So it was a bit thrilling to hear them pattering on the porch pillars and raining on the roofs. I could write a hundred pages on this ridiculous and pathetic war; the maneuvers of the armies were like those of the stage armies in a comic opera. But this is not the place to begin.

"We took many delightful trips into the country to marvelous old monasteries whose ancient court yards were thick with moss and lichens, and whose sacred pop-eyed gold fish were hundreds of years old; we climbed old White Cloud mountain – holy ground because of its thousands of graves; we browsed among incredible junk shops hidden in the fascinating, twisting, granite-paved streets of the real Canton of the Kings; we loitered on the beautiful Pearl River in luxurious house-boats as guests of amiable English and American business people. In the summer some of us fled from the tropical heat to Juliang, a resort in the mountains some hundred miles up the China coast. There, one night, we saw a whole village burn while a raging typhoon rocked the earth. The low hanging mountain-mists reflected the light of the flames until it seemed as though the whole world was on fire. It was impressive and terrifying, for no one could live to go down the mountain in such a storm to offer help.

"Coming home down the China Coast a typhoon struck us. Our old tub apparently heaved up to the stars and then plunged toward the center of the earth. We pictured our bones glistening whitely in the pale moonlight on some treacherous coral-reef. We all said our prayers.

"If I could express China in a word it would be 'Incongruity'. Things are incongruous. The contrasts are too great to be imagined. The exquisite and the hideous are forever rubbing elbows. The lotus flowers near the cess-pool; the leper suns himself by the wall where the pomegranate blooms; one smells the sweet odor of burning incense and sandal wood in streets whose stench cries to heaven.

"As it is nearing Christmas I am reminded of the way it is celebrated at Hackett. There are students, and tiny village waifs, and about a hundred patients, and half as many institutional servants, and last of all ourselves to have Christmas parties for. Each set have their own celebration so there is something doing for many days.

"If you had looked in on us about this time last year, you would have seen the faculty all sewing madly on bags. Bags for the young, the middle-aged, the old and toothless, hundreds of bags. A great many of these, fortunately, are given by Westminster Guilds, otherwise, the faculty would be bagging all year. There is a great demand for these reticules, and their delectable contents of say, a wash-cloth, piece of soap, thread and needles, handkerchiefs, pencil, and sweets.

"Consequently, one is not surprised to see new faces appear at the meetings or in the dispensary a few weeks before the great day of distribution. One old woman, fat and rotund as a cream pitcher used always to come for medicine just a day or so before she imagined the celebrations would begin. She invariably had six or eight grandchildren in tow, all of whom were entitled (she hoped) to presents. We knew her methods well, but she was such a naïve old soul, and had such an expectant look, that we always took her to our hearts and let her battalion of pseudo- descendants take well filled bags to theirs. She was affectionately called Old Drug Pot and at this very moment no doubt, she is standing at the Dispensary window asking for medicine which she doesn't need, and incidentally getting valuable information regarding the exact hour of distribution. Now, C.L. you can see the Washington Guild need never worry about sending too many bags, for there are always Old Drug Pots with attendant's strings of urchins who are thrilled over any surplus.

Homeward Bound

"Some other time perhaps, I'll tell you a little about our trip home via Suez. It is wonderful to be home again where I can see the children. Perhaps some of you do not know that I have a blue-eyed Elizabeth who will be eight in March, and a sunny-haired Wilbert who is hurrying joyously toward seven. It would be better perhaps not to be too frank about my opinion of their superior gifts; I just mention in passing, therefore that they are both perfectly adorable. On the dock Billy-Boy remarked that his mother had 'changed'. When questioned as to how she had changed, he answered, 'Well, just as anyone would change in two years'. Not only in Washington is diplomacy used!"

CHAPTER 17

The Gold Star Wife

Coming back to New York on March 2, 1922 had a bittersweet ending. The itinerary was a full agenda with her father, Mother Jean, Eddie, Mary and Christine as they began their furlough in America for a year. Christine, or "Mitty", as she preferred to be called, was a missionary in Canton. Originally from West Chester, Pennsylvania, Mitty, was going home on furlough with health problems that prohibited her from returning to her position in China. The plan was to return by way of the Suez Canal enroute to the USA, but her passport list Straits Settlement, India, Italy, Switzerland, Germany, Holland, Belgium, France and England, Holy City of Jerusalem, Palestine, and Egypt. She acquired a visa to enter Palestine on April 8, 1922. The news spread that Howard Carter had opened the tomb of King Tutankamen on November 1, 1921, with the most spectacular cache of artifacts. Whether this was the reason they decided to tour this region is unanswered, but they spent several days riding camels at the site and buying souvenirs before heading to Paris, Germany, Switzerland, and London.

The world tour ended in London. After that, Elsie was faced with several dilemmas. She would realize that the reunion with her children would be bittersweet after Aunt Helen developed a lifelong co-dependent relationship that couldn't be changed. She had to pay for her trip. She had to find a job.

Elsie was having health issues and in early February 1923, Elsie wrote a letter to Dr. White. What she received back was coded language, "I have your esteemed favor…among other evidences of the failure of the strawberry cake to proceed rightly along the pneumo-gastric is the fact that the communication is undated. Then I observe a slight tremor evident in the use of the pen. I trust that the crisis is passed and that you are assured of calubrious and prophylactic years referred to in the last paragraph…So far as volcanoes are concerned, I should prefer hearing a lecture on the active volcanoes in Hawaii, to being compelled to take up my abode on the top of one threatening to break forth…Trusting that neither you nor I are or ever will be in such a predicament." A person can only surmise what was meant by volcanoe.

In July of 1923, Jean and Edward Machle were preparing to leave Wooster, "We spent from Wednesday to Saturday at the Bell's near Millersburg and made a round of Miss Johnston's relatives who feasted us and wound up our stay with a picnic at the school grounds in the country with a beautiful circle of hills around us." The plan was to spend a month with Edward's brother Harry, while visiting Victor and other relatives. He was disappointed that he missed Elsie because she was hospitalized and too weak to visit friends or family. She was living with two other girls in Belleville, New Jersey, close to St. James Hospital where she was employed. A visit to Wooster was out of the question until she gained her strength. Yet, there were expenses from her return trip that needed reconciled and Edward needed the money, so while she was recuperating, he wrote her a letter asking for payment.

By September, Edward and Jean were in Hong Kong. Jean reported that, "Fighting started up with the Yunanese, and that put a stop to work in the city, so I seized the opportunity to take the children to Cheong Chow for ten days. Eddie was coughing and Mary had rather high fever the day we went, and both developed into a kind of whooping cough, that went on gaily day and night...I left them on the island and hurried up to Canton for Mission Meeting, only to hear that the Consul had ordered us all out of Canton. I packed up things as fast as I could, and as Yau Tsai had already been turned over to the Chinese to run, your father and I, with the cook and washerwoman, caught the Saturday morning boat...when it was time to *hoi shaw*, all the seamen and boys walked off, followed by all the Chinese passengers and some of the foreigner's servants, among them our cook! These latter were scared off...certainly *A Wa* did not go on strike...we finally got out of Canton Harbor on Saturday evening on a Chinese S.S. crowded with foreigners. We got down here to find a strike on here, engineered by the powers in Canton...The house we had taken for July for our summer vacation had eleven people in it, and I had to turn in and cook for the crowd, being the only one that knew anything about cooking. Mr. Rogers did the 'coolie' work, and everybody helped with the dishes. But cooking three big meals over a hot coal stove in blazing June and July weather was no joke, although I really felt it less than most folks would... bit by bit, things eased up, and the last week or two in August I only had ourselves to cook for. No American President Mission School or College will open till after October 15 and Dr. Hofman came back this week to take on his job again, so your father does not need to worry so much about *Jau Tsai*. All the Mission are scattered about Hong Kong, Cheong Chow, and Baguio, and other Missions likewise. The Consuls will not allow us to go back yet, as the Bolshevist Russians and the Strike Committee still rule, or misrule, at Canton, and Shameen and Hong Kong are still strictly boycotted. It would take pages to tell the state of affairs. The Bolshevists planned the whole thing from the beginning and have lied continuously. The papers say there are 1,500 Russians up there now, daily putting a tighter grip on Canton and the Province, and they are frankly out to 'kill' Hong Kong in the process...kill Kwong Luing, but that does not matter a bit to them. What they are after is to break the other Powers, and they are beginning with Great Britain as the biggest. If something is not done soon, many of the Hong Kong firms will go to the wall, and that will mean a big lot of suffering in England and other places. But, as always, it is the Chinese themselves who are suffering most...Shameen Gates are still closest, and any Chinese found selling vegetables or fruit or fish or food or anything at all to them is severely punished, placarded, and marched up and down the Bund...The whole thing was cooked up by the Russian Bolshevist, with a few Chinese drips. The whole thing is really awful, and other nations have no idea how wonderfully the British have 'held their hand' under the most flaunting insult and provocation." But by December, Mother Jean expresses her concern that, "The Reds are getting their own medicine in frightful doses, and Canton just now is simply horrifying."

Elsie entered Miss Alston's by November for her health, "My dear girl", writes Amelia Wood, "How my heart ached to know all that you were going through there. Please tell me what Dr. Bainbridge found." Dr. William S. Bainbridge had offices at 34 Gramercy Park. Mrs. W. W. White was billed $400 for an examination, operation and calls from April 3-28, 1923, a substantial amount of money for a woman who wasn't employed. Amelia elaborates, "Please tell me what Dr. Bainbridge found and what he did...So your friend Miss Quinn is married...Did she marry a minister? She is a very charming and remarkable young woman."

Then Elsie received an invitation from Helen to come to Silver Bay for Christmas. It was unusual for the family to go up there in winter, but it was a new experience and, "Quite different from summers...most of the time we are quite comfy in the house. Tis beautiful outside...today tis melting, rainy, and since starting this letter have heard two slides of snow fall off the roof...Yesterday we finally decided to stay up here for Christmas. The family seems to think it wiser for this year...we will go down to New York before New Years', toward end of Christmas week (Elizabeth is out this week on Friday or Saturday and returns January 3). Then, Wilbert's school in New York opens about that time, so we want you to spend Christmas with us here if you possibly can! It will all, must needs be, a very simple celebration, but I hope there will be snow for the children and they can have a happy time. You said you had a 'job' but didn't tell us what it is or where...hoping you are feeling better physically and that Dr. Bainbridge is helping."

Quinnie

Beginning at 541 Lexington in 1912, through World War I, Quinnie's role in Elsie's life was important. It was Quinnie that taught Billy shorthand. She was in the Red Cross in France and saw Billy shortly before his death. Not to mention her close ties with Dr. White which possibly go back many years. Nina R. Quinn was an important part of Elsie's life. She was a friend and confidant. The White family held her in high regard which will become obvious.

Quinnie married Jon Sigurd Melby on September 8, 1923 in Washington, D.C. Having met Si in Minneapolis when she had the tea room, Sig, as he was called, was Dean of Men at Augsburg College and Head of the Christianity Department in Minneapolis, Minnesota. Quinnie is settled in Minneapolis though looking for a smaller place. Sig and Quinnie finally find a small two room apartment, "Think possibly the readjustments of the season have somewhat unsettled my brain, and that my cerebellum is where my cerebrum used to be. Anyway, it is all bum now. Have had many up-rootings in my life, but the replanting has always been on native soil, as t'were. So, while I am and always will be the same to you, I have a sneaking idea that smpin's up in my subconscious parts that can't as yet be analyzed. Shall try not to worry about it unduly however, but probably this is the reason why I have grown actually detestably lazy, without ambition, hate to write, don't know what to say when I do write, and believe me, when I do get a chance to sit in the rocker, pocket my chin in my hand and stare out of the window, thinking of anything and everything…Now, can you analyze my case? Don't get obstreperous or hasty…Am expecting J.S. home tonight about midnight. The new school term began today, and so he will have to go at things with special 'veal and sigor' tomorrow…am so interested in the new job at Newark." She became a lecturer to nurses in bacteriology shortly before her hospitalization, "I suppose you deemed it discreet to give up as Hedley's 'secretary'… also have been so interested in your meeting Hedley's family and am so delighted that some are friends and that you seem to know at first glance who is not, so as to know how to aim your guns. Also, the ring! Dear, oh dear, can just see you at Tiffany's – venture the old clerk more a smile. Also, glad about your good Christmas…I think I have told you that we are not in a home of our own as yet, and probably will not be until fall. We have a furnished six room house, furnished with fumed oak, and all that stuff that – as one girl expressed it – makes a beautiful setting for a funeral. That is mean though – it really is quite nice, and we are proud of it…we will need everything from a dishrag to a piano and automobile. Except, we won't need candle sticks. We just need one more to make the buffet look like an altar. Thought I'd get a job of some kind to help while away the passing hours, as well as perform other useful service, but there are no jobs for married women any more than there are hen's teeth. And there are not many for the young and beautiful and single. So, thinks I to myself, will try the insurance game—but somehow or other after trying to persuade a hundred or more that they positively were going to die and that they should have money to meet their funeral expenses, felt that perhaps salesmanship was not my line, and then couldn't do my duty socially and follow that as closely as it should be at the same time, so have done nothing lately...Next summer J.S. and I are thinking of walking to Yellowstone – impossible probably, but we will or may walk somewhere. He needs a change terribly physically and I need one some other way...All chickens on the roadside, take warning!"

Surprise Announcement

On March 17, 1924 Elsie received a letter from Mother Jean and her father. Since we left Cincinnati, no, Wooster:--we have only had one short letter from you, and it didn't tell us anything about yourself, anyway—only that you had moved out to Belleville, and are living with two other girls—so this morning's letter surely is a welcome one. Your father won't see it till he gets home, but I know how glad he'll be to find it here.

First of all, though, what am I to say about that engagement of yours. Dear Elsie, I do hope you are really and truly happy. For your sake I do hope he is a good, fine man, with character and education enough to make him a real companion for you, and gumption enough to understand and appreciate you. I quite believe he thinks he does—they all do--but he sure will be in trouble some if he does not! You don't tell us very much about him, but I wonder if he is English, or of English parentage? "Hedley

Vickers" was a name very well known in my father's house, as his "memoirs" was a favorite book…Does he belong to New York or Philadelphia, or where? Certes, Elsie, why didn't you write reams about him while you were at it! I'm just as curious as can be to know everything that you would care to tell us—only of course you know I don't want to pry into things that are your own private property.

I am glad to hear the children are well, and was so glad to hear of Vic. We had not heard a word from him since we left U.S. and didn't know where he was. Ida said he had lost his position in Cincinnati shortly after we left, and had gone to Cleveland, but he did not know whether he had work there, or where he was.

We are all well, except for colds, and busy, of course. The children are both in school—Mary going daily to Pak Hok, and Eddie to kindergarten at Mrs. Kwaan's. They are both growing fast, and Eddie is the same old lady killer he used to be, with his brown eyes and rosy cheeks. They both seem to be keeping up the family reputation for brains.

Things political are in a worse tangle than ever here, and the soldiers, who simply overrun the place, are awful. Yau Tsai seems to wag along in the same old way. Dr. Taylor is by way of being engaged to Dr. Ross, but "it may be for aye—and it may be for never!" She is not sure herself. He is away just now to Honolulu, etc. getting funds for the hospital for the insane—expected back in June or July.

Her father wrote her a note on April 21, 1924, Jean put this on my desk some days ago requesting me to write a few lines, so here goes the few lines while I wait for a member of a committee to go see our new chapel in a suburb of Canton City.

I was glad to receive your letter and to hear that you will in the course of a year precipitate yourself into the gulf of matrimony with an osteopath who knows how to fool with bones and plastic tissues.

I hope he is the one for you and I feel he needs congratulations from your dad and mother. I wish I could be present at your wedding so as to have the honor of giving you away…send us his photo, or better, a photo of both of you". There is little evidence the relationship with Hedley lasted except for a short note from his sister.

Despite having a job at St. James, Elsie looked elsewhere for employment and examined her options of getting an M.A. at Columbia University. Without steady employment, supporting the children would be impossible. Her only means of transportation were buses or trains. Then Dr. White sent a warning. "Ease up on the night work idea…let enclosed be between us. Shall cooperate in every way possible. Give me any hint of what I can do…children are better – pardon haste." Elsie received gifts on occasion but why it was a secret is unknown. There was a payout from Billy's insurance policy however, it is unclear who received it.

Then in 1925 Quinnie wrote Elsie another prose about her life as a faculty wife, "Mr. Melby is just about in the notion of studying for his Ph.D. in New York next year, but of course don't know yet. This is not due to any urging of mine especially either. But don't say anything about it until we know for sure. If we do come, we may have a family of three daughters – one 21, and two 17 – two of my nieces and Bollie's niece – the little girl who helped me so royally when I was here in the tea room. Wouldn't that be exciting to have such a big family? I think it would be good for both of us – would liven us up… Sig and I also went to see Janice Meredith during Christmas week…I dragged him down but haven't decided whether it was done cleverly or not. We were on our way, when I was telling him that there were at least three movies that I did want him to see this year. Then he drew his usual lost face and began to say he was handicapped by the rules of the school…we got into an argument that landed us back home in about half an hour without seeing the show. I had appealed to his historical sense in telling him about it – he teaches U.S. history. The next night I was determined I would see Peter Pan…he wouldn't let me go by myself, and so we started, but rather than see something that he didn't know anything about, he suggested that we try Janice – and so we did. I missed Peter Pan altogether, for which I have been sorry ever since. Perhaps you are familiar with little arguments that will come up in the best regulated family – eh, what?" She concludes her letter by saying, "don't wait too long to begin that work for your M.A. wherever you are going to do it."

Quinnie's letters were quaint in their approach to life, much the same way as Elsie's, "Am playing hooky from the game tonight…Sig seems to think I ought to go to everyone…but evidently are doing as well as the other colleges their first Conference year…another one Monday night with Macalester across the river." Quinnie is having medical issues, "Went to the hospital this morning at 8:30 for an x-ray treatment and didn't get away until 10:30, although only half an hour on the table – you have to wait so long. As a result, am feeling pretty starched up tonight. Have had a mean and miserable pain in my chest which seems to run clear through to the back, and I was a bit worried about it for a while, but he 'floroscoped' me this morning with favorable report, am thankful to say. No doubt it will disappear of itself as so many others have done." But by March she says, "Have not been out of the house today. Have a terrible chest – no joking. Have not known what it was for two or three weeks but have about decided it is a hard chest cold with a touch of pleurisy – which I have never been introduced to before, and for this reason am a bit uncertain as to facts. Anyway, that for one reason kept me indoors."

It was two months later when she wrote, "It hasn't been a good year for me, and particularly since February, the program has been mostly the doctor and the couch. That sounds dreadful, doesn't it? I mean – to go to see the doctor and loll on the couch at home. Leave it to me to make the breaks, but you know me, Al. The last week or ten days though have been feeling much better, even though am still under doctor's orders and some very strict. The one doctor quibbled and quibbled (although he was awfully nice and did the best he could) and threatened me with all sorts of big sticks, and then finally the other day sent me to a specialist – this last has given me much comfort together with the fact that I'm feeling better. However, I'm still under suspicion, though at times look the picture of health. At least seems to me I never looked so well."

Quinnie left Minneapolis and went to New York City. On May 23, 1925, she died at the age of 38. Her eulogy and funeral were held at 541 Lexington Avenue. Quinnie's death impacted Elsie deeply. There were so many deaths in Elsie's life that were hard to comprehend and she began to feel the loss.

In the midst of a busy schedule, Dr. White writes that he is going ahead with the Neighborhood House. His energy was put into the memorial for his son, Wilbert, although the donations were dribbling in, "Have made up my mind this morning that I shall not allow correspondence thus to accumulate. It is a difficult thing to clear one's desk every day and yet it is the proper thing to do. I hope that I shall be able to carry out my determination. I am reminded in this connection of a Sir James somebody, who explained his inability to rise in the morning in this way: He said, 'I find it easy to make up my mind but difficult to make up my body.'...At any rate, I am acquainted with a few who manifest the same disability… In September Dr. White writes to Elsie at 70 Morningside Drive where she has an apartment, "I think I appreciate the situation. Life is made up of a series of problems. I will enclose check for $100, in case I can lay my hand on the checkbook before this goes. It will be best, I think, to have the checks passed through in the regular order. Let me know when I can help you. I have to have things brought to my attention these days. Am glad that Miss Forsyth was so much of a comfort…Let us both try to commit our way most completely to the One whose we are and whom we serve…The children have had a great summer. Betsey is developing wonderfully. Billy is full of life. We must plan to keep him occupied."

There were changes in Elsie's plans based on the 1923 decision to form Gold Star Mothers, "A commission was formed by act of Congress to honor the dead of the American Expeditionary Forces of World War I. The commission selected top architects of the day to design the 18 war memorials and construction of the cemeteries began by 1925. In the spring of 1930, the final resting places of 30,800 American soldiers were ready for visits from the mothers and widows of those interred. The American Gold Star Mothers of the World War was formed by the unification of many small-town groups just as the Battle Monuments Commission was progressing with their European duties. In 1929, the 70th Congress approved the act to enable the mothers and widows of the deceased soldiers, sailors and marines to make a pilgrimage to the cemeteries". In the years following the war, Gold Star Mothers dedicated trees to those who made the supreme sacrifice and marched in parades as tributes to those who served, and each parade was full of pageantry throughout the United States.

On March 2, 1929, the 70th Congress approved the act to enable the mothers and widows of the deceased to make a pilgrimage to the cemeteries. Since the end of the war, mothers of the fallen had been taking part in Memorial Day processions. They were referred to as Gold Star Mothers and participated in the pageantry which included G.A.R. veterans. Parades were pretentious and had processions that included 25,000 marchers, all representing different units and organizations. The New York tribune on May 31, 1921, described two parades in Brooklyn honoring the heroes. In the reviewing stand with a place of honor were the gold star mothers and widows of men.

Elsie applied for her passport and left on June 19, 1931 on board the President Roosevelt. She had an identity card issued by the Headquarters in Europe for the American Pilgrimage Gold Star Mothers and Widows. Her address in Paris was Hotel Ambassador, Boulevard Haussmann with a notation that if needed they should be ready, "giving her aid or assistance if needed." Her special passport was stamped "Trip completed, May 11, 1931." She received Certificate No. 4098 and Medallion No. 4126. The specially minted medallion was given to the mothers and widows by the United States Lines, the shipping company which brought the Gold Star mothers and widows to Europe. It was bronze, 38mm and designed and manufactured by Tiffany & Company. They were presented on a red-white-blue neck ribbon, with an observe showing a three-quarter view of a steamship in the open sea, at the stern the Statue of Liberty, and at the bow the Eiffel Tower. In the sea below the ship is the date of the first voyages, 1930; above the ship is a five-pointed gold-plated star. The gold star is a separate thin flake, which is struck into the bronze in the correct design position. The extra medal of the star was then darkened to conform with the bronze area around the star. The reverse has the legend: Gold Star, Pilgrimage to the Battlefields of The World War.

Elsie was pictured next to Billy's cross. Words came into her mind. She sat down and wrote this poem,

"My life was like a peaceful, mountain pool,
That in a golden swoon lay 'neath the sun;
No ripple of emotion stirred its cool,
Smooth waters, and when day was done,
Sometimes it held upon its placid breast,
The cold, chaste whiteness of the moon;
On its serene, bright bosom sank to rest,
Wan, silver stars from heaven's blue lagoon.
Then Love, like a white stone, pierced it still deeps,
Tossed there by you, as stone into a stream
By thoughtless youth. Stirred thus, the water leaps;
Lost stars and moon; peace is a broken dream...
You have forgotten that tossed stone, and yet,
Sine gemmed spray leaps in joy, can I regret.

CHAPTER 18

Elsie White 1927-1939

She was taking a course at The Biblical Seminary in New York. She begins 1927 writing a paper on the Origin of Art, and Father White compliments her on the fine work, "The other day I came across the following definition or description of poetry ascribed to Edgar Allen Poe. 'The origin of poetry lies in a search for a wilder beauty than the earth supplies.' I am wondering if this has a bearing on the origin of art as discussed in your paper". But this is only the beginning of a difficult year. One in which she is plagued with illness, surgery, disappointments, and confrontations. Maybe this is a turning point in her life where she understands that some things are not in her control as she had thought.

In February, Elsie spent two weeks in the hospital, "I was so proud of your progress when the nurse wrote. It was so good of you to have her write" says Amelia, "I certainly am hoping that this operation will set you up in fine shape. I hope the other is not serious and can wait a good long while...I haven't glimpsed Dr. Rosenberger for months. The last day we met dear Dr. De Rivas which was at an evening lecture from 7:00 to 9:30, after his last eulogy on the previous parasites, he turned to me suddenly before the whole class and said, 'Has Mrs. White been in Philadelphia recently?' I was so delighted. That is devotion, my dear." In 1918, one of her instructors at the University of Pennsylvania was John Fogg. The two of them became friends. Besides teaching at the University of Pennsylvania, Dr. Fogg was a dentist at 1907 Chestnut Street. He was going through a difficult period in 1921 and referred to Elsie as a, "Dear Friend, back in what seems like the dim past, but was probably about October, I wrote you a letter. A sort of one. Since then I have been on a long, dark journey and I am just now on my way back. Twas to a place called hell, I journeyed, and it's a long way home. The nervous break against which you cautioned me did finally come. Was coming, I guess, when you warned me. Insidiously for a while and then with a smack. The old optimism sure got it in the neck. I tried to keep it to myself, for instance, I saw Betty two or three times and don't think she was aware of my condition, but now...I am getting a bit better". Before ending the letter, he explains he is going away for some time and hopes to begin writing to her soon. He signs it Uncle Jack and that seems to end it. But Dr. John Milton Fogg and Elsie began writing letters regularly in October 1921. There are other connections when she discovers he knows her cousin Betty Elliott who lived at 3615 Chestnut Street. Amelia Wood and Dr. Fogg seemed to have a proposition for Elsie to stay in Philadelphia. Amelia sent a note to Elsie in the fall of 1927, "Dr. Fogg and I do heartily agree that it is more than worth a salary to have you with us. This is not a salary, it is merely a part of that over which we must not waste words. You will please me not to mention it in anyway." And the two of them conspired to support Elsie financially.

On March 16, Amelia inquires, "I'm believing that you may be in your little white bed at Miss Alston's. If you are, just as soon as she can, will your nurse please write me a nice note letting me know how you are...I am so glad you are having the gall bladder and appendix out. When you told me of your x-ray, I could see what would readily account for all that pain." Recovery from the surgery took away her energy to do anything else. Dr. Bainbridge prescribed Ovoferrin, which was an iron supplement, to increase her energy level. Her resume lists 1927-28 as a year of recuperation from health issues which indicates how difficult it must have been to maintain enough strength to look for employment. She spent her time recuperating by reading and writing. She loved to write poetry but began writing a book on Shanghai. It was a fiction novel. Her first love was writing poetry and hoped that she would publish a book o poetry some day.

Irene Mott, Kathleen Carter and Aunt Elizabeth sent get well notes in March. Irene, "I was so sorry to hear you'd been parted from most of your internals". Kathleen sent this note, "A letter from Hedley informs me of your illness and operation." Then from Aunt Elizabeth, "I do hope you will not have any setbacks and will soon be strong and well." Her friends and family were concerned, yet none of the children's letters mention her recent surgery and illness. Was it a lapse of information or their busy schedules?

In the midst of it all, Elsie was completing her academic requirements for graduation from Columbia when she received this letter from an old friend from 541 Lexington, Ethel Irving, "I am glad that you are going to Battle Creek and do hope it will do you worlds of good...Do hope that they will help you marvelously and that you will get entirely well...I am grieved if your heart is not yet at peace. Please let me know if I can do anything for you and what." Battle Creek Sanitarium was located at Battlecreek, Michigan. Established in 1876 by John Harvey Kellogg and W. K. Kellogg, it was known as a health resort for the rich and famous using diet, exercise and meditation as part of their therapy program.

It is important to note that this was the last time Hedley's name was mentioned in her correspondence. The relationship probably ended shortly after it began although she continued her friendship with his sister, Kathleen Carter.

Friction in the Household

Father White was also struggling with challenges when he wrote this letter to Elsie after a confrontation. It was dated April 10, 1927, This morning I imposed upon myself a penalty for some words over the phone yesterday which I was sorry I used. The trouble was chiefly in the tone. The person spoken to was provoking. That had its effect on me and I went back at him. As a consequence, while I felt and yet feel, that there was reason for what I said as well as for the how of it, I went on foot many blocks before breakfast this morning and apologized. He was very gracious. Said there was no need, etc. This penalty I paid largely to chastise myself – to punish myself so I may be the less likely to do the like again.

Why am I passing this on to you? That I may do the part of friendship in the truest sense. When one takes the risk of losing in order to help, is it not evidence of deepest interests.

Surely you must realize to some extent how much people of our temperament and temper lose by our sharp words and often by our manner alone. You see that I clearly intended to write on these. This in all sincerity, for I am a great sinner in this respect. It is a life struggle with – what shall I call it – a hereditary disability? That would be blaming it on ancestry. We do not do that. Whatever it's origin, it is to be overcome. Not in our own strength, but by grace. This is available and abundant for our need. You have come through a great deliverance. I know a bit about the enormity of it. I have discerned that deep down in your life is the greatest loyalty, and disposition to sacrifice for others.

This, you very well know, is not always revealed. I don't want to preach to you. I'll not write a bit more. You'll forgive any wrong I [sic] you. But I long to have you do yourself less harm, even more at all by. You must know what I mean. I purpose crucifying 'the flesh' in days to come with a vigor yet unequaled. Shall send…in strictest confidence and warmest love and sympathy.

At the same time Victor's letter captured his struggles with his physical disability.

> *1795 E. 19ʰ*
> *Cleveland, Ohio*
> *July 10, 1927*
>
> *Dearest Sister Elsie,*
>
> *Have been away on a trip to Cincinnati (I should have said Moscow, Ohio). Three other persons and myself motored down there from here. Talk about trouble, we certainly had our share. When I returned your card was waiting for me. I was more than delighted to get it.*
>
> *Things aren't so rosy at the Machle's. Uncle Harry must give up work indefinitely or he'll drop over. This giving up work means, selling out his interest in his business, (wholesale dry goods) and selling their home, which had just been remodeled and retiring to their summer home in Moscow, Ohio. Their city home was mortgaged to raise funds for the business so after everything is straightened out, I don't believe there'll be much left. If you owe Aunt Ida a letter, please write her. I'm sure it will be very much appreciated. I realize none of the Machle's are much on*

letter writing. That includes you and me, but I really do enjoy writing, providing, of course, the second party takes time to write me. Now Sis – I need you more than ever now. If you'll write me once a week, I'll promise you I'll reciprocate. What do you say? You asked for dad's letter. I'll send it, but you must return it. There's not much news in it, as you'll see for yourself.

Received the most terrible shock of my life the past week. The young lady I was engaged to, broke our engagement after I had told her of my affliction. Had been leading up to it the past six months testing out her love for me, and when she said nothing could ever separate us, I thought the time was ripe to tell her. Result: the break. In a way I'm sorry I ever told her, then again I realize if she did love me as much as she claimed, nothing could ever separate us. I had heard all these wild tales about never hurting a woman, but, thought as we all do at times, it wasn't time, but here's one I'd die for.

Remember, Sis dear, some time ago I wrote you about undergoing an operation. Well, this is going to take place sometime within the next year. First, I must raise the funds. I'm sure dad will help me although I hate to ask him, but I must go through with this if I ever wish to marry. God help me!

I'd give up the hope of ever marrying this girl if you and I could get together and live. You say we have nothing in common, we're of the same flesh and blood and surely you're not ashamed of your brother. Let me hear from you on this subject.

Four weeks ago yesterday, another chap and I motored to Wooster. We went to Vesper Service in the afternoon which was very delightful. I took a time exposure of the interior of the Chapel in the morning and several other snapshots. I am enclosing same for your approval. Must close now. Let me hear from you as I miss you more than ever now.

Love, affectionately,

Vic

P.S. Address all correspondence to Box 413, Cleveland, Ohio"

In June, the summer activities at Silver Bay had begun and Wilbert took time to drop a line to his mother, "I am having a wonderful time here...The lake is cold now but it will be warm soon...The cookies you sent me were very nice and I thank you. I caught my first lake trout two days ago with Emory Decker. It was only 2 ½ lbs. but it was good. I wish you were here to enjoy the raspberries."

Billy is enjoying his summer at Silver Bay and tells his mother, "I know you will be thinking about my birthday soon but please don't get me much. All I'd like is Tenhunes latest dog book, *Gray Dawn*. I have been reading a lot these days. I have read *Lad* and *Wolf* already." He follows up with a note that he read *Gray Dawn* in three days. "It was very interesting. The candy and cookies are very nice too. I had a nice birthday. Aunt Helen gave me and Betsey the set of pictured encyclopedia which is very interesting. We have had a nice time here and hope you will be up in time for the Regatta."

While setting up a schedule of college presentations for the school, Dr. White received a letter from Dr. McMichael at Monmouth College of an opening in the biology department for one year and wonders if his daughter-in-law(Elsie) would be interested in a short-term appointment." Helen informs her on August 14, "From all reports, you have had a full schedule with study, 20 hours is it? How much longer does Columbia last, and then are you going to be able to come and see us? It seems impossible that we are half through August, though again it seems we have been here a long time" in Silver Bay. "On the new job – it sounds most interesting surely – and a big challenge. You will be going into a great W.P. community. Mother has always, naturally, been interested in Monmouth as her Uncle David Wallace was President (cousin Lizzie Taggart's father, you know). I hope you are going to like the work, the people…and be happy there…the children are both well as can be. Haven't yet had a sick day. We have great times trying to keep Elizabeth from eating quite all the time! How she loves to eat! She weighed 129 lbs. the other day. Of course, is taller, but is getting larger. It doesn't distress her enough to give up food. We have great fun. I must stop. Hope you will be able to get done the things you want, before leaving and that you will let us know when and if you could come our way."

By summer, the Academy Award winning movie *Wings* was in movie theatres around the nation. She received a letter from Elizabeth Irving, Secretary to the President of Monmouth on July 30, "You were very courageous to take your children to see *Wings*, it was certainly self-sacrificing and I hope that they appreciate it…I marvel at you. I looked at the pictures in the program and nearly wept, so that I would not read the story, but have it here." In the beginning of the movie, one of the characters is mourning the loss of a fellow pilot named, "Whitey" who was killed in aerial combat. There is reason to believe it was in reference to Wilbert W. White since John Monk Saunders knew men in the 147th Squadron and stories about Wilber. *Wings* was an American action silent film about two World War I fighter pilot friends, both involved with the same woman. It was produced by Lucien Hubbard and directed by William A. Wellman and released by Paramount Pictures. The screen play was written by John Monk Saunders. It starred Clara Bow, Charles "Buddy" Rogers, and Richard Arlen. It is implied that "Whitey" was Lt. Wilbert W. White.

She makes plans to begin her duties on September 7. But before she leaves New York on September 2, she receives a letter from Dr. White,

> *"Dear Elsie,*
>
> *I have just learned in note from Donald at 3 o'clock Saturday afternoon, that you got off yesterday. Later on we may consider the pros and cons quietly together which issued in such a general fiasco in respect to your getting off. It has been a keen disappointment to us as well as to you, in more ways than one. We shall not allow ourselves to be disturbed just now by any detailed discussion. We are so anxious with you that everything shall get started well out there.*
>
> *Monmouth is a college which, next to my own Alma Mater, I am personally interested in. My friends have been there through all these years. I am sure that you are planning to meet and will succeed in meeting every expectation. The opportunity is a rare one. It will be very testing to you with your temperament, experience, tastes,*

and the rest, but I am depending upon you to fight the good fight, and to win the crown.

Please write me freely and fully about the financial situation. I would not have allowed this thing to happen had you been open and above board with me. I did not suspect that the situation was as it was.

Please remember us cordially to inquiring friends.

Affectionately yours,

Father"

The problem became clear that Elsie had limited spare time. Surgery and hospitalization placed her in a weakened condition which made it difficult for her to work for any length of time but created anxiety when she was unable to see the children before she left for Monmouth. While the family was at Silver Bay Donald managed the office at school, leaving Elsie alone to pack. A letter from Ethel Irving on September 8 clarifies what Elsie experienced that day, "Perhaps you can imagine how grieved I was on reading your letter Friday. And how I did wish that there were no miles between us so that I could be with you and help even a little. You poor dear, I am so sorry, sorry that the packing was too much…so I can readily understand it's upsetting you so soon after the operation and immediately after the strenuousness of Summer School…It does seem so tragic that you had to journey without seeing your children for I know it was hard. It was just too much but I know that you were brave about it and are not going to dwell upon it now but eagerly look forward to Christmas time when you will all be together and it will be here before you know it...Surely, I can sympathize with you when you say 'Spent most of yesterday lying on the bed and considerable more of today' for that is my story these days! I try not to be discouraged and trust that sometime, I can step from the sidelines and get into the race again and 'press toward the prize', not that I am thinking of the prize though.

"I am thinking of you today as you are arriving in Monmouth. I hope that the campus, the town, the people will all seem attractive and to your liking. Blessings on thee, my dear. Remember I am on the sidelines cheering! I sometimes wonder if I will ever be anywhere but on the sidelines. I do hope that you will enjoy it all and that everything will go along beautifully."

By the end of September The Biblical Seminary of New York opened a new building on 49th Street dedicated to Billy. The Lieutenant White Memorial Neighborhood House and Religious Education Center of the Biblical Seminary in New York opened on September 25, 1927 for the purpose of religious training to be combined with recreation and occupational study. Boys and girls clubs would use the house as well as 600 former students and other friends of the Seminary. Among those were 115 foreign missionaries who agreed to pray and work for $1000 for the permanent assets of the institution. The brochures were widely distributed and Dr. White hoped that Bible class members in local churches would join the group and help to make the number higher.

Helen informed Elsie in early October that they located another school for Wilbert, Riverdale Country School in Riverdale, New York. Mr. Hackett, Head Master, was a member of their last group of men at Silver Bay. "He took great fancy to Wilbert which resulted in his coming down night before he left and offering enough scholarship to make it possible with care, for us to send Wilbert there. He lives there during the week and spends weekends at home. It's a beautiful school, up on a hill beside Van Courtland Park, about 250th Street, they have 12 or 14 acres and it's like country. There are about 100 boys live there and that many more come in by day. A Christian atmosphere and fine boys. Lots of outdoor life and real advantages…Wilbert and I came down two weeks ago today having hustled up there, getting mother and Rhoda James settled in Wilson House…We got his clothes tagged and visited the school…They have single rooms. They make much of singing…It was hard to let him go, and he wasn't keen one bit to leave home, but it's near and weekends make it seem right when he is only eleven. He needs boys so badly and had almost no children at Silver Bay, so we felt that was important…Betsey is fine…She was so very well all summer and her grades are going up. She is getting art study."

Elsie is at Monmouth but keeps in touch with her friend Ethel, "I am so sorry that you have had a sick time. Please be careful and please take care of your precious self. I wish you did not have such a heavy schedule—does it have to be? Couldn't you have one less class and let some husky man have one more? I think it is a shame that they have put so much on you and feel that it will not pay for you to be working so hard after your operation—so soon after…I know that the outside things make it hard and it must be difficult to be agreeable out in the evening when you know you have to work far into the night when you get back. Please cut down on those things where you can…So glad to hear about Billy's new school and feel it is an excellent thing all the way around."

She went to New York for Christmas and returned to Monmouth after the New Year in 1928. Shortly after her arrival Mother White's letter arrived, "I wonder Elsie if you struck the blizzard when you went back. We saw by the papers that they were having one. It was pretty cold here for a few days but quite warm again now, too warm for winter." By March 25, Mother White reports that Billy is home with, "A bad cold and was in bed three days up at school in the infirmary, not very sick, but a little temperature. Friday, we had him brought home. He will not go back until after vacation though he is seemingly all right now." She inquires as to whether Elsie will be having some vacation soon?

At the end of the school year, Elsie left Monmouth and returned to New York City. Elsie was located at Riverside Drive and wrote to Ethel in March of 1930, "Tuesday night I had dinner with Hedley's sister in Brooklyn. Wednesday, I enjoyed a very much belated dinner with Helen Lehman – one of the girls with whom I had lived in Belleville. An emergency came in to the laboratory at five fifteen which left me working until seven! But Helen was game. She stayed and seemed interested in watching me make the necessary cell counts, cultures, and bacteriological examination's on the spinal fluid that was in question...I lunched with my cousin, Betty who happened to be up near the Medical Center and in the evening, my own Billy escorted me to the Flower Show...Saturday Hedley's sister and I saw *Bedeley Square* together and today I am trying to do everything that should have been done during the week."

Wilbert White III

"I received your letter today and was delighted to find out that you would give me a collie puppy", writes young Wilbert on a Sunday afternoon, "I told the family about it and they thought that it would be very nice to have it for the summer. We are doubtful though about the winter because Alma does not want a dog." They named the puppy, Nancy.

Billy continues to write to his mother throughout the year and keeps her informed about his health, school and his activities,

"I passed in French and am now in French II with all A's in all subjects. I have math the first period, English the second, then Latin, French and the period after lunch I have history. They are giving us a lot of homework so am working very hard to get them all done.

"I am interested in some new cars which have a front drive instead of a rear. The Cord car is one, which made by the Auburn Company and the Ruxton is the other." As he continues to write to Elsie, he starts using Billy as his signature instead of Wilbert, "I was sorry you lost your job up at the hospital. However, you were lucky to get another one so quickly and I hope you will like it very much…My marks for the last two weeks have come up a little. My English came up to an 80 which wasn't so bad. My biology and French were also 80, while my Latin was 98 and my algebra was 87. These gave me a weighted average of 80.95 or 81."

By fall semester, 1931, Billy was at The Hill School in Pottstown, Pennsylvania, struggling with his grades when Dr. White received a letter from James Wendell. "I am pleased to inform you that we have removed Wilbert's condition in Fourth Form Latin… Wilbert's good work in this subject for the past month has deserved this recognition on our part, and we are hopeful that he will carry this course successfully for the remainder of the year." In the spring of 1932, he isn't feeling well, "I personally have had a mean cough for over a week. It gets me so damn mad when I can't sleep or do anything and the doctor can't do a thing apparently as I am thoroughly gripped." About a week later, "I'm glad to hear that you are out of New York and now in a place where you can enjoy yourself a little and get a breath of fresh air. What! No cellophane!..I've been in the 'San' from Monday till Friday with bronchitis. I still have a cough but I'm feeling fine."

Elsie wants to visit Billy but relies on friends for transportation. Visiting her children is difficult and relying on others becomes cumbersome. In the midst of it all she made plans to pick up Billy for a visit to Philadelphia, "I can leave with you in the car when you can come Thursday evening. Will that be okay? Get here as soon as possible, for I think you might like to see the school if possible...I passed everything. I was a little disappointed in biology for I only got a 68, but I got a 75 in Latin and an 83 in algebra...wish me luck in my exams. With love, until I see you Thursday evening...It really is awfully good of Mrs. Baldwin (Mitty) to take the trouble to come up here and get me. I won't forget to thank her. Damn I can't write with my roommate bothering me. He's a pest most of the time."

The summer at Silver Bay for a fifteen-year old was an outlet from the usual school work and schedule, "A group of us went up Brown Mountain on a picnic hike. It is the place where the blueberries are so abundant. We, Betsey and I, were with the Penfield's, and the Hume's. Several other friends came along also. We had a swell time, and it was a perfect day. We were tired when we got home but a swim pepped us up...we're planning another trip today up to Fort Frederick, but it poured and we couldn't go...one of the daughters of the people at the Lodge, has had many visitors. She had three girls from Englewood up here about a week ago. They stayed several days, and before they left, I was on excellent terms with all of them. We had a lot of fun swimming...the girls were a couple of years older than I am, but they didn't know it."

The children were good about writing to Elsie and a week later, "Don and grandfather drove up from New York Tuesday. On Wednesday grandfather and I started at about noon for Canada. He felt that he must see Uncle John (Mott) about some matters concerning the seminary...so we started. I drive a large part of the way up and all the way back. On the way up, we made Montreal in four hours and averaging well over 36 miles an hour.

We reached Uncle John's at about 7:30 p.m. Yesterday, we had a big aquatic meet at the community boat house in our bay. The cottagers and everybody that wanted to, entered the competition. I was in everything that I could enter. The twins and I entered our sailboat and won by a nose in a very exciting race. It was called a tie because it was so close…Bill Arms and I won the canoe tilting…I won the canoe planning race in which one person gets up on the back of the canoe and jumps up and down…I was in the 100-yard free style swim. I took a close second." Billy is as competitive as his father and is involved in all the Silver Bay activities during the summer.

Elsie was staying with Mitty Baldwin in Cockraneville when Billy writes to his mother on October 20, 1932, "I was surprised when I got your letter from Spruce Lawn Farm…For the last eight days, beginning on Friday, about 50 members of the female sex were here to brighten the dark lines of The Hill School boys. It was the fall term dance. I didn't go to any of the dances for these good reasons. I didn't have a 'tuck'; I didn't feel like forking over $10 for the dances; and I can't dance very well. I'll have to learn before long though because the Glee Club is going to the Baldwin School to give the girls there a treat on December 3 and I'll probably go since I'm in the first 36 and also the choir."

On March 31, 1935, Dr. and Mrs. White celebrated their 50th Anniversary. It may have been a quiet celebration but Elsie honored them with a poem addressed to Father and Mother White on their golden wedding anniversary.

An article about Elsie appeared in a local paper describing how she was writing stories that described adventurous tales with exotic Oriental settings for her own amusement. She was helping with publicity for the Women's University Club, playing bridge and keeping up with biology by reading medical journals. But there wasn't a full-time position in biology and her son Billy was putting pressure on her, "I've been wondering whether Fred Mott couldn't help you. I'm sure he could, or at least put you in touch with somebody who could. You certainly should be able to make use of your bacteriology these days. Or how about writing some of father's old friends that you know. Surely, they would do anything they could to help. Or I'll write them if you prefer. Just tell me whom you'd like to have me contact and I'll do it. But let's get something on the fire."

It was 1939. The World's Fair was in the Flushing Meadows-Corona Park. Many countries around the world participated in the year-long festivities. It was futuristic, with an emphasis on the theme, "Dawn of a New Day" and a look at tomorrow. Elsie prepares her tax return in March of 1940. She is living at 2211 Delancey Street in Philadelphia creating more confusion about her return address of 2007 Walnut Street, or 2007 Delancey. Sometimes you can tell a lot about a person's life style when you read a tax return. We know she filed as a single person, had personal exemptions, and donated to the church and Red Cross as well as paid interest on a loan. While attending the World's Fair in 1940, she meets Roy Tasco Davis, President of National Park College in Forest Glen, Maryland and meets with him to discuss a possible faculty position but that meeting was just "a meeting."

In July 1942, Elsie's son Billy shares his frustration with the school and those in charge since his grandfather retired, "Regarding the Seminary – I'm not particularly happy about it. As far as I'm concerned the place isn't worth a damn right now as far as professors, students, or finances go. It's strictly "B" class – always has been since grandfather left and even before for a few years. And how are they going to run the place anyway? It's like raising money to buy a new car – then not having anybody who knows how to drive and no fuel or money to buy fuel. The people who have given to help the Seminary get out of this hole are certainly owed a lot in return – in results and reorganization. I'm sick of the damn place, and care very little what happens to it. It's not the place that you know. I believe grandfather feels pretty much the same way, although it is his life – and he hates to say die. He's so far ahead of anybody else down there that he's like a master mechanic trying to work with a bunch of bricklayers…I can't possibly finance your trip to New York until after the 20th. Then you'll have to take it easy because I'm in a hellava[*sic*] spot with my apartment."

Elsie becomes assistant to Dr. de Rivas at his Laboratory of Clinical Medicine and Pathology at 1831 Chestnut Street in Philadelphia. On February 26, 1943, Betsey wrote, "I was so glad to know that you are now working. I would love to watch what you are doing in the hospital. Will I have permission to watch you? I hope someday…I am working now, but on a different job where I can sit down. The job is to decorate such things as rattles, brushes and combs, etc. with painted flowers, in a variety of designs. I like it all right, but I have trouble with my back, a sharp pain between my shoulder blades and vertebra, nearest to the vertebra, at my left side as you know I am left-handed as an artist…The same old pain of many years makes me so cross and have tried to get rid of it. I bought an electric vibrating machine to relieve the pain. It does not seem much of a help – I was told that the only way to stop the pain was to be operated…I had one letter from Billy a few days after he arrived in California. He must be busy now to make up all the studies he missed." There is reason to believe Betsey inherited this condition from her mother since Elsie often complained about her back problems.

Victor sends Elsie birthday greetings, "Thanks a lot of Betsey's picture. I see that she favors her mother. She is a mighty fine good-looking girl and why not, her dad and mother were a good-looking couple."

CHAPTER 19

Elsie Co-Authors book:
Our Friends, The Chinese,
1945

Elsie was writing poetry with hopes of publishing a book of poetry. In the midst of writing *This Ravaged Heart,* she received a note from a friend. Josephine Budd Vaughan, a friend she met at Columbia who made an offer she couldn't refuse, "I am going to wish a job on you. If it is asking too much please just say, 'No' in capital letters. But you did such a good piece of work the other day for me that I need more help...Would you mind going through this material and checking on its weak spots and there are plenty for instance, involved sentences, also wherever the presentation is weak, just say so. I am a bit discouraged about it and doubt if it is good enough or up-to-the minute enough to meet the market – would that I could write a short story as you do or even a grand long article. And then I just might spend some extra thousand hours on it and low we would find ourselves in war with Japan, then where would this stuff be?" While Elsie continued writing poetry under the pen name Vivien Sterling the rejection letters kept coming making Joie's offer appealing.

She received a story written by Joie who expected her to edit her work, "You help me criticize this and I will try to help you sell those stories which are a thousand times better than anything I can do, so get them to me quickly. I hope probably by the end of next week we can get together again." Elsie and Joie made a deal. "Blessing on you, old dear and I still hope nothing more than popcorn is to be found in the interiors."

Elsie continued to have health issues and had surgery at Johns Hopkins on June 9. After recuperation she accepted the offer and begins meeting with Joie regularly to develop ideas for the book yet the premise of the book would come from Bill Vaughan's experience in Japan. Elsie would become a ghost writer for Bill who didn't want to jeopardize his position.

She continued to keep in touch with Billy and Betsey through letters. Elsie received news on April 9, 1943 from her son Billy that he was a navigator, ...The writing portfolio which you mentioned sounds very nice, but really mother, I don't need things...I certainly don't want you to think that you should buy me things." But by September, he shares news, "I'm in Chicago! I'm here... for a very good reason! For some time now I have been contemplating the big step of matrimony – the lady willing. Now it is blossoming into reality, and Wednesday we intend to officially announce our engagement. The young lady in question... is Nancy Freund, the daughter of Mr. & Mrs. F. C. Woodward of Chicago, Illinois. She has been living for some time in San Francisco at the same place where I have my room and is without any question absolutely wonderful...I love her and her family very much. The reason for not having let you know sooner is quite simple – we didn't quite know either. As for the wedding – that will be in the future sometime when arrangements can be made. Tentatively we plan to be married in Chicago sometime around Christmas time but that is all dependent on my schedule and transportation problems. We aren't particularly worried about the details since they can be ironed out rather easily. Naturally, we plan to live in San Francisco or the vicinity as long as my work keeps me there, but beyond that our plans are few. I know you'll love Nancy. She's a wonderful girl and comes from a wonderful family. I'll keep you posted as to any further developments."

By October, they were still indefinite about their plans. The letter is very upbeat and urges her not to spend money on them, but she should take care of herself. By November 18, he is thanking her for sending an evening bag to Nancy, "Our plans are finally materializing into something which looks as though it might be pretty definite. Barring any unforeseen happenings, Nancy and I are to be married on Wednesday, December 15. I am leaving San Francisco with her on the train this Sunday and will be with her family until the day of the wedding. After that we are going to New York and spend a few days, and then start back to San Francisco. I have been very lucky in regards to getting time off. The company has given me my vacation for the last two weeks in December and are allowing me to skip a trip between now and then, since I could not go out on another trip and still have time to take my vacation this year, which is in the regulations."

Betsey informs Elsie that she is going to be the maid-of-honor, "As yet, I have not heard of the definite date for Billy's wedding...I've always thought you knew that Nancy had asked me to be a maid-of-honor and her sister is to be a matron-of-honor... grandfather is wanted to be in Chicago before December 12, and I have to go with him and Aunt Helen on the 10th. I have to be there early enough to have time to have my dress fitted and to buy some things which Nancy wants me to get for the wedding... I have some good dresses here I can wear. I plan to stay there till the following Friday and I have some friends whom I would like to see. Grandfather is taking care of the reservations. You are lovely to want to get the tickets as your treat for me and I thank you very much. I appreciate it all...We will have a very quiet Thanksgiving and we have no plans for the day, perhaps, eating less, sleeping more and seeing some movies...I am more than sorry that this is disappointing you. There is no other way."

On December 1, Elsie receives some final plans for the wedding, "The show itself ought to be a good one as everything down to the smallest detail has been thought out. I hope you can arrange to get here by Sunday as we are having the bridal dinner that night. Let me know if you need any help in getting a reservation as I might be able to do something – but it's pretty hard from this end...I'm having a bit of an usher problem. I asked six and two dropped out but guess there's a large enough supply here to make it possible for me to get someone else. Let me hear from you soon so that I can plan to meet you...I'll be seeing you in a few days."

A newspaper clipping of the wedding states that Mrs. Wilbert W. White was unable to arrive in time for the Sunday party, but will be present for the wedding. She wore an elegant mauve crepe gown, hat and gloves. At the wedding dinner, she was placed next to a bachelor by the name of Jay Halla, who was one of the ushers, making the event, more palatable in a very uncomfortable situation. Elsie took out a loan for $156. The note was created on December 3, 1943 with The Morris Plan Bank of Philadelphia.

Elsie has a new job by March 7, 1944 and news from Billy that the family is growing, "that less than four months from now Nancy and I will be responsible for a third member in our family." The news comes in May and he plans to stay at home until the baby arrives, "I'm interested to learn a new book is in the making. I trust it will be a big success." Elsie sent Billy money for his birthday present and went on to New York to see Betsey. Betsey wasn't there. There must have been lack of communication because

Betsey was on vacation and wouldn't arrive back until August 17. She was visiting grandfather and Aunt Helen and was sorry she missed her mother.

There is a question whether Betsey was able to visit Dr. White and Aunt Helen since news of his death made front page headlines. On August 12, 1944, Dr. Wilbert Webster White died at the Hotel Commodore. He and Helen had checked in on August 7, and as usual, he sat down at the desk and was in the midst of writing a letter to Helen when he had a heart attack and died.

In June, 1945 Billy announces that Nancy is expecting another baby in December. On August 8, Billy expresses his thoughts about his mother moving to the country, "I can picture you today gathering together your accumulated what-nots and packing off for the country. I'm glad to hear that you are giving up Philadelphia for a while...It's no place for a human being...your transition from city to country life will, I'm sure, be enjoyable... I'm glad to hear that you are interested in getting back to your writing as a permanent, rather than a sideline job. I know that your ability to write should pay dividends and give you a lot more pleasure to boot." On November 18, 1944, Billy announces the birth of their son, "The nurse does most of the work for the baby and also takes good care of us in between feedings...David is really quite a boy. He looks, I believe a little bit like father did, though I only have one picture of him when he was a boy about five." Elsie keeps in touch by telephone, "It was wonderful to hear your voice over the phone Tuesday...I was sorry to learn that you had a tumble downstairs. I hope you're not suffering any ill effects now." She also receives a letter from Betsey thanking her for sending $10 and, "Now you are grandmother and I am aunt. David Walton, very pretty name, isn't it?"

She kept Betsey and Billy informed about her decision to leave Philadelphia and move to the country. Elsie accepted an invitation to live with her friend Mitty at Spruce Lawn Farm in Cochraneville where Mitty and Bill Baldwin had, "160 acres, 30 in woodland. A sixty-acre meadow is watered by the Octoraro[*sic*] Creek, where there is a dividing line between Chester and Lancaster Counties. Ancient black spruces give it its name. Principally it was a dairy farm. A few chickens, ducks, goose, and guinea fowls are raised, and some pigs, of course. Corn, oats, wheat, alfalfa, clover and timothy are grown for feed" but it was the peace and quiet Elsie needed to be creative. She continued to describe her surroundings, "The house is stone, built some two hundred years ago and the original crane and pot are still hanging in one of the vast fireplaces." Yet, as she prepared to leave Philadelphia, she packed her belongings and left without contacting Amelia Wood or other close friends who arrived at her apartment and realized that she was gone. Not only did she have the phone disconnected but left nothing behind to indicate where she had gone.

Grandma Elsie

Billy was now called "Snowey" by his friends and Elsie became grandmother again when Billy and Nancy had a baby girl. On January 3, 1946, Constance arrived at 6:45 p.m. weighing 8 lb. 5 oz. They would call her Connie as Billy expresses his impression of her, "I believe, she resembles her mother, but as the Children's Hospital does not permit visitors to see the babies, I had only a brief glimpse of her. She looked healthy and fair but had a more difficult time than with David." Elsie, an accomplished needle-work artist, knitted a set of sweater and booties for both grand-children bringing a comment from Harriet Woodward that they, "are the most beautiful ones I've ever seen. I should think you could make a fortune selling them."

In September 1945, Joie and Elsie are busy working on the book. The book emphasized, "their concept of international industrialization and the very modern idea of the outstanding responsibility engineers assume in the development of foreign countries, i.e. Japan and China, guiding the hands that plan and develop the concept of people-minded engineers." Or, the book examines the American engineer. Those were mainly Bill's ideas. At the time Bill Vaughan was in the Economic and Scientific Section. He was the first special staff group to be created independently of the AFPAC Military Government Section assigned control over Japan's economic affairs and advised SCAP on labour, finance and industry, both in Japan and Korea. All of these ideas were jumbled into what if, who, and how are we going to do it before they settled on, *Our Neighbors, the Chinese*. A story about the Chinese people and how they transitioned from peasants to soldiers during WWII. Once, Joie exclaimed, "As for titles, I am still hunting desperately and go around mumbling nouns and verbs, hoping one will jump out a me." And combined the last names to become Vaughan White, the author of the book about the startling extremes of Chinese life.

Joie even set up a meeting with Alex Taub, the British born Engineer who worked with Chevrolet, who went on to design the engine for the Churchill tank. They met with Alex over dinner at the Warwick Hotel in Washington, D.C. He had a diary in his possession of his recent trip to China with Nelson that they could use as they saw fit. Joie suggests that Elsie have an outline ready for their meeting when she came to Mt. Holly for a week to work out the details. Joie gave Elsie a check for $10 to cover paper, postage and the typing, assuming that the going rate was $.10 a page.

By 1950, Bill was in Tokyo. After two years, he was loaned from the Italian Government where he was acting as their Technical

Adviser to the Executive Branch where he was on the top level of planning for all that goes on under SCAP. There were contacts with Nora Waln, Elsa Troedsson, Elizabeth Vining, Marje Aimie, and Myra Olive.

While at The Dodge Hotel in Washington D.C., she exclaims in her exuberance, "Blessings on you, old ear. I've got something coming your way for Christmas Day but maybe Uncle Sam will be slow. Don't you dare send me anything except some more manuscript. Santa Claus never visits hotels but writers are regular lounge lizards and love them. You know those type. Would be writers. That's me. I wish somebody had started me off on the poetry of the bible when I was three rather than to Sunday school and the Presbyterian Church!"

By 1946, the book was published by Rinehart. It sold for $2.75 with descriptive advertising in newspapers and magazines. One article describes, "A new book on the psychology and philosophy of that allied nation, scheduled to be released this month by Rinehart & Co., Inc. of New York." Mrs. Vaughan, who is the wife of William Vaughan, chief of the Foreign Economic Administration's technical specifications division spent ten years in China doing sociological and psychological research and teaching of two universities in that country. There were two reviews. One in *The Free World* and one in *The Saturday Review.* Currently, the book is located in 160 libraries throughout the United States. There were offers to speak, radio work, and a study group.

As word went out that Elsie's husband was a pilot in WWI, inquiries about her background came in requesting information, "My husband was a 1st lieutenant…doing the work of a Captain but was killed before his Captain's commission came through. He trained with the Royal Flying Corps, flew with Vernon Castel, and accounts of his exploits have appeared in numerous magazines, and books such as *Heroes All, the Flying Circus* by Eddie Rickenbacker, *Up and at 'Em* by Colonel Hartney, etc. I suggest that no mention be made of the Congressional Medal until I can give you the data concerning it which you have asked for. I have written for this information. Also for copies of his citations as I myself am confused as to the specific acts for which he was honored by the award of The Distinguished Service Cross with Oakleaf Clusters and the Croix deGuerre with palms. I believe he was the ranking Ace of New York State." It was interesting to note that she didn't know the details of his awards, or his ranking as an Ace. He was the top Ace with more kills than any other pilot at the end of the war.

She was even asked to have a picture taken with Eddie Rickenbacker, "I certainly would not object, quite the contrary. I have always admired him...I heard him on *We The People*...it would certainly be interesting to appear on *We The People*." When asked if she had hobbies by Mr. Geddes she replied, "My hobby is bird study. I like biology, major league baseball, opera, mystery novels, Chinese food, philosophy, air travel, biographies, the St. Louis Blues, heavy-weight boxing bouts, but dislike modern love stories, getting up early, seashore resorts, puddings, problem plays and problem movies, news commentators (except Lowell Thomas and Raymond Swing) serial stores, and questionnaires." The half share royalties from the sale of the book was approximately $50. Hardly enough to live on.

Along with the celebrity status was pressure to write another book. There were many suggestions and Elsie began to outline Joie's ideas, but the pressure from Joie to continue writing went awry. She didn't finish writing the second book. Four years later in July, Joie wrote that it was clear, "I know you haven't written as you should and for that I am sorry probably a bit selfishly sorry for as the days and months go by and I get no inspiration from your written word from that gifted brain of yours which has always sent me back to grubbing some more in the hope that I might produce something a wee bit better than before, when that inspiration does not come my desire to try to write grows weaker and more and more I find myself letting other things take the place of going ahead with the writing...I've lost my inspiration in not having you share your thoughts with me." Perhaps it was lack of time, or lack of interest, but she continued to write poetry which was never published.

Victor wrote to Elsie with stories of lost money, stolen items, burning his dinner, or losing his job. He seemed to find misfortune. Yet on January 1, 1945, "It's 4:00 a.m. I'll write a while and then off to bed...I want to thank you for the wonderful gifts I received from 2400 Spruce Street, everything is swell...the slippers are a couple sizes too large." She was always buying the wrong size regardless if it was Victor, Billy, or Betsey, "The pajamas are a little tight...The tie is gorgeous, you have excellent taste, and the sox are nice too." In return he sends her, "The playing cards caught my eye, rather expensive but I said, 'Nothing is too good for Sis'...I hope you enjoyed the basket of goodies, also nuts and cigarettes...LIFE and Nature magazines are renewed for another year." Within a month, he makes a proposal, "I really don't see why we should be separated and...if I could secure a job in Philadelphia, well, we could get a nice seven room apartment with the money we both are spending on separate places we ought to be able to get something nice." He continues to detail his finances and how it would benefit them.

It was about this time in 1949 that Elsie and a friend from Philadelphia, Elizabeth Brinton decided to move to Monument Street in Baltimore, Maryland. Elsie went to the Maryland Employment Center and applied for a job as a laboratory technician at Church, Home and Hospital, where she worked for three years. They bought a house at 501½ 42nd Street in 1950. It was a brown clapboard with white trim on a tree lined street with a backyard. It had two apartments. One for each of them.

Vic writes on August 18, 1950, "You say your friend, which I suppose is Elizabeth Brinton, is going to Baltimore, too. From what I gather, although you don't come right out and say so, you are more or less a nurse or governess, or companion, in other words you are taking care of her." Imagine his surprise when she tells him in a letter that she was, "taking 14 medicines a day for a week, then 11 per day the next week. Whatta you got…I do hope it will make you feel like a new person."

Elsie and Victor received word that their stepmother, Jean Mawson Machle, died on August 25, 1952 in Tacoma, Washington. They did not make the trip for the funeral but sent a message to Mary Cooke and family.

She taught Chinese at Grace & St. Peter's Episcopal Church in Baltimore's historic neighborhood until 1965. On May 2, 1965, Jimmy, David and Raymond Lee had a birthday celebration for her 75th birthday. One child, Jimmy Lee asked, "Are you going to eat the whole cake yourself Mrs. White?"

It was after 1958 when Victor moved to Baltimore. Elizabeth Brinton moved into a nursing home in Oxford, Pennsylvania, leaving Elsie her half of the house. She jotted a note that she(Elsie) shouldn't put her things on the second floor. There were applications to various department stores for clerk positions, but social security and a small salary from Grace & St. Peter's were her only source of income.

SNOWEY, NANCY, CONNIE AND DAVID WHITE

RANDY, WENDY, GEORGENE SEARFOSS WITH ELSIE MACHLE WHITE IN 1977

CHAPTER 20

Our Neighbors, Elsie and Victor

Now, Wooster, Endeavor, New York and Philadelphia were somewhere in the past. There were three of us sitting in the Johnson-Fosbrink Funeral Home listening to the eulogy for Elsie Machle White. The casket was placed in a room that felt cold and unfriendly and much too large for a small intimate memorial service. Her body, dressed in a blue lace dress, didn't seem appropriate for the woman wearing it. It was a solemn service attended by the power of attorney, her husband, as well as myself, the wife of the minister who conducted the service. Internment was held in an idyllic setting in Moreland Cemetery off Loch Raven Boulevard in Baltimore, Maryland. Within a few months, Elsie's brother, Victor would be buried beside her.

A will had been drawn up by her attorney leaving the house and property to Victor, all the clothes, linens, books, pictures to a stepsister, Mary Cooke, who lived in Tacoma, Washington; with a codicil that she was not leaving her children anything in the Will because they were adopted by their aunt when they were 5 or 6 years old and would inherit from her. However, no document was found to verify this. The document appointed Mrs. Cosimo Portera (the power of attorney) Executors of the Estate, but the document was never signed. After Elsie's death,

Charles H. Dorn, her lawyer who handled the half-interest purchase of her home in 1967 from Elizabeth Brinton, a long-time Philadelphia friend, informed Mrs. Portera that her authority ceased and they could not proceed with the sale of the property as she had planned. Under the law the only one who could sell the property was the Personal Representative of the estate. The Personal Representative appointed by Mr. Dorn was Elsie's estranged son, Wilbert W. White, III.

One day early in July, Mr. Dorn stopped by our home with Elsie's son, Wilbert, who had come from Denver, Colorado to view the house and belongings at 501½ E. 42nd Street.

Wilbert's letter of July 26, 1978:

"Dear Pastor Searfoss,

"Thank you for taking the time to visit with me and Mr. Dorn the other day. I must admit that it was quite a shock to discover that mother's house had been so completely ransacked. I suppose it was to be expected, under the circumstances, but I'm certain that many things were ruined or taken in the process.

"I certainly appreciate all you and your wife did to assist Elsie and Victor over the past four years. I'm sure they had some difficult times. Also, thank you for your suggestions about cleaning up and disposing of the property. I hope Mr. Dorn is able to work things out and that the house and property will again have life and loving care.

Sincerely,

Wilbert W. White"

He returned to Colorado with instructions to the lawyer to contact Dave Green, the neighbor on the west side of the property, who offered to buy it for $7,000, and arranged to begin cleaning out the house. Anne and Dave Green were community activists involved in entrepreneurship, and education. Dave was a physics professor at Towson University and Anne ran a private school for a short time before returning to the private sector. The large white columned manse on the property, once a funeral home, housed students, artists and musicians in a coffee house, Halloween Haunted House, energy co-op and boarding house. Acquiring the Elsie White house gave the couple another opportunity to assist college students with housing.

There were the Sunday afternoon visits when Anne and I took Elsie out on the porch for some fresh air and she would tell us stories from her life. It wasn't easy to interpret her stories although Anne was better at it than I was. But it became more common to visit her on those days.

One Sunday afternoon a year earlier I spent time with Elsie. There were many letters in Elsie's dresser drawer; letters from her parents and husband. I gave her a bath and did her laundry while we talked. Elsie spoke in a thickly voice as she told me she was born in China. She spoke of her parents, her time in China and bowing low, low, low when she met the Empress. She was expressive when she talked about her love of birds and flowers, and very proud of the book she co-authored, *Our Neighbors, The Chinese* under the pen name Vaughan White. Conversations with Elsie were strained. It was necessary to listen carefully to understand her because her mind wandered, perhaps that is why she never talked about her children or her husband. But there were several memories that pained her. One was Victor's kidnapping by a Chinese bandit who castrated him and placed him on the auction block. It was painful to hear her describe how her mother and sister were killed in the Lien Chow Massacre. She became hysterical and enacted the drama by flailing her arms when she described how they flung her sister in the river. On one occasion after her bath, I was looking for underwear in her dresser when I found a drawer full of letters. I asked her who they were from and she said, "My husband." Then I asked, "What happened to your husband," and she looked up at me and said, "He died." She seemed different when she spoke about him, calmer, more solemn, almost soulful, which gave me the impression that she didn't want to talk about it anymore. It would be some time before I would understand her response.

Sometime later we received a call from Victor that Elsie was missing. We combed the neighborhood looking for her without success. We looked all over the first floor of the house, never looking any further since there were so many items on the steps it seemed impossible that she could make her way up to the second floor. The police were called. Yet their search provided no clue as to what happened to Elsie. Later that day Victor called saying he found her upstairs sitting in a chair reading letters. It was remarkable that she was able to maneuver her way upstairs through the clutter on the steps.

When the Green's offered us an opportunity to take items from the house, I looked for the letters, but the letters in the dresser were gone. However, there were others in a hallway cupboard. It was in the basement that I found an old deteriorating trunk, soaked with water from a water pipe leak weeks before, partially full of letters. I gathered as many as I could, at least the ones that weren't falling apart when I lifted them up from their resting place. There were also two small pairs of Chinese baby shoes; one was a blue cat with whiskers, the other a red lion-type face. Both were soaked with water, colors running together; but I knew, if dried out, they would still be a treasure. After collecting many letters, documents, and pictures, I took them home and laid the wet letters out on the basement floor to dry. Each one was water-logged, some beyond hope of saving, but after drying, were put back in the envelopes and saved. They were saved for forty years before this author began to type them into a readable image which turned into an eight-year project. Besides the clutter everywhere, the house was packed with garbage bags of cards and letters. Magazines were piled high, furniture was misplaced and everything had a layer of dirt and grime.

We're talking about Greenmount Avenue where it meets York Road at 42nd Street. Once a tree lined street with lovely homes in an upscale area, one can imagine that it was the suburbs of a rapidly growing city where the old city line met Baltimore County at Boundary Avenue and why the church across the street was named Boundary Avenue Methodist Episcopal Church, later renamed Boundary United Methodist Church. Boundary was a beautiful stone church formed in 1891, was rebuilt in 1916 with an impressive stained glass window that once held a large congregation of 900 plus members. In the mid 1940s Rev. C. E. Seymour, blinded in a hunting accident, led the congregation to buy the house on the corner of Greenmount and 42nd for a parsonage, purchased hymnals in Braille, giving the church an outreach to the blind that no other church in the city offered. Boundary became known for this service. Once Helen Keller visited Baltimore and chose to attend Boundary. Between the large parsonage and church was a carriage house with a circular driveway lined with roses and a garden in the middle of the circular driveway. Parishioners often told the story about the blind pastor raising prize dahlias in the space. Since Elsie's house was across the street she had a picturesque view of the church grounds. It lies north of Waverly near East 33rd where Venable

Park, also known as Memorial Stadium was located, an area targeted by "block busting" by unscrupulous real estate agents in the 1960s.

One Sunday in December, I invited Elsie to my house for tea while the children baked Christmas cookies. She could no longer wear shoes over her swollen feet, so she wore slippers which made it hard for her to walk. She was excited to go and always wanted to see the inside of the large Victorian three-story parsonage. Years earlier she was friends with the clergy family that lived there but never had the opportunity to go inside. Once inside the house, she exclaimed, "it's just as I had imagined it." While I did her laundry and the children baked cookies, an announcement came over the television that there as a small private airplane crash on the stadium premises. The excitement was too much and Elsie wanted to go back to her safe haven.

The changing neighborhood created tensions in the communities bordering Greenmount Avenue and those west of Ellerslie Avenue. Martin Luther King's death and funeral in April, 1968, triggered unrest and violence in Baltimore. Looting and burning was all over the city, but it gradually moved up Greenmount Avenue to 22nd Street, then to 25th, and eventually close to 42nd Street. Whether that was the day teenagers roamed the streets looking for trouble is unknown, but one day they came to Elsie's house robbed the elderly couple, broke her glasses, stole her wedding ring, and broke the windows on the first floor. Incidence like this occurred more frequently as gangs of young people moved around the community. Although some of the homeowners stayed, others moved farther out in the suburbs because they felt unsafe so most of Boundary's congregation were gasoline Christians. Victor's response to the damage was to board up the windows which gave the appearance of an abandoned home, added to that was the inability to care for the landscape around the home, while the yard in back displayed a tangle of overgrown vines and bushes. By 1978 property values fell making the value of the home less than $2600.

Once you entered the house, a small hallway and stairs greeted you with a doorway on the left that led into the living room. A path between the wall of magazines and an overstuffed chair led to the dining/kitchen area. As your eyes adjusted to the darkness it became clear there was a chair which sat next to a small side table where a lamp cast a dim light, a phone and a worn address book lay next to it. Elsie became accustomed to sitting in the chair which had become her bed as well; her bedroom unused because she was afraid of the rats that came out at night.

Elsie suffered from congestive heart failure which caused her legs to swell from sitting too long. Her physician ordered her to elevate her legs more often after her hospitalization on March 7, 1974 for heart failure. She refused to go to the hospital until she had the social worker contact Mr. Dorn regarding the Will. She sent a message that she would like to meet with him and turn the Will over to him. She told him what she wanted and he drew up the will. Her Will stipulated that she wanted her body to go to research at Johns Hopkins, with a list of items to be distributed to relatives, one large silk screen oriental picture to the Baltimore Chapter of the Kappa Kappa Gama, but once again, she didn't sign the Will or have it witnessed. After making her bed with clean sheets, pillow cases and covers, she decided she was more comfortable in her favorite chair which led to another hospitalization at Union Memorial Hospital where she died on January 29, 1978.

Victor had arranged for his barber's wife to be their power of attorney. Victor would turn the porch light on once a week so they could make their way up the cement steps, drop off groceries, check the mail for bills or checks while Victor got a haircut.

Their step-sister, Mary Machle Cooke kept in touch with Elsie and Victor in later years by telephone and correspondence. During the late 70s, Mary's daughter Mary Margaret and Kevin Brewer spent time in Baltimore with Elsie and Victor. During that visit, Victor shared his story about his abduction, castration, placed on the auction block as a eunuch, and recovery as a child. This was verified during a visit by Pastor Searfoss when Victor fell during the night in the bathroom and substantiated by Victor's sharing the story with Mary Brewer.

Mary Cooke shared her thoughts, "I felt good about the Will. Elsie had told me that she wanted me to have certain things and told me some things she wanted given away. Then, Mary Margaret did ask her when they were there, but it was a kind of a token question, as Elsie was certainly not in command of her mind, though she did say, "Yes." Now, the Will bears it out, so I guess it is all right, even though the Will is not valid because it wasn't witnessed. And why didn't the nurse witness it? With the two statements before Elsie's death, I am just going to consider matters closed about what the youngsters sent. There is nothing of any great value. Most of it is just of family interest. Even the manuscript is taking a great deal of editing and re-writing because it is written in an older style. The descriptions are very fine, but the conversations are somewhat stilted. The background material is excellent, and the frame of the story is quite good, but the action is clogged by wordiness and unnecessary conversation. If we ever print it, it will be the achievement of three- Elsie, myself, and Mary Margaret. We will print it as written by Vivian Stirling- the pen-name Elsie has on the title page- and Mary Brooke- a combination of Brewer and Cooke."

Although she set aside money for Victor's care in a home, the property taxes failed to be paid. At one point, Mrs. Portera said that Elsie had inherited some money which kept her soluble, otherwise, she didn't know how they could continue to live in the house. Between the power of attorney and Victor, confusion about whether he would be kept in the home after Elsie's death lingered when it became evident that he would have to leave the home since she didn't finalize her Will. To neighbors this was an indication that someone was checking on their welfare but their sister Mary discovered that their involvement was limited and requested assistance from Social Services. Mary, Mary's daughter, Mary Margaret and Kevin came east to clean out the attic and check on Elsie and Victor's welfare. It was in the attic that they found Wilbert W. White's medals from WWI. It was Elsie's wish that the medals would go to her son.

It was hard to imagine how someone could live in a dilapidated house with the windows boarded up, until I reviewed her life. Until 1952, she never had a home of her own. She moved from apartment to apartment, in different cities, never knowing where she belonged. Often living with friends, but never having a place to call home. Over the years most of her belongings were in storage. Finally, she had a place of her own. She fulfilled the promise to her mother that she would look after Victor and she was able to settle down. That old boarded up house was home.

Bibliography

Books

Ball, J. Dyer. *Things Chinese; or Notes connected with China.* Hong Kong: Kelly & Walsh, 1903.

Bartlett, John, Kaplan, Justin. *Bartletts Familiar Quotations.* 16th Ed., Boston: Little Brown and Co. 1891.

Ballard, J. S., Parks, James John. *The 147th Aero Squadron in World War I.* Aiglen: Schiffer Ltd. 2013.

Coryell, Deborah Morris. *Good Grief, Healing through the Shadow of Loss.* The Shiva Foundation. 1998.

Flexner, Stuart Berg. *Listening to America.* New York: Simon and Schuster. 1982.

Fosdick, Harry Emerson. *The Manhood of the Master* New York: Association Press. 1915

Franks, Norman. *American Aces of World War I.* New York: Osprey Publishing Ltd. 2001.

Gerhold, Henry D. *A Century of Forest Resources Education at Penn State.* University Park: 2007.

Glass, Shirley P. *Not "Just Friends".* New York: The Free Press. 2003.

Hartney, Harold E. *Up and At Em.* Edited by Stanley M. Ulanoff, Lt. Col. USAR. New York: Doubleday & Company, Inc. 1971.

Hynes, Samuel. *The Unsubstantial Air.* New York: Farrar, Strauss & Gerous. 2014.

Illich, Joseph S. *Pennsylvania Trees.* Bulletin 11, Reprint of Fifth
　　Ed. Of 1925. Harrisburg: Pennsyvlania Department of
　　Forestry and Waters. 1925.
Lewis, W. David. *Eddie Rickenbacker: An American Hero in the
　　Twentieth Century.* U.S. Air Services, Vol. 2.
Maltby, Richard M. (Ed.) *Passing Parade: A History of Popular
　　Culture in the Twentieth Century.* New York: Oxford University
　　Press. 1989.
Monroe, Paul. *China: A Nation in Evolution.* New York: The
　　Chautauqua Press. 1927.
Reed, James. *The Missionary Mind and American Asia Policy, 1911-
　　1915.* Boston: Harvard University Press. 1983.
Sanger, Margaret. *Woman and the New Race.* New York:
　　Brentana's Publishers. 1920.
Tennyson, Alfred Lord. *The Poetic and Dramatic Work of Alfred
　　Lord Tennyson.* Boston: Houghton, Mifflin and Company.
　　1899.
Wilson, Woodrow. *On Being Human.* New York: Harper &
　　Brothers. 1916.

Articles and Manuscripts
Cornell University Library. "Board of Foreign Missions of the
　　Presbyterian Church: Historical Sketches of the Missions,
　　1897".
Cornell University Library. "Annual Report of the Board of
　　Foreign Missions of the Presbyterian Church, 1904-1906".
　　43,50,51.
Cornell University Library. "Report of the Board of Foreign
　　Missions, 1913-1914".
Cornell Alumni News. "Meissner '18' Becomes Ace". vol. XX: 40
　　(August 1918): 462-463.

Ennis, Frank S. *"National Museum of the U.S. Air Force"*. Posted October 9, 2014.

Ferris State University. "The Coon Character, Jim Crow Museum of Racist Memorabilia". January, 2016.

Hallmark, Harrydell. "A Story of Two Grateful Chinaman". *Sunday Philadelphia Press.* (August 1900).

Honolulu star-bulletin. (1912, July 18). 2.

Huston, James A. "The Sinews of War: Army Logistics 1775-1953". Washington: *United States Army: Army Historical Series: Center of Military History, United States Army.* 346-347.

Johnson, R. Park. "The Legacy of Arthur Judson Brown". *Bulletin of Missionary International Research.* April 1986.

Little Falls Herald. "Dr. E. C. Machle, a Presbyterian missionary". (1907, June).

Maurer, Mauren. "The U.S. Air Service in World War I". Washington: *The Office of Air Force History, Headquarters U.S.A.F.* (1978): 1.

Miller Center of Public Affairs. "William Taft: Life Before the Presidency". February 2016.

Northwestern Christian Advocate. "One of the Causes of the Lienchow Massacre". Rev. H. Olin Cody, D.D. of West China Mission. vol. 53.

One Hundred Year Biographical Directory of Mount Holyoke College 1837-1937. Bulletin Series 30, No. 5, published and compiled by the Alumni Association of Mt. Holyoke College. Massachusetts.

Rockwell, Tim Osage. "A Request for Reconsideration of the Medal of Honor for Lt. Wilbert W. White". *Mercersburg Academy.* 9-12, 182-185.

Ross, John F. "Enduring Courage: Ace Pilot Eddie Rickenbacker and the Dawn of the Age of Speed". (April 1917). 244.

Scott, Eberhardt. "Performance Analysis and Tactics of Fighter Aircraft from WWI". *American Institute of Aeronautics and Astronautics*, (A1AA Paper 2005).

Speer, Robert E. "Report on the China Missions of the Presbyterian Board of Foreign Missions, 1897". (July 1902). 80,81.

Spence, Jonathan D. "Our Mission in China". (September 1984).

The Daily Telegram. "No decision". (December 1912). 10.

The Evening Post. "Fighting Forces Urged to Take Out Insurance". (November 1917).

The Evening World. "Aviator Who Won American Cross and His Wife and Two Children". (November 1918).

The Forest Republican(Tionesta, PA). "Wedding of White and Machle". (1912, December 8).

The Hawaiian Star. "Money Paid". (June 1907).

The Washington Herald. "Society section". (November 1911).

The Washington Times. "Chinese Mobs Menace American Engineers". (April 1903).

White, Wilbert Webster. "The American Dead in France and the Skylark". *U.S. Air Service*. (February 1926). 21-24.

Wilhelm, Samuel A. "The Wheeler and Dusenbury Lumber Company of Forest and Warren Counties". (November 1952).

Web Sites

Bath Treatments. The Clifton Springs Sanatarium. (2016, May 6). Retrieved from http://www.fostercottage.org/menu/bath_treatments_4.htm.

Benson, Ian. *The Wooster Voice*. The whirlwind history of Greek Life at Wooster, revealed. Retrieved from http://

thewoostervoice-spaces.wooster.edu/2012/02/03/the_whirl-wind_history_of_greek_life... (2013, March 16).

Bio on Dr. Amelia Talitha Wood. (1970, March 18). Ball State University Libraries, Muncie, Indiana. Retrieved from http://mail.google.com/mail/u/0/?ui=2&ik=bb3d68c8a7&view=pt&search=inbox&th=14d.

Bunner, Henry Cuyler, (2010, January). The Way to Arcady. Retrieved from http://www.bartleby.com/102/233,html.

Elsie Machle, 1911. U.S. Yearbook record, University of Wooster, Wooster, Ohio. (2013, April 21). Retrieved from http://search.ancestry.com/content/viewespf.aspx?h=235839186&db=YearbookIndex&is--...

Evening Star (Washington, D.C.) 1854-1972. (1905, November 3). Women Seized Chinese Image. Retrieved from http://chroniclingamerica.loc.gov./lccn/sn83045462/1905-11-03/ed-seq-2/print/image_68... (2015, October 1).

Evening Star (Washington, D.C.) 1854-1972. (1915, July 31). Will Become President of Wooster University. Retrieved from http://chroniclingamerica.loc.gov/lccn/sn83045462/1915-07-3/ed-1seq-20/print/image_6...

Hollenden Hotel. Retrieved from http://en.wikipedia.org/loc/index.php?title=Hollenden_Hotel&olded=5810809964. (2017, January 21).

Hudson, James J. History of the 1st Pursuit Group. Gorrell Histories, Air Service, American Expeditionary Forces. (2014, January). Retrieved from http://www.Airpower.maxwell.af.mil/airchronicles/aureview/1972/jan-feb/hudson.html (2016, May 3). Series C, 1X 6.

Johnson, R. Park. (April, 1986). The Legacy of Arthur Judson Brown. Retrieved from http://www.bu.edu/missionalogy/missionary-biography/9-c/brown-Arthur-judson-1856_1963/.

Long Island History – World War, 1914-1918. Patchogue-Medford Library, New York. (2014, November 14). Retrieved from http://www.pmlib.org/likestorywwi.

Tangelder, Johan D. Reformed Reflections: John Bunyan's Doubting Castle. Retrieved from http://www.reformedre-flections.ca/bibliography/john-bunyan.html (2016, January 31).

The Bourbon news. (Paris, KY) 1895-1922. Amy Machle, the doctor's 10-yr old child carried off and flug alone into the river. Retrieved from http://chroniclingamerica.loc.gov/lccn/sn86069873/1905-11-14/ed-1/seq.-7/print/image_68... (2016, March 29).

The College of Wooster. Historical Presbyterian Collection and College Archives Collection. Retrieved from http://www.wooster.edu/academics/libraries/collections/Collections/historical/Historical .   (August, 2016).

The Forest Republican (Tionesta, PA) 1869-1952. (1908, June 24). Penn State University Libraries, University Park, PA. Retrieved from http://chroniclingamerica.loc.gov/lccn/sn84026497/1908-06-24/ed-1/seq.-3/...

The Forest Republican (Tionesta, PA) 1869-1952. (1909, November 11). Retrieved from http://chroniclingamerica.loc.gov/lccn/sn84026497/1909-11-03/ed-1/seq.-3/print/image_68... (2016, June 19).

The Harrisburg Telegraph. America's Ace of Aces Stuns Large Audience.
(1919, April 18). Retrieved from http://chroniclingamerica.loc.gov./lccn/sn85038411/1919-04-18/ed-1/seq.-17. (2016, March 31).

The Hawaiian star (Oahu) 1893-1912. Was with Doomed Christians in Lien Chou Province last October when infuri-ated Chinese Mob murdered Five People – Goo Kim Fought with Mob and Finally Escaped was wounded in the Fight. (1906, August 16). Retrieved from http://chroniclingamerica.loc.gov/lccn/sn82015415/1906-08-16/ed-l/seq-1. (2016, March 30).

The Hewes Library. Monmouth College. Retrieved from http://en/wikipedia.org/wiki/Monmouth_College. (2015, May). 2.

The Lexington Dispatch(Lexington, S.C.). Indemnity Paid by China, May 23, 1906. Retrieved from http://chroniclingamerica.loc.gov/lccn/sn84026907/1906-05-23/ed-1/seq-3 (2015, February

The Presbyterian Historical Society Blog. LoMo: The Beloved Mother of Chinatown. (2016, March). Retrieved from http://www.history.pcusa.org/blog/2016/03/lo-mo-beloved-mother-of-chinatown (2016, April).

The Saint Paul globe (St. Paul, Minn.) 1896-1905. (2015, January). Retrieved from http://chroniclingamerica.loc.gov/lccn/sn90059523/1905-01-14/ed-1/seq.-10. (2016, June).

The Times Dispatch 1903-1914. Campbell White Here To-morrow. (1909, October 22). Retrieved from http://chroniclingamerica.loc.gov/lccn/en8503861/109-10-22/ed-1/seq-10/.

Camp Mills. (2014, November 14). Retrieved from http://en/wikipedia.org/wiki/Camp_Mills.

Camp Taliaferro (Fort Worth, Texas). Retrieved from http://en/wikipedia.org/wiki/Camp_Taliaferro.

Christian Moerlein Brewing Co. Retrieved from http://en/wikipedia.org/wiki/Christian_Moerlein_Brewing_Co. (2017, January 17).

History of Cincinnati. Retrieved from http://en/wikipedia.org/wiki/History_of_Cincinnati. (2016, December 21).

Lake George (New York). Retrieved from http://en/wikipedia.org/wiki/Lake_George_(New_York) . (2013, September 3).

Otago Daily times, Issue 13493. The Lien Chow Massacre. (1906, January 17). Retrieved from http://paperspast.natlib.govt. nz/cgi-bin/paperspast?a=d&d=ODT19060117.2.49. (2014, February 3).

Philaphilia Empty Lot of the Week: Pat's and Geno's Shame Lot. (2013, June 11). Retrieved from http://citypaper.net/ Blogs/PHILADELPHIA-Empty-lot-of-the-Week-Pat's-and-Geno's-Sha... (2015, November 25).

Progressive Party (United States, 1912). Retrieved from http:// en/wikipedia.org/wiki/Progressive_Party_(United_ States,_1912). (2016, July 1).

Si Melby Hall, Augsburg College Athletics. (2014, April 5). Retrieved from http://Athletics.Augsburg. edu/sports/2014/4/5/30/facilities-simelbyhall. aspx?path=general&ta... (2015, April 27).

The "Mish Kids" and Canada's Post-War Asia Relations. (2013, August 20). Retrieved from http://www.thegoddards.ca/ alexgoddardblog/?p=380.

The Sagamore. Retrieved from http://en/wikipedia.org/wiki/ The_Sagamore. (2016, January 17).

Wheeler & Dusenbury. (2016, June 19). Retrieved from http:// www.randgust.com/wdscenes.htm.

Wooster Hack Line, July 26, Wooster July 26, 1871. The States and Union (Ashland, Ohio) 1868-1872. Retrieved from http:// chroniclingamerica.loc.gov./lccn/sn83035174/1871-07-26/4d-1/seq-3. (2016, May 18).

YMCA, History of Silver Bay. Retrieved from http://www.silver-bay.org/index.php/ourheritage/history. (2013, September).

Suffragette. Retrieved from http://en.wikipedia.org/wiki/ Suffragette. (2016, June 30).

Other:

Advertisement Card. Yut Cheong, Canton, China, No. 10 Sai Hing Street.

Alumni Class Directory. Penn State Forestry Camp, 1912: Forestry Education in Pennsylvania. 204, 206.

Diary of Elsie Machle (1908-1909). Date of entry, February 8, 1909, description of first date. U of WSHD. Collection of Rebecca Davis, N.C.

Directory of Protestant Missionaries in China, Japan, & Corea for the Year, 1904. *Yale Divinity School Library.*

Obituary of Dr. White, 81, Dies; Founded Seminary.

New Yorker Newspaper. Dr. W.W. White Presbyterian Minister Dies. Founded Biblical Seminary Retired as It's President in 1939 after 39 years. (1944).

Rawleighs. Good Health Guide and Almanac Cookbook. *W. T. Rawleigh.* (1921): 20.

Archives:

Speer, Robert E. 1795-1947 Papers. The Burke Library Archives, Columbia University Library. Union Theological Seminary, New York, 1.

White, Wilbert Webster 1878-1945 Papers. The Burke Library, Columbia University Libraries, New York. Retrieved from http://www.Columbia.edu/cu/lweb/archival/collections/Idpd_7188365/. 2.7. Series 2, Box 2, Folder 23.

Letters:

Edward and Ella Machle, Elsie Machle and Wilbert White Collection of letters of Mary Margaret Brewer

Wilbert White, Elsie White, Victor Machle collection of letters of Rachel Davis

Endnotes

1   An article by Rev. H. Olin Cody DD of West China Mission details one of the causes of the massacre, "Such a tragedy as the massacre at Lien Chow does not occur ever in China without a pre-existing condition of popular feeling that may be quite apart from the immediate occasion of the tragedy. It is my desire to call attention to a specific incident that has had its confluence in creating the condition that made the murder of these missionaries possible.

On September 20, 1904 in the city of Canton, capital of the province in which Lien chow is situated, a squad of sailors from an American man-of-war which lay in the harbor of Canton seized a compredore (business manager) of Battlefield and Swire as he was passing over a bridge and slinging him over the parapet of the bridge, suffocated him in the slimy mud of the canal. For this crime, no one was punished. An inquest was held before the Chinese magistrate and the British consul general, as Butterfield & Swire, is a British firm, and the foregoing facts there substantiated. But when the complaint was lodged before the American consul general he found himself hampered so it was then currently reported by the unwillingness of American naval officers to assist in procuring the evidence necessary to identify the individual members of the crew who were participants in the crime. To foreigners as well as the Chinese there in Canton it seemed clear that the officers could easily have found out if they did not already know, what members of the crew were on shore at that time.

Finally, some indemnity was offered to the family of the murdered man. The local papers were full of the affairs. As one of them said, 'Are the Chinese less men that they should be treated like this?' For months afterward, the affair was discussed in the shops and native papers, and it was no uncommon thing to hear well educated men refer to that murder with extreme bitterness and to remind the foreigners that while the life of a foreigner, if taken by the Chinese, must be atoned for by sundry Chinese lives and the degradation of officials, if a Chinese is killed there is no fuss and only a few dollars given as an atonement. This feeling, says a correspondent of the North China Herald is very general throughout the province and bodes no good for the foreigners and especially the Americans.

The indifference of the American naval officers seems to the Chinese the more inexplicable because in China the civil magistrate is held responsible for crimes committed against foreigners in his jurisdiction, and the military and naval officials are held to a personal accountability for the conduct of the subordinates."

2   Jean Mawson was born November 21, 1876 in Purakaui, Otago. She trained as a Deaconness at the Presbyterian Women's Training Institute Dunedin and ordained on November 14, 1905. She was one of the first graduates of PWTI and one of the two Deaconesses accepted for Mission service to South China She studied Cantonese with Rev. Alexander Don in Dunedin from September 1904. She was appointed to Canton Villages Mission, South China 1905, arrived Canton December 29, 1905. She resigned in 1910 to marry Dr. Machle of the American Presbyterian Church South China Mission but continued to serve as a member of the A Mission in education work for women and children until they both retired in 1929. She died August 25, 1952 in Tacoma, Washington, USA.

3   Beta Theta Pi, University of Wooster, Flower, American beauty rose; Color: Light shade of Pink and blue: Fraternity Brothers: Jumbo (E.N. Chalfant); Robert A. Bobby Elder; Pal; Paul L. Harvey; Satan Gregg; Carrots Harris Vance, George Hackett, Ralph Fulton; Jack John Mateer, Ken Johnson; Fritz Kilpatrick; Baalone; Ajax; Hat John S. Hattery, Clarence Cummings, Horace C. Emergy, Chester C. Mellen, Morgan P. Jones, John G. Loy, James R. Dunlap, Frederick L. Phelps, R. K. Fentey, Fran Taggart, and Harold Fulton.

4   In 1912, Lewis Severance, a wealthy donor to The College, issued an ultimatum threatening to withdraw his support from the school if national Greek life persisted, stating in a letter, "what I do on this million dollar effort, with the General Education Board, will pledge only on condition that the fraternities surrender their charter at Wooster." Severance's opinion and ultimatum regarding Greek life was foreshadowed in a 1910 letter to

President Holden, saying that he was "decidedly opposed to them," and suggested that they disband their efforts and energies should be used towards the creation of two new dorms on campus. Due to Severance's threat, the Board of Trustees voted in February of 1913 on the matter, resulting in a 13-10 vote, with four members absent, to abolish the current Greek system. Angered by the results of the vote, three of the dissenting trustees resigned following the meeting. Within a year, Greek life returned to the campus in the form of "sections."

5   The poem is about love conquering wisdom through life to the golden years: Love must kiss that mortal's eyes, Who hopes to see fair Arcady. No gold can buy you entrance there; beleggard[sic] Love may go all are—No wisdom won with weariness; But Love goes in with Folly's dress—No fare wit could ever win; But only Love may lead Love in.

6   This was the first time women or suffragist, became involved in the Election of 1912 and was a general term for members of the suffrage movement. They advocated the right to vote in public elections for women. Leaders of the movement were often associated with the Progressive Party, but in general women associated with this movement were advocating for better conditions of workers, the poor and immigrants. Jane Addams, a NAWSA vice president, was nonpartisan. Rev. Dr. Anna Howard Shaw was anti Roosevelt and denounced TR for supporting woman suffrage only when it was politically expedient to do so. It was a complicated movement with Roosevelt in favor of woman suffrage if the women voted to have it, while Wilson insisted that suffrage was a state, not a national, matter and Taft escaped being heckled by not speaking in New York, so he didn't need a reply to the issue.

7   Elizabeth Worthington White, known as Betsey, was born March 2, 1915 in New York and died on September 3, 2009 in Lititz, Pennsylvania. She was an accomplished painter and expert in needle point. She attended Montrose School for Girls, Montrose, Pennsylvania, Clarke School for the Deaf and Art Student League in New York. She at tended the Wayman Adams Class of Portraiture in Elizabethtown, New Jersey.

8   Rev. Henry Jowett (1863-1923) was born in Yorkshire and educated at Edinburgh University and Mansfield College, Oxford. He came to Fifth

Avenue Presbyterian Church from Carr Lane Congregational Church in Birmingham, England in 1911. He was an author, the greatest preacher in America, and a non-conformist. He founded Digbeth Institute in the poor part of Birmingham. In 1917, he was called by Westminster Congregational Church of London, accompanied by representative of grand church, he felt he must give it consideration. There were personal appeals from Premier Lloyd-George and the King. He never took out citizenship in this country. Located at 5th Avenue & 55th Street, Fifth Avenue Presbyterian Church was created in 1808 in lower Manhattan on November 6. The current building was completed in 1875 in gothic revival. Known as the "church of the Patriots" its pulpit and pews have been filled with passionate voices that have paralleled the nation's growth. Rev. John Henry Jowett served from 1911-1917.

9   The Registrar's Report #331-99-22-A lists the date as June 5, but the WWI Officer Cards his enlistment at 45C at Mineola L I N Y on July 6. He was called into active service on February 7, 1918 from ERC.

10   The Evening Post: New York had an article, "Fighting Forces Urged To Take Out Insurance"...Application must be made at Washington Bureau Before February 12 – Text of Secretary's Address. November 21 – All offices and enlisted men and women in both Army and navy were urged in an address by Secretary McAdoo to apply to the Bureau of War Risk Insurance at Washington for Government Life Insurance before February 12 next. Failure to apply by that date, he explained, would bar them from the benefits of what he characterized as "the greatest measure of protection ever offered to its fighting forces by any nation in the history of the world...To provide adequate protection until February 12, 1918 during the period when the soldiers and sailors are learning the details of this law, the Government automatically insures each man and woman commissioned or enlisted in the military service of the United States. It pays the man $25 a month during total permanent disability, if he dies within twenty years, it pays the rest of 240 monthly installments of $25 each to his wife, child, or widowed mother." NOTE: there was only one copy of his insurance application among the documents in Elsie White's possession. It was a hand written copy of an application done while Wilber was in France. After his death, there are no records showing she received a death benefit from the government although it was mentioned in a letter from Dr. White to Elsie that he was settling a financial

commitment to her from the government. That money seems to have been in the accounting records of The Biblical Seminary of New York.

11   Camp Taliaferro was named after 1st Lieutenant Walter R. Taliaferro, a U.S. Army aviator who was killed in an accident at Rockwell Field, California on 11 October 1915. The first winter of 1917-1918 was difficult. Many men lived in tents in this snowy winter. In six months, 1,960 pilots were trained, completing 67,000 flying hours on the Curtiss JN4 Canuck (also known as the "Jenny", a two-seater biplane weighing 2,100 lbs. with a maximum speed of 75 mph. During the winter there were 8 deaths due to influenza and 39 RFC personnel died as the result of aircraft accidents, influenza, or other illnesses.

12   Norman L. Hummel was born in Snyder County, Pennsylvania on December 16, 1888. He was first married to Edna, and later to widow Alice N. Niebel. He served United Methodist churches in State College, York, and Williamsport, Pennsylvania. He graduated from Albright College and Biblical Seminary of New York City. He died on August 22, 1980 at the age of 91 after serving as Conference Superintendent for 20 years.

Made in the USA
Middletown, DE
25 October 2020

22732978R00265